The Emer

D0235148

University of the
West of England

BRISTOL

**ST. MATTHIAS
LIBRARY**

This book should be returned by the last date
stamped below.

UWE, BRISTOL   F334.08.03
Printing & Stationery Services

STUDIES IN MODERN HISTORY

General editors: John Morrill and David Cannadine

This series, intended primarily for students, will tackle significant historical issues in concise volumes which are both stimulating and scholarly. The authors combine a broad approach, explaining the current state of our knowledge in the area, with their own research and judgements: and the topics chosen range widely in subject, period and place.

Titles already published

[Titles not currently available, 1998]

The Emergence of a Ruling Order

English Landed Society 1650–1750

JAMES M. ROSENHEIM

Longman
London and New York

Addison Wesley Longman Limited
Edinburgh Gate,
Harlow, Essex CM20 2JE,
United Kingdom
and Associated Companies throughout the world

*Published in the United States of America
by Addison Wesley Longman Inc., New York*

First published 1998

ISBN 0 582 087422 CSD
ISBN 0 582 087414 PPR

British Library Cataloguing in Publication Data
A catalogue record for this book is available from the British Library

Library of Congress Cataloging-in-Publication Data
Rosenheim, James M.
The emergence of a ruling order : English landed society,
1650–1750 / James M. Rosenheim.
p. cm. — (Studies in modern history)
Includes bibliographical references and index.
ISBN 0–582–08742–2. — ISBN 0–582–08741–4
1. Great Britain—Politics and government—1603–1714.
2. Political leadership—Great Britain—History—17th century.
3. Political leadership—Great Britain—History—18th century.
4. Great Britain—Politics and government—1714–1760. 5. England—
Social conditions—17th century. 6. England—Social
conditions—18th century. 7. Land tenure—England—History.
8. Upper class—England—History. 9. Landowners—England—History.
10. Gentry—England—History. I. Title. II. Series: Studies in
modern history (Longman (Firm))
DA435.R67 1998
306.2′0941′09032—dc21
97–32454
CIP

Set by 35 in 10/12pt Baskerville
Produced by Addison Wesley Longman Singapore (Pte) Ltd.,
Printed in Singapore

Contents

Contents

Acknowledgements

The author Henry Wiggen once offered '1 word of advice to any sap with the itch to write a book – do not begin it in the first place'. Having ignored this injunction, I none the less concur with the learned lefthander's further observation that authorship has little to do with get-up-and-go: 'It is the sit down and stay that gets books wrote.'

Several groups at Texas A&M University helped me with this project. The members of the Interdisciplinary Group for Historical Literary Study provided me much intellectual stimulus in pursuit of questions that I came quickly to recognize were not at all tangential to my concerns. Participants in three senior seminars and three graduate seminars in the Department of History surely studied English landed society and culture more intensively than they expected, but very much to my benefit. My comrades in 'QT' may not know that they allowed me the academic and personal context without which this work could not have been completed.

I gratefully acknowledge the support extended to me by Texas A&M University in the form of a faculty development leave, an honours teacher-scholar award, and several honours curriculum development grants while I worked on this book. I am pleased to have been affiliated during 1991 with both the Centre of East Anglian Studies at the University of East Anglia and the Centre for British Studies at the University of Colorado at Boulder. I also received generous grant assistance from the American Philosophical Society in 1991. A fellowship from the American Society for Eighteenth-Century Studies allowed me to visit the William Andrews Clark Library in 1994. Over the years I have been extended the warmest possible welcome at Raynham Hall. I continue to be deeply indebted to the Marquess Townshend of Raynham for permission to consult and cite the manuscripts there.

Many individuals have helped me with the 'sit down and stay' of this book by unstintingly offering advice, diversion, encouragement, and sympathy. It would be invidious to suggest what measure of which was supplied by whom. I am pleased to thank David Anderson,

Lee Beier, Julia Kirk Blackwelder, Cynthia Bouton, Albert Broussard, Garrett Brown, James Busby, Robert Calvert, Jeffrey Cox, Edward and Marilyn Evans-Lombe, James Haddan, Larry Hill, Brigid Howell, Mary Johnson, Marjorie McIntosh, Charles Middleton, Jane K. Linnstaedter Mims, the late Jay Poole, Bruce Redford, Clare Rosenheim, Brian Stagner, Victor Stater, John Stevenson, Lawrence Stone, Jude Swank, Susan Whyman, Susan Williams, and the entire Wingate family.

Edward Rosenheim read the manuscript with a keen eye, especially for my 'other-handism'. He helped me sort out many obscurities (including those in my prose) and tacitly encouraged me to reflect on what the figures he knows so well – Atterbury, Pope, Swift – would have made of my argument. I am not certain I have done justice to them, or to a father's generosity, but I have tried. Larry Yarak's scholarship, qualities of mind, and friendship have influenced me in uncountable ways: I hope he will disown none of them. Newton Key kindly read the entire manuscript, and his insight, suggestions, references, and frankness have been enormously helpful. David Cannadine, John Morrill, and Andrew MacLennan gave sharp, scrupulous readings of a work even more imperfect than it remains. At an early stage in this project Kevin Graham gave me indispensable support, without which I may have abandoned it and for which I cannot be sufficiently thankful. Samuel Gladden has graciously abetted my work in ways as constant and diverse as they have been sustaining. Finally, Mary Ann O'Farrell, Andrew Rosenheim, and Jeremy Webster will not need me to tell them why I single each of them out. The many shortcomings of this study are mine.

Abbreviations

Cherry Walker, eds, *Northamptonshire Record Society* 36 (1990 for 1988).

Grassby, *Business Community*
Richard Grassby, *The Business Community of Seventeenth-Century England* (Cambridge, 1995).

Habakkuk, *Estates System*
John Habakkuk, *Marriage, Debt, and the Estates System: English Land Ownership 1650–1950* (Oxford, 1994).

Hainsworth, *Stewards*
D.R. Hainsworth, *Stewards, Lords and People: The Estate Steward and His World in Later Stuart England* (Cambridge, 1992).

Heal and Holmes, *Gentry*
Felicity Heal and Clive Holmes, *The Gentry in England and Wales 1500–1700* (Stanford, 1994).

Holmes, *Augustan England*
Geoffrey Holmes, *Augustan England: Professions, State and Society, 1680–1730* (London, 1982).

Holmes, *Seventeenth-Century Lincolnshire*
Clive Holmes, *History of Lincolnshire*, VII, *Seventeenth-Century Lincolnshire* (Lincoln, 1980).

Isham Diaries
The Diary of Thomas Isham of Lamport (1658–81) kept by him in Latin from 1671 to 1673 at his Father's command, N. Marlow, trans. and Sir Gyles Isham ed. (Farnborough, 1971).

Jenkins, *Making of a Ruling Class*
Philip Jenkins, *The Making of a Ruling Class: The Glamorgan Gentry 1640–1790* (Cambridge, 1983).

Langford, *Public Life*
Paul Langford, *Public Life and the Propertied Englishman 1689–1789* (Oxford, 1985).

Lowther Correspondence
The Correspondence of John Lowther of Whitehaven 1693–1698: A Provincial Community in Wartime, D.R. Hainsworth, ed., *Records of Social and Economic History*, new series, 7 (1983).

Montagu Letters
The Complete Letters of Lady Mary Wortley Montagu, Robert Halsband, ed., 3 vols (Oxford, 1965–76).

Nicolson Diaries	*The London Diaries of William Nicolson Bishop of Carlisle 1702–1718*, Clyve Jones and Geoffrey Holmes, eds (Oxford, 1985).
Prideaux to Ellis Letters	*Letters of Humphrey Prideaux sometime Dean of Norwich to John Ellis sometime Under-secretary of State 1674–1722*, Edward Maunde Thompson, ed., *Camden Society*, new series, 15 (1875).
Richmond–Newcastle Correspondence	*The Correspondence of the Dukes of Richmond and Newcastle 1724–1750*, Timothy J. McCann, ed., *Sussex Record Society* 73 (1984 for 1982–83).
Roebuck, *Yorkshire Baronets*	Peter Roebuck, *Yorkshire Baronets 1640–1760: Families, Estates and Fortunes* (Oxford, 1986).
Rosenheim, *Townshends of Raynham*	James M. Rosenheim, *The Townshends of Raynham: Nobility in Transition in Late Stuart and Early Hanoverian England* (Middletown, Connecticut, 1989).
Schwoerer, *Lady Rachel Russell*	Lois G. Schwoerer, *Lady Rachel Russel: 'One of the Best of Women'* (Baltimore, 1988).
Stone, *Crisis of the Aristocracy*	Lawrence Stone, *The Crisis of the Aristocracy 1558–1641* (Oxford, 1965).
Stone and Stone, *An Open Elite?*	Lawrence Stone and Jeanne C. Fawtier Stone, *An Open Elite? England 1540–1880* (Oxford, 1984).
Walpole Correspondence	*The Yale Edition of Horace Walpole's Correspondence*, W.S. Lewis et al., eds, 42 vols (New Haven, 1937–83).

For my parents –
inspirations, exemplars

Counties of Wales

A Anglesey
B Caernarfonshire
C Denbighshire
D Flintshire
E Merioneth
F Montgomeryshire
G Cardiganshire
H Radnorshire
I Brecknockshire
J Pembrokeshire
K Carmarthenshire
L Glamorganshire
M Monmouthshire
(technically an
English county)

Counties of England

1	Northumberland	14	Rutland	27	Hertfordshire
2	Cumberland	15	Norfolk	28	Essex
3	Lancashire	16	Herefordshire	29	Somerset
4	Westmorland	17	Worcestershire	30	Wiltshire
5	Durham	18	Warwickshire	31	Berkshire
6	Yorkshire	19	Northamptonshire	32	Greater London
7	Cheshire	20	Huntingdonshire	33	Surrey
8	Derbyshire	21	Cambridgeshire	34	Kent
9	Notttinghamshire	22	Suffolk	35	Cornwall
10	Lincolnshire	23	Bedfordshire	36	Devon
11	Shropshire	24	Gloucestershire	37	Dorset
12	Staffordshire	25	Oxfordshire	38	Hampshire
13	Leicestershire	26	Buckinghamshire	39	Sussex

Counties and principal centres of England

CHAPTER ONE

Introduction

England's large landowners have drawn the attention of historians for generations, an interest that has not abated with the notice paid to other strata of English society since the second world war. Because the landed order remained rich, powerful, and influential into the twentieth century, explaining its persistence is crucial to tracing the trajectory of the history of modern England. That explanation is complicated by the landed's self-awareness, the order's social indistinction and even permeability, its cultural adaptability in the face of religious and intellectual change, and its flexibility with regard to the agrarian regime on which it depended.

When the landed gentry emerged in the shires in the fourteenth century as coherent groups with significant roles in national politics, local communities, and county affairs, it was a social stratum quite distinctive from the nobility. By the middle of the seventeenth century, this was far less the case, whether in terms of education, wealth, political power, or maybe even the conduct of daily life. The increase in the size of England's landed classes from the mid-sixteenth to mid-seventeenth centuries, which outstripped total population growth and was vastly disproportionate among the untitled, contributed to some of this convergence. The 'inflation of honours' that more than doubled the size of the titled nobility between the death of Elizabeth and the late 1620s, the creation of the non-noble but hereditary title of baronet in 1611, and the continuing accretion of large amounts of land by gentry also narrowed some of the cultural distance between them and the peerage proper. The preoccupations of the gentry and nobility – the landed elite – and their relations with the crown, church, and other social strata

1

grew increasingly coincident with one another.[1] The experience of landed life, already in 1650 significantly different from what it had been, continued to change through the next century, this book will argue, resulting in a more homogeneous and hence more hegemonic landed class than England had ever experienced – a true ruling order.

The argument to make this case will rest on those figures, almost exclusively men, who dominated their societies on account of the land-based wealth, status, and power they enjoyed. This domination was something that, in common with landowners before and since, those of this era took for granted. Their consciousness was marked by what has been called, in reference to nineteenth-century landowners, 'a collective awareness of inherited and unworked-for superiority',[2] and the century from 1650 to 1750 was crucial for cementing the collective character of that awareness. Moreover, what hardened the cement during this century, compared with the years 1750–1850 or even 1750–1914, was not the landed's confidence in a future based on their persistence through time but rather a sense among the landed of anxiety and even fear.

The traumas of the mid-seventeenth century contributed to this concern. They did so in part by effecting a deep separation between popular and elite political cultures,[3] partly by raising the prospect of a divided elite made vulnerable to popular challenge. In the aftermath of revolution and civil war, England's aristocrats recognized the fragility of the social order on which their privileges rested. Their gestures and displays (hanging portraits, landscaping grounds, decorating houses, adorning themselves with à-la-mode clothes), even though some of them were not highly visible to the lower social orders, are explicable as the deployments of cultural claims to superiority intended to fortify their social position against challenge.[4]

Anxious, challenged, and insecure though some of them were, in their own eyes these landowners were also still aristocrats. And as

---

1. M.L. Bush, *The English Aristocracy: A Comparative Synthesis* (Manchester, 1984), ch. 3; G.E. Mingay, *The Gentry: The Rise and Fall of a Ruling Class* (London, 1976), ch. 1; Stone, *Crisis of the Aristocracy*; Heal and Holmes, *Gentry*, pp. 11–12; C.G.A. Clay, *Economic Expansion and Social Change: I, England 1500–1700, People, Land and Towns* (Cambridge, 1984), ch. 5.

2. David Cannadine, *The Decline and Fall of the British Aristocracy* (New Haven, 1990), p. 24; what follows is informed by his discussion of the hierarchies of wealth, status, and power on pp. 8–25.

3. David Underdown, *A Freeborn People: Politics and the Nation in Seventeenth-Century England* (Oxford, 1996), pp. 8, 10.

4. Jeremy Black, *The Politics of Britain 1688–1800* (Manchester, 1993), pp. 17–18.

the Greek *aristokratia* means 'rule of the best', this study is preoccupied both with the ways in which the landed ruled and with the ways in which they thought of themselves and set themselves apart as 'the best'. Being 'best', unless it involves only a single individual outstripping all others, is a subjectively measured achievement, which subjectivity makes it more understandable that the ruling order discussed in the following pages is in the main defined descriptively rather than quantitatively. Whether that gentility which set apart the aristocrat derived from honourable behaviour, learning, profession, or countenance and bearing, none of its defining characteristics (unless only descent was allowed) rested on clearly measurable criteria.[5]

That is not to say that this work is blind to quantitative questions, and at the outset the issues of movement into the ranks of the landed and the matter of rank and order among the landed themselves need to be addressed. Expansion after all had characterized the ranks of the landed through the latter part of the sixteenth and first half of the seventeenth century. Then, with a drying up of new land, a drop in population size, and falls in agricultural prices in the second half, the establishment of new landed families of gentle status slowed dramatically and may not have kept up with demographic wastage. There was no substantial recruitment in the early eighteenth century to make up for loss either. While fortunate cadet branches of landed families found themselves coming into major estates with the extinction of direct lines, there was nothing comparable to the sixteenth-century influx of new-made gentlemen rising from the yeomanry or from careers in law and business. At least for the period 1650–1750, this was not a pronouncedly open elite.[6]

In terms of ranks, who were the landed elite? Embracing the titled and untitled, the true magnates controlling dozens of separate estates and lesser gentry who lived off a single one, the landed order had its grades, distinct in some ways and indistinct in others.[7] They ranged at the bottom from somewhere between ten and twenty

5. J.P. Cooper, 'Ideas of gentility in early-modern England', in Cooper, *Land, Men and Beliefs: Studies in Early-Modern History*, G.F. Aylmer and J.S. Morrill, eds (London, 1983), pp. 43–77.

6. John Cannon, *Aristocratic Century: the Peerage of Eighteenth-Century England* (Cambridge, 1984), ch. 1; Stone and Stone, *An Open Elite?* esp. pt 4; Grassby, *Business Community*, pp. 373–88. For a 'miscellany of purchasers' among 'new moneyed men', however, see Habakkuk, *Estates System*, pp. 413–76.

7. For a useful comment on the problems encountered when defining the upper class, see Ellis Archer Wasson, 'The House of Commons, 1660–1945: parliamentary families and the political elite', *English Historical Review* 106 (1991), pp. 635–51, esp. 635–7.

thousand gentlemen and several thousand esquires, to about seven hundred to nine hundred and fifty baronets, somewhat fewer knights, and about two hundred peers at the top.[8]

This is not a book about this last group alone, the peerage, for any number of reasons, but not because titles were meaningless. Members of the gentry (and other social groups, for that matter) aspired to them, although it is notable that Sir Robert Walpole only took one when he fell from power and that the fabulously wealthy Sir James Lowther died without one. On an individual basis, status, wealth, and power did by and large fall in greatest measure to the peerage, but to focus on them alone as England's unequivocal social, economic, and political rulers would give a skewed and in-adequate picture of that rule. Peers were not numerous enough to demand separate consideration from the gentry on that basis alone, and titles as such did not define their holders nearly as much as their status as landed rulers did. Nobility in England did not bestow substantial legal or economic privilege and most importantly only accrued in a strict sense to the heads of families. Titles did not denote a vast income that automatically set their holders apart from others in the landed classes, and some of the kingdom's wealthiest subjects, like Lowther, like Sir Stephen Fox, like any number of London merchant plutocrats, never received or were even considered for peerages.[9]

While it might next seem logical to include knights and baronets with the nobility and associate rule only with the limited numbers of the titled, there were simply too many of the 'plain' gentry hold-ing too many important positions in all three of English society's hierarchies of wealth, status, and power to do so. Yet understand-ably scholars have sought to distinguish among the thousands of non-noble landed. Some have discussed them in terms of greater, middling, and lesser gentry, roughly broken down along the lines first of baronets and knights, next esquires, then gentlemen. This divi-sion provides a rule of thumb for economic analysis, at least among Tudor and early Stuart gentry, but seems less usefully employed in other narratives.[10] Many a not-so-plain esquire had claims to stand

8. All calculations seem doomed to imprecision: see, for example, Beckett, *Aris-tocracy*, pp. 26–40 and esp. the appendix, pp. 482–95 for his painstaking efforts. See below chapter 2 for my attempt.

9. Peers numbered about 120 in 1658, 160 in 1688, 170 in 1714, and around 190 or under in 1720–60: Beckett, *Aristocracy*, pp. 27–8; Cannon, *Aristocratic Century*, p. 15. On plutocrats see Grassby, *Business Community*, pp. 247–9.

10. Heal and Holmes, *Gentry*, pp. 13–15; Mingay, *Gentry*, pp. 11–16; Beckett, *Aristo-cracy*, pp. 26–40.

as a county member of parliament far exceeding those of the head of a diminished baronet line. And the ordering of the commission of the peace that put nobles before baronets, and baronets before knights before esquires, none the less placed a privy councillor who was only an esquire ahead of his county's most senior baronet.

Non-noble landowners have also been distinguished as national, county, and parish gentry. These designations supposedly acknowledge the limits of spheres of influence and daily activity, but too much is known about the broad contacts even insignificant parish gentry had for these distinctions to carry too much weight as descriptors of social or political life.[11] And one of the contentions advanced here is that it became increasingly more difficult and less likely even for squires of limited ambition and contacts to be insulated from metropolitan influences. So this book eschews three-fold divisions of the landed because they do not seem to accord fully with contemporary experience and are not suitable to the ana-tomizing of a ruling order, but not because there were no important differences between minor squire and great magnate.

Minor squires are discussed less in what follows than greater gentry and nobles largely because the former had a smaller part in ruling and, more significantly, in defining what rule meant and what a ruler was over the course of this period. The lesser squire who was a justice of the peace, however, *is* here; so too the minor figure who managed to send his son on a tour to Europe; likewise the man who found his daughter or son a marriage partner by exploring the prospects offered in Bath or London. These examples of shared enterprise, however, do nothing to indicate that land-owners comprised a monolithic body, only that they had common experiences. And where something as precise as titles guided behavi-our by eliciting deferential acknowledgement of titular superiority (the doffed hat, the ordered entrance, the arranged seating), it is not clear that the landed of the mid-eighteenth century observed all these niceties of precedence in private and among themselves or did so in a way that erased those commonalities. There was no homogeneity, yet the great chasms in English society did not exist between different elevations within the landed order but between the landed and everyone else.

---

11. Clive Holmes, 'The county community in Stuart historiography', *Journal of British Studies* 19 (1979–80), pp. 54–73. Much of what Holmes says about the county community could be applied, *mutatis mutandis*, to the parish. See also Anthony J. Fletcher, *A County Community in Peace and War: Sussex 1600–1660* (London, 1975), esp. ch. 2.

The landed order had its gradations and its common attributes both, and these characteristics of attitude, taste, interest, and material well-being brought landowners together because they set them apart from the rest of society. In being propertied, for example, the elite were not alone, but they were set apart from the business community of the day. To begin with, all the subjects studied here were people of leisure – which is another way of making William Harrison's point that a telling attribute of gentility was the ability to 'live idly'.[12] Aristocrats did not pursue a single activity in order to earn income. The bulk of them lived predominantly off the rent of land they owned in the countryside and from largely conservative, non-commercial investments. They also spent their money, when they had any, in generally predictable and distinctive ways – on land, on their country seats, and on personal possessions likely to be wrought with self-conscious artistry rather than just craft. Their divergence here from the patterns of consumption of other wealthy folk is also clear, especially with respect to houses and land.[13]

In addition, the landed were the governors of England, individuals who took on the most important offices and positions of power in the kingdom. They were set apart from other persons of property, whose numbers were growing in the eighteenth century and who were taking an increasing part in public life,[14] precisely in the measure of their rule. This was in some arenas an increasingly participatory society, but of course not one where all participants in a single process or forum carried anything approaching equal power in making or implementing decisions. Many of those mentioned in this study are men with disproportionate weight in the public realm, especially the parliamentary one, and they include many members of what Ellis Wasson has called the 'parliamentary families', those supplying more than three members to the kingdom's legislative bodies between 1660 and 1945. Because service in the Commons bestowed 'the most certain measure of rank apart from a heritable title', members of parliament clearly constitute part of the political elite.[15] But in a study that, unlike Wasson's, spans only a century, those with status enough to be candidates (successful or not) or to play important roles in elections must also be counted among the political elite, and not just those who became members of parliament.

Moreover, the ruling elite under scrutiny here must include people other than those who held sway in the public realm of politics

---

12. Cited in Heal and Holmes, *Gentry*, p. 7.
13. Grassby, *Business Community*, ch. 11.   14. Langford, *Public Life*.
15. Wasson, 'The House of Commons, 1660–1945'; quotation on p. 637.

and office. Otherwise it would be an examination only of the victors of struggles for power. And although in some sense this *is* a study of victors, they are victors in an economic, social, and cultural struggle more than a political one. The 'rule' analysed here is rule that members of the landed order exercised in myriad ways and over a wide array of people in different forums. It is, to begin with, the rule that landlords exercised over property, a rule found in the way, as Corrigan and Sayer put it, that 'liberty and property were – simply – *there* for some men: gentry, governors, rulers, regulators'.[16] In concrete terms, this discursive appropriation translated into sway over tenants, a rule that varied depending on the amount and location of one's land, on past relations between tenants and landlords, on agricultural regimes. Yet it was rule in which landlords across the kingdom experienced similar imperatives for good management, were comparably placed vis-à-vis tenants and employees, and had needs for income and produce from their lands that were very much alike.

The landed classes held sway in a world of law and order as well as one of property. Sometimes they did so through office, as legislators who made the law and as justices of the peace who enforced it. They also did so by taking opponents of various kinds to court, by asserting their privileges and using their arcane knowledge, and by extracting their due through legal process or the threat of it. The legal system was more than a mere instrument of class rule. Yet its ceremonial, its deference to precedent, its domination by figures of landed status, and its increasingly protective attitude to property during the eighteenth century all made it congenial to landed interests, to say the very least. It did not take service as a single justice dispensing summary judgement and punishment for members of the gentry and nobility to act as *amici curiae* and as agents of the rule of law in ways as beneficial to them as they could be inimical to the interests of (non-landed) others.[17]

Less clearly, the landed ruled in a high cultural realm. This does not mean that the elite imposed their taste on the rest of society, or

16. Philip Corrigan and Derek Sayer, *The Great Arch: English State Formation as Cultural Revolution* (Oxford, 1985), p. 96.

17. This is not to suggest that the landed did not use the law against one another, only to point out the ways in which the landed ruled through law. Classic expositions of the relationship between law and the landed can be found in Douglas Hay, Peter Linebaugh, John G. Rule, E.P. Thompson, and Cal Winslow's, *Albion's Fatal Tree: Crime and Society in Eighteenth-Century England* (New York, 1975); E.P. Thompson, *Whigs and Hunters: The Making of the Black Act* (London, 1975); idem, 'Custom, law and common right', in Thompson, *Customs in Common: Studies in Traditional Popular Culture* (New York, 1991), pp. 97–184.

that they wanted to do so. Nor does it mean that the standards they set were unthinkingly striven after and mimicked by their social inferiors.[18] At the same time, wealthy families constituted an essential element among the growing body of consumers in an increasingly commercialized world. They provided a principal market, both appreciative and mercenary, for the artistic creations of master architects and master painters, of poets, composers, essayists, and historians alike. They bought, spoke of, and sought more of the novel porcelains, exotic fabrics, and innovative designs that proliferated in the eighteenth-century 'world of goods'. The landed elite may not entirely have ruled this world of consumption – arguably they were ruled by it – but it was in these its early years more shaped by the elites' presumed desires and putative needs than by those of any other group.[19]

In the intellectual world too, the landed joined and welcomed movements that were redefining acceptable modes of thought and behaviour. The antiquarians who produced works of local history and archaeology partly for a market among the genteel disdained to use oral tradition in doing so. In the same vein, the turning from astrology, rejection of witchcraft beliefs, and the acceptance of calendar and nascent weights-and-measures reform by educated women and men all marked a slow seeking, neither inevitable nor unimpeded, of experimentally verifiable and rational grounds for (all but religious) beliefs and social practices. These grounds would provide the foundation for the emergence of a pervasive and powerful discourse of science and technology that did much to sustain aristocratic (although also spawning bureaucratic and technocratic) rule.

This itemization of some facets of landed rule may clarify, if not entirely excuse, a number of lacunae in what follows. A principal one is the absence of full consideration of the impact of location and geography on the landed experience. Geography helped shape regional affinities; it determined the pace and extent of the

18. Colin Campbell, 'Understanding traditional and modern patterns of consumption in eighteenth-century England: a character–action approach', in John Brewer and Roy Porter, eds, *Consumption and the World of Goods* (London, 1993), pp. 40–57.
19. Neil McKendrick, John Brewer, and J.H. Plumb, *The Birth of a Consumer Society: The Commercialization of Eighteenth-Century England* (Bloomington, Indiana, 1982); Jean-Christophe Agnew, 'Consumer culture in historical perspective', in Brewer and Porter, eds, *Consumption and the World of Goods*, pp. 19–39; Louise Lippincott, 'Expanding on portraiture: the market, the public, and the hierarchy of genres in eighteenth-century Britain', in Ann Bermingham and John Brewer, eds, *The Consumption of Culture 1600–1800: Image, Object, Text* (London, 1995), pp. 75–88; John Brewer, '"The most polite age and the most vicious": attitudes towards culture as a commodity, 1660–1800', in ibid., pp. 341–61.

penetration of crown edicts as well as London fashions. But mere distance from London or a provincial town did not determine the extent to which a particular landed family was in contact with or affected by things metropolitan. Even if one could account for the manner in which inland waterways, coastal routes, and turnpikes eased communication and travel, it would be impossible to chart the exact effect on thousands of families, whose receptivity to what was accessible is equally unknowable. Perhaps the most important point to remember when trying to establish the impact location had on landed life is that made by Jeremy Black, that in politics at least it may make more sense to talk in terms of metropolitan and local dynamics that interacted to constitute the national.[20]

In many ways, elite women played crucial roles in the mediation of the metropolitan and the local, and they exercised much authority and power in landed society, most notably in the spheres of education in the home, religious observance, material consumption, and household (as opposed to estate) management. They none the less have a low profile here. Partly this is because the arenas where they held most sway did not impinge so directly on the exercise of rule as those considered in the chapters that follow. Moreover, for a work like this that depends so greatly on the scholarship of others, the published material on education or religion in the home or on domestic consumption and management remains too sparse to allow for full and credible synthesis. In other areas, studies of politics, both parliamentary and popular, focus on men. So do those, for example, of county gentry, estate management, landscape design, justices of the peace, and elite professions.

Women would feature more prominently in an account of landed society written differently, one that emphasized the margin where public and private meet, as has been done in a recent account of the middling sort in Halifax, Yorkshire.[21] Because so much of my story, however, attempts to identify the way the landed elite positioned themselves to rule, it is necessarily taken up with the public side of landed life. And with this aspect, women legally, formally, theoretically, and even practically had much less to do than men. In addition, women took limited recorded part in the management and disposition of the kind of economic resources and assets discussed here. Their low profile in this study should not suggest, however, that theirs was a less weighty or an historically less calculable

20. Black, *Politics of Britain*, p. 62.
21. John Smail, *The Origins of Middle Class Culture: Halifax, Yorkshire, 1660–1780* (Ithaca, New York, 1994).

part in the shaping and exercise of landed rule than that of men. Recent work on the influence of political change on the gender order (and vice versa), studies of women in intellectual circles, exemplary case studies of Restoration and eighteenth-century women of influence and power[22] – all demonstrate the need for a truly two-gender study of the ruling order.

The forging of a ruling order that shared approaches to the navigation of English society began in a climate that did not seem conducive to any journey. As chapter 2 points out, in the wake of the threatening social disorder that marked the interregnum, demographic hardship beset the landed classes at the end of the seventeenth century. They survived testing times not by widening their ranks but by taking steps to reinforce them. These included expanding the geographic range in which marriage partners were found and allowing prospective partners more say in marriage choice, a strategy that did not guarantee but did nothing to lessen the chances of congenial and productive matches. In the realm of education, a reaction against both grammar schools and universities as potential sites of subversive teaching increased the number of landed children who were schooled at home or in academies. Foreign travel for young men grew common. Along with instruction in the classics (which persisted despite some questions raised about it) it supplied an important index of gentility and affirmed the unique status of the landed. In reaction to circumstances that posed questions about the nature and viability of their pre-eminent positions, the landed responded by reasserting old and creating new kinds of bonds among themselves.

English aristocrats confronted economic hardship as well as demographic crisis, and reacted here with more imagination and daring, in both agricultural and non-agricultural realms (chapter 3). They gave up the remnants of their traditional roles as husbandmen to local agrarian communities and with knowing management of their land sought above all to make it productive. By the mid-eighteenth century, when prices began to pick up again, the adoption

---

22. Susan Amussen, *An Ordered Society: Gender and Class in Early Modern England* (Oxford, 1988); Anthony J. Fletcher, *Gender, Sex and Subordination in England 1500–1800* (New Haven, 1995); Margaret J.M. Ezell, *The Patriarch's Wife: Literary Evidence and the History of the Family* (Chapel Hill, North Carolina and London, 1987); *The Poems and Prose of Mary, Lady Chudleigh*, Margaret J.M. Ezell, ed. (Oxford, 1993), pp. xvii–xxxiv; Marilyn Williamson, *Raising Their Voices: British Women Writers, 1650–1750* (Detroit, 1990); Schwoerer, *Lady Rachel Russell* (Baltimore, 1988); *The Diaries of Lady Anne Clifford*, D.J.H. Clifford, ed. (Stroud, 1990); Frances Harris, *A Passion for Government: The Life of Sarah, Duchess of Marlborough* (Oxford, 1991).

of hard-nosed attitudes toward tenants and profits and the acceptance of novel techniques and crops were characteristic of many gentry and nobility and their employees. Eagerly embracing the spirit of improvement, landowners shared enthusiasm, ideas, plants and seeds with one another, creating strong ties across the land. In other economic realms, they shared a growing involvement in the national financial markets that arose out of the wars of the late seventeenth and early eighteenth centuries. Where members of the elite possessed the resources, they also participated in the proto-industrial expansion of the extractive sector.

These strong involvements with agriculture stand as a counterpoint to a disengagement from other countryside activities, as shown in chapter 4. Although activities of the country, and especially those around the country house, continued to have deep meaning for landowners, they resonated differently with them than in the past. Participation in local governance now seemed too onerous and possessed of too little reward of any sort to attract many of the gentry and nobility resident in the countryside. County reputation, which still mattered to the landed elite, none the less rested increasingly on figures' ability to bring to the locality the benefits of metropolitan or some other extra-local connection. And concern for that reputation vied with the desire to cut a figure in London, in a provincial town or national resort. In any event, direct interaction with tenants or other social inferiors constituted a less essential and less desirable element of country life in the mid-eighteenth century than it had a hundred years before.

Country life itself was shaped by a realm of party and metropolitan politics, examined in chapter 5, that further broke down dichotomies between centre and province. The attention of the landed as politicians rested heavily on local matters. But it was from central institutions, both parliament and agencies of the crown, that relief or instruction or power increasingly came, at least initially. Many contentious issues had local ramifications but often originated from considerations of a grander scale: religious policy, dynastic succession, levels of national taxation, the conduct of war and terms of peace. Landed politicians had to be national and party politicians to be successful. Yet for all that party divided and defined landowners, the lurking spectre of past revolutions persuaded the landed to limit the range in which partisanship operated. At times of crisis, the need to maintain social order and retain the reins of social power encouraged the landed to reflect on the interests that they held in common.

The metropolitan pull of politics as exercised in parliamentary elections, at Whitehall and Westminster, and through centrally administered patronage widened a gap between the elite and other social groups that was evident in other areas too. The next two chapters lay out the many cultural manifestations of this separation (chapter 6) and locate many of them in an urban and especially the metropolitan setting of London (chapter 7). In the country-side, the gentry and nobility lived privately and effectively hid themselves from their non-gentle neighbours and neighbourhoods. They rarely graced the communal activities in which landlords had more frequently participated in the past. They turned away intellectually from popular beliefs, and they very effectively used the landscape to create artificially 'natural' worlds to their own liking.

In town the aristocracy were more visible but still able to place distance between themselves and those beneath them. They were catered to by urban professionals and in turn made full use of the increasing resources, luxuries, and entertainments that towns and cities afforded. As much as did landed estates, the urban sites of England gave aristocrats fertile grounds in which to cultivate their lives. And although by the mid-eighteenth century an urban renaissance had given great vitality to several dozen provincial towns, London constituted the kingdom's metropolis and as such contributed uniquely to the pruning and shaping of elite identity. It also offered to the landed order, as did its privileged status more generally, a profusion of opportunity, for good and ill, to shape the identity of an entire nation.

CHAPTER TWO

Birth, Marriage, and Education

Introduction

In the hundred years after 1650, a combination of relatively stable components and of two different kinds of solder (marriage and education) helped to weld England's provincial elites into a composite ruling order. This process saw a relative weakening of local and countywide connections in landed culture. These had enjoyed large places in the ethos of landed life in the sixteenth and early seventeenth centuries, and if the landed order had grown as rapidly after the mid-seventeenth century as it did between the Reformation and civil war, they might have continued to do so. As it was, the number of English landed families in 1650 and 1750 were roughly the same. This similarity, however, masks a demographic regression that became apparent at the end of the seventeenth century and, although temporary, contributed to a kind of siege mentality and collective identity within the ranks of English landed society.

In the face of this crisis, one that left many elite families without sons to inherit family estates, the landed persisted in marrying overwhelmingly among themselves, but they increasingly found partners from across the kingdom in a marriage market of wide scope. This broadening market helped to link the elite together, as did education, especially of the males among the elite. This education had always insisted on a socially distinctive, Latin-based instruction, and now the employment of private tutors, and the popularity of European travel to finish young men's schooling, intensified the unique character of elite education. This chapter explores the ways in which patterns of demography, marriage, and education reinforced an inclination among gentry and nobility alike to look for and acknowledge the characteristics that distinguished them from

13

those below them in the social order. These same characteristics reminded them that despite their differences of religion and party, rank and place of residence, they were also in important ways much like one another.

Demographic crisis?

Historians agree that the landed order in late Stuart and early Hanoverian England experienced no substantial growth and shrank for several decades after the middle of the hundred years under study. Yet they have found it difficult to establish precisely just who belonged to this landed order and how many individuals made it up. Titled members of the landed elite – dukes, marquesses, earls, viscounts, and barons among the nobility, baronets and knights among the gentry – can be counted with some accuracy, but the absence of comprehensive sources makes it impossible to identify esquires and gentlemen as precisely. Materials that seem to provide potential guides to the wealthy and especially the landed wealthy – the records of the nationwide poll, hearth, and land taxes – are unreliable or unusable. They vary widely in their rates of survival and in the accuracy with which they identify persons taxed. Heralds' visitations that supposedly recorded families entitled to bear arms fell into abeyance after the mid-seventeenth century. Sources that seem to include virtually all substantial landowners are unsatisfactory too: the land tax of 1702 named some 32,000 commissioners, apparently few below the rank of gentleman and all of whom were meant to have £100 p.a. in land. But in 1723 there were no more than 13,000 commissioners named outside London and Middlesex, although no one would suggest that there were thousands fewer landed families than twenty years before.[1]

For the same reasons that they can be counted, the titled members of the landed loom large in the chapters that follow: their wealth, their prestige, and their power made them visible and audible. They include the owners of England's most extensive estates and largest houses (many still extant), and they have historically

1. Stone and Stone, *An Open Elite?*, pp. 53–60; Beckett, *Aristocracy*, pp. 33–4; Langford, *Public Life*, pp. 289, 422–3; Dennis Mills, 'Survival of early land tax assessments', in Michael Turner and Dennis Mills, eds, *Land and Property: The English Land Tax 1692–1832* (New York, 1986), pp. 219–31. See also J.P. Cooper, 'Social distribution of land and men in England, 1463–1700', in Cooper, *Land, Men and Beliefs: Studies in Early Modern History*, G.E. Aylmer and J.S. Morrill, eds (London, 1983), pp. 17–42.

left the best preserved and most accessible archives, through which they have been made to speak loudly about the landed experience. But esquires and gentlemen speak too, and the experience of the most prominent estate owners was shared in many ways by others in the landed class. There were, moreover, untitled men who ranked among the 'parliamentary families', the 'governing class . . . at the national level', who from 1660 to 1755 provided between 65 and 80 per cent of all members of the House of Commons.[2]

Although the labels 'gentleman' and 'esquire' carried imprecise meanings and their use was ineffectively policed, they were precise enough in our period (as in earlier ones) in their denotation of comportment rather than income, of presumed standing rather than legally defined rights and privileges. Clearly, incomes and acres calculated in the thousands enabled their possessors to carry themselves more grandly and stylishly than those who possessed only hundreds. But the average income of £400 p.a. that John Chamberlayne accorded to squires and gentlemen in 1669, and the £450 and £280 Gregory King respectively assigned them for 1688, still allowed them to consume at a level that set them off from the nongentle.[3] Even though they could not keep up with the age's Dukes of Omnium, thousands of country squires embraced a mode of living and set of values that left no doubt that they were persons of quality, a cut above virtually all of the rest of society.

When it comes to assessing the size of the squirearchy, the absence after 1650 of some of the features that characterized the preceding era of gentry expansion indicates shrinkage in their ranks. The decline in enrolments at universities, partly attributable to a new outlook on education (just as the expansion had been), may also speak to a less pressing supply of gentry sons. The relative decline in the price of land and the activity of the land market in the late seventeenth and early eighteenth centuries, although attributable to many causes, may reflect a drop in demand that has a demographic component.[4] More significantly, however, the failures

---

2. Ellis Archer Wasson, 'The House of Commons, 1660–1945: parliamentary families and the political elite', *English Historical Review* 106 (1991), p. 637, and table 1 (p. 647). This 'hereditary political elite' (p. 643) is comprised of members of families who produced three or more MPs between 1660 and 1945, and so its hereditary character is most evident retrospectively and less so from, say, 1750.

3. The figures derive respectively from G.E. Mingay, *The Gentry: The Rise and Fall of a Ruling Class* (London, 1976), p. 11 and Joan Thirsk and J.P. Cooper, eds, *Seventeenth-Century Economic Documents* (Oxford, 1972), p. 780.

4. *AHEW*, V, pt 2, pp. 170–6, esp. table 14.1; C.G.A. Clay, *Economic Expansion and Social Change: England 1500–1700*, I, *People, Land and Towns* (Cambridge, 1984), pp. 162–3; Grassby, *Business Community*, pp. 335, 373–8.

of family after family in the direct male line signals a crisis of numbers unprecedented in previous generations.

The era of the gentry's great expansion stretched from the early sixteenth to mid-seventeenth centuries, altering the kingdom from one where many parishes lacked resident gentle families to a society where such families proliferated. The years of growth saw limited increase among England's few hundred magnate families, but the generality of gentry expanded to number from fifteen to twenty thousand families around 1650. They held at that point about half of the kingdom's land and constituted about two per cent of the population. While the substantial rise in gentry numbers up to the mid-seventeenth century seems proven, there is no evidence for continued growth in the hundred years that followed. Surviving impressionistic evidence is in agreement with what can be established for particular counties or areas of the country. If the proportion of landed families within the total population remained constant, then at one-fiftieth of the population, these families numbered about 105,000 persons in 1650 and 10,000 more in 1750. If family size among the elite was something like 4.75, then these aggregate figures would indicate that 22,000 to 24,000 family units made up the landed order during this century.[5] These figures correspond to the higher estimates in Gregory King's 'Scheme of the Income and Expenses of the Several Famillies of England', which he compiled in the 1690s. There, in different versions, he enumerated 160 holders of noble titles, 800 baronets, 600 knights, 3000 to 4000 esquires and 12,000 to 20,000 gentlemen, for a total ranging from under 17,000 to over 25,000 landed aristocratic families.[6]

England's population increased over ten per cent during that century, from 5.23 million in 1651 to 5.77 million in 1751.[7] Considering the landed elite's problems in directly transmitting estates through the generations between the mid-seventeenth and mid-eighteenth centuries, it is likely that the landed population did not rise in the same proportion. In other words, the shifts and transformations within the landowning elite that are the subject of this study were not forged in times of demographic expansion for the

---

5. Clay, *Economic Expansion and Social Change*, I, pp. 142–58; Heal and Holmes, *Gentry*, pp. 11–12; Mingay, *Gentry*, p. 59.

6. Thirsk and Cooper, eds, *Documents*, pp. 766–8, 780–1; G.S. Holmes, 'Gregory King and the social structure of pre-industrial England', *Transactions of the Royal Historical Society*, 5th series, 27 (1977), pp. 41–68.

7. E.A. Wrigley and R.S. Schofield, *The Population History of England 1541–1871: A Reconstruction* (Cambridge, Massachusetts, 1981), table 7.8.

group. The shrinkage in numbers, which coincided with a perception dating from the Restoration that the landed elite was under attack, began around the late seventeenth and extended to the mid-eighteenth century. For reasons that continue to prove elusive, reduced nuptiality and fertility, along with high infant mortality, combined to reduce the size of elite families, to lower the average age at inheritance, and to appear to threaten the survival of male lines.

These lines failed markedly among the titled and gentle orders of late Stuart and early Hanoverian England; names and patrimonies were preserved but direct lines of male descent were not. The tight gentry community of Glamorgan 'was destroyed by demographic changes' that saw one-third of greater and one-quarter of lesser gentry heads of estates between 1660 and 1760 fail to produce male heirs. None of the four families of Yorkshire baronets closely chronicled by Peter Roebuck for the period 1640–1760 experienced continuous direct transmission of inheritance. And in Hertfordshire, Northamptonshire, and Northumberland, by the mid-eighteenth century less than two-thirds of estates were passing by direct inheritance from grandfather or father to a son.[8] Among the titled, such difficulties led to extinction. Titled families (peers, baronets, and knights) collectively numbered 1546 in 1700, but only 1096 fifty years later. Although the decline grew partly from a curtailment of knighthoods after the many creations in Charles II's reign and again after 1714, the number of baronets (whose titles were hereditary) dropped from 860 in 1700 to 651 in 1750, despite the creation of over 160 new titles during this period.[9]

The role of mortality in this picture of demographic crisis is much less easy to delineate than evidence for delayed marriage and decreased fertility, but two circumstances distinct from those operating among the population at large (which in the mid-1690s was $3^{1}/_{2}$ per cent below its level of 1650) may have been at play. First, England's military involvement in continental wars beginning under William III created an officer corps full of gentry offspring who

8. Jenkins, *Making of a Ruling Class*; Roebuck, *Yorkshire Baronets*, pp. 271–88; Stone and Stone, *An Open Elite?*, pp. 106–7.
9. Figures calculated from Beckett, *Aristocracy*, tables A1–A3, A5 [total (iii)], A6–A7, and see pp. 97–8. See also Stone and Stone, *An Open Elite?*, pp. 86–104; *AHEW*, V, pt 2: pp. 165–66; John Habakkuk, *Estates System*, p. ix; T.H. Hollingsworth, *The Demography of the British Peerage*, supplement to *Population Studies* 18 (1964); Lloyd Bonfield, 'Marriage settlements and the "rise of great estates": the demographic aspect', *Economic History Review*, 2nd series, 32 (1979), pp. 489–91.

were exposed to harm in battle and, far more dangerously, to disease. Second, the migration of the landed to London had attendant health hazards. Although the quality tended to live in the more spacious parts of town, in newer housing that was provided with better (if still not high-quality) water, they were none the less exposed to rates of mortality far higher in the metropolis than in the rest of the country. These were somewhat mitigated because the landed were part-time residents and lived in areas less exposed to the airborne pollution that exacerbated common lung ailments. Westminster, much favoured by aristocrats, was also a district with a relatively low incidence of smallpox, and the more salubrious accommodations of the gentry and nobility may have protected their offspring from the diseases of infancy that in 1675–1775 caused a third of the deaths recorded in the Bills of Mortality. But then again, aristocrats were quite likely to be resident in town during high mortality months like January, February, and March; aristocratic women often purposefully came to London to give birth; and the mortality rates of neighbourhoods where the elite generally lived are lower only in the context of the metropolis as a whole.[10]

Although unlikely to be aware of periods of higher mortality in their ranks, some contemporaries worried for the actual survival of a landed order. Their fears took root in memories of the revolutionary years and in the potential for future political conspiracy and social upheaval. The Marquess of Halifax wrote in Charles II's reign that the world had grown 'saucy' around him,[11] but the times held graver dangers. Open challenges and resistance to the socially and politically prominent, most seriously in the form of seditious conspiracy but also through attacks on deer parks, opposition to the hearth tax, and the defiant behaviour of dissenters, had the cumulative effect of creating suspicion and raising alarm among many gentry and nobility.[12] And this psychologically embattled group, perhaps finding comfort by closing ranks, may also in pessimism have felt less inclination to marry and propagate.

10. John Landers, *Death and the Metropolis: Studies in the Demographic History of London 1670–1830* (Cambridge, 1993), pp. 70–2, 94–8, 206, 321–4 and *passim*.
11. Cited in John Spurr, *The Restoration Church of England, 1646–1689* (New Haven, 1991), p. 219.
12. David Underdown, *A Freeborn People: Politics and the Nation in Seventeenth-Century England* (Oxford, 1996), pp. 122–3, 130; Ronald Hutton, *The Restoration: A Political and Religious History of England and Wales 1658–1667* (Oxford, 1985), pp. 183–4; Richard L. Greaves, *Deliver Us from Evil: The Radical Underground in Britain, 1660–1663* (New York, 1986), p. 7; idem, *Enemies Under His Feet: Radicals and Nonconformists in Britain, 1664–1677* (Stanford, 1990), ch. 4.

The anxieties of the landed should be taken seriously, especially as they illuminate the changing self-conception of this social group. Yet even if they help to explain the order's demographic downturn, that decline was borne well. Landowners remained pre-eminent in English society. There was no significant recruitment of outsiders for the landed order, into whose lower ranks by 1700 there was 'a significantly reduced rate of recruitment . . . compared to that of 1600 or 1640'.[13] Any demographic breaks in the integrity of existing communities did not fundamentally modify the landed's continuous possession of land or their basically unassailable local social domination. Sometimes breaches led to the infusion of more broadly British families than hitherto, as with the Morgans of Tredegar in Monmouth, whose huge inheritance passed in the eighteenth century to an in-law with Kentish origins, who took the family name and tried to disguise a lack of local connection by securing the title Lord Tredegar.[14]

Such a strategy exemplifies the painstaking efforts, widely employed and somehow successful, that landed elements made to preserve both a family name and estate. Yet it seems a move likely to do a limited amount to counter the dissolution of any community feeling that rested on long association of regionally connected families. Where gentry cohorts in particular counties suffered loss of old-established lines, the introduction of distant relatives did little for local social cohesion, however it sustained family names and houses. And because such truly insular gentry communities were rare, the entrance of indirect heirs probably worked more often to intensify an already emergent sense of membership in a more nationally extensive community of the landed.[15]

The movement of outsiders into counties underscores the fact that provincial elites were continuing to lose the county-defined character they had in the sixteenth and even still in the early seventeenth century, leaving the way open for them to think of their fortunes and futures in terms of the kingdom as a whole.[16] Although 'completely new'[17] in the sense of never having lived in the regions to which they moved, the late seventeenth- and eighteenth-century

13. Clay, *Economic Expansion and Social Change*, I, p. 163.
14. J.P. Jenkins, 'The demographic decline of the landed gentry in the eighteenth century: a south Wales study', *Welsh Historical Review* 11 (1982), p. 36.
15. This and the next paragraph follow the argument in Stone and Stone, *An Open Elite?*, part II.
16. Linda Colley, *Britons: Forging the Nation 1707–1837* (New Haven, 1992), pp. 156–8.
17. Jenkins, 'Demographic decline', p. 45.

landowners who took up estates where established families failed in primary lines usually obtained them through intra-familial inheritance and not by purchase. Far from being recruited outside the gentry, individual inheritors were outsiders only because they were less often direct male heirs and more often heiresses, nephews, cousins, or sons-in-law. In the interests of continuity, the men changed their names and engaged in other tortuous, self-deluding, and even devious strategies to perpetuate a particular family appellation and maintain ancestral acres whole.[18]

In addition to these strategies of inheritance and patronymic, new economic tactics enabled even debt-ridden, financially vulnerable landed families to persist, if a head of family could be found to carry on the family name. Sales of estates for the purpose of liquidation were relatively few, and when they occurred, they mostly had landed buyers. Where gentry did sell their estates, therefore, the action may well have made the landed order more homogeneous and broader in outlook. Demand for great estates by the non-landed wealthy was limited, and landed estates grand enough to establish a gentle interest on the part of social climbers were actually not often available.[19] When monied men bought, they most commonly acquired urban property. Sir Stephen Fox, who broke the mould and spent nearly £100,000 between 1670 and 1716 amassing land in the West Country, none the less had no interest in living the landed life.[20] From the 1690s, development of 'the institutional framework for a monied elite' meant that businessmen seeking investments had less need to be involved in the land market even as holders of mortgages.[21]

Where direct male heirs failed but sale was avoided, the descent of properties through heiresses or indirect male heirs encouraged the growth of bigger estates, because heiresses themselves most often married husbands who possessed some property of their own, and indirect male heirs usually already possessed landed estates, albeit modest ones.[22] The prosperity that more property brought

18. Heal and Holmes, *Gentry*, p. 46; Roebuck, *Yorkshire Baronets*, pp. 277–87.

19. Stone and Stone, *An Open Elite?*, pp. 212–25; *AHEW*, V, pt 2, pp. 170–98; Clay, *Economic Expansion and Social Change*, I, pp. 160–4; Habakkuk, *Estates System*, chs 6, 7; idem, 'The rise and fall of English landed families, 1600–1800, II', *Transactions of the Royal Historical Society*, 5th series, 30 (1980), pp. 213–17; idem, 'The rise and fall of English landed families, 1600–1800, III', *Transactions of the Royal Historical Society*, 5th series, 31 (1981), p. 217.

20. C.G.A. Clay, *Public Finance and Private Wealth: The Career of Sir Stephen Fox 1627–1716* (Oxford, 1978), pp. 161–76, 334–5.

21. Grassby, *Business Community*, pp. 375–7; quotation on p. 377.

22. H.J. Habakkuk, 'The rise and fall of landed families, I', *Transactions of the Royal Historical Society*, 5th series, 29 (1979), pp. 189–94.

and the economic flexibility that the greatest landowners enjoyed stimulated not insularity but the extroversion so manifest in trips abroad or to Bath, in the building, decorating, and entertaining at country seats, in an extroverted consumerism that had the effect of creating and designating a community of cultural interest. In its way, a demographic crisis partly the result of the gentry's own actions, one which assisted the consolidation of estates and made clear that the age of the gentry's growth in numbers had come to an end, may have worked to enhance the common identity and solidarity of the landed order.

Marriage

Links forged through marriage had long been one of the ways in which individuals and families in the ranks of landowners came together and expressed their common interests. In the latter part of the seventeenth century, as both cause and consequence of demographic crisis, the elite's usages in marriage and courtship assisted its slow development as a cosmopolitan and more nationally oriented social group. Some of these practices were new or had new currency, like the greater voice children expressed in marriage choice and the ever sharper tendency to make marriages from a geographically widespread pool of possible partners. Other practices continued past observances but with different meaning, like the propensity for the landed to marry others from landed society.

NUPTIALITY

To begin with, delay in first marriages, reduced rates of remarriage, and an unexplained decline in lifetime nuptiality all added to the crisis in aristocratic numbers in the middle of our period. Among the nobility the median age at first marriage rose steadily from the later sixteenth to the eighteenth centuries, reaching a peak in the late 1730s of over twenty-five and a half years for females and a peak at mid-century of thirty-three and a half for males.[23] Among a sample of male country-house owners, a group who tended to marry earlier than their younger brothers and one that largely excludes younger sons, the median age at first marriage rose from roughly twenty-four for those born between 1600 and 1649 to twenty-six for the cohort born a century later.[24]

23. Hollingsworth, *Demography of the Peerage*, p. 18.
24. Stone and Stone, *An Open Elite?*, p. 96 (fig. 3.3) and table 3.3.

Where many delayed marrying, others rejected matrimony entirely, and the numbers of offspring among the landed elite who never married were drawing negative comment by the end of the seventeenth century. Apparently their behaviour constituted not a particular but a national problem. One of *The Spectator's* female correspondents lamented in 1712 that 'Celibacy is the great Evil of our Nation', and suggested that bachelors be fined like convicted papists. 'Now-a-days', she complained, 'we must be contented if we can get Creatures which are not bad, good are not to be expected.'[25] The appearance of two editions of *The Bachelor's Directory* in the mid-1690s, attempting to persuade unmarried men of the need to enter the marital state, suggests that at least one publisher believed there was a readership looking to be persuaded of 'the excellence of marriage'.[26]

These contemporary perceptions of marriage-shyness are borne out by historians' research. Nearly a quarter of females in the peerage cohort born between 1675 and 1699 and over a quarter born between 1700 and 1724 were unmarried at age fifty, compared with just 16 per cent for the cohort born between 1650 and 1674. Over one-fifth of the combined male peerage cohorts born between 1675 and 1699 and between 1700 and 1724 also never married. Among a group of country-house owners from three counties there was a three-fold rise in the proportion of the unmarried between those born in the late sixteenth or early seventeenth century and those born between 1650 and 1750: 15 per cent of the latter remained unmarried.[27]

The reasons for the rise in bachelorhood and spinsterhood remain mysterious, although the latter to some extent derived from the former. Some have suggested that the percolation of Lockian ideas promoting individual freedom gave young men and women in the early eighteenth century greater liberty to seek emotional fulfilment where they wished, and not necessarily in matrimony.[28] The active subculture in early eighteenth-century London of what today would be labelled the male homosexual, although mostly

25. *The Spectator*, Donald F. Bond, ed., 5 vols (Oxford, 1965), IV, pp. 382, 385.
26. *The Bachelor's Directory: Being a Treatise of the Excellence of Marriage . . .* (London, 1694; 2nd edn, 1696).
27. Hollingsworth, *Demography of the Peerage*, p. 20 (table 11); Susan Staves, *Married Women's Separate Property in England, 1660–1833* (Cambridge, Massachusetts, 1990), pp. 278–9, n. 36; Stone and Stone, *An Open Elite?*, pp. 88–91 and table 3.2.
28. Lawrence Stone, 'Libertine sexuality in post-Restoration England: group sex and flagellation among the middling sort in Norwich in 1706–07', *Journal of the History of Sexuality* 2 (1991–92), p. 525; Habakkuk, *Estates System*, pp. 158–9.

populated by those from the lower and middling orders, included some gentlemen too. That an observer at the turn of the century attributed to 'Italian . . . moralls' one squire's reluctance to wed signals this commentator's awareness of homosexual practices in his society and displays his theory as to their originary influence. In fact, the association between Italy – the increasingly likely destination of young gentlemen on tour – and male homosexuality was common in the late seventeenth century. The explicit connection made a few decades later between homosexuality and Italian opera, much attended by young aristocratic males, is further suggestion that men – perhaps even groups of men – behaving in some recognizably 'homosexual' manner were identifiable in the upper reaches of Augustan society, specifically in London. It may be proper to impute to them a disinclination to marry.[29]

Probably more important in explaining the decline in nuptiality is the fact that a higher mortality among heads of households increased the number of heirs acceding to family seats when still unmarried: in the absence of paternal pressure these heirs more freely postponed or even rejected marriage. Over half the heirs inheriting during the period 1700–59 in one group of gentry married after their fathers' deaths.[30] Proportions of remarriages also fell after 1650, and the increasingly common provision in marriage settlements for jointure payments to terminate on widows' remarriage may have played a part in this trend.[31]

Unwillingness to marry or remarry can also be attributed to the expectations many of the landed had of marriage. A companionable and affectionate partnership was in this period more requisite (or at least desirable) than had historically been the case. Some likely candidates for matrimony may have put it off as they awaited the seemingly necessary sensation of love. Because parents more frequently gave weight to love and to their children's personal preferences as the eighteenth century wore on, some offspring were freed not to marry at all and others insisted upon second or further choice of spouses. Besides emotional expectations, financial

29. Rictor Norton, *Mother Clap's Molly House: The Gay Subculture in England 1700–1830* (London, 1992), chap. 2; Randolph Trumbach, 'The birth of the queen: sodomy and the emergence of gender equality in modern culture, 1660–1750', in Martin B. Duberman, Martha Vicinus, and George Chauncey, Jr, eds, *Hidden from History: Reclaiming the Gay and Lesbian Past* (New York, 1989), pp. 129–40; Bruce Redford, *Venice & the Grand Tour* (New Haven, 1996), pp. 22–5. For the reference to Italian morals see *Prideaux to Ellis Letters*, p. 193.

30. Stone and Stone, *An Open Elite?*, pp. 102–3 and table 3.9.

31. Ibid., pp. 123–4; Staves, *Married Women's Separate Property*, pp. 100–1, 215–16.

considerations might diminish nuptiality. The rise in the size of acceptable marriage portions during the course of the seventeenth century led some heirs with unmarried sisters to postpone their own marriages until they provided their siblings with portions. And sisters whose brothers could not produce adequate dowries were in danger of being effectively prevented from ever securing husbands.[32]

MARITAL GEOGRAPHY

Among the peerage, geographical distance was no impediment to marriage. Considering the restricted number of noble families, those who sought partners from other titled families had to seek them widely. For the gentry of many counties as well, marriage was by the middle of the seventeenth century decidedly exogamous, that is, made with partners from other regions. Endogamy none the less notably persisted in the north and northwest, also in East Anglia and peninsular counties like Kent: here more than 60 per cent of gentry marriage alliances were made within the county.[33] But the ensuing century saw only developments that would weaken this insular pattern.

As will be seen, extra-local marriage markets flourished under the later Stuarts and early Hanoverians, and, given the relative scarcity of suitable partners brought on by the demographic dip and by reluctance to marry, few parents could insist on finding a spouse within the county. Lesser gentry remained most likely to marry locally, and if they did so abroad, they understandably and often found partners in adjacent counties, as did greater gentry like the prosperous Sir Richard Newdigate of Arbury in Warwickshire who wed Mary Bagot from adjacent Staffordshire. Yet Cumberland (in the person of Sir John Lowther of Whitehaven) could marry Surrey (in the person of Jane Leigh), and no principle whatsoever stood in the way of marrying further afield.[34] When southerners 'hesitated before committing a child to the remote fastnesses of Wales',

32. Lawrence Stone, *The Family, Sex and Marriage in England 1500–1800* (London, 1977), chs 5, 7; Heal and Holmes, *Gentry*, pp. 60–8; Habakkuk, *Estates System*, pp. 128–9, 147–8; Jenkins, 'Demographic decline', pp. 41–2. Staves, *Married Women's Separate Property*, pp. 118, 203–4 notes that provisions made in settlements are no guide to the portions eventually paid.

33. Heal and Holmes, *Gentry*, pp. 61–2; Ralph A. Houlbrooke, *The English Family 1450–1700* (London, 1984), p. 51.

34. Vivienne Larminie, *Wealth, Kinship and Culture: The Seventeenth-Century Newdigates of Arbury and Their World* (Woodbridge, Suffolk, 1995), p. 59; Beckett, *Coal and Tobacco*, p. 210.

it seems to be the fact of Wales and not distance that put them off. Mary Wynn, a Welsh heiress, had no problem securing a match in the Bertie family of Lincolnshire, and of the four 'Gentlemen of Quality' who hoped to marry the daughter of John Evelyn of Surrey, one came from Cheshire and another from Staffordshire.[35] Even where partners came from the same county, as in the case of Walter Calverley's 'sister Ramsden' and her husband, consecration of the marriage in London gave it a non-local and even slightly exotic colouration, and implicated the couple in a far-reaching social milieu.[36]

Whether marrying across a large or narrower geographic spectrum, a significant majority of landowners stayed within the social confines of landed society when choosing partners. In counties immediately adjacent to London, like Hertfordshire, there was a rise in matches with monied daughters in the early eighteenth century, coinciding with an expansion of consumer-driven commerce, a legitimation of the world of high finance in the eyes of the landed, and a depression of grain prices that affected landed incomes. Under the later Stuarts, numerous daughters of London aldermen married gentlemen and '[t]he successful merchant . . . was frequently targeted by impecunious landed families' – with, however, no guarantee of success, since landowners generally used marriage to preserve social boundaries. The most desired match was one that linked land with land, a preference nearly universal among the nobility and one successfully attained by most of the landed. The continuing desire to marry with the landed if possible expressed the essentially common cultural values of landowners seeking to preserve the integrity of a social order stretching across the kingdom.[37]

An analysis of the 'politics of matrimony' rather ironically bears out this point, not because it shows marriages taking place across political lines but because it demonstrates that the search for politically appropriate partners transcended geographical considerations. On the political score, where wives' party allegiances can be determined, over 80 per cent of a sample of tory and whig members of parliament from 1715 to 1754 married like-minded women. On

---

35. Heal and Holmes, *Gentry*, pp. 67–8; Houlbrooke, *English Family*, pp. 70–1; Ann Hughes, *Politics, Society and Civil War in Warwickshire, 1620–1660* (Cambridge, 1987), pp. 39–40 and n. 53.

36. 'Calverly memorandum book', p. 71.

37. Grassby, *Business Community*, p. 307 for the quotation. See also Stone and Stone, *An Open Elite?*, pp. 247–51, 289–92, and table 7.9; Hollingsworth, *Demography of the Peerage*, p. 9; David Thomas, 'The social origins of marriage partners of the British peerage in the eighteenth and nineteenth centuries', *Population Studies* 26 (1972), pp. 99–111, esp. tables 3–6, 9, and 11.

the count of geography, however, by the 1740s Roman Catholic Jacobite gentlemen from the south of England looked to the north to find wives and in-laws of a similar persuasion.[38] Insofar as political allegiance was a significant term in the equation of marital choice, the desire to marry like-minded partners tended to encourage geographical exogamy among the politically convinced gentry and nobility.

The identification and selection of suitable marriage partners could therefore be complicated by politics, demographic circumstance, financial pressures, and insistence on free choice, a situation that encouraged members of landed families to look far afield for partners. This breadth of search constitutes another example of the orientation to the national plane that characterized so many facets of elite life by the mid-eighteenth century. Families undoubtedly continued to have an interest in making alliances within a familiar region or county, and because 'propinquity breeds familiarity', marital endogamy never disappeared, especially in northern counties where it was more expensive and difficult to enter the marriage markets of London and Bath. Yet the development of national and regional social networks had been expanding families' horizons and altering their marital patterns since the sixteenth century, and among the nobility and greater gentry purely local marriages were already rare in the early seventeenth century.[39] The development of better communications and the multiplication of reasons for landed men and women to travel away from their places of origin and principal residence worked similar changes even among lesser gentry, especially by drawing them into marriage markets far larger than the county.

MARRIAGE MARKETS

A national marriage market offering a wide choice of potential spouses accompanied the decline in county and regional marital endogamy. From the last quarter of the sixteenth century an aristocratic marriage market existed in London, an important site to garner information about potential partners, and one that afforded some social contact between eligible young men and women around the royal court. During and after the late seventeenth century,

38. Paul Monod, 'The politics of matrimony: Jacobitism and marriage in eighteenth-century England', in Eveline Cruickshanks and Jeremy Black, eds, *The Jacobite Challenge* (Edinburgh, 1988), pp. 24–41.

39. Stone and Stone, *An Open Elite?*, pp. 38 (for quotation), 40; Heal and Holmes, *Gentry*, pp. 61–2, 67–8; Stone, *Crisis of the Aristocracy*, pp. 623–5; Habakkuk, *Estates System*, pp. 170–93.

improved communications and transport, the heightened centrality of London-based services in landed life, and the appearance of new arenas for social interaction intensified this metropolitan influence and expanded its range beyond the nobility to the prosperous gentry. By the mid-eighteenth century, provincial marriage markets flourished across the countryside in towns that had benefited from an urban renaissance, and a truly national one thrived in London and Bath.[40]

Of all the venues for matrimonial negotiations, London had pride of place. It was a nexus for many activities of aristocratic life. The political attraction of the court and then of the state bureaucracy, along with frequent (and after 1689 annual) sessions of parliament, enticed many members of landed society to town. The capital's allure as a centre of cultural and social activity also increased, and the elite's demographic crisis, by reducing marriage opportunities in the countryside, made it sensible to seek a partner in the kingdom's largest and fastest-growing urban centre.[41] Development of a predictable London season, not very discernible much before the end of the seventeenth century, played a significant role in making matches. The entry on 'wooing' in *The Ladies Dictionary* of 1694 clearly implies that the proper, most effective courtship of a woman entailed a round of activities focussed on London. And as the preliminaries to marriage grew more complicated after the mid-seventeenth century with adoption of the strict settlement, so did dependence on London lawyers for the documentation involved.[42] This focus on the metropolis in matters matrimonial, as in so many aspects of elite life, encouraged members of the landed order also to focus on – and find commonalities with – one another.

Despite London's pre-eminence, it is important to remember that those among the landed elite who did not make choices of partners within their 'home' county or region did not necessarily find the people they married in a London market. The marriage market in which they shopped ramified beyond the metropolis and depended on information retrieved from the whole kingdom. Although a man like the patriarch of the Lowther family in Westmorland regularly learned about projects and London's marital

---

40. Stone, *Family, Sex and Marriage*, pp. 316–17; Houlbrooke, *English Family*, pp. 29, 65–6.

41. Roger Finlay and Beatrice Shearer, 'Population growth and suburban expansion', in A.L. Beier and Roger Finlay, eds, *London 1500–1700: The Making of a Metropolis* (London, 1986), p. 39.

42. Staves, *Married Women's Separate Property*, pp. 58–9.

'practise' from a nephew in town, intelligence moved from country to town too. Accurate calculation of prospects depended on detailed and reliable information from the provinces, secured through the same networks of friends and relatives who initially helped to identify possible grooms and brides. The landlords who increasingly insisted on reliable, professional accounting on their estates coincidentally facilitated better assessment of prospective spouses' financial expectations.[43] The emergence after 1650 of many provincial gathering places and resorts played its part, and even in county towns with limited cultural outlets, such as Bury St Edmunds and Winchester, identifiable marriage markets developed by the first third of the eighteenth century.[44] The provincial press of that era further testified to the national exchange of marital news by recording noteworthy marriages. These notices appeared as early as the 1720s in the *Ipswich Journal*, and from its inception in 1744 the *Bath Journal* ran accounts of weddings that had recently occurred throughout the kingdom, accounts that often indicated the size of the bride's portion.

For the gentry and nobility who were finding marriage partners in a broadening arena, it is difficult to imagine where alliances could have been so readily made besides London or a national gathering spot like Bath. Local occasions like assizes or fairs drew many gentry but at most from a multi-county and still proximate region: the denizens of Sussex were unlikely to find much of interest at, say, Gloucestershire assizes. By contrast, the presence of marriage opportunity in London was as well acknowledged as its place in fixing marriages was unique. The proposed match between young Bellair and Harriet Woodvill in *The Man of Mode* (1676), while negotiated by their parents in the country, none the less depended upon the couple's successful interview in town.[45] London provided the forum where Sir Ralph Verney's godson learned of a match worth £6000 in 1672. A Lincolnshire landowner who enlisted the help of financier Robert Clayton to find him a rich bride succinctly noted around the same time that 'you have all the money and women at London'.[46] A similar sentiment resonates in the counsel given Oliver Le Neve,

---

43. D.R. Hainsworth, 'Fathers and daughters: patterns of marriage and inheritance among the later Stuart gentry', in L.O. Frappell, ed., *Principalities, Powers and Estates* (Adelaide, 1979 [recte 1980]), p. 17.

44. Peter Borsay, *The English Urban Renaissance: Culture and Society in the Provincial Town 1660–1770* (Oxford, 1989), p. 245.

45. George Etherege, *The Man of Mode; or Sir Fopling Flutter* (1676), in John Harold Wilson, ed., *Six Restoration Plays* (Boston, 1959), pp. 102, 115.

46. Miriam Slater, *Family Life in the Seventeenth Century: The Verneys of Claydon House* (London, 1984), p. 76; Frank T. Melton, *Sir Robert Clayton and the Origins of English Deposit Banking, 1658–1685* (Cambridge, 1986), p. 48.

a recent widower visiting town in 1696, who was advised that 'if you meete with a handsome & sound girle pray be not backward but trust stoutly & spend lustely' since similar prospects were 'not here [in the country] to be had'.[47] London's 'market reach' expanded throughout the eighteenth century, but by the nineteenth the city's sheer size may have made it a less efficient site for identifying prospects than provincial towns. Jane Austen's novels, for example, as preoccupied with marriage as they are, depict no more than ephemeral plans to find husbands in the metropolis and instead present London as a place where marriages are endangered.[48]

THE MAKING AND MEANINGS OF MARRIAGE

A visible and widely used marriage market caught the attention of the wealthy landed, another enticement to draw their vision beyond county and region. But attitudes toward the institution of marriage itself – its purpose, making, and meaning – also shifted in the century after the civil war. This alteration was attended by changes in the meaning of the family, and together they had the effect of diminishing the provincial and enhancing the cosmopolitan outlook of England's landed order. The 'waning obsession' with family lineage meant that marriages were construed more as the union of a couple and the inception of nuclear families, and less as the joining of dynasties. This waning coincided with an end to the practice of denominating the components of the landed household (relatives, servants, and employees) as 'family', a practice that had the effect of eliding the separate standing that each group enjoyed. In the late seventeenth century the distinction between nuclear unit and others in the household became stronger and clearer, and an emotional basis for the former unit was seen as desirable.[49] Such changes projected the landed into the world as atomized individuals readily configured into a collectivity more amorphous yet larger and more complex than a dynasty, kin group, or collection of 'county' families.

In prior ages, marriages made predominantly to perpetuate family lines had not necessarily been emotionless partnerships, and the second half of the seventeenth century did not usher in an entirely

---

47. G. Bladwell to Le Neve, 9 December 1696 and 11 January 1697, British Library, Egerton MS 2718, fols 344, 369.
48. I am grateful to Mary Ann O'Farrell for this point.
49. Heal and Holmes, *Gentry*, pp. 38–42, 53. Chapter 4 below notes some of the changes this distinction wrought in domestic architecture.

new era of affective relations between wife and husband and in the immediate family. Yet starting early in the seventeenth century, guided in some measure by affection, landed parents granted greater weight to their children's wishes regarding marriage partners. These particular desires continued to be subordinate to familial interests, but children exercised vetoes over objectionable proposals ever more commonly and with fewer repercussions or parental protests.[50] As we reach the polite society of the early eighteenth century envisioned in *The Spectator*, prospective partners significantly determined their own marital fates. Ideal partnerships occurred 'where two Persons meet and voluntarily make Choice of each other'. Young women with more than one suitor were assumed to have fundamentally free choice between them, so much so that a 'virtuous Woman' was jocularly advised to 'reject the first Offer of Marriage, as a good Man does . . . a Bishoprick'.[51]

In some measure, children's emotions could be given play and parental control could afford to be relaxed because a national marriage market enlarged the range of potential partners who would be acceptable in parents' eyes. The burgeoning aristocratic social life in country house, provincial town, and London gave the young 'increasing opportunities to meet, under discreet surveillance, contemporaries of their own rank at such gatherings as dinners, music parties, balls and race meetings'.[52] When the landed were marrying within relatively closed circles, suitable mates were few and parents had strong incentive to direct their children's choice to a specific individual. In the eighteenth century, the presence of a wider selection of qualified candidates allowed parents to relax their insistence on a particular person – if not their vigilance as to the prospect's circumstances and character. Children took more initiative in the choice of partners than had once been the case, although specific circumstances dictated where this was so, and it probably occurred more rarely among the peerage (where dynastic considerations still claimed great attention) than among non-noble landowners.

The demographic crisis enhanced freedom of choice – including the freedom not to marry – by bestowing inheritances on unmarried young men and liberating them in their selection. Changing views on the nature of marriage, which gave greater weight to the

---

50. For this and the next paragraph see Stone, *Family, Sex and Marriage*, chs 7, 8, 9; Houlbrooke, *English Family*, ch. 4; and Habakkuk, *Estates System*, ch. 3.
   51. *The Spectator*, II, pp. 87–8; I, p. 379. See also II, pp. 515–16 and IV, pp. 357–60.
   52. Houlbrooke, *English Family*, pp. 65–6 for quotation; see also Lawrence Stone, *Road to Divorce: England 1530–1987* (Oxford, 1990), p. 60.

sentiments of the parties involved, played their part too. One daughter observed that 'man and woman must run a great hazard of living misserably all their lives, where there is not a mutual inclination beforehand',[53] and sensitivity to such an inclination appears frequently among the eighteenth-century landed classes. It appeared regardless of wealth or status but depending to some degree on the birth position and sex of the children involved: eldest sons, whose marriages most affected the future of an entire family, were most likely to feel and respond to pressures to give less credit to their feelings.[54] Sir Edward Dering accepted for his daughter Mary a suitor with only a modest estate but whose family he knew, who had expectations, and was civil, likable and 'seemed to love [Dering's] daughter very well'. When it came to his eldest son, however, Dering twice rejected financially inadequate proposals, the second offered by a mother who apparently thought Dering would be inclined to accept merely because the young man 'had an affection for her daughter'.[55]

The importance placed on emotional compatibility between prospective partners none the less grew over the period. Parents expected children to advance reasons for spurning a match but also recognized that rejections could entail 'too nice points for yong women to give reasons in, fancy being often the greatest reason'.[56] Marriages were therefore increasingly rarely put together without the assenting, even heartfelt, cooperation of the parties. Sir James Simeon wanted his son to marry expeditiously and identified a potential bride of decent estate and connections, but in line with current attitudes he refused 'to be too pressing' on his son. As a consequence that match fizzled and his son uncooperatively ignored 'all discourse of any proposall [of] changing his state'. Despite his father's hopes, he remained unmarried his entire eighty-seven years.[57] In preliminary negotiations the prospective groom and bride, and even a parent, might be ill informed by those trying to make a match, but once terms had been broached between families, it was necessary to 'let the yong people see how they like one another' before proceeding to a firm settlement. The match-making process entailed reciprocity. So when the Earl of Halifax faced a possible match for his son about 1680, he looked for a cue to the boy, whose

53. *Banks Papers*, p. 15.   54. Habakkuk, *Estates System*, pp. 154–5.
55. *Dering Diaries*, pp. 112–13.   56. *Banks Papers*, p. 18.
57. [Draft] Sir J. Simeon to M. Weld, 20 January 1705, Bodleian Library, MS D.D. Weld.c.13/5/18.

own 'wish for [Halifax's] approbation' would have 'great weight' in the earl's decision.[58]

This widely endorsed approach that insisted on 'mutual inclination' ensured that children's vetoes were accepted with less quarrel than were their unsuitable enthusiasms. It also made it reasonable to try to cultivate 'mutual inclination' in an open field, to broadcast one's eligibility widely. Similarly, insofar as considerations of affection did not wholly displace those of material interest ('Trains and Equipage, and all the showy Parts of Life' had a place in marriage too),[59] it was sensible to search broadly for the best location to secure that interest and to employ anyone to do so. Making a marriage was a family affair, and one where the women of a family – mothers, grandmothers, and other female relatives – had much say. Both where they were as powerful as Sarah Duchess of Marlborough and in the case of more typical 'weaker vessels', women often instigated matches. They worked avidly to find suitable partners, consulting acquaintances and writing directly to interested parties. Despite the fact that arranged marriages involved large numbers of people, not all related to one party or another, mothers often received the credit as the figures who made a match succeed or fail.[60]

In two of the three negotiations that Sir Edward Dering made for his heir in the 1670s, for example, he dealt with the prospective brides' mothers, in one case a widow but in the other a woman who had remarried yet negotiated by herself for the daughter of her first marriage.[61] The courting strategy of one man-about-town in the 1690s relied crucially on his potential mother-in-law. After securing his prospective bride's consent, he approached her mother in the hope that she would agree to the match herself and then 'mould the Father into a complying temper'.[62] Among the Verneys, Sir Ralph's wife proposed in the 1640s to help the Earl of Warwick's daughter to a good match, and in 1672 Sir Ralph's godson, although seeking his godfather's advice, also considered 'a proposal made to my aunt for me'.[63]

How much of this activity on the part of gentlewomen continued a traditional but unstudied role for women in elite life is unclear.

58. *Banks Papers*, p. 8; Habakkuk, *Estates System*, p. 163.
59. *The Spectator*, II, p. 515; see also II, pp. 545–6.
60. Margaret J.M. Ezell, *The Patriarch's Wife: Literary Evidence and the History of the Family* (Chapel Hill, North Carolina, and London, 1987), pp. 20–2; Habakkuk, *Estates System*, p. 153; Schwoerer, *Lady Rachel Russell*, 201–6; Larminie, *Wealth, Kinship and Culture*, pp. 79, 83, 91–2.
61. *Dering Diaries*, pp. 112–13, 114, 116.   62. Houlbrooke, *English Family*, p. 71.
63. Slater, *Family Life*, pp. 62, 76.

But if women were coming into a sphere they had previously explored little, this boldness may be explained by the mid-seventeenth-century dislocation of earlier social patterns when male heads of household were away at war, which absence allowed elite women to take leads in these areas.[64] Of greater significance in tracing the expansiveness of landed society, it was presumably only because women's social networks were at least the equivalent of men's that mothers and aunts, godmothers, grandmothers, and female cousins made such powerful marriage-brokers – and did so regularly across all levels of landed society. This function was facilitated by the landed's broadening engagement with more and more of those of similar standing, and by their increasing recourse to provincial towns and the metropolis, all features characteristic of the ruling order in this period.

Education

For men of the landed order, more than for women, the process and institutions of education created bonds among them, widened their prospects and assisted in the coalescence of the social networks that dictated so much of what made up gentlemanly conduct. In several ostensible ways, elite education in the century after 1650 departed from its earlier patterns. Elite attendance at universities and inns of court diminished, grammar schools came under attack for their harshness and vice, and challenges were even raised to the unquestioned pre-eminence of classical learning. Some among the landed therefore turned to alternative forms of education, to private tutors and travel abroad.

Yet educational institutions showed some ability to adapt to changing times, and the content of the education of the elite – perhaps males in particular – expanded to include new matter rather than omit the classics that had long lain at its core. Many among the landed of the mid-eighteenth century went to the same school and university as their grandfathers and great-grandfathers had attended. There was no full-scale abandonment of Eton and Westminster, Oxford and Cambridge, or the inns of court, and both public schools and universities experienced a new influx of landed students toward the middle of the eighteenth century, after their late seventeenth-

---

64. R.T. Spence, 'Lady Anne Clifford, Countess of Dorset, Pembroke and Montgomery (1590–1676): a reappraisal', *Northern History* 15 (1979), pp. 43–65.

and early eighteenth-century slumps. If educational experience among landowners was somewhat more heterogeneous in 1750 than a century before, the experience was comparable to the past as well. It too shaped lives in common ways, helping to generate similar outlooks, visions and values among its recipients.

THE VALUE AND VALUES OF EDUCATION

Whether the landed elite were taught in formal institutions, under private tuition at home, or when travelling, parents took seriously the education of their children, 'the best way of [their] being formed and instructed'.[65] They were especially (although not exclusively) concerned with the shaping of male offspring to pursue the calling of gentlemen. The express objects of this education may seem to have remained essentially constant during the seventeenth and eighteenth centuries: to inculcate virtue and public spiritedness, to provide intellectual training and impart knowledge, to aid in good breeding, and to equip one for experience of the world. But the different emphasis and changed means used to attain these objects gave a different effect to elite male education after about 1650. Previously, the inculcation of 'civic' values had been pre-eminent among the goals of an education that was most importantly pre-paring young men for active governance of their households and communities. Although this goal was not abandoned after the Res-toration, perhaps 'the very completeness of the gentry's political success . . . made it less necessary to invoke learning as a route to power'. Now 'civil' concerns – social and cultural accomplishments – loomed much larger in the education of a gentleman.[66]

As a result of this shift, the continuing debate about the prepar-atory value of book-learning as opposed to experience of the world gave the latter the upper hand until toward the very end of our period, although even in the mid-eighteenth century experiential learning was still highly valued and comported well with the image of the landed as men of action.[67] In the form of touring the Con-tinent and even in that of revelry and debauchery, experience had the added virtue of very efficiently performing education's less

65. John Locke, *Some Thoughts Concerning Education*, J.L. Axtell, ed. (Cambridge, 1968; originally published 1693), 'Epistle dedicatory'.
66. This paragraph adopts the argument of Heal and Holmes, *Gentry*, ch. 7; quota-tion on p. 275.
67. George C. Brauer, Jr, *The Education of a Gentleman: Theories of Gentlemanly Edu-cation in England, 1660–1775* (New York, 1959), chs 1–5.

explicit objective, that of distinguishing the true gentleman from those who would mimic him. Latin provided a secret language, and classical texts provided a shared set of stories, references and even values. But unlike them, 'experience of the world' was unaffordable to many who could acquire language and learning, as were the artwork and antiquities acquired on a foreign tour to symbolize accomplishment of this cultural ritual. Experience like that tour provided a shared initiation into a sphere closed to women and closed to all men but the select few.[68]

Whether using tutors or established schools, landed parents expected that much of their (male) children's education would rest on study of the classics. Insofar as some of the sons of the elite intended to proceed to university – but probably not to study rigorously there – they required a classical training to do so. Even in the absence of such ambitions, exposure to the ancients' wisdom and acquisition of fluency in Latin not only provided timeless and useful lessons but was a distinctive mark of gender and social status for landed men. Such education was the stock in trade of the grammar schools, and late seventeenth-century country gentry did not turn their backs on the provincial institutions their ancestors had attended (and endowed) and which had laid the foundation for the Tudor and early Stuart 'educational revolution'. It is true that vernacular studies, especially French and mathematics, began to take more space in the curriculum, and by the eighteenth century even grammar schools were showing themselves flexible, providing 'practical', non-classical, instruction and accepting its availability on an extra-curricular basis. But classical education continued to have its hold on the male members of English landed society. Its cultural value overrode other considerations. For all the ambivalence expressed about institutional education in the middle of the period discussed here, its function as a marker of social distinction was too great for it to be abandoned.[69]

While schools continued to be valued for their success in imparting Latin language, literature and tradition, there were a number of reasons for some of the landed to spurn institutional education,

---

68. Anthony J. Fletcher, *Gender, Sex and Subordination in England 1500–1800* (New Haven, 1995), ch. 15; Redford, *Venice & the Grand Tour, passim.*

69. W.A.L. Vincent, *The Grammar Schools: Their Continuing Tradition 1660–1714* (London, 1969), *passim;* M.V. Wallbank, 'Eighteenth-century public schools and the education of the governing elite', *History of Education* 8 (1979), pp. 14–16; Brauer, *Education of a Gentleman,* pp. 82–90; Rosemary O'Day, *Education and Society 1500–1800: The Social Foundations of Education in Early Modern Britain* (London, 1982), pp. 204–16; Fletcher, *Gender, Sex and Subordination,* pp. 299–302.

as they did before 1700. Rising costs played a part in discouraging some landed parents from sending their male offspring. Declining endowments forced some grammar schools to raise or initiate fees. At the inns of court, the expense of membership was not burdensome, but students felt obliged (regardless of their circumstances) to live in a high style, which increased the cost of maintenance by over half between the Restoration and 1700. This rise to £100 p.a. at a time when profits from agriculture were under pressure made a stay less affordable for gentry families who a generation or two before would have expected to send their sons to the inns.[70]

The same story obtained at the universities. According to tutors' accounts from St Catharine's College, Cambridge, the expenses for a run-of-the-mill student more than doubled between 1680 and 1744. Rises took place both in basic fees like chamber rent, tuition and payments to the college steward and in expenses with tradesmen.[71] In the first years of the eighteenth century, Sir Nicholas L'Estrange complained that he was paying much more to support his two sons at university (one at Oxford, and one at Cambridge) than he had laid out for himself at Christ Church, Oxford, between 1677 and 1680. Without mentioning the inflation of extra-mural costs, he noted that entrance fees had risen by half and that a new species of 'Sub-tutors' charged £6 a year to teach 'Algebra, Euclid, & . . . practicall Mathematicks', which a primary tutor had done in Sir Nicholas's day. The new 'Pupillmonger' also sent his students to select (and expensive) tradespeople who in return for the referrals gave him 'good Gratuityes' and kicked back to him any abatements made on the accounts. In all L'Estrange laid out £320 for the two boys in the academic year of 1706–7.[72]

Other criticism aimed at several targets. Life at school could be barbaric, socially demeaning, and corrupting; pedagogic methods were harsh and boring. John Aubrey in the 1670s observed that entering school enabled a boy 'to be beaten by his school fellows, to be falsely accused, to be whipped by the master . . . 'Tis here he begins to understand the world, the misery, falseness and deceitfulness of it.'[73] As salutary as such lessons might appear to some,

---

70. Vincent, *Grammar Schools*, pp. 3, 40–1; O'Day, *Education and Society*, p. 198; David Lemmings, *Gentlemen and Barristers: The Inns of Court and the English Bar 1680–1730* (Oxford, 1990), pp. 23–5, 29–30.

71. St Catharine's College, Cambridge, MSS L55, L63 and L67 (photocopies courtesy of Lawrence Stone).

72. Sir Nicholas L'Estrange's account book 1700–13, Norfolk Record Office, Le Strange P13, pp. 123–6.

73. Fletcher, *Gender, Sex and Subordination*, p. 307.

others were put off by them. Revulsion against corporal punishment (perhaps especially on the part of mothers) may have diminished elite enrolments in the older grammar schools like Westminster, where Dr Richard Busby was notorious for vehemence, or Eton, from which, one claimed, victims of beatings 'have run . . . and were never heard of afterwards'.[74] Their rowdiness may have too, although the shared experience of harsh regimes could forge solidarities among young men of the landed order. The social mixing (and consequent inadequate respect of status) that occurred at some newer, urban grammar schools like Colchester made them less desirable than they once had been. The same might apply for 'free' grammar schools that took in pupils regardless of social background.[75]

The failure of the universities to provide instruction in most modern subjects probably diminished attendance as much as did their reputation as places where little study at all took place. There were desirable non-academic attainments to be gained while at university, and the inns of court beckoned for this purpose but only until the cessation of legal readings and learning exercises, which took place before 1680, diminished the value of a sojourn there. After all, young men could also become skilled in mathematics, acquire French or Italian or Spanish, learn to fence and handle arms, sing, dance, paint, and the like, during residence in London, or when touring abroad, or even in a provincial town. The popularity of academies, like those that thrived in London in the Restoration, grew from their provision of just this array of offerings.[76]

Signs of disenchantment had appeared before the civil war, and that era of upheaval had also occasioned fears that higher education, especially in the university, was subverting the dominant values of the social order. Even grammar schools suffered from this reaction, and John Locke's arguments in favour of private tuition and against public classical education in *Some Thoughts Concerning Education* expressed existing elite uncertainty about the wisdom of consigning their children to schools and universities. Although it did not halt the establishment of further girls' boarding schools in provincial towns like Oxford, Leicester, and Manchester, this

74. Vincent, *Grammar Schools*, pp. 64–6; O'Day, *Education and Society*, pp. 196, 201, 287 n. 28.

75. O'Day, *Education and Society*, pp. 36–7; Vincent, *Grammar Schools*, ch. 3.

76. Brauer, *Education of a Gentleman*, ch. 7; Vincent, *Grammar Schools*, pp. 198–201; O'Day, *Education and Society*, pp. 62–4; Fletcher, *Gender, Sex and Subordination*, p. 305; Lemmings, *Gentlemen and Barristers*, pp. 25, 78–92; Heal and Holmes, *Gentry*, p. 260; Locke, *Some Thoughts*, §164.

uncertainty seemed to pull landed males away from institutional education – over one-third of Nicholas Hans's selection of some seven hundred gentry and nobles born between 1685 and 1785 were schooled at home.[77] Higher education's decline during the late seventeenth and early eighteenth centuries can be measured numerically in terms of enrolment. From early seventeenth-centuries highs, matriculations at the two universities and first admissions to the inns of court all fell. These institutions experienced slight upturns just after the Restoration, the understandable result of more stable times than the 1640s or 1650s, but the next half century saw decreases. At the same time, total enrolments also dipped at grammar schools, which had problems drawing a 'monied clientele', but numbers there too began to recover after 1700. In general, elite attendance dropped in concert with decreases in overall numbers, but these declines did not signal decisive abandonment of traditional educational institutions.[78]

If these formal channels had become less attractive, for many they remained necessary conduits for essential training. Among country-house owners from Hertfordshire, Northamptonshire, and Northumberland, a return to formal higher education occurred in the generations born after 1700, leaving the lowest proportion educated at schools to be found among those born from 1650 to 1699.[79] As for members of parliament, 48 per cent of those sitting between 1660 and 1690 attended an English university, but so did 45 per cent of members between 1715 and 1754.[80] Only the number of members who attended an inn of court fell sharply between the parliamentary cohorts for 1660–90 and 1715–54, mirroring the decrease in attendance identified for the inns overall.[81] By contrast, the proportion of the nobility among university matriculants actually

---

77. Vincent, *Grammar Schools*, pp. 75–82, 194–8; Brauer, *Education of a Gentleman*, pp. 197–208; Nicholas Hans, *New Trends in Education in the Eighteenth Century* (London, 1951), pp. 26–7; O'Day, *Education and Society*, pp. 187–8, 196–208.

78. Lawrence Stone, 'The size and composition of the Oxford student body 1580–1909', in Lawrence Stone, ed., *The University in Society*, 1, *Oxford and Cambridge from the 14th to the Early 19th Century* (Princeton, 1974), pp. 91–2 (tables 1A–1B); Lemmings, *Gentlemen and Barristers*, p. 10; O'Day, *Education and Society*, p. 201.

79. Stone and Stone, *An Open Elite?*, table 7.4.

80. Basil Duke Henning, *The History of Parliament: The House of Commons 1660–1690*, 3 vols (London, 1983), I, p. 4; Romney Sedgwick, *The History of Parliament: The House of Commons 1715–1754*, 2 vols (London, 1970), I, p. 139. The former figure counts only once those MPs attending both universities; the latter figure apparently counts them twice. Ibid., I, p. 111 says that '[a]pproximately two-fifths of the Members returned to each Parliament had received a university education.'

81. Henning, *House of Commons*, I, p. 5; Sedgwick, *House of Commons*, I, p. 145; Lemmings, *Gentlemen and Barristers*, pp. 9–10.

doubled over the eighteenth century, and the proportion of the peerage who had received some university education rose from nearly a third of those alive in 1701 to nearly two-thirds in 1799.[82]

REVIVAL

Even if caused by disenchantment, the drop in the elite's attendance at educational institutions was temporary, largely a phenomenon of the late seventeenth and early eighteenth centuries.[83] As such it may reflect the demographic difficulties the landed then faced, but in any case lower attendance did not constitute complete abandonment. Grammar school, university, and inn of court all played important parts in forming England's ruling order, intellectually and socially. The classical training provided by these schools, however sceptical some were about its universal educational value, was believed highly suitable for those landed pupils destined to rule. When successfully inculcated in them, it instilled diligence and competitiveness, encouraged both rationality and sociability of behaviour, and developed their rhetorical skills.[84]

A continued need for signs of social distinction like these first generated a boom in private tutors. It then played the stronger part in the revival of a small group of fashionable boarding schools in the early eighteenth century, where in fact decline had never been as severe as at other endowed grammar schools. By the late 1720s, Eton, Westminster, and Winchester were between them teaching almost a thousand boys at a time.[85] What later became the nine Great Public Schools of the nineteenth century were 'fortunate exceptions' to a more general decline of grammar schools in the eighteenth century, and all of them drew aristocrats. About two-thirds of the sons of peers attended these most exclusive schools during the eighteenth century, and a group of forty-seven ministers holding office in the twenty-five years after 1775 (and educated as early as 1721) overwhelmingly went to Eton and Westminster.[86] Of members of parliament, those who attended public schools comprised

82. John Cannon, *Aristocratic Century: The Peerage of Eighteenth-Century England* (Cambridge, 1984), pp. 48, 52.

83. Ibid., pp. 40–1.

84. Wallbank, 'Eighteenth-century public schools', pp. 2–17; O'Day, *Education and Society*, pp. 204–5; Brauer, *Education of a Gentleman*, pp. 82–90.

85. Geoffrey Holmes, *Augustan England*, pp. 46–7.

86. Vincent, *Grammar Schools*, pp. 16–22, quotation on p. 21; Wallbank, 'Eighteenth-century public schools', pp. 1–2. The nine schools were Charterhouse, Eton, Harrow, Merchant Taylors', Rugby, St Paul's, Shrewsbury, Westminster, and Winchester.

17 per cent of members sitting between 1660 and 1690, about one-fifth of those sitting between 1715 and 1754, and more than a third of those chosen between 1754 and 1790.[87] And more than school-boys were touched by the culture of these institutions: it took in their parents as well, figures like the 'great number of nobility and gentry . . . [in] upwards of one hundred gentlemen's coaches' who attended the performance of a play by Terence at Hackney School in 1751.[88]

Even if unhappy with their own past education, or sceptical about their children's prospective one, landed parents could not allow their male offspring to remain ignorant of book-learning. Instruction was meant to inculcate in the eldest son a willingness and ability to undertake the duties involved in managing an inheritance; it was meant to equip younger males with tools to help them secure a livelihood.[89] Society demanded that the next generation, heirs and younger sons alike, display a modicum of learning. In the mid-1740s Horace Mann wondered in dismay how the noble father of a young visitor to him at Leghorn 'could . . . let the education of any son of his be neglected so'.[90]

Although agreed on the need for study, the landed took eclectic rather than focussed, pragmatic, or vocational approaches to it, and calls for a more specialized education for the landed were generally ignored.[91] From the late seventeenth century education served more as a hallmark of status than as a rigorous training for life. 'Education' involved the shaping of character and moulding of children in ways that books did not teach. Sir Ralph Verney did not worry too much at his son Edmund's disinclination to study in the final phase of his development, believing that 'A meere Schollar, is but a woefull creature'.[92] Yet if sons were expected to dabble, they were also meant to make progress, and Sir Francis and Lady Drake in 1712 grew a little impatient with their eldest boy's sojourn at the Inner Temple, aware that his schooling was incomplete and that they had to find some other place 'to set him for another little while next'.[93]

87. Calculation from Henning, *House of Commons*, I, p. 4 and Cannon, *Aristocratic Century*, p. 42. These figures may be affected by the disruption of the civil war and by better record preservation over time. The figures after 1715 may underestimate landed school-going, because of changes in the Commons' membership to include Scottish members and more merchants and military officers.

88. Wallbank, 'Eighteenth-century public schools', p. 14.

89. Cannon, *Aristocratic Century*, p. 37.   90. *Walpole Correspondence*, XIX, p. 169.

91. Brauer, *Education of a Gentleman*, pp. 95–100.

92. Mark Motley, 'Educating the English gentleman abroad: the Verney family in seventeenth-century France and Holland', *History of Education* 23 (1994), p. 254.

93. David Lemmings, 'The student body of the inns of court under the later Stuarts', *Bulletin of the Institute of Historical Research* 58 (1985), p. 155.

Private tutors who could mix the learned with the utilitarian provided an alternative for parents suspicious of or impatient with schools, and home instruction in the late seventeenth century flourished by contrast with institutional education. The potential disadvantages to children of home education – improper familiarities with household staff, the potentially malign influence of the tutor, the loss of socialization provided in school, the indulgence of parents – had to be set against the lower costs, the emotional rewards of living with one's family, the avoidance of public school vices, and the benefits of parental influence.[94] On this last point, one tutor in 1701 suggested at the end of a stay abroad that his charge had absorbed all he could from formal education there. He flattered the boy's father with the observation that the son could now 'be no where so well as under your own tuition . . . that your instructions animated by what he will see in your self will be of greatest force to accomplish him'.[95]

Evidence about the schooling of young women remains patchy, but parents' interest in their children's education extended beyond that of their sons alone. A clerk in the Prince of Wales' household assured a country friend in 1733 that no one would question his lodging in an inconvenient part of the town of Lincoln to be near his daughters' school, since it demonstrated that their education was 'one of the things of the highest importance to [him] in life'.[96] Provision for daughters was quite clearly getting no worse between the mid-seventeenth and mid-eighteenth centuries, and may have been improving. The successful performance of men's tasks by elite women during the civil wars demonstrated women's capacities. It helped to stimulate and justify calls to improve women's education (although these had an earlier history too), made in works like Bathshua Makin's *Essay to Revive the Ancient Education of Gentlewomen* (1673), Mary Astell's *Serious Proposal to the Ladies* (1694) and Judith Drake's *Essay in Defence of the Female Sex* (1696). The advertisement in Makin's essay for her own establishment 'lately erected for gentlewomen' also testifies to the vitality of girls' schools in the later seventeenth century, at least some of which provided much more than instruction in 'womanly' and domestic pursuits. Young women, however, were more likely to obtain serious learning at home than in such schools, and as private tuition aimed at the sons of the landed intensified, the daughters shared in it. Near the beginning

94. Brauer, *Education of a Gentleman*, pp. 209–18; Locke, *Some Thoughts*, §§90–4.
95. G. Webbe to Sir J. Simeon, 16 February 1701 [NS], Bodleian Library, MS D.D.Weld.c.13/3/45.
96. *Banks Papers*, p. 150.

of his *Some Thoughts on Education*, for example, John Locke assumed that daughters should receive an education similar to that of their brothers, and most of those accounted to be the age's 'learned ladies' were educated privately. Some evidence of daughters' education is thus surely buried in that of their brothers. Lord Townshend's extensive household accounts from the 1710s to 1730s make it appear, for example, as if only his boys were being schooled, but this visible impression is contradicted by another, the accuracy and confidence with which at sixteen his daughter Dorothy (b. 1714) began to keep his domestic books.[97]

FOREIGN TRAVEL

The moderate decline in elite acquisition of formal higher education was short-lived, and even at the slackest times a substantial portion of the elite continued to congregate with one another in educational institutions. The formal lessons of university and legal education may no longer have seemed as valuable to the elite as they once had, but along with formal schooling sons of the elite gained connections and broader knowledge about their own kind. Elite education remained a composite of book-learning and of polishing, and as the eighteenth century progressed, the mix increasingly contained ingredients acquired outside printed materials, educational establishments, and even irregular instructional institutions like dancing schools. In an era in which Great Britain's place in the world was expanding dramatically, presenting opportunities, challenges, and even threats to older ways of landed life, a propensity to seek education by exposure to things foreign quite understandably grew as well.

Foreign travel, although not without its critics or its abusers, especially in its most grandiose forms, had by the mid-eighteenth century become a popular, accepted, and valued element in gentlemanly upbringing. Bruce Redford's elegant recent account of Venice's special place in the Grand Tour persuasively identifies the years 1670 to 1700 as ones of growing popularity, and the decades from then to 1760 as the heyday of Italian touring.[98] In its developed

97. Ezell, *The Patriarch's Wife*, pp. 11–15, 111–18; Kate Aughterson, ed., *Renaissance Women: Constructions of Femininity in England* (London, 1995), pp. 167–8, 186–91; O'Day, *Education and Society*, pp. 187–8; Locke, *Some Thoughts*, §6; Schwoerer, *Lady Rachel Russell*, pp. 17–18; Raynham Hall, Norfolk, household accounts 1730–37, uncatalogued bound volumes.

98. Redford, *Venice & the Grand Tour*, pp. 14–15; this study has decisively shaped what follows. For further discussion of foreign travel see chapter 6 below.

form – which lasted for two or more years, entailed a tutor, and had an itinerary with Rome at its heart – the tour followed the pattern outlined as early as 1670 in Father Richard Lassel's *The Voyage of Italy*, a work consciously aimed at 'the Gentry of our Nation'.[99] Even before the mid-seventeenth century, however, journeying abroad for the purpose of education had had its proponents, commentators who recognized travel's cultural and moral effect in shaping character and broadening perspectives on one's national identity.[100] Its edifying impact, which appeared all the greater when associated with exposure to the classical world, justified European travel; in the post-Restoration era its utility as an educational option and its function as a socially distinctive 'maker and marker'[101] of gentility almost demanded it.

Not to travel deprived young gentlemen of a variety of benefits. Tourists were expected to improve themselves and to learn better what it meant to comport themselves as gentlemen. The pleasures travel afforded were tacitly assumed though largely unmentioned: edification was its publicly acceptable *raison d'être*.[102] An acknowledged motive for going abroad was to acquire finish – taste, self-possession, modest self-confidence – through a variety of social interactions. By study, through observation, conversation, and even reading, the traveller obtained 'useful knowledge' as well. This ranged from insight into foreign agricultural and commercial practices to illumination of Britain's political system. Exposure to other nations' customs and manners made young Englishmen more cosmopolitan and simultaneously made them conscious of their home country's virtues. Either way, their encounters with the Continent marked them distinctively and set them apart from their untravelled sisters, from the hard-working merchant and stay-at-home professional man. A foreign tour helped to distinguish the kingdom's elite from mere aspirants. Foreign travel also figured prominently in the self-fashioning of young men of the landowning order as a final rite of passage in the transition from child to adult. 'The last part usually in Education', said Locke, 'is Travel, which is commonly thought to finish the Work, and compleat the Gentleman.'[103]

99. Ibid., pp. 9–12 and p. 14 for the components of the tour; see also H. Waugh's review of M. Bence-Jones, *The Catholic Families* in *Times Literary Supplement*, 18 September 1992, p. 17.

100. John Stoye, *English Travellers Abroad 1604–1667: Their Influence in English Society and Politics*, revised edition (New Haven, 1989).

101. Redford, *Venice & the Grand Tour*, p. 15.

102. Jeremy Black, *The British and the Grand Tour* (London, 1985), pp. 233–44.

103. Redford, *Venice & the Grand Tour*, pp. 15–16, 28–39; Black, *British and the Grand Tour*, pp. 233–41; Locke, *Some Thoughts*, §212.

The expense of European travel denied it to gentry who were struggling economically but did not confine it to the super-rich, and cost did not impede its growing popularity. In Lincolnshire after the Restoration, what had once been reserved to magnates became a common experience for the heirs of wealthy gentry. In 1673, Sir Justinian Isham recruited a servant, probably a Frenchman, who took it for granted that Isham's son would go abroad – and he with him.[104] Among early travellers from Norfolk, Henry Lee Warner, Hamon L'Estrange, and Ashe Windham came from prominent but not inordinately grand families, and offspring of urban gentry, like Henry Partridge of King's Lynn, who made a brief excursion to the Low Countries in autumn 1732, could also travel affordably.[105] Sir Charles Hotham did not let his indebtedness deprive his eldest son of a stay abroad in the 1710s; decades later travel was so much taken for granted that the Court of Chancery allowed £800 p.a. from this son's estate to pay for the extensive European tour of Sir Charles's grandson after he left Westminster school in 1750.[106]

Travel was not without its critics. Everything the tour was meant to do could backfire: exposure to foreign governments could breed republicanism or worse; encounters with different religions, above all Roman Catholicism, could seduce travellers from the Church of England; too much time devoted to cultivating moral and aesthetic sensibilities might turn young men from their mundane responsibilities; and sowing sexual wild oats with the wrong people might unintentionally cultivate disease, effeminacy, and homosexuality.[107] Defences of travelling countered these anxieties, but they mostly ignored the overtly xenophobic and also the economic criticisms.[108]

Involving greater planning, risk, and expense than any kind of domestic education, the tour was clearly more than a means to get landed youth conveniently out of the way. Seen as a valuable formative experience, it also became a widely accepted social practice whose completion was one of the expected features of elite male education. Thus not only in their subjection to pedagogic discipline and spartan conditions, in their study of classic authors, or in

---

104. Holmes, *Seventeenth-Century Lincolnshire*, p. 77; *Isham Diary*, pp. 209–10.
105. Andrew Moore, *Norfolk and the Grand Tour: Eighteenth-Century Travellers Abroad and Their Souvenirs* (Fakenham, Norfolk, 1985), pp. 19–24.
106. Roebuck, *Yorkshire Baronets*, pp. 81–2, 101; the boy went to France, Switzerland, Italy, Russia, Denmark, Sweden, Prussia, and most of the German principalities.
107. Redford, *Venice & the Grand Tour*, pp. 16–25.
108. Black, *British and the Grand Tour*, pp. 242–4.

their experience of schoolroom declamation and written composition did male members of the English aristocracy undergo a shared upbringing for prolonged periods. For many – and for increasing numbers in the reigns of George I and George II – the tour also provided a common foundation on which a national ruling order was built.

Conclusion

The identity that demographic accident, marital union, and education helped to make possible in the Restoration and early Hanoverian landed elite was not based on entirely new connections. The English landed order always had been both set apart from other social groups and unified in its own ranks by marriages to one another and by similar training and breeding. Even in the early seventeenth century, attendance at the universities had significantly encouraged the 'country' sentiments and values shared by many gentry across the kingdom:[109] the 'nationalizing' impact of education under the late Stuarts and first two Georges was not unprecedented. But for much of their history the landed had manifested their common characteristics locally and regionally; this was increasingly less true after the mid-seventeenth century. And the generations after 1650 saw new developments that had a cumulative effect in suppressing the provincial and elevating the metropolitan and cosmopolitan profiles in the complex identity of the landowning classes.

Partly this effect was the result of the retrenchment of a social group suffering demographic and cultural assault, people who felt threatened in the transmission of their lands and in the preservation of a way of life inimitable by lesser folks. Part of the national scope of social relations within the gentry grew from the width and strength of their marital connections, which by 1750 were more than ever knotted before the scrutiny of observers and to the awareness of readers across the entire kingdom. The elite's brief but notable turning away from traditional educational institutions and their inclination to pursue education for the ends of civility rather than civic duty constituted other departures from past practice. A partial rejection of local grammar schools in favour of private tutors was a self-conscious gesture of separation from those below. The temporary flight from the universities because of the taint of

---

109. Victor Morgan, 'Cambridge University and "the Country" 1560–1640', in Stone, ed., *The University in Society*, 1, pp. 183–245.

rebellion that hung over them after 1660 necessarily meant that academic study of the sort associated with attendance at Oxford and Cambridge was not a defining element of gentility. What turned out to be the landed's more permanent shunning of the inns of court and their diminished exposure to the rudiments of law which Elizabethan, Jacobean, and Caroline gentry had typically obtained discouraged local service as justice of the peace and encouraged landowners to put entirely into the hands of professionals their increasingly arcane legal affairs. Yet if the shunning of schools by some constituted a means of separation, so, paradoxically, did the embrace of schools. The continued hold of specifically classical education lay in its much publicized suitability for the society's landed rulers and in its evident capacity to mark them out from others and to provide them with a shared cultural ground.

Whether following or diverging from the most popular educational tracks of their forebears, and whether at the beginning or somewhat further down the path of education, more and more young gentlemen found a finishing experience of foreign travel served extremely useful ends. It exposed them to other ways of life to compare with their own and to breed in them a conviction of the excellence of the current English way of governing and prospering. It allowed them to behave with licence, and even scandalously, without consequences as serious as would have attended such behaviour at home. Travel was also an important mechanism for the well-to-do landed to differentiate themselves from those of non-landed wealth who could imitate the demeanour and some of the actions of the landed, but for whom an extended tour of Europe was out of the question. (Travel served this end within the ranks of the landed too.) And finally, the pleasurable, tempting, challenging, dangerous, and alien encounters that defined continental travel generated companionship, cooperation, and solidarity among those who returned from abroad to take up positions as a social order ruling over estates, families, and kingdom.

CHAPTER THREE

Agriculture, the Landed Estate, and Business

Introduction

The economic activities of the landed elite played a major part in forging its identity, and the circumstances of landownership and landlordship, although they varied from region to region, provided an important common ground in the process. So did the operation of the markets in which landowners participated, particularly those in agricultural goods, which were growing more integrated and nationally extensive in the years after the mid-seventeenth century.[1]

This emerging nationwide marketplace was created in several ways. Improvements in transport brought by turnpikes made for better land routes, commercially connecting areas like the east Midlands and the southwest more directly to London.[2] The activities of middlemen who sold into the metropolis and provincial urban centres augmented and even displaced the importance of regional markets and fairs for some producers. A rising demand for luxury goods and garden produce, and the establishment of government bounties on grain exports, injected new supra-local considerations into the agricultural calculations of landowners. These developments encouraged cultivation of specialized crops, flattened out price ranges across the kingdom, and promoted economic integration.[3]

By 1750 the English economy possessed great diversity and regional specialization in agriculture, a strong home market, and an increasingly potent manufacturing sector. Landowners doing

---

1. This and the next two paragraphs rely on *AHEW*, V, pt 2, ch. 17.
2. Ibid., pt 1, pp. 90–2, 376.
3. On specialization see ibid., pt 2, pp. 302, 570–81; for prices and markets see pp. 27 and 459–65 respectively.

business in an economy becoming inescapably national and international had to take ever greater account of economic forces outside
their estates and regions and gained broader perspectives on the
economic world as they pursued their own material well-being.[4] This
was additionally the case because expanding business opportunities
outside the realm of agriculture served for the landed as increasingly
important outlets for investment – and as sources of profit and loss.

Elite participation in a national market of agriculture and business helped to connect landowners with one another across local
and regional lines. Major avenues of connection, in economic life
as elsewhere, ran through London, which occupied a place in the
kingdom's economy as well recognized as it was large. London provided the standard by which local goods were compared for price
and quality (not always unfavourably for the provincials), and such
comparisons extended even to the labour force.[5] The patterns of
sea and land trade and the routes of carriers, whom the gentry
employed proportionately more than other economic actors did,
radiated from the metropolis and also joined other communities
and regions to one another, spreading commodities throughout
the kingdom. Other connections grew from the common obstacles
and opportunities that landowners faced in sustaining their economic positions, which led them to adopt common strategies and
undertake similar activities in response. During the Restoration and
early Hanoverian eras, the landed notably embraced agricultural
improvements, modified the management of their estates, and both
adapted to and participated in the changing worlds of commerce
and finance. These activities reflected and engendered shared attitudes toward investment, expenditure, estate management, and agricultural practice, attitudes that helped give to the landed order its
metropolitan and cosmopolitan character.

The century after 1650 saw no fundamental alteration in the
economic basis or characteristics of the wealth of the landed order.
Landowners remained predominantly reliant on rents for the income they derived from the lands they possessed.[6] The items that
the land yielded and that they sold themselves – whether cattle or
corn, hops or timber or hay – had long been vented in a cash

---

4. Ibid., V, pp. 501, 587; John Rule, *The Vital Century: England's Developing Economy
1714–1815* (London, 1992), p. 52.

5. *Fitzwilliam Correspondence*, pp. 71, 109, 111.

6. The term 'rents' includes fines paid on lease renewals, which in some areas
were more significant sources of income than annual rents, but whose payment was
liable to the same influences: see Barry Coward, *The Stanleys, Lords Stanley and Earls
of Derby, 1385–1672: The Origins, Wealth and Power of a Landowning Family*, Chetham
Society 3rd series, 30 (1983), p. 79.

marketplace. And insofar as that marketplace was nationally consti-tuted, London had been its hub for generations; since at least the mid-sixteenth century landowners had also found in London the financial services their wealth demanded. As receivers of rents and of land-derived profits, elite landowners had also historically known that their estates needed careful management. Whether by them-selves or through their employees, landowners had been involved in making agricultural improvements well before 1650, although not on the scale of the succeeding century. They had always fol-lowed non-agricultural pursuits (also on a smaller scale), whether those based on the land they owned – exploitation of mineral re-sources, development of urban tracts – or those into which they placed available capital – like trading ventures and money-lending.[7]

Despite these elements of continuity with the past, however, the later seventeenth and early eighteenth centuries did not present the same secular economic conditions to the landed elite as the previous century had done. Where inflation and a growing popu-lation had boosted land prices, rents, and gentry prosperity for a hundred and fifty years before 1650, after this point prices and rents both stagnated. Although the landed continued to prosper as a group they did so in a less generous economic climate and with more struggle than before.

During a century of lower return on land that started around 1640, when grain prices dipped more than ten per cent, many land-owners faced financial trouble. Some only maintained their aristo-cratic style of life by using their resources to borrow, and in critical instances only access to the new mortgage markets forestalled bank-ruptcy. More commonly, the landed elite survived stringent times by calling upon their significant resources of land, capital, and credit in new and newly energetic ways: by taking up innovative crops and agricultural methods and by employing the novel managerial skills and accepting the financial risks these involved.[8] As a result, the level of farm rents in the mid-eighteenth century even slightly exceeded that of a hundred years earlier, despite the depressed prices for agricultural commodities that had obtained in the intervening years.[9]

The expansion of England's business community in the seven-teenth and eighteenth centuries offered alternatives to landowners who hoped to provide the basis of a livelihood for their children. By presenting more career opportunities for estate owners' younger

7. Stone, *Crisis of the Aristocracy*, ch. 7.
8. *AHEW*, V, pt 2, pp. 552–3, 558–9, 578–9; for regional examples and variations see ibid., pt 1, pp. 96–9, 160–2, 250–6, 297–9, 358–66.
9. Ibid., pt 2, p. 73.

sons, the expansion allowed owners to resist the temptation to break up their holdings and apportion some of their lands for those children's support, a once-common practice that became 'increasingly unusual'.[10] No longer so much bothered by traditional strictures against business as a calling, young members of the landed elite regularly entered apprenticeships in business. Entry into the ranks of businessmen required capital and connections, both broadly available among the landed. It is not surprising that as much as a third of the business community derived from the ranks of country and urban gentry.[11] Similar cash and connections helped to place gentry sons into careers in government and military service, as well as the church and the law, all of which outlets had the advantage of helping fathers to keep estates intact.

The movement into business and the new attitudes accompanying it were congruent with the elite's search for places to invest not only their progeny but also their agricultural profits, when they realized them. The investment opportunities with which an eighteenth-century landowner was presented – whether in enlarged financial markets, emerging industries, or the unprecedentedly booming arena of domestic and international commerce – played their part in widening his outlook on what were economic activities appropriate for a gentleman. Partly as a result, the economic fortunes of the landed at large rested by 1750 on a broader base than at any previous time in its history. The widening scope of landed economic interests in the three or four generations after the civil war firmly set aristocratic economic experiences in a cosmopolitan context. The development of a national economy, perhaps not ineluctable but proceeding palpably over a long period, played a substantial part in enlarging the ruling order's horizons. This chapter assesses the ways in which the economic roles of the elite as landlords, agriculturists, industrialists, entrepreneurs, and investors all helped to generate common identity among them.

Pressures on income

Following a period that brought inflation-led prosperity to most landowners, it became more difficult after the mid-seventeenth

---

10. C.G.A. Clay, *Economic Expansion and Social Change: England 1500–1700*, I, *People, Land and Towns* (Cambridge, 1984), p. 160.
11. Richard Grassby defines businessmen as those full-time, self-employed managers of non-agricultural endeavours possessing at least £500 of equity and £1000 in working capital: *Business Community*, pp. 10–11, 170, and more generally chs 3 and 5.

century for many of them to generate the necessary income to support the expenditures expected of persons of quality. These grew: trips to urban centres, overseas tours, the employment of private tutors, implementation of architectural and interior improvements, and enjoyment of fashionable consumer items of every description were nothing if not costly. Even for those landowners who avoided such disbursements, particular conditions made ends difficult to meet at several points. The interregnum brought unprecedented taxation to all landowners, and income dropped sharply for those whose property suffered wartime damage, as well as for royalists whose lands were sequestered or had to be sold as the price for political delinquency. In the early eighteenth century, the land tax fell on landowners everywhere, and especially so on those in the south and east, where a disproportionate amount of the national burden was assessed.[12]

In addition to these disruptive material considerations, the task of enhancing income was complicated psychologically by the nagging sense that true gentility was inconsistent with a preoccupation with wealth, especially when it affected relations with one's tenants and employees: paternalism died hard. Was it proper, as two modern historians ask, for the owner 'to treat his landed estate simply as an economic unit'? The tension that arose between the duties of paternalism and the demands of earning enough to live as an aristocrat none the less was most often resolved on the side of the need for wealth. In the same way that landowners willingly engaged in business ventures that once would have been socially inappropriate, so they adopted business-like approaches to their estates and exchanged their tenants' loyalty for their tenants' rents.[13]

These rents did not seem to be so readily forthcoming after the mid-seventeenth century, mostly because of changing economic conditions. Tenants' profits predominantly derived from arable farming or from the raising of livestock in pastoral regions. Obviously, then, the market in grains, sheep, and cattle had a fundamental impact on the income of both tenants and of the landed elite to whom they paid rent. On a national scale, the market for and production of livestock held stable over the period, but crop specialization and new methods of farming were producing larger yields on arable

12. C.G.A. Clay, *Economic Expansion and Social Change*, II, *Industry, Trade and Government* (Cambridge, 1984), pp. 263–6; Ann Hughes, *Politics, Society and Civil War in Warwickshire, 1620–1660* (Cambridge, 1987), pp. 262–71.

13. Heal and Holmes, *Gentry*, pp. 163–5; quotation on p. 164; see also Stone, *Crisis of the Aristocracy*, pp. 42–4.

land, and with a relatively static population, enhanced productivity brought lower prices for grain. These declined some 12 per cent between 1640–79 and 1710–49, presenting landowners with problems unlike those their recent forebears had faced.[14]

In fact, for more than a century before the English civil war, the demand for cereals and other foodstuffs had been high enough so that 'most farmers could garner substantial profits, and most landlords could secure substantial increases in rent, without undertaking improvements'.[15] Now, depressed prices for grain compromised landowners' ability to raise or even sustain rent levels where their tenants' principal crops were cereals. This 'fall of rents' worried landowners off and on well into the eighteenth century and featured in the agricultural depression of the 1730s and 1740s, although few seem to have understood the cause of the trend. Instead of identifying its origins in the reduced profits tenants were reaping, late seventeenth-century landlords blamed the inability to pay rent on the lack of specie in the provinces, on their tenants' wilful nonpayment, and on the indolence and dishonesty of rent collectors.[16] Whatever the cause, however, landlords faced an economic difficulty of serious proportions.

Rent arrears accumulated on estates across the kingdom after the mid-seventeenth century, even where conscientious tenants were overseen by vigilant landlords and their diligent employees. While the slump in rents became widespread starting in the early 1660s, in some places the decline dated from the civil war. War damage to many properties noticeably affected rent levels in Northumberland, Durham, Bedfordshire, and Hertfordshire. Overdue payments on the Earl of Suffolk's lands, mostly in East Anglia, totalled nearly an entire year's rent by 1650, and the Earl of Salisbury lost three years of income between 1642 and 1650 because of reduced and unpaid rents, uncollectable fines, and wartime repairs. In Warwickshire the Earls of Middlesex, and lesser figures elsewhere, experienced similar difficulties.[17] After the Restoration and absent the effects of war, arrears accumulated further, despite efforts to counter the trend, and estates as carefully managed by professional agents as those in the care of the London scriveners Clayton and Morris suffered

14 *AHEW*, V, pt 2, pp. 1–4 and appendix III, tables I–XXVII.

15. Clay, *Economic Expansion and Social Change*, I, p. 123.

16. Hainsworth, *Stewards*, pp. 54–5.

17. *AHEW*, V, pt 1, pp. 44–5, 239–40; Lawrence Stone, *Family and Fortune: Studies in Aristocratic Finance in the Sixteenth and Seventeenth Centuries* (Oxford, 1973), pp. 150–2, 291; Hughes, *Warwickshire*, pp. 265–7.

deficits in the 1670s. The author of a manual for estate employees assumed that most 'rent-gatherers' would also necessarily be managers of 'a Stock of Cattle, Sheep, &c. upon Lands in hand: a thing which happens upon most Estates, since the Fall of Land in every County'.[18]

Christopher Clay suggests that 'almost all landlords experienced some loss of income in the 1670s and 1680s', a judgement confirmed in the case of Horatio Lord Townshend. He watched obsessively over his lands in Suffolk and Norfolk but feared he would be ruined 'let mee take what care I can', as unpaid rent mounted to a full year's income in these decades, despite his confrontation with delinquent tenants and his dismissal of three inept stewards. His servants recognized that persistently low grain prices and failure to keep reliable tenants did more to explain rent deficiencies than any individual's shortcomings, one observing on the eve of conflict with the Dutch that the 'noyse of a sea warr has . . . dampt the prises of all Corne'. At the turn of the century, Robert Walpole's steward similarly connected low prices and high taxes with the difficulties tenants had in making their payments.[19]

When unable to pay rent, tenants sometimes voluntarily fled their farms, but eviction was relatively rare, since delinquent tenants were preferable to taking an untenanted farm 'in hand', which meant that a landlord had to pay to have it farmed with labour he hired. John Wyndham of Dunraven tried to keep his son from dismissing tenants in the 1690s because he knew they would be difficult to replace, and Sir Ralph Verney was 'glad at any rates to get tenants'. The complaints of the Fullers of Brightling Park in Sussex, whose rental income fell seriously short of its nominal value after 1710, show that these problems in places persisted early into the next century.[20] Indeed, a return of low grain prices in the 1730s

18. Frank T. Melton, *Sir Robert Clayton and the Origins of English Deposit Banking, 1658–1685* (Cambridge, 1986), pp. 192–7; [Stephen Monteage,] *Instructions for Rent-Gatherers Accompts &c. made easie* (London, 1683), p. 10.

19. Clay, *Economic Expansion and Social Change*, I, p. 162. See also Rosenheim, *Townshends of Raynham*, pp. 98–103; the quotations are respectively from 'Monyes Respited in the Accompts for . . . 1681', Raynham Hall uncatalogued estate manuscripts, tempus Horatio Townshend; C. Spelman to Townshend, 12 December 1664, Raynham Hall box files, 'Horatio Townshend, miscellaneous'; and J. Wrott to Walpole, 13 January 1703, Cambridge University Library, Cholmondeley (Houghton) Correspondence, #275.

20. Jenkins, *Making of a Ruling Class*, p. 49; Heal and Holmes, *Gentry*, p. 118; R.V. Saville, 'Gentry wealth on the Weald in the eighteenth century: the Fullers of Brightling Park', *Sussex Archaeological Collections* 121 (1983), pp. 133–5.

and 1740s (with the exception of 1739–41) created depression in areas where arable farming predominated and again presented landlords with the problem of non-paying tenants.[21]

Three other significant considerations besides low prices for grain and the fall of rents affected landowners' ability to make ends meet. A substantial jump in the size of the portions that landed fathers were expected to provide for daughters, and also some increase in the provision they made for their younger sons, together constituted one of these, although not the most significant one.[22]

The need to maintain an appropriately aristocratic way of life made up a second, and it was arguably a more expensive proposition to meet this requirement in 1750 than in 1650, both in real terms and because of downward pressure on incomes in the period. It is true that the aristocratic provision of hospitality was restrained compared with medieval practices of open-house, and the employment of smaller household staffs in country houses and in town was another common feature of the transition into the eighteenth century for the landed.[23] These economies lowered expenditure for some. But they were overshadowed by the new and newly heightened costs of life in towns and cities, by the sharper demands of fashion, and by the vastly wider array of commercially marketed goods that tempted elite consumers. Architectural and decorative displays of status, less manifest in entirely new building or structural renovations than in the landscaping, decorating, and furnishing of residences, also continued to comprise a major and often growing element of aristocratic consumption. The late seventeenth-century fashion for covering walls and ceilings with painted scenes is just one example of new and costly taste in interior decoration.[24]

---

21. *AHEW*, V, pt 2, pp. 75–82; Margaret Gay Davies, 'Country gentry and falling rents in the 1660s and 1670s', *Midland History* 4 (1977), pp. 86–96; J.V. Beckett, 'Regional variation and the agricultural depression 1730–1750', *Economic History Review*, 2nd series, 35 (1982), pp. 35–51; R.V. Jackson, 'Growth and deceleration in English agriculture, 1660–1790', *Economic History Review*, 2nd series, 38 (1985), pp. 333–51

22. Habakkuk, *Estates System*, pp. 97–108; Clay, *Economic Expansion and Social Change*, I, pp. 147–8.

23. Mark Girouard, *Life in the English Country House: A Social and Architectural History* (New Haven, 1978), pp. 138–43. As Lord Chancellor, the Earl of Shaftesbury maintained at Exeter House a household of thirty-six, where Lord Burleigh had accommodated eighty: K.H.D. Haley, *The First Earl of Shaftesbury* (Oxford, 1968), p. 206.

24. Peter Borsay, *The English Urban Renaissance: Culture and Society in the Provincial Town 1660–1770* (Oxford, 1989), p. 231; Beckett, *Aristocracy*, pp. 325–37; Stone and Stone, *An Open Elite?*, pp. 355–6.

All these developments occurred, as Peter Roebuck notes about landowners in the north, where agricultural depression may have made less of a dent than elsewhere, 'long before rents, the permanent and major component of most incomes, resumed an upward trend'.[25] Among the fortunate whose income did rise, therefore, were those who understandably succumbed to these pressures and increased their life-style expenditures. Sir John Bright, who 'presided over one of the most remarkable family success stories in seventeenth-century Yorkshire', had plate valued at £160 in 1657 and over £1200 some thirty years later. Some individuals spent more than their access of wealth strictly warranted. The income of Sir Edward Dering, member of parliament and public official, more than doubled between 1648–58 and 1668–79, but his expenses still outran it.[26]

A third and unfamiliar term added to the equation of elite spending was the burden of central government taxes, whose unprecedented volume and scope during the civil wars introduced a new component into the personal economy of landowners.[27] The Restoration brought only moderate relief from the tax patterns of the 1640s and 1650s. Reluctantly and after efforts to disguise its character, the monthly assessment introduced during the civil war was employed under different names and different circumstances, but there was no disguising it as a property tax, apportioned county by county, to yield fixed sums levied predominantly on realty.[28] A national levy, finally designated a land tax, was perfected during the Nine Years' War (1689–97), and although it was not imposed exclusively on land and fell unevenly on different regions, it was purposefully laid on landowners rather than their tenants.[29]

In the early eighteenth century the assessment at three or four shillings in the pound did literally amount in places to a 15 or 20 per cent levy on landed income. In gross terms, government tax revenues tripled between the mid-1670s and 1715, and the proportion of national income taken in by government grew from about

25. Roebuck, *Yorkshire Baronets*, pp. 32, 61.
26. Ibid., pp. 220, 222, 332–4; *Dering Diaries*, p. 28.
27. Hughes, *Warwickshire*, pp. 187–90 illustrates the impact of war taxes on one county.
28. C.D. Chandaman, *The English Public Revenue 1660–1688* (Oxford, 1975), ch. 5, esp. pp. 140–7 and table 2 (p. 158).
29. W.R. Ward, *The English Land Tax in the Eighteenth Century* (London, 1953), section I; *AHEW*, V, pt 2, pp. 119–23, 224–5; Michael Turner, 'The land tax, land and property: old debates and new horizons', in Turner and Dennis Mills, eds, *Land Tax and Property: The English Land Tax 1692–1832* (New York, 1986), pp. 1–3.

3.5 per cent to more than 9 per cent. In the first quarter of the eighteenth century, the English paid double what the French did *per capita*, with the gentry and nobility taking a heavy burden. After 1713 the land tax rates fell until the 1740s and the tax load shifted from direct to indirect, relieving to some extent members of the landed order. Even with this relief, however, and while recognizing that owners were affected differently by taxes (depending on place of residence and amount of income derived from taxable sources), the burden lay heavily on landowners in the formative period of what John Brewer has called the fiscal-military state. This imposition, and its origin in central government actions and institutions, increasingly intruded that government into the landed elite's consciousness. In doing so it exemplified the way that the emerging agencies of the modern state were beginning to populate, and thus define, the horizons of English life.[30]

Landowners laboured by and large successfully to cope with the pressures that were placed on their landed incomes by the fall of rents, the need to spend amply to maintain status, and the demands of central government: farming could be made profitable. The smaller return that grain yielded did not necessarily make its cultivation unprofitable, and low profits could be overcome by adopting a strategy of agricultural improvement in the face of these pressures. But tenant-farmers and landlords both had to employ new energy and skill in order to prosper. When they did and farmers continued to earn profits, landlords benefited in two ways. First, they received the steady payment of agreed-upon rents. Second, landlords who assisted their tenant-farmers, either by way of capital investment or by way of allowance for improvements that tenants made, could condition that help on a concomitant or subsequent increase in rent. They also imposed other lease conditions on improved lands than higher rent alone, terms which were intended to ensure that the improvements made would not be lost in the future through poor husbandry.

The economist Peter Bowden has conceived several notional farms in order to assess where profitability lay in agriculture. His work shows that tenants and landlords were most likely to be rewarded by cultivating wheat, and that a greater return could usually be obtained

30. R.A.C. Parker, 'Direct taxation on the Coke estates in the eighteenth century', *English Historical Review* 71 (1956), pp. 247–8; Clay, *Economic Expansion and Social Change*, II, pp. 263–9; John Brewer, *The Sinews of Power: War, Money and the English State, 1688–1763* (Cambridge, Massachusetts, 1990), pp. 88–91, 95–101 – Brewer displays patterns of imposition graphically in figure 4.2 (pp. 96–7).

from beef production rather than dairying, while sheep-raising was a vulnerable and relatively weak pillar of the farm economy.[31] Signs abound that in this context new approaches to agriculture brought material reward even in hard times. Many landlords in the north were actually able to raise their rents in the years between 1680 and 1750, annual leases allowing for rapid rent adjustments became characteristic of the Downs in the south at this time, and the elevation of rents occurring in Hertfordshire in the late seventeenth and early eighteenth centuries derived from improvements. Some of the innovative aspects of progressive agriculture bore rich fruit, and a specialized crop like hops could yield net profits as high as 30 per cent.[32]

Agricultural advances (as opposed to new purchases or conversion of directly farmed land to leaseholds) accounted for over 40 per cent of the increase in value on the estates of the second Viscount Townshend between 1701 and 1737. Rents per acre rose on some of his farms from seven to ten shillings over the course of a few years, and Lord Lovel simultaneously raised rents from 6s to 8s 6d per acre after a course of marling on some of his Norfolk lands. Despite land sales, improvement between 1670 and 1745 increased by two-thirds the income from lands the Viscounts Windsor held in Glamorgan.[33]

In the end, Bowden's exercise reveals that profitability in farming lay wherever 'good fortune, an enterprising disposition, and sound business acumen' were joined together.[34] Enjoying almost by definition a measure of material good fortune, many of the landed elite of England were able to invest in agriculture and to profit from the investment. An enterprising disposition, however – at least with regard to agriculture – seems important by its absence from many of the elite. Unwillingness to provide sufficient oversight and management on their lands was a dire failing of many aristocrats, from which some were saved only because of income that came from other directions. The last of Bowden's three attributes, business acumen, was more prevalent, at least in the form of the attention landowners paid to agricultural income and in their willingness to try to enhance it, if only by following others' advice about how to do so.

31. *AHEW*, V, pt 2, pp. 83–118.   32. Ibid., V, pt 1, pp. 45–6, 244–5, 332.
33. Rosenheim, *Townshends of Raynham*, pp. 142 (table 4.4), 147, 155; R.A.C. Parker, *Coke of Norfolk: A Financial and Agricultural Study 1707–1842* (Oxford, 1975), p. 41; Jenkins, *Making of a Ruling Class*, pp. 50–1.
34. *AHEW*, V, pt 2, p. 118.

In the final analysis, the combination of characteristics necessary for exceptional success eluded many landowners, especially at the end of the seventeenth century. But failure resulting in a retreat from gentility was also rare: incurring debt was common, bankruptcy much rarer. And although other sources usefully and perhaps even essentially augmented income for landed family after landed family, the judgement reiterated in study after study is that rent receipts – the landed aristocracy's profits from the land – exceeded these contributions to family wealth.[35] The economic difficulties faced by many landed families during this era did nothing for their confidence but the challenges these posed was a shared adversity. Moreover, both the landed elite's prosperity and its continued dominance of English society well past the eighteenth century testifies to its success in finding solutions to the difficult problems of making ends meet and to doing so in ways that also helped to reinforce its transformation as a national ruling order.

The context of improvement

Maintaining the profitability of agriculture raised the most serious but also the most tractable of these problems, which landowners faced with an array of vague ideas, concrete plans, and even legislation. Individual landlords devised strategies to cope with falling rents and low prices on a case-by-case basis, in ways appropriate to their specific estates and needs and thus sometimes haphazardly or even in contradictory ways. Yet they addressed their singular dilemmas in a common intellectual climate that made economic policy the object of growing public debate and of parliamentary scrutiny and legislation. Moreover, they sought solutions to unique problems while none the less confident that their particular cares could also be addressed as those of the nation at large.

The body of literature that addressed landowners' common agricultural concerns grew so much in both size and specificity after about 1650 that the century's mid-point seems to mark a watershed in the intellectual environment that surrounded the aristocrat as agriculturalist. This increase in publications that dwelt on the practical improvability of the land was informed by and occurred in the wake of a shift in the literary representation of agriculture.

---

35. Roebuck, *Yorkshire Baronets*, pp. 218, 270–1; Haley, *Shaftesbury*, pp. 207–9; Jenkins, *Making of a Ruling Class*, pp. 45–8; Rosenheim, *Townshends of Raynham*, pp. 137–40, 156–60; Beckett, *Aristocracy*, pp. 288–94.

Sixteenth-century pastoral depictions of agriculture had projected an agrarian moral economy in which members of the landed elite figured as stewards of an unchanging natural landscape of beauty and bounty. The views found in early Stuart surveyors' manuals, chorographies, and rural poetry were contrastingly informed by a georgic vision giving priority to expansive and improving cultivation of the land. Where the ploughman had once been a symbol of the manorial community, he nearly drops from sight in this and later literature, remaining largely as an instrument of the landlord, whose profile rises. Presented in ways that stressed his individuality (as in county chorographies that catalogued family after gentry family), the landlord was also shown as the motivator and supervisor of a rural productivity that arose from acres whose property was insistently and clearly defined as his.[36]

A literature of improvement constituted one of the keys to productivity and full exploitation of one's resources. Although agricultural practices varied from region to region across the kingdom, an assumption that underlay much of this body of work was that landlords everywhere did or ought to acknowledge 'the *duty* of improving their estates'.[37] Some writers sought broad readership by addressing topics like tree-planting, which would be adaptable by and interest any agriculturalist. Just one element of this agricultural literature, gardening books, produced a hundred titles in the seventeenth century, eighty of them after 1650; the next century saw six hundred more. The 1660s and 1670s saw the publication of John Worlidge's 'influential general handbooks' *Systema Agriculturae* (1669) and *Systema Horti-Culturae* (1677). Up to 1700 the Royal Society's *Philosophical Transactions* carried over forty articles on agriculture, a pace more rapid than in the next fifty years. Sir John Lowther, who owned a set of *Transactions* and promised to extract its most valuable information for his steward, observed in 1698 that it contained 'many useful accounts relating to agriculture, planting, mines, salt works, etc.' Much published material was unoriginal and even the plagiarized product of unqualified authors, and readership of specialized works remained limited until the late eighteenth century, but this literature had its influence in the countryside, partly because it drew the attention of the squirearchy and nobility.

36. *AHEW*, V, pt 2, ch. 16; Andrew McRae, *God Speed the Plough: The Representation of Agrarian England, 1500–1660* (Cambridge, 1996).
37. Christopher Hill, *The English Bible and the Seventeenth-Century Revolution* (London, 1993), p. 159, citing *The Whole Duty of Man* (1704).

The Duke of Kent (1671–1740) was not alone in having a large collection of books on gardening and husbandry in his library.[38] The rather eclectic literature of improvement, even where it derived from experience gained in a particular locale, largely ignored county boundaries. Some writers in fact believed that regional isolation obstructed advances in agriculture and hoped to give readers information to overcome their retrograde provincialism.[39] William Ellis, whose writings and agricultural experiments of the 1730s through the 1750s focussed on Hertfordshire and the Chilterns, acted as a conduit for dispatches from all over and earned a national audience. John Houghton's *Collection for Improvement of Husbandry and Trade*, published weekly and issued cheaply after 1681, gave current agricultural prices and offered suggested reading and information about new agricultural methods. It specifically aimed to demolish county barriers that prevented the spread of useful agricultural knowledge. In Cumberland, Sir John Lowther's steward planned sales of his master's coal with the help of prices Houghton published, and he was similarly guided in agrarian matters by garden books and by John Evelyn's *Sylva* (1664).[40]

Besides obtaining knowledge about farming through the published word, landowners learned from one another, exchanging ideas at assizes and sessions, in county towns and country houses. Among the gifts that gentry frequently exchanged with one another, live plants figured along with harvested meats, fish, and fruits. Gentry supplied each other clover seed in East Anglia in the late seventeenth century, and in the southwest Midlands small coteries of gentlemen promoted schemes for fruit-growing, cider production, and even industrial development. Public places like the Botanical Gardens at Oxford provided visible evidence of new plants and innovative practices, as did visits to private residences, whether to renowned gardens at Wilton or to obscure nursery gardens like that of Sir Justinian Isham's cousin Poulton.[41]

London, whose gardening fashions, for example, spread into the Vale of Evesham in the 1640s,[42] remained a primary locale for the

38. Keith Thomas, *Man and the Natural World: Changing Attitudes in England 1500–1800* (Harmondsworth, 1984), p. 225; Pamela Horn, 'The contribution of the propagandist to eighteenth-century agricultural improvement', *Historical Journal* 25 (1982), pp. 319–21; *AHEW*, V, pt 1, pp. 262–3; ibid., pt 2, p. 569; Joshua Lerner, 'Science and agricultural progress: quantitative evidence from England, 1660–1780', *Agricultural History* 66 (Fall 1992), p. 23; *Lowther Correspondence*, pp. 551, 559.
39. *AHEW*, V, pt 2, p. 569.
40. Ibid., pt 1, pp. 263–5 and pt 2, p. 338; *Lowther Correspondence*, pp. 383, 471.
41. *AHEW*, V, pt 1, pp. 160–3, 223 and pt 2, p. 569; *Isham Diary*, p. 99.
42. *AHEW*, V, pt 1, p. 168.

interchange of ideas and had a concentration of sites to visit. During the interregnum the pioneers Walter Blith and Samuel Hartlib stood at the centre of metropolitan circles of like-minded men, encouraging landowners to share their experiences with each other, in part by writing accounts for publication. After the Restoration, the Royal Society's Georgical Committee and later its Committee for Agriculture provided institutional venues for discussion; by 1700 a botanical club met in the Temple Coffee House and by the mid-eighteenth century physic gardens existed at Chelsea and Kew.[43] Where the immediate audience for these gatherings may well have been small, it was dominated by the landed elite and 'to contemporaries it went almost without saying that influence *must* spread out from London because only there could groups of interested people from different counties meet to talk, exchange experience, and advance their practice'. The Hanoverian kings' court itself served as a forum for 'extending, intensifying, and perhaps making fashionable a lively interest in improved farming', objects that were assisted by gestures like the gifts of turnip seed and buckwheat made to the second Viscount Townshend by the German favourites of George I.[44]

Agrarian issues received expression in parliament and the halls of government that demonstrated their importance in the public discourse of England's rulers. During the civil war and interregnum, the harsh economic times and the fertile climate for proposals of social amelioration stimulated discussion about agricultural policy. Parliament, by meeting recurrently, played an important role in the conversation then and thereafter. Throughout the next hundred years, public agricultural debate revolved around efforts to encourage and diversify production, to improve land, to regulate enclosure, and (more grudgingly) to provide for the poor. On the whole, little legislation was passed to effect these or other agrarian aims: enactments generally intervened only indirectly in agriculture, by addressing matters of marketing more than of production.[45] Particular crises, however, whether the fall of rents in the later seventeenth century or the occurrence of cattle plague in the eighteenth, led to acts such as those prohibiting the import of Irish cattle or encouraging the export of grain with bounties.[46] A ban on

43. Ibid., pt 2, pp. 562, 566–7; Thomas, *Man and the Natural World*, pp. 227, 271.
44. *AHEW*, V, pt 2, pp. 566, 575; Townshend household extraordinary accounts 1719–23 (26 June 1721) and 1723–5 (10 February 1724), Raynham Hall, Norfolk, uncatalogued bound volumes.
45. *AHEW*, V, pt 2, pp. 303–4 and pp. 298–388, *passim*.
46. Joan Thirsk and J.P. Cooper, eds, *Seventeenth-Century Economic Documents* (Oxford, 1972), pp. 155–6, 162–4; *AHEW*, V, pt 2, pp. 346–61.

Irish cattle imposed in 1667, although it exposed differences of interest between cattle producers and corn growers among landowners, none the less tackled what was presented as the kingdom's problem. Other legislation similarly spoke to the common interests of the gentry. The game statutes of 1661 and 1670, for instance, which coincide with the decline of gentry involvement in deer-stealing and other kinds of poaching, were the first of a group of laws (augmented under Queen Anne) 'which steadily and purposefully extended the gentry's control over foodstuffs that had once been much more fairly shared by all'.[47]

Debates about the fall of rents and decay of trade were national debates reflecting the interests and outlook of landowners and farmers. Action on the central stage helped to bring the concerns of landowners to the attention of one another, even if they differed from one another. This held equally true when no statute was enacted, as was the case with proposals introduced between the 1660s and 1690s to ease and regulate enclosure. Regardless of what was passed into law, the reading of bills, appointment of committees, and discussion of proposals in parliament spread both facts and opinions regarding agrarian policy well beyond Westminster.[48] This dissemination made it more likely for landowners to see themselves as members of a ruling order rather than of a county community or purely regional society.

Solutions

Landowners addressing common difficulties within a shared intellectual environment had to solve their own specific problems by themselves, yet they had similar motives and employed similar tactics to do so. Some landlords consolidated farms and turned to fewer and larger tenants in response to falling rents, some turned necessity to advantage by enclosing properties that lost tenants, in hope of making them more profitable and attractive, and some followed conscious policies of innovation by investing in material improvements and repairs and by experimenting with new crops, methods, and rotations. They did not act solely from economic motives, as Sir John (later first Baron) Ashburnham indicated in 1698: 'We ought to improve our talents and not waste or destroy

47. Roger B. Manning, *Hunters and Poachers: A Social and Cultural History of Unlawful Hunting in England, 1485–1640* (Oxford, 1993), p. 234; *AHEW*, V, pt 2, p. 368.
48. *AHEW*, V, pt 2, pp. 325, 378–80.

nor bury them uselesse in a napkin; this is true in land as well as in grace.' 'Lyming or marling', he added, 'are the wordes and must be the workes in fashion to preserve the peace and quietnesse amongst us and prevent the effusion of Christian money, by which our tenants will be gainers as well as savers.'[49]

More prosaically, however, landowners were called upon to apply more careful and rational management to their landed estates. Profits were simply harder to wring from land after about 1640 than they had been beforehand, when 'only the particularly unfortunate or the very incompetent' among private landowners experienced a long-term drop in the purchasing power of their agricultural incomes. After mid-century, landowners had to work harder at being rural landowners in order to prosper, and they responded to this challenge.[50]

Because all landlords shared the need for tenants who faithfully paid rent and did nothing to reduce the value of the farms they hired, one strategy for prosperity was to persuade tenants who had shown their reliability in those terms to rent increasingly large holdings. A scarcity of such tenants slowed this process, but it did not prevent movement toward large farms in many regions of the country – Hertfordshire, the southeast, the Downs, northwest Norfolk, east Yorkshire, to name a few. Probably not the consequence of a policy of dispossession, sometimes this development was the result of strategies of acquisition by new owners, sometimes the result of a change in leasing practices.[51] Consolidation of existing but disparate holdings, like that urged by the Earl of Carlisle's steward to enhance both agricultural fertility and rents,[52] could also lead to the creation of large tenant farms. And reorganization took place for non-economic reasons, like recreation or aesthetics, which was just as well when larger farms were not necessarily more efficient or

49. Colin Brooks, 'John, 1st Baron Ashburnham and the state, c.1688–1710', *Historical Research* 60, no. 141 (1987), p. 65.

50. Clay, *Economic Expansion and Social Change*, I, p. 147. Among the studies that emphasize their subjects' business-like management see Haley, *Shaftesbury*, p. 210; Roebuck, *Yorkshire Baronets*, pp. 89, 212; Jenkins, *Making of a Ruling Class*, p. 57; and Rosenheim, *Townshends of Raynham*, pp. 64–5.

51. Rule, *Vital Century*, p. 66; Clay, *Economic Expansion and Social Change*, I, pp. 81–2; G.E. Mingay, 'The size of farms in the eighteenth century', *Economic History Review*, 2nd series, 14 (1962), pp. 475, 477; *AHEW*, V, pt 1, pp. 144–5, 244, 295, 332; Rosenheim, *Townshends of Raynham*, pp. 145–7; Saville, 'Fullers of Brightling Park', p. 135; J.R. Wordie, *Estate Management in Eighteenth-Century England: The Building of the Leveson-Gower Fortune* (London, 1982), pp. 160–4; Roebuck, *Yorkshire Baronets*, p. 214.

52. *AHEW*, V, pt 1, p. 51.

profitable ones. The Duke of Kingston bought land from copyhold tenants in the mid-1730s for the purpose of extending his park, and one steward recommended a new farm layout merely to 'bring the park pale into a straight line which now runs very uneven'.[53]

The landlord owning an estate characterized by large farms (perhaps newly created) that were leased at market rents to substantial tenants confronted considerations of management different from those posed by an estate comprised of numerous smaller, often customary tenancies. Worrying about the leasing and oversight of farms each worth several hundreds of pounds in rent differed greatly from trying to bring in myriad small quit rents from copyholders. The former conditions suggested several new managerial tactics, like giving significant rent abatements for the kind of major capital improvements that only large tenants could make, and they fostered the adoption of more rational methods of accounting by more clearly professional estate employees. Both of these practices tended to standardize the experience of landlords, tying together in a common bond of modern landlordship the great magnate, the prosperous baronet, and the affluent squire, otherwise separated by politics or geography or religion.

Some landlords took significant parts in the direction of estate affairs, and some estate accounts preserve signs (like corrections to the arithmetic) of intimate engagement by owners, which may have been more forthcoming when a shortage of tenants meant that land had to be farmed by the landlords' employees. The rent rolls of the second Baron Gower suggest that in 1723 he displayed most unusual interest in his estate and tenants by receiving the rents in person. Sir John Ashburnham employed no steward at all and wrote hundreds of letters a year to employees scattered in Wales, Bedfordshire, and Sussex. He gave them advice on farming techniques and carefully supervised his tenants, his iron furnace, and his coal mines when in the country. From London, Paul Foley sent directions to his steward in Herefordshire that even included orders about which branches to prune on an apple tree in his kitchen garden. Whether they were this particularly involved or not, landowners placed large, sometimes new demands on their employees. They wanted more detailed, informative, and realistic reckonings of their affairs, like accounts that were shorn of irrecoverable and

53. A.D.M. Phillips, 'A note on farm size and efficiency on the north Staffordshire estate of the Leveson-Gowers, 1714–1809', *North Staffordshire Journal of Field Studies* 19 (1979), pp. 30–8; *AHEW*, V, pt 1, p. 120; Wordie, *Estate Management*, p. 161.

ancient rent-arrears that had been uselessly carried on the books for decades.[54]

The announcement in the *Ipswich Journal* during 1727 of an estate audit for the Earl of Tankerville, and advertisements for tenants in the eighteenth-century regional press, exemplify the adoption of methodical approaches to estate management. Stephen Monteage's *Instructions for Rent-Gatherers Accompts* assumed that most landowners would not be their own rent-collectors, but still claimed to provide 'the Gentry of this Nation' and even their children with a 'plain Method' to take accounts.[55] Regardless of who actually applied these procedures, landowners would benefit from learning them because they would be able to look knowingly into the details of their country business and interpret and check the accuracy of the accounts they received.

The efforts to make estate management clearer and simpler were aimed at saving administrative energy and at maintaining income, and they were adopted partly in response to the economic burden that war taxation imposed after the 1690s, although the financial strain these taxes placed on landlords varied by region and according to the individual owner's financial position. In some instances the fact that improved lands were not usually reassessed for the tax may have given an inducement for improvement and made the tax's impact indirectly beneficial. More negatively and universally, the 'administrative repercussions' and general inconvenience of the tax fell on landlords, especially because tenants virtually everywhere received allowances for the land tax payments they made.[56] Not only did landlords or their surrogates have to keep an eye on the way their lands were assessed, but they also had to be vigilant that tenants were making legitimate claims for abatements. In response to new circumstances like these, aristocratic landlords across the country turned toward similar, eventually standard solutions.[57]

Often these developments in management procedures involved changes in personnel, and, where the landlord thought himself

54. Wordie, *Estate Management*, pp. 33–5, 39; G.E. Mingay, *English Landed Society in the Eighteenth Century* (London, 1963), pp. 61–6; *AHEW*, V, pt 1, p. 177; Rosenheim, *Townshends of Raynham*, p. 122.

55. *Ipswich Journal*, 23–30 September 1727, p. 4; J. Sendall to R. Britiffe 12 February and 2 March 1748, Norfolk Record Office, NRS 21089, 71x3; [Monteage,] *Instructions for Rent-Gatherers Accompts*, pp. 33, 3.

56. Brooks, 'Ashburnham and the state', p. 76; Roebuck notes several instances in Yorkshire where tenants were made to pay national taxes: *Yorkshire Baronets*, pp. 120, 152, 228.

57. Beckett, *Aristocracy*, p. 144.

expert, the instruction of new employees. On the Leveson-Gower estates between 1690 and 1720, four under-agents serving a single steward took over the work of a dozen tenant-bailiffs. From 1650 to 1680 the first Viscount Townshend reduced nine different positions to three. A landlord who remained directly involved in administration of his land, Townshend also drew up detailed instructions for the employees he retained on 'how to looke after my Estate'; these were used long after his death. Lord Fitzwilliam, disappointed in 1704 that his steward could not recall which tenants had paid him their rents, urged on the man a regular system of daily record-keeping, warning that '[w]ithout such a method you must have all things in great confusion I feare.'[58]

In a manner that reflected the emergence of a kingdom-wide pool of trained employees on which landowners could draw, Monteage encouraged landlords not to employ local men as their stewards, favouring instead 'a sober Citizen, who is a good Accomptant, than ... another that is not so, though versed in Country-Affairs'. Confirming their Anglophilia, members of the Glamorgan gentry employed as stewards men whose English surnames suggest that they were not native to the county.[59] Employment of such outsiders is evidence of broader changes occurring in the households of the landed, where objective qualifications for such appointments began to outweigh subjective ones like traditions of family service or a prospective employee's connections in the surrounding community. Where once a local manorial official had sufficed to serve as a measurer of land, in the early seventeenth century the land surveyor emerged as a 'specialized, temporary employee, who impose[d] new standards of knowledge and order upon preexistent structures of land management'.[60] Similarly in the latter part of the century, the estate steward went from being seen as part of the household to being perceived as a member of a profession, one whose actions as his master's surrogate carried weight not simply through the transference of the landowner's status and authority to him but on the basis of the steward's own knowledge and skill. Most clearly when functioning as an accountant, the estate steward was no longer a household officer 'in the neo-feudal sense' but a salaried employee,

58. Wordie, *Estate Management*, pp. 18, 27; Rosenheim, *Townshends of Raynham*, pp. 96–104, 121–2; *Fitzwilliam Correspondence*, p. 153.

59. [Monteage,] *Instructions for Rent-Gatherers Accompts*, p. 7; Jenkins, *Making of a Ruling Class*, p. 56.

60. McRae, *God Speed the Plough*, p. 176.

a transformation of role that injected a 'less familial note' into the relationship of master and man.[61]

By adopting more strictly business-like relations with those they employed, landlords were party to the diminution of their own paternalist authority, a decline engendered in part by procuring more unified management of their estates and in part by an attitude toward their agricultural accounts that stressed financial over social calculation. The willingness and even eagerness of the landed to employ such figures as the full-time estate steward suggest that aristocrats were coming to see their control of land less in fiduciary terms and more in strictly economic ones. They saw theirs less as lordship over a unique trust and more as ownership of a possession, even if a special possession with singular characteristics. These developments make up part of the reconstitution of elite identity that saw landowners yielding the social power that ownership gave them over their tenants in medieval times for the economic power that ownership gave them within society at large as a modern aristocracy.[62] When deciding to proceed with a scheme of unpopular enclosure, for example, owners were rejecting the 'reasons of conscience, family pride, popularity, and politics' that otherwise encouraged them to keep their small tenants around.[63] In return they could hope to gain income or to open up acreage for the kind of consumption or landscaping project that enhanced, if not their political might, then their social power and cultural prestige.

Although some landowners, like Sir John Ashburnham, continued to see themselves as husbandmen to their own estates, for substantial numbers of the gentry and nobility involvement in estate management became increasingly vicarious into the mid-eighteenth century, perhaps as a way of dealing with the local and psychological stress created by abandoning some of the elements of paternalist agriculture. At the least, by employing deputies the landed avoided the tedious routine of so much farming business, theoretically gaining the benefit of 'meticulous management' through the labour of others.[64] Gentry whose Elizabethan and early Stuart forebears had ridden over their estates in careful supervision of agricultural life were in the mid-eighteenth century riding over their own and others'

61. Hainsworth, *Stewards*, p. 261.
62. David Cannadine, *Lords and Landlords: The Aristocracy and the Towns 1774–1967* (Leicester, 1980), pp. 21–5.
63. *AHEW*, V, pt 1, p. 117.
64. Holmes, *Seventeenth-Century Lincolnshire*, pp. 71–2; see also Roebuck, *Yorkshire Baronets*, p. 319.

lands in pursuit of the fox or in appreciation of the landscape architecture they had created. They also could distance themselves from activities that no longer seemed entirely suitable for aristocrats: the decline of the once-ubiquitous East Anglian foldcourse, which gave landlords rights to graze sheep on their tenants' lands, has been attributed to such a cause and to the rise of 'rentier estate management' between the 1640s and 1680s.[65]

Absenteeism

The distancing of landlords, although explicable, was considered lamentable by contemporaries. Much more than any formal written directions, the owner's simple attendance in the countryside was thought to have a beneficial effect on estate affairs, a traditional view traceable to classical times. Edward Laurence, author of a well-known manual for stewards, 'always found [the landlord's] Presence to [be] . . . a constant Cheque both upon Steward and Tenant, as to any *unjustifiable* Connivances or private Bargains'.[66] This published observation only underlined a commonplace echoed again and again: Lord Fitzwilliam lamented in 1697 that nothing got done on his Northamptonshire estate when he was gone; in 1726 the Earl of Cardigan's steward reported that a tenant challenged his authority to collect rent and refused to pay 'till your Lordship comes to receive it your self'. In the 1740s a steward told his master that in his absence it was 'impossible to carry on with the same success as if you were here'.[67] Landlords, however, more and more often were not on their estates, a fact that played its own part in shaping elite identity. Where their predecessors were criticized for a wrong-headed stewardship of the land displayed both through covetousness and excessively possessive attention to their property,[68] late seventeenth- and early eighteenth-century landlords were more likely to be made targets because they were ineffective and uncaring trustees.

65. *AHEW*, V, pt 1, pp. 229–30.

66. McRae, *God Speed the Plough*, pp. 140, 192–3; Edward Laurence, *The Duty and Office of a Land Steward: Represented under Several Plain and Distinct Articles* (2nd edition, London, 1731; reprinted New York, 1979), p. 90.

67. *Fitzwilliam Correspondence*, p. 9; *Eaton to Cardigan Letters*, pp. 30–1; J.V. Beckett, 'Absentee landownership in the later seventeenth and early eighteenth centuries: the case of Cumbria', *Northern History* 19 (1983), p. 95.

68. McRae, *God Speed the Plough*, chs. 1, 6.

Because the interregnum displaced so many, the mid-seventeenth century constitutes a landmark, a point of acceleration in the history of landlord absenteeism. Military service, exile, the regularity of parliamentary sessions, and the expansion of the state together drew landlords away from their estates (perhaps only temporarily but still consequentially and in unprecedented fashion) to battlefield, the Continent, London, and elsewhere. In later years, the growth of extremely large estates in the eighteenth century also encouraged absenteeism. Minorities among heirs, common because of high mortality at the turn of the eighteenth century, abetted it further, since these children tended to be sent away to school or to some relative's house. Landlords who possessed acres scattered across numerous counties would necessarily be absent from one estate even if resident on another, and this phenomenon was intensified when marriage alliances outside county or region brought far-flung lands into individual owners' hands. Normal socializing with family and friends and the new popularity of foxhunting brought gentlemen to their friends' estates and away from their own for what could be substantial periods of time. The development of national and regional centres of pleasure, Newmarket and Bath, York and Bristol and Tunbridge Wells, also lured landowners from home, even in the case of those who lived in remote areas: apparently the majority of larger Cumbrian landowners were absentee. It is further noteworthy that a hypothetical set of estate accounts published in the 1680s to illustrate accounting methods included in its expenditures £50 for 'my Lord's Bill of Exchange from the Bath' and £10 paid 'my Lady at her going out of Town'.[69]

London was to some extent a newly potent attraction. Although nobles had for many years spent considerable time there, before 1640 gentry were less likely to go, nor did they go for so long. After the mid-seventeenth century, London's role as centre of consumption, as location of marriage, financial, and land markets, developed markedly and continuously. The Restoration re-opened the capital to all but a few proscribed republicans, parliament met regularly, and the royal court's magnetic attraction was felt again.

69. Stone, *Crisis of the Aristocracy*, pp. 385–92; Peter Roebuck, 'Absentee landownership in the late seventeenth and early eighteenth centuries: a neglected factor in English agrarian history', *Agricultural History Review* 21 (1973), pp. 11–12; Hainsworth, *Stewards*, pp. 13–17; J.V. Beckett, 'Estate management in eighteenth-century England: the Lowther–Spedding relationship in Cumberland', in John Chartres and David Hey, eds, *English Rural Society, 1500–1800: Essays in Honour of Joan Thirsk* (Cambridge, 1990), p. 58; [Monteage,] *Instructions for Rent-Gatherers Accompts*, p. 19 for the quotations.

Yet the landed's prolonged absence from their estates did not equate to lack of interest or necessarily cause neglect of estates, which, as their primary capital assets, landowners had strong incentives to maintain. Increasingly reliable and professional substitutes played their part, perhaps even performing better than resident gentlemen, who were not demonstrably superior managers to their surrogates, if the case of Cumbria is anything to go by. The growing income of the Yorkshire baronet Sir Charles Hotham has, for instance, been attributed in significant measure to his employment of a steward. And when the Duke of Buckingham's debts forced him to put his lands into a trusteeship, its entrepreneurial land management and 'metropolitan control' made him a most successful *rentier*.[70] Absentees might visit regularly, employees could satisfactorily fill the vacuum created by an owner's absence, and correspondence with those on the ground kept some owners surprisingly well informed. Although Sir John Lowther visited his Cumbrian lands only eight times between 1666 and 1698, his interest in them never dropped, and from offstage he abetted the exploitation of his collieries, the development of the port of Whitehaven, and the increase of his rentals. In the late seventeenth century Sir Ralph Verney's steward wrote to him daily, John Spedding wrote to Sir James Lowther thrice weekly from the 1720s to 1750s, and Lady Diana Feilding claimed when writing to an employee in 1709 to 'know more at this distance then you that live on the place'.[71]

All the same, the detriment of absenteeism to estate management and the economic development of the countryside appears obvious today: decay of estates in the absence of owners' direct supervision, which allowed tenants to exploit holdings to their own rather than the landlord's benefit; little occasion for absentee landlords to pursue improving methods on their land; opportunity for employees to cheat their masters; and the drain of money and loss of rural employment as landowners pursued leisure and pleasure elsewhere. To take just one example, during Sir Marmaduke Constable's long sojourn in Europe between 1730 and 1746, customary services fell into abeyance, property on his Yorkshire lands fell into disrepair, and tenants 'stole, poached, organized hare-coursing on the estate' and used his bull to serve their cows.[72] In the final analysis,

70. Beckett, 'Absentee landownership', pp. 87–107; Roebuck, *Yorkshire Baronets*, p. 89.

71. *Lowther Correspondence*, p. xviii and *passim*; Beckett, 'Estate management', p. 65; Feilding to [T.] Wilkinson, spring 1709, Norfolk Record Office, HOW 731/11, 349X; I am indebted to Dr Susan Whyman for the information on Verney.

72. Roebuck, *Yorkshire Baronets*, pp. 189–92; quotation on p. 190. Despite these developments, and regardless of long-term consequences, Constable's 'general financial and economic circumstances did not decline': p. 192.

disadvantage rather than benefit was more likely to accrue from absence. Life away from one's country estate inevitably distracted the sheer attention that was the most important asset landowners could bring to their estates. Yet for all its potential consequence, this drawback did not matter enough to most absentee landlords to get them to come home, Constable serving as a prime example. The greater frequency of their absences is a sign of the elite's re-evaluation of its place in the countryside. As such, absenteeism played a part in establishing common practices of and attitudes to estate management that showed landowners their mutual interests and common fates.

In this context, the estate steward played an important part.[73] Well-paid and carefully chosen, successful stewards received the confidence and support of their employers, and some made fortunes and established landed families. Ideally these men possessed a range of skills and served an array of roles, and they affected estate operations in myriad trivial and significant ways. Matters as small as the practice of numbering and docqueting letters, providing interim accounts, and making them clearer and simpler (by converting from roman to arabic numerals, for example) exemplify the approach to estate administration that landlords sought from these men. Stewards helped to reorganize farms, recruit and retain worthy tenants, and promote new techniques and courses of husbandry. They also crucially preserved and enhanced landlords' local interests at elections, and they maintained the physical integrity of estates, defending against encroachment. These valuable services – even if they were not all performed equally well – uniquely insulated landowning employers from at least some of the evils of absence. And if the benefits these professionals brought were confined to the landed elite, so were the problems that the quarrelsome, venal, or incompetent generated.[74] Yeoman farmers who did their own bookkeeping, rent collection, and negotiation with tenants never had to deal with the serious disruption such employees could cause. The common tasks of landownership for gentry and nobility, however, included recurrent, often fraught, dealings with these subordinate yet absolutely essential (and thus potentially insubordinate) figures.

Whether or not specific individuals were honest, sober, loyal, and efficient, the position itself tended to standardize the practices

---

73. Hainsworth, *Stewards* is the essential source for what follows, but see also Beckett, 'Estate management'.
74. Mingay, *English Landed Society*, p. 59; Jenkins, *Making of a Ruling Class*, pp. 54–7.

of landlords' estate management, what David Hainsworth calls 'England's largest collective business',[75] in part because the terms of these practices were readily available in print. Stephen Monteage offered twenty-three pages of model accounts in his *Instructions*; Edward Laurence's handbook contained an appendix with 'General Rules and Directions for the Management and Improvement of a Farm'.[76] Works of this kind, moreover, encouraged landlords to see their farming enterprises not as unique but as comparable to those of other estate holders in other places, even if off the printed page and on the ground farming systems varied across the kingdom, and methods had to be adapted accordingly.

Clearly, stewards appear to be particularly prominent because the most usable materials for writing the history of estate management consists of correspondence between them and landlords. Resident landowners did exist and must not be overlooked,[77] although stewards were also for them pre-eminent employees, helping materially in the making of elite livelihoods rather than in an auxiliary position of making life prettier, more delectable, or more entertaining, as with others whom the elite hired. Absenteeism – the situation that gave rise to doubts that it was 'possible to transact such an affair as ours at 60 miles distance one from another'[78] – none the less amplified the steward's significance and was the most important of the three reasons that stewards' roles in landowners' lives grew as they did. Owners' economic problems also placed a premium on the expertise of stewards, and the less deferential and more contested nature of politics required new degrees of electoral management that they provided. But the extensive and growing absenteeism of landlords, often taken for granted in works on estate management,[79] pushed these men most to the fore in the late Stuart era. Although an old phenomenon, absenteeism's new scale into the eighteenth century signalled an approach to landed life not necessarily uninterested, but both more remote and also differently mediated from that of the resident landowner.[80]

Late Stuart and early Hanoverian landlords relied confidently on specialists, and for elite men and women alike, the pursuit of

75. Hainsworth, *Stewards*, p. 28.

76. [Monteage] *Instructions for Rent-gatherers Accompts*, pp. 10–32; Laurence, *Duty and Office*.

77. Beckett, 'Absentee landownership', p. 93.   78. *Banks Papers*, p. 175.

79. Laurence, *Duty and Office*, pp. 25, 80, 90, 119.

80. Roebuck, *Yorkshire Baronets*, pp. 52–6; Frank T. Melton, 'Absentee land management in seventeenth-century England', *Agricultural History* 52 (1978), pp. 147–59; Roebuck, 'Absentee landownership', pp. 1–17; Beckett, 'Absentee landownership'.

leisure away from home was a growing demarcator of aristocratic status and one that increased the need for surrogates of many sorts.[81] Specialized needs could not be filled by locals recruited from the neighbourhood, but only by individuals who were identifiable on a national canvas as trained and expert gardeners, surveyors, designers, even gamekeepers.[82] Indeed, part of what it meant to belong to the landed elite was to be able to find out and afford to employ the services of such people.

Making money

In the early modern era England's landed elite was distinguished by its attachment to the land, yet the transformation it underwent during the seventeenth and eighteenth centuries into a kingdom-wide ruling order involved economic activities and developments beyond the purely agricultural realms already discussed. Even in the seventeenth century, few landowners 'from the courtiers downward were completely divorced from the business world'.[83] These involvements, however, were generally not high-risk ventures in uncharted spheres. Members of the elite recognized their estates 'as part of the wider economy beyond the park walls' and on the whole favoured commercial undertakings that used the resources lying on their land or under it. Their 'entrepreneurial activities . . . [and] undertaking of new business concerns, were limited to the exploitation of their estates'.[84] Beyond these projects and efforts to extend one's landed property, the economic opportunities that landowners typically grasped were to make provision for younger daughters to marry and for sons to go into respectable enterprises, to advance money for loans secured by mortgages, and, more occasionally, to deploy capital into turnpikes or other local projects. The landed elite was selective about its forays in the commercial world. Few took the initiative to join in what many still deemed the suspect, unproductive commerce of paper (rather than that of goods) except as incidental investors. Gentry were not great projectors except in the political realm. Wariness about the monied interest and the newer trades led younger sons into commercial

81. I owe this point about leisure to Newton Key.
82. Thomas, *Man and the Natural World*, p. 225; Lord Townshend to Sir Edward Harley, 3 February 1678, British Library, Additional MSS 70012, fol. 260.
83. Grassby, *Business Community*, p. 9.
84. Beckett, *Aristocracy*, p. 207; Mingay, *English Landed Society*, p. 190.

careers (and some of their fathers and elder brothers into commercial interactions) restricted mostly to marketing the output of landed estates, to dealing in goods obtained in exchange for estate-grown products, and to joining well-established companies engaged in overseas trade. A number of sons of the elite became quite notable merchants, like John Verney and Dudley North, and something of the ethos of business surely penetrated into the country house via the paths these children's careers described. Although relatively few entered foreign trade, the connections forged there made up another set of radiating avenues linking landed families to the international economy, the kingdom's metropolis, and one another.[85]

While the aristocratic contribution to the early days of industrial development has recently been reassessed favourably, the members of the landed elite were ultimately insignificant as proto-industrialists in this era (and only marginally important in sterling terms as creditors to the government).[86] Advocacy of industry, investigation of new commercial byways, the conscious cultivation of portfolios of financial paper as alternatives to land – none of these was a common feature of the ruling order of the late Stuart and early Hanoverian age. Yet the broader worlds of industry, commerce, and high finance increasingly overlapped with the aristocratic agrarian one, reordering and reconfiguring the context in which gentry and nobility carved out their identities and places in English society.

The change over the period 1650–1750 in these three economic spheres – industry, commerce, and finance – is well known. Commercial activity exploded, and although manufacturing was in no sense driving the national economy, by 1700 it 'already exceeded the level usually associated with economic underdevelopment'.[87] In finance, the late seventeenth century saw the establishment of the Bank of England, the long- and short-term funding of a national debt, and an extensive growth in the number and value of joint-stock companies in which those with spare capital could invest. For the landed, this variety of business and investment opportunities demanded and allowed different degrees of personal involvement, ranging from the active supervision of mineral extraction to the passive placing of cash in the safest money markets.

85. Grassby, *Business Community*, pts 1–2, *passim*; Stone and Stone, *An Open Elite?*, pp. 233–9; Heal and Holmes, *Gentry*, pp. 127–8.
86. This and the next paragraph follow Beckett, *Aristocracy*, pp. 206–37; see also Mingay, *English Landed Society*, pp. 189–201.
87. Rule, *Vital Century*, p. 93.

Landowners possessed natural resources beyond their arable lands in amounts that varied as much as did their ability to seize the economic opportunities these presented. Timber was the asset that the greatest number possessed, and even those relatively indifferent to estate management tended to keep track of it. Of Edward Laurence's thirty-six instructions to estate stewards, that about woods was the second longest, indicating the significance he assigned to care of timber lands.[88]

As with sculpting the landscape, displaying portraits, or maintaining a deer park, to cultivate (and harvest) one's woodlands in this era was to perform a function more nearly essential to the persona of a landowner than demanding a particular crop rotation or requiring the application of so many loads of manure an acre. Planted and preserved for many reasons besides financial ones (to beautify, to aid the state with ship-timber, to mark social status), trees were economically exploited for use about one's estate, for annual income, and for sporadic infusions of cash. Individuals had long planted trees, but planting by policy appeared only in the reign of Charles II, which may have led contemporaries and later historians to believe that cultivation for the sake of timber began in the late seventeenth century. The national debates and the occasional legislation which arose from them during the period reflect timber's importance to the estate economy and in elite culture. The Leveson-Gowers expected to receive £5000 for timber from charcoal burners in the five years after 1720, and timber's value for charcoal was enhanced by the demands of ironworks for cordwood and by the growing requirements of the furniture trade for fine wood starting at the end of the seventeenth century.[89]

After timber, landowners' resources varied. For the fortunate few who possessed exploitable acreage in or near towns, urban development could yield important income. The Earls of Salisbury derived 16 per cent of their gross landed rental from London rents in the mid-seventeenth century, increasing that amount to 30 per cent in 1677 and nearly 40 per cent by 1720, primarily the result of the enhanced value of property they improved in St Martin's Lane and the Strand. The Earl of Southampton's income from his London holdings similarly accounted for over a third of his total rental in 1668. Rents on the property of the Dukes of Bedford in Covent

---

88. Laurence, *Duty and Office*, article xxvi; the longest section addressed surveying.
89. Thomas, *Man and the Natural World*, pp. 198–9; *AHEW*, V, pt 2, pp. 291–2, 309–11, 374–8, 447–8; Wordie, *Estate Management*, pp. 133–4.

Garden and Bloomsbury soared from £3500 after the Restoration to about £18,000 in the 1750s. Most of the rewarding urban development in the rest of the country occurred after the end of our period, but the Lowther family's control of the village of Whitehaven helped them to develop it into an industrial town and harbour, which made possible their fabulous exploitation of coal on surrounding property they owned. By contrast, Viscount Yarmouth's failure to develop profitably his lands in Southtown, across the River Yare from the town of Great Yarmouth where the corporation obstructed him, is a reminder that urban investments could be as risky as any others.[90]

Industrialist aristocrats who used rural land for purposes other than farming tended to be more involved in the extractive industries than in manufacturing. The experience of those like the Lowthers, who made unsuccessful excursions into cloth manufacture and glassworks,[91] may have discouraged others from emulating them. Industrial entrepreneurship and manufacturing moreover demanded resources, assets, and inclination that were not widely available. Exploitation of minerals had its costs, but significant yields too. The truly unusual Sir James Lowther in 1754 received £9000 from his collieries out of a total income of £25,000 that year, and on his death the next year he left a personal estate of £375,000 that derived from coal.[92] Thomas Pitt in 1721 worried that he would be cheated of profits from mines on his Cornish lands, and in the Peak District families like the Dukes of Devonshire and Rutland and gentry like the Eyres, Bebingtons, and Gells all made money from the lead industry.[93] On a modest but by no means negligible scale, Hugh Boscawen, who mined tin and copper on Cornish lands, earned enough to spend £17,000 on land in Lincolnshire and Cornwall in the 1660s and 1670s, and the iron sold by the Archers of Stratford-upon-Avon comprised a tenth of their annual income at the turn of the century. A number of families in the Weald benefited significantly from iron interests – the Pelhams, Sackvilles, Gorings, and Filmers among them – although the industry was declining by the end of the seventeenth century.[94]

90. Stone, *Family and Fortune*, pp. 114, 242 and ch. 3, *passim*; Beckett, *Aristocracy*, p. 281; Perry Gauci, *Politics and Society in Great Yarmouth 1660–1720* (Oxford, 1996), pp. 112–48; Beckett, *Coal and Tobacco*, ch. 7. See also Roebuck, *Yorkshire Baronets*, pp. 36–7 and on later developments Cannadine, *Lords and Landlords*.
91. Beckett, *Coal and Tobacco*, pp. 137–9, 143–5.   92. Ibid., pp. 218–19.
93. *AHEW*, V, pt 1, pp. 140, 389.
94. J.T. Cliffe, *The Puritan Gentry Besieged, 1650–1700* (London, 1993), p. 166; Heal and Holmes, *Gentry*, p. 123; *AHEW*, V, pt 1, p. 309.

Some landowners like these leased out existing mines, ironworks, and quarries and had outsiders risk the search for unexploited mineral resources, while others personally managed whatever industrial activity took place on their estates. The Leveson-Gowers, who after the late eighteenth century grew hugely wealthy on mines in Shropshire and Staffordshire, adopted both tactics, changing periodically. In the 1670s they leased out mining rights for twenty-one years and in 1691 drew about eight per cent of their gross revenue from these sources. Thereafter they apparently spent twenty years exploiting the minerals directly and making capital improvements in the mining operations. From 1715 to 1748 they acquired new, mineral-rich property but let others develop and work it and pay them. In 1730 these sources yielded the same percentage of a gross income that had doubled, but when the first Earl Gower became an entrepreneur himself after 1748 he did well, raising industrial returns to 13 per cent of gross, and 22 per cent of net income, in 1760.[95] Where agricultural strategies tended toward indirect exploitation, then, ones that avoided the tedious and expensive business of providing labour and supplies to farm one's own land, 'industrial' strategies were more diverse. What was entailed in being an aristocratic industrialist was less clear and less constrained, economically and culturally, than what it meant to be an aristocratic agriculturalist.

Where they undertook them, the landed approached their non-farming economic activities with an unequivocally commercial outlook and what J. P. Jenkins has characterized as 'total opportunism'.[96] The commercial dealings of John Berney of Westwick in Norfolk illustrate on an individual level just how much these views enmeshed landowners in national and international economic systems. A well-off but in no way grand landowner with a landed income of £400 p.a. in 1710, Berney took part in overseas and domestic coastal trade that grew out of his agricultural interests. He sought out purchasers for his corn and malt, shipping the latter to Sweden (along with small batches of cloth that were difficult to sell) for iron bars and lumber. These commodities, along with imported wine and more of his malt, he sent to London, where an agent purchased goods for him from the proceeds. His profit cannot be calculated from surviving documents, but the gross amount he realized from such sales came to substantial sums: £800 in ten months during 1713 and £4300 for two years from 1718 to 1720.[97]

95. Wordie, *Estate Management*, pp. 95–112, 133–42.
96. Jenkins, *Making of a Ruling Class*, pp. 57–8.
97. Norfolk Record Office, PET 566, 99x2 and PET 845/20, 262x4.

The sums involved indicate that Berney was doing more than dabbling when he plunged into the import–export business, and the prosperity of the Lowthers and Leveson-Gowers exemplifies the way that mineral wealth in particular could be translated into flows of revenue. For many more landowners, however, the return from industrial enterprises even in good years made up too small a proportion of total income to justify continued investment when costs rose or profits diminished. While some massive fortunes were accumulated from other sources, land continued to provide most landowners with the majority of their income, and despite the exceptional cases, the significance of industry for the economic well-being of the landed elite as a whole was decidedly secondary.[98] In the history of industry and industrialization the aristocracy's part may well have been 'vital and sustained', as John Beckett suggests,[99] but in the history of the Restoration and early Hanoverian ruling elite entrepreneurial activity plays a smaller part. The seizure of opportunities by those advantageously placed to do so was not a signal of changing elite experience in the way that taking the Grand Tour was. Yet it demonstrated that arable land was not the only acceptable outlet for elite economic energies, and that the concept of gentility had to allow room for the gentleman-industrialist, just as it did for the absentee country magistrate or the landed devotee of the metropolis.

Investing

The majority of landowners who had surplus income for which they sought opportunities of profit did not put their money into trade or industry, although they were eager that it should work for them: to have money 'lying dead' was detestable.[100] Much surplus went to the improvement of existing estates or to acquire new land, outlets that would one day presumably yield a return but not necessarily quickly. The landed also invested at a further remove from themselves but in venues meant to provide immediate or short-term income, in public funds, private mortgages, and more rarely in speculative ventures, joint-stock and individual.[101]

98. Beckett, *Aristocracy*, pp. 230–7; Mingay, *English Landed Society*, pp. 51, 65, 191–3, 201.

99. Beckett, *Aristocracy*, p. 208.

100. Brooks, 'Ashburnham and the state', p. 65.

101. Mingay, *English Landed Society*, p. 72; Roebuck, *Yorkshire Baronets*, pp. 36, 41–2; for an illuminating example of individual ventures see *Dering Diaries*, pp. 113, 117.

The use of private mortgages grew dramatically, as did the state securities market, where the number of public creditors (drawn foremost from London and the Home Counties) doubled from about 5000 in the mid-1690s to 11,000 in Anne's reign, 40,000 in 1720, and some 60,000 on the eve of the Seven Years' War. The landed elite as a group had many reasons to support state institutions, and the number of landowners among these investors may have been increasing disproportionately even while the landed contributed only a tiny portion to public loans. Nobles accounted for less than 1 per cent of government stock outstanding in 1719 and less than 2 per cent of that in 1750. Only nineteen of several hundred gentry families in Warwickshire held Bank of England stock between 1694 and 1730.[102] The extent and profitability of the elite's speculations are hard to measure but probably rose and fell as booms in the 1690s and early 1720s punctuated an otherwise slowly growing array of investment opportunities in the kingdom's stock market.

Elite landowners none the less responded to the speculative lure cautiously and in restricted numbers up through the first decades of the eighteenth century. Some virtually ignored the siren song. Sir Stephen Fox, Paymaster to the Forces, a lord of the Treasury, and the richest commoner in three kingdoms, had an 'investment portfolio' that came to nearly £400,000 in 1686 but seems to have included no joint-stock ventures. Sir John Lowther of Whitehaven (1642–1706), who had substantial capital tied up in coal mining, shunned almost all commercial investments outside that trade, even during the heady 1690s. He heeded his steward's advice to invest only 'where trade shall be managed upon a joynt stock' and in no local venture 'unless built upon the basis of coal fuell', since other projects would 'end in stock-jobbing, as many new experiments of late years have done'.[103] Thomas Pelham-Holles, Duke of Newcastle, apparently owned no Bank, East India or South Sea stock at all between 1714 and 1730, and the first Duke of Kingston, with an annual income of nearly £14,000 in 1726 when he died, left only about £6000 in South Sea Annuity and Bank stock.[104]

102. P.G.M. Dickson, *The Financial Revolution in England: A Study in the Development of Public Credit 1688–1756* (London, 1967), pp. 254, 260, 262, 273, 285, 302; *AHEW*, V, pt 2, pp. 178–9.

103. C.G.A. Clay, *Public Finance and Private Wealth: The Career of Sir Stephen Fox, 1627–1716* (Oxford, 1978), pp. 190–1, 213–14; *Lowther Correspondence*, pp. xx, 59, 93–6 and pp. 57, 364 for quotations.

104. Ray A. Kelch, *Newcastle A Duke without Money: Thomas Pelham-Holles 1693–1768* (Berkeley, 1974), pp. 38, 53–4; Mingay, *English Landed Society*, pp. 67–70.

Investors or not, few among the landed order could have been unaware of the growth of joint-stock companies, especially when they proliferated between 1692–5 and 1719–20.[105] Some applauded and some condemned the 'projecting spirit' and 'moneyed interest', but like it or not, both spirit and interest had entered into and were reshaping the gentry's world. Condemnation of projecting and stock-jobbing, even when crashes confirmed their dangers, neither negated nor more than briefly retarded the changes occurring, which by the mid-eighteenth century had made market investments unremarkable for the landed. Stock-jobbers who profited by manipulating prices continued to be unpopular, yet 'by advertising the opportunities of the stock market they helped in the long-run to widen the circle of investors and speculators, to create habits of investing instead of hoarding'.[106] When plays like the anonymous *Exchange Alley: or the Stock-Jobber Turned Gentleman* (1720) found their way to the stage, they raised awareness of activities to which people might otherwise have been unexposed. While tories and Jacobites complained about the evil that stock-jobbers perpetrated, that disapproval did not keep these critics from exploiting for their own benefit the new world of high finance. Moreover, attacking jobbers as scapegoats prevented discredit from falling on stocks or their market: not the system but its perverters were to blame. The 'nostalgia' associated with the toryism of the second third of the eighteenth century could conjure up but not reinstate the simpler, pre-Exchange world of commerce and trade.[107]

The vastly wealthy like the Duke of Chandos, who invested in over half a dozen of the popular ventures of the 1720s, may have taken part in stock ventures because their riches somewhat insulated them from the risk attached to any single enterprise.[108] Landowners resident in Westminster, and perhaps most notably those of them in parliament or in government service, were necessarily aware of the metropolitan financial world nearby in the City, which offered varied economic opportunities. They also were most likely to be touched by the insistencies of colonization, an activity 'indissolubly

105. W.R. Scott, *The Constitution and Finance of English, Scottish and Irish Joint-Stock Companies to 1720*, 3 vols (Gloucester, Massachusetts, 1968; originally published 1912).
106. Charles Wilson, *England's Apprenticeship 1603–1763*, 2nd edn (London, 1984), pp. 314–17, 324–7; quotation at p. 327.
107. Paul Kléber Monod, *Jacobitism and the English People, 1688–1788* (Cambridge, 1989), p. 281; Isaac Kramnick, *Bolingbroke and His Circle: The Politics of Nostalgia in the Age of Walpole* (Ithaca, New York, 1992), p. 67; Langford, *Public Life*, pp. 308–9.
108. Joan Johnson, *Princely Chandos: James Brydges 1674–1744* (Wolfeboro, New Hampshire, 1989), pp. 53–61, 102–5, 155.

linked' with trade. It is not surprising, therefore, to find the first Earl of Shaftesbury investing as miscellaneously as he did: not just in Carolina but in the Hudson's Bay and Royal Africa companies, and domestically in the Mines Royal and Prince Rupert's new metallurgical process.[109]

For those further off, the new world of commercial investment might be mysterious and less well known, but the appearance of published information in the reign of William III widened an audience that personal correspondence or handwritten bulletins had ably supplied so far. Specific information was sufficiently available in the 1690s for John first Baron Ashburnham, whether on his lands in Sussex or in Bedfordshire, to remain entirely abreast of the markets with which he had dealings.[110] At the same time, John Castaing's *The Course of the Exchange and other things* was appearing twice a week and providing exchange rates. John Houghton's *Collection for Improvement of Husbandry and Trade* gave prices for eight different shares in 1692, and for sixty-three companies only two years later. London newspapers also printed share prices in the 1690s, as did provincial papers as soon as they appeared in the next century, and a monthly like the *Gentleman's Magazine* included them from its inception in 1731. These stock quotations can scarcely have been aimed primarily at people who frequented Change Alley or even the London coffee houses. Although instead meant for commercial groups in provincial towns, the *Gentleman's Magazine*, Houghton's publication, and London papers also all explicitly appealed to landed readers for part of their audience.[111]

The presence of stock prices in these publications points to a perceived or presumed interest not to be dismissed by the historian, even though landowners were not great suppliers of venture capital in the risky world of the later Stuarts and first Hanoverians. The translation of intellectual interest into material ones is illuminated by many provincial figures, though it was cautiously and slowly undertaken. The careful father of the Yorkshireman John Liddell-Bright would not place £3200 in the funds for him in 1718 'without the advice of the most judicious I know in these matters'. In the first decades of the eighteenth century Sir Wilfrid Lawson I and Sir Wilfrid Lawson II in Cumberland judiciously invested in a mix of

109. Haley, *Shaftesbury*, pp. 207–9 and ch. 12, *passim*; quotation on p. 227.
110. Brooks, 'Ashburnham and the state', p. 67.
111. S.R. Cope, 'The stock exchange revisited: a new look at the market in securities in London in the eighteenth century', *Economica* 45 (1978), pp. 18–19; Wilson, *England's Apprenticeship*, pp. 222–3.

mortgages and government paper. During 1712 Edward Lombe of Weston in Norfolk put £600 into lottery tickets, £550 in East India stock, and £1425 in two ninety-nine year annuities. Two years later he laid out over £1400 on lottery tickets, East India and South Sea stock. Neither was a terribly risky mixture. Sir Charles Hotham's personal estate on his death included mortgages and bonds worth £600, more than £4000 of New South Sea Annuity stock, and an assignment of a note for military supplies worth £2800.[112]

Such examples show that even those residing in distant parts of the kingdom could and did participate in a single national investment market, and one that drew their financial attentions to the metropolis. Government finance had always been based there, and joint-stock schemes generally emerged in London too, although the range of their operations spread into the reaches of a growing empire. A proposal like the one for a London to Norwich stagecoach company in the 1690s might have appealed strongly to East Anglian investors, but such provincially oriented projects were rare. Even during the South Sea craze the schemes proposed included almost none that could be considered provincial rather than national in their aims. Of 190 recorded projects promoted in 1719 and 1720 only half a dozen had a distinctive provincial purpose.[113]

The initial favourable clamour and later laments generated during the South Sea Bubble played an important part in spurring landed society's awareness of speculative investment options. Considering the volume of new or newly revived undertakings being publicly promoted, a contemporary would have been well insulated to have remained unaware. Of the 30,000 individuals, groups, and corporations (only a small minority of them landowners) who were affected by the South Sea scheme alone in 1720, the majority lived in or near the capital, and those drawn to London were both 'best placed to take advantage of the mania, and at the same time were least well situated to view the matter in a rational light'.[114] Yet landowners from all parts of the land participated, and those left out thought they were missing a great adventure. 'I cant without great regrett reflect', moaned Lady Elizabeth Germain, 'that for want of a little mony I am forctt to lett slip an Opertunity which is never

---

112. Roebuck, *Yorkshire Baronets*, pp. 91–2, 230–1; J.V. Beckett, 'Cumbrians and the South Sea Bubble, 1720', *Transactions of the Cumberland and Westmorland Archaeological Society* 82 (1982), p. 147; Norfolk Record Office, EVL 648, 463x8.
113. Scott, *Joint-Stock Companies to 1720*, I, pp. 333, 335, III, pp. 445–58.
114. Dickson, *Financial Revolution*, p. 271; Beckett, 'Cumbrians and the Bubble', p. 144.

like to happen again.'[115] However slowly, investment perspectives
for the landowner were expanding from the southeast to embrace
the entire kingdom, and the fact that investors mostly lived near
the metropolis serves merely as a reminder of the capital's role as a
site of cultural diffusion.

The crash of 1720 also seemed to affect everyone in genteel
society. As one contemporary observed, 'the undone people [were]
so many & in so great Familys'. 'South Sea has made Misfortunes
. . . Familiar to almost all the best family's in England', lamented
another.[116] The collapse of the Bubble made some potential landed
investors suspicious of stocks and more likely to seek the safer
havens of mortgages or newly purchased land. John second Baron
Gower as late as 1730 had almost nothing to do with commercial
investments, although he apparently had held (and before the crash
disposed of) £20,000 of South Sea stock. The family even had no
bank account until 1734, leading their chronicler to wonder if the
South Sea disaster had turned many aristocrats besides them 'against
the idea of investment in any kind of commercial or industrial
undertaking'.[117]

The answer, however, seems to be 'No'. If they left them, families came back to City markets. The scheme to rescue the South Sea
Company's investors and the measures to prevent future débâcles
reassured many, and the collapse's financial consequences for aristocrats may have lasted longer than landowners' wariness. John
Liddell-Bright in the autumn of 1721 was placing money in the
lottery, where he felt 'more than safe'. Although the crash ruined
one of her sons and so tangled her own affairs that she could not
draw up her accounts, Katherine Windham received stock quotations and lottery tickets sent from London in the mid-1720s and
looked again at 'laying out . . . money to advantage' in the market
rather than 'letting it lay by'.[118] This strategy aimed not at windfall
fortunes but at finding a way to bank one's profits, and a lack of
provincial outlets to lodge capital in this manner may have accelerated a return to London investments, private and public. A group

115. Lady Elizabeth Germain to George Berkeley, 17 October 1720, Henry E.
Huntington Library, HM 6664.

116. J. Windham to A. Windham, 3 January 1721, Norfolk Record Office, WKC 7/
28/22, 404x2; [draft, c. 1721,] H. Howard to K. Churchill, Huntington Library, HM
6676.

117. Wordie, *Estate Management*, p. 138.

118. Roebuck, *Yorkshire Baronets*, p. 231; J. Windham to K. Windham, 27 February
1725, Norfolk Record Office, WKC 7/26, 404x2; R.W. Ketton-Cremer, *Norfolk Portraits* (London, 1944), p. 82.

of Cumbrian landowners all had substantial paper holdings in town by mid-century, and after 1723 Sir James Lowther transferred his profits from the north to the City, where he possessed assets of nearly £140,000 in 1755. The second Earl of Warrington, who first had to dig himself out from a mass of debt, died in 1758 with nearly £23,000 earning interest in a conservative set of holdings, including £15,000 in Bank of England and 3 per cent government annuities.[119]

In the case of Sir Marmaduke Constable, problems placing money in Yorkshire and his unwillingness to lend money unsecured made him order his London banker in 1737 to invest 'in some of the public funds'.[120] Not surprisingly, government paper seemed a wise haven for those re-entering or first entering the market, as it was comparatively quite secure and financially rewarding. Even if one did not strongly support a particular ministry and, like Lord Ashburnham, was 'not *concerned* to do it, . . . [felt] no question of moral obligation', it seemed natural enough to lend to the government.[121] Such an investment, precisely because it could be made through a gesture stripped of partisan meaning, played its part in reconfiguring elite attitudes. The 'quality of *permanence* in the public debt', which became apparent after 1692, broadened elite horizons. The landed had new options before them – to accept or reject – when making financial decisions. And sufficient numbers accepted them so that by 1750 'the buying and selling of government stock [was] reduced to a routine'.[122]

Betting on stocks was acceptable, government instruments were generally safe and increasingly popular locations for landed folk's capital as the eighteenth century progressed,[123] but loans made on the security of mortgages, increasingly common after the mid-seventeenth century, were productive, safe, and the most popular of all investments. The amount of money landowners invested in the mortgage market through bankers surely outstripped the value of any other of their metropolitan investments. Aristocrats at all levels invested in mortgages, from William Windham, whose £9300 'disposed of' at interest in 1689 included nearly £8000 in mortgages,

119. Beckett, 'Cumbrians and the Bubble', pp. 149–50; idem, *Coal and Tobacco*, pp. 207, 215–16; J.V. Beckett and Clyve Jones, 'Financial improvidence and political independence in the early eighteenth century: George Booth, 2nd Earl of Warrington (1675–1758)', *Bulletin of the John Rylands Library* 68 (1982–83), p. 29.

120. Roebuck, 'Absentee landownership', p. 10.

121. Brooks, 'Ashburnham and the state', p. 67, emphasis in the original.

122. Wilson, *England's Apprenticeship*, pp. 314, 324, emphasis in the original.

123. For example, Roebuck, *Yorkshire Baronets*, p. 326.

to the first Duke of Chandos, who had £80,000 lent out in this way in 1720, and Sir James Lowther, who died with £125,000 secured mostly by mortgages in the London money market.[124] This London mortgage market, dominated by the goldsmith bankers, experienced strong growth in the 1650s and 1660s and was larger, better organized, and safer than regional ones. Sir William Coventry had this comparison in mind when he explained around 1670 that a 'lender scarce thinks he can have a security well drawn (for the money he lends) but in London'. Sir James Lowther, although claiming both in the 1710s and 1730s that he wanted to advance money to 'gentlemen of the country', took caution from the fact that when lending locally 'one does not know who to trust, if one be not also on the spot'. As an absentee, he avoided the 'hazard and trouble in meddling with mortgages in our country' by looking in the capital, where he had his 'choice of the whole town to deal with and meet no disappointments'.[125]

Although the national availability of mortgages beginning in the mid-seventeenth century helped many straitened landowners to overcome economic difficulties (whether brought on by the civil wars or by mismanagement, personal extravagance, and the like), Lowther's attitude contributed to the problems of those who sought to borrow rather than lend. Sir Bassingbourne Gawdy, faced with a local creditor calling in an outstanding mortgage, frantically sought 'any body in town that wold take the morgage, [because] . . . it will be dificult . . . to doe it in the country'.[126] Except perhaps in the north,[127] the evidence of rural credit markets suggests that some gentry (but probably fewer titled or vastly wealthy grandees) lent extensively in their counties but usually did so without requiring land as security, which accounts for their lending insubstantial individual sums.[128] Large sums were far more likely to find a borrower in London than in the country. For the landowner with a surplus to lend, the market in town was thus more attractive than that in the country, a phenomenon that helped to direct the financial focus of

---

124. Norfolk Record Office, WKC 5/152, 400x, p. 178; Mingay, *English Landed Society*, p. 75; Beckett, *Coal and Tobacco*, pp. 216–19.

125. Clay, *Economic Expansion and Social Change*, II, pp. 274–5; Thirsk and Cooper, *Documents*, p. 83; Beckett, *Coal and Tobacco*, pp. 216–17.

126. Gawdy to O. Le Neve, 19 May, 4 June and 2 July 1711, British Library, Additional MSS 27397, fols 209, 210, 218.

127. Roebuck suggests that the 'bulk of surplus capital [in Yorkshire] circulated locally' via bonds and mortgages: *Yorkshire Baronets*, p. 326.

128. B.A. Holderness, 'Credit in English rural society before the nineteenth century, with special reference to the period 1650–1720', *Agricultural History Review* 24 (1976), pp. 97–109, esp. 102–4.

the more solvent among the elite to the metropolis, where by the mid-eighteenth century mortgages could be routinely, easily, and cheaply obtained.[129]

Innovations in the development of mortgage finance made the instrument more available and made lending relationships more sophisticated, complex, and depersonalized, with the London-based banker serving as a broker between parties unknown to one another. Mortgage-lending was far more secure than the old-fashioned way of lending on penal bond, since land itself provided the debt's security, but the broker of the mortgage needed to be certain of the value of that land. A banker's business reach thus extended into the countryside itself, where he sought out information about properties before accepting them as security or taking on landowners as creditors. These new financial practices, pioneered by Sir Robert Clayton and William Morris in Charles II's reign, had consequences for rural society and the relationship of landlords and tenants, by compromising the freedom of the former to control their estates as they wished, since lending arrangements were controlled in the City. This meant that on some occasions rents were actually remitted directly to London to pay mortgage interest, which altered and attenuated the economic and social interaction between landlord, tenant, and neighbourhood. Rent values in the country also had to be precisely determined to justify the size of a mortgage loan, which encouraged professional surveying and accounting and undercut remaining paternal relations of landowner and occupant. It had been controversial in the late sixteenth and early seventeenth centuries for an owner to be too much occupied with 'knowing his own' by surveying his acres with mathematical precision. But at least such activity had been associated with policies of improvement that purportedly kept the landowner engaged with his locality. In the following century, ever more intrusive efforts at knowing – not only surveying in the fields but enquiring about rent levels and payments in tenants' homes, the manor court, or the local alehouse – when made by unfamiliar figures for unknown reasons, undercut landlord–tenant relations even further.[130] Here, then, is an example of the way that the development of more modern financial markets contributed to the distancing of rural landowners from their localities, a process laid out in detail in the next chapter.

129. Melton, *Sir Robert Clayton*, chs 2–3, 8; Habakkuk, *Estates System*, pp. 341–2.
130. D.M. Joslin, 'London private bankers, 1720–1785', *Economic History Review*, 2nd series, 7 (1954–55), pp. 167–86; Melton, *Sir Robert Clayton*, p. 206; McRae, *God Speed the Plough*, ch. 6.

Conclusion

The financial activity of England's landowners, like their agricultural practices, had come far indeed in a century. In both cases, the forces of a national market, whether for grain or mortgages, impinged on what might otherwise have been more isolated economic lives. Although landowners had always been players in whatever degree of national market existed, they had played neither as willingly nor with as significant consequences to their sense of identity and social place as they did in the century after 1650. For in this period their involvement in common enterprises with like figures across the kingdom helped to forge a common awareness that to live prosperously off the land as *rentier* landlord, whether in Kent or in Cumberland, was to be set apart from the rest of society as a member of a distinctive social order.

Moreover, due to the gentry's and nobility's willing embrace of novel financial developments, the 'old, simple assumptions about the line of demarcation between land and commerce' had become blurred by the third decade of the eighteenth century, mixing together 'the supposedly distinct worlds of finance, trade, and agriculture' in a way that by the 1730s gave life to a perception that there existed 'a broad commercial consensus' within English society's upper reaches.[131]

Within the agricultural component of that consensus, where elite landowners dominated, common opinion can be discerned about approaches to managing land and marketing its produce. Despite older claims to the contrary,[132] it seems clear that greater efficiency contributed to the good management of the land and the profit of farms, and in part made possible the economic advantages estates derived from new crops, new techniques of farming, and sheer size. Even where efficiency was lacking, the landowner who employed new men and methods in new ways was both adopting and announcing a different outlook and attitude towards his identity as landowner. In the evolution of the landed's sense of function and purpose, the adoption of a new posture toward management – one that relied on others' expertise, that favoured consolidation of farms, and that encouraged more standard treatment of tenants – had more consequence for the landowners who controlled the countryside than did any increased profits.

---

131. Langford, *Public Life*, p. 308.   132. Mingay, *English Landed Society*, p. 71.

A more careful, rational, scientific, and professional approach to estates tended to put landlords at a further remove from tenants and employees, although it did not make them ignorant of what those tenants and employees were doing. It tended to sever paternalist bonds and erase traditional attitudes about the landowner's trust and responsibility for the land and its occupants. None of these tendencies was fully realized in the eighteenth century (if they ever were), and landowners of 1750 would not have been unrecognizable to their equivalents of a century before. As ensuing chapters will show, by exploring the landowner's engagement with his locality and local culture, with the political and governmental world around him, and with the looming presence of London and things metropolitan in everyday life, a complex congeries of changes in early modern England was only slowly and imperfectly creating from thousands of individual experiences a truly national ruling order.

CHAPTER FOUR

The Transformation of County Identity

Introduction

Much has been made of the county orientation of England's landowners in the early modern era. On the one hand, identification with a particular county and with shire-directed concerns evidently contributed much to the self-awareness of many of the elite, particularly under the Tudors and to a lesser degree under the early Stuarts and their successors. On the other hand, even in the late fifteenth century, different identities, both smaller and larger than the county orbit, also influenced the way the landed saw and described themselves. And at some time in the seventeenth century, the county ceased to be the primary point of reference or realm of activity for most landowners. For those with houses in several counties, for those who lived a good deal of the year in London or provincial towns, and even for those who had a single country residence where they spent most of their time, the social world was not introverted and 'involved them in relationships and attitudes' that extended well beyond county borders.[1] Although some historians have placed this shift in the first half of the century, seeing it as part of the explanation for the gentry's political behaviour in advance of civil war,[2] this chapter will note a number of benchmarks which suggest that however broad the perspective of England's rulers in the early Stuart era, the second half of the seventeenth century and first half of the next produced circumstances that turned

---

1. Holmes, *Seventeenth-Century Lincolnshire*, pp. 79, 83–7.
2. See notably idem, 'The county community in Stuart historiography', *Journal of British Studies* 19 (1979–80), pp. 54–73 and Ann Hughes, 'Local history and the origins of the English civil war', in Richard Cust and Ann Hughes, eds, *Conflict in Early Stuart England* (London, 1989), pp. 224–53.

attention away from county and countryside in novel and more decisive ways.

The 'relationships and attitudes' in which the landed were caught
up became much more open during the century that concerns us,
which is not to say that county identification had historically been
the defining characteristic of the landed elite. Precisely because the
landowners under study were governors and rulers as well as landlords and rural residents, they had travelled and lived outside the
bounds of the local region. Prior to the seventeenth century, especially its second half, they were less likely to have spent substantial
slices of time outside the 'cultural provinces' in whose terms some
cultural anthropologists view the early modern era. These regions
may have bounded the experiences of Tudor and early Stuart landowners, but the landed of the later period were much less affected
by the 'distinguishable cultural traits' characterizing these areas. In
particular, the elite did not share the mutual 'susceptibility to the
same outside influences' that define cultural provinces. Landowners'
unique response to and embrace of outside influences in fact actually helped to set them apart from the rest of any local community.[3]
The place of county identification in the cultural make-up of gentry
and nobility must be seen from the perspective of their identification with others like them across the kingdom.

As an analytic concept, 'the county' is most useful for explaining
the workings of politics and civil administration, rather than for
understanding cultural, social, or economic life. Even in the former
two arenas, where the county served as the fundamental unit of
organization, county identity underwent a transformation in substance and meaning during the course of the century after the English civil war. While gentry continued to be identified (by themselves
and others) through association with specific counties, after the
mid-seventeenth century the pull of central government, national
economy, and metropolitan culture increasingly gave gentry new perspectives and involved them in new activities that extended beyond
the shire's limits. These involvements reduced the county's prominence in defining what it meant to be a member of the landed elite.
They did so extensively enough over the course of several generations
as to reduce county and provincial identification to a secondary
position with the landed gentry, not for all of them and not equally,

---

3. Charles Phythian-Adams, 'Introduction: an agenda for English local history', in
Phythian-Adams, ed., *Societies, Cultures and Kinship, 1580–1850: Cultural Provinces and
English Local History* (Leicester, 1993), p. 9.

but in many discernible ways. This shift was both particularly visible and symbolically potent in the arena of county governance, which had always presupposed loyalties and outlooks both narrower and broader than the county boundaries, but which had directed the public gaze to the polity of Everyshire all the same. By the mid-eighteenth century, the enterprise of ruling in the locality had changed its very nature, with profound consequences for the self-perception, vision, and behaviour of England's landed rulers. This chapter seeks to explain why this development occurred.

Country life: the country house

The landed order's attachment to localities is evident in many ways, in its devotion to rural pursuits, its involvement with institutions of county governance, and its attention to country-house establishments. Clearly, had country life not mattered profoundly to the landed families of England, they would not have devoted the time, energy, and money that they put into it, and especially into their residences. Owning a country house 'was an essential qualification for membership of the local elites' and one's local seat, grand or more modest, served as 'a power centre, a showplace for the display of authority'.[4] It also provided an important site for sustaining landed cultural identity during the hundred years between the mid-seventeenth and mid-eighteenth centuries, however much a family was absent from it.

During the century after 1650, country houses were being refined as well as created; they were rebuilt, renovated, and redecorated as well as started from the ground. None the less, the century from 1650 to 1750 saw the erection of an extraordinary number and quality of new houses.[5] In parts of southern England the great wave of country-house building had apparently subsided by the mid-seventeenth century,[6] but elsewhere it kept up, fed in part by political success and ambition: members of parliament and noblemen built most of the more than a hundred houses started 1710–25.[7] The new building that occurred produced some of the most stylistically influential and some of the best-known private residences of England: Coleshill, Clarendon House and Belton House among the former, Blenheim Palace, Castle Howard, Houghton

---

4. Stone and Stone, *An Open Elite?*, pp. 295, 299.   5. *AHEW*, V, pt 2, pp. 600–19.
6. Stone and Stone, *An Open Elite?*, pp. 359–62.   7. *AHEW*, V, pt 2, p. 609.

Hall, Moor Park, and Holkham Hall to name the grandest of the latter. Whether in the form of fresh starts or of renewals, building was the order of the day. In part this was a matter of keeping up with modern fashion, whether by replacing a double entrance with a central doorway or casement windows with sashes.[8] More significantly, the rough half-century from 1680 to 1730 or thereabouts witnessed a reassessment of the proper size of a country seat and, as a consequence, a good deal of renovation involved expansion. The largest houses built over the century were all begun from 1700 to 1725.[9]

Fashionable entertainment of the period increasingly took the form of the assembly, which involved several activities – like card-playing, music, and dancing – that occurred simultaneously in different rooms, and which required ampler and more flowing space to allow circulation of people. The proper display of artwork demanded additional space as well, and the popularity of the unimpeded interior view across a house encouraged additions of corridors and even galleries.[10]

The changes introduced through new building or remodelling – especially the use of space in the house – reflect changes in the social and personal meaning of gentility. Three principal shifts draw attention: new means of display, partly in the placement of houses in their environments (discussed in chapter 6), partly in spatial arrangements and the way the contents of houses were made visible; allowances for the privacy of residents and guests; and a turning from the use of the house as a neighbourhood focal point.

The emphasis on privacy and on the separation of servants and employees from other inhabitants of the house contributed to the impulse to remodel. House owners fed their staff no longer in the great hall (absent from most new houses of the era) but rather in a separate dining area. In line with the influential ideas of the architect Sir Roger Pratt (1620–84), this 'little hall', along with the kitchen, buttery, and other areas that servants used, was shifted into a half-basement. Servants' sleeping quarters now sat at the top of the 'double-pile' house that Pratt made popular, and the introduction in many such houses (and others) of back stairs and of service

8. Rosenheim, *Townshends of Raynham*, pp. 173–7; Colin Platt, *The Great Rebuilding of Tudor and Stuart England: Revolutions in Architectural Taste* (London, 1994), pp. 36, 44, 116.

9. *AHEW*, V, pt 2, p. 600.

10. Stone and Stone, *An Open Elite?*, pp. 371–4, 378–81; Platt, *Great Rebuilding*, pp. 46–8, 127–8.

corridors literally removed from the view of the landed those men and women who made the house run.[11]

The country house had always made an assertion about the character of its occupants, but this differed in the later seventeenth and early eighteenth centuries from what had been said in the past. Now the statement spoke more to the owner's taste than to his power, expressed his and his family's character through quality more than quantity, through possessions rather than the amplitude of the house (three-storey dwellings largely gave way to two-storey ones)[12] or household itself. Display of possessions was nothing new, but in the sixteenth and early seventeenth centuries, the typical, rather haphazard collections of *objets* and paintings reflected a fascination with the curious and exotic, reflecting the freshness of a recently expanded 'new' world.[13] Many sixteenth-century houses, moreover, had few pictures and books, and even in the second half of the seventeenth century a special room for books warranted comment. Now the matter on display in a house was gathered more coherently, in a conscious attempt to express the owner's refinement. By the mid-seventeenth century free-standing cabinets of curiosities exemplified such efforts and statements. Books and pictures occupied more space, and many houses had both private studies and communal libraries (which served as living rooms) stuffed with the former, and galleries and 'cabinets' displaying the latter. Certain kinds of pictures began to seem suitable for particular rooms – fowl pieces and still lifes in dining rooms, portraits in bedrooms, for example – and by contrast with older houses, the display of pictures was an important consideration from the beginning at places like Chiswick House and Houghton Hall.[14]

11. Stone and Stone, *Open Elite?*, pp. 343–7; Mark Girouard, *Life in the English Country House: A Social and Architectural History* (New Haven, 1978), pp. 136–8; Platt, *Great Rebuilding*, pp. 41–2, 99; *AHEW*, V, pt 2, pp. 610–12; Gervase Jackson-Stops, *The English Country House in Perspective* (New York, 1990), pp. 59–60.

12. *AHEW*, V, pt 2, p. 608.

13. Adrian Tinniswood, *A History of Country House Visiting: Five Centuries of Tourism and Taste* (Oxford, 1989), ch. 3.

14. Girouard, *Life in the English Country House*, pp. 164–80; Barbara M. Benedict, 'The "curious attitude" in eighteenth-century Britain: observing and owning', *Eighteenth-Century Life* 14, new series (1990–91), pp. 67–75; Marcia Pointon, *Hanging the Head: Portraiture and Social Formation in Eighteenth-Century England* (New Haven, 1993), pp. 13–36; Francis Russell, 'The hanging and display of pictures, 1700–1850', in Gervase Jackson-Stops, Gordon J. Schochet and Lena Cowen Orlin, and Elisabeth Blair MacDougall, eds, *The Fashioning and Functioning of the British Country House, Studies in the History of Art* 25, Center for the Advanced Study in the Visual Arts, Symposium Papers, vol. 10 (Hanover, New Hampshire, 1989), pp. 133–5, 138–9.

The decorative objects in a country house – fine wood furniture, porcelain, silks, carpets, lacquer, works of the Old Masters – themselves reflected the width of the cultural catchment area from which the proper aristocrat drew, embracing London necessarily but also France, Italy, Turkey, Persia, China, Japan, and the New World. Goods from these regions had all been found in houses of the previous century, but in much smaller volume and much less frequently than in this era, when, for example, competition between China and Japan lowered prices and increased the availability of porcelain ware.[15] For owners who had ventured abroad, houses became repositories of the *spolia* – statues, paintings, medals, books – that they acquired while travelling. These signs of breeding and sensibility, displayed for the approving view of one's peers, testified to the owner's cultural legitimacy and his past participation in the class ritual of the Grand Tour.[16]

Social life in the counties: the country house

The use of the country house to assert membership in a relatively homogeneous cultural elite coincided with, indeed led to, a shift in the social function of the house as a site of entertainment. That shift was reinforced by campaigns of land consolidation that many owners undertook in the later seventeenth and early eighteenth centuries. These efforts to concentrate holdings within a single county or region undid the scattered ownership of land that often accompanied its acquisition by marriage or indirect inheritance. Landowners willingly sold distant estates and purchased others near their principal seats, and many created 'ring fence' estates of land that surrounded their mansions and parks in protective (and often extensive) circles of farms.[17] This accumulation of coherent blocks of acres into a primary landed estate, for those who owned several, focussed attention on one area and one house. It reduced the travel needed to oversee lands and allowed the principal domain to take on the character of a rural retreat for the many landowners who were, ironically, increasingly absent from their country estates.

15. Oliver Impey, 'Eastern trade and the furnishing of the British country house', in Jackson-Stops et al., eds, *Fashioning and Functioning*, pp. 177–92.

16. Bruce Redford, *Venice & the Grand Tour* (New Haven, 1996), pp. 15–16; see also Jeremy Black, *The British Abroad: The Grand Tour in the Eighteenth Century* (New York, 1992), pp. 261–8.

17. *AHEW*, V, pt 2, pp. 179–84, 196–7, 208.

Whatever the economic reasons to effect consolidation, there were psychological, social, and cultural ones too, and the consequences of this consolidation reverberated in the changing place of the country house in landed life.

When considering that place, however, it is necessary to recognize that the duration of the landed elite's residence at primary country seats declined during the later seventeenth and especially the eighteenth century. Where it was most commonly the greater gentry and nobility who spent half the year and more in the capital, making country visits, or at resort towns, by the mid-eighteenth century gentry of more modest means found affordable and comfortable accommodation in many county towns (where some even bought houses)[18] and themselves often ventured further afield, to London or Bath, for weeks and months at a time. Diminished time in residence at a country seat was not the same as abandonment of it, however, and even landowners in the thick of national politics contrived to spend substantial stretches in the counties, sometimes during the less hospitable winters but usually in the fair weather that facilitated rural recreation. Whatever the myriad attractions of London, when summertime made it virtually uninhabitable the well-to-do fled to the country for respite. One correspondent observed that the capital was 'extreme empty' in late summer 1700, and while it would rapidly fill after George I's death in June 1727, it emptied just as quickly thereafter. Even as, or perhaps because, life in the capital grew more and more diverting and jolly, its aristocratic denizens needed breaks. In the 1740s Horace Walpole noted London's emptiness in summer and early autumn, at Christmas, and even on weekends. More than seventy years before, the Earl of Shaftesbury had entertained himself in London by imagining changes he would make around his Dorset seat, thinking of a 'bathing-room' here, chimney-pieces there, a private chapel elsewhere.[19]

Plans such as these, or other ones Shaftesbury had for a 'stair . . . out of the designed dining-room into the terrace in the garden',

18. Adrian Henstock, 'Town houses and society in Georgian country towns, Part 1: architecture', *Local Historian* 14 (1980), pp. 68–74 and 'Part 2: houses and society', ibid., pp. 151–2.

19. Stone and Stone, *An Open Elite?*, pp. 324–5; G.E. Mingay, *English Landed Society in the Eighteenth Century* (London, 1963), p. 158; Platt, *Great Rebuilding*, p. 142; Peter Borsay, *The English Urban Renaissance: Culture and Society in the Provincial Town 1660–1770* (Oxford, 1989), p. 140; *Ipswich Journal,* 17–24 June, 22–9 July 1727; *Walpole Correspondence*, XX, pp. 63–4, 89, 163, 209; K.H.D. Haley, *The First Earl of Shaftesbury* (Oxford, 1968), p. 210.

were appropriate for a house more private than a typical Tudor country seat, where the great hall served for dining, and other functions too. By the mid-eighteenth century, the country house served relatively rarely as a gathering place for those of lesser ranks or a site for the intentionally awe-inspiring reception of tenants and charity-seekers. House owners built or set aside separate stewards' rooms and tenants' halls to accommodate those who came to the country seat on business and with whom the landed might once have mingled. Servants' halls now ably provided for the occasional dinners provided to the lesser sort at Christmas or some other celebration, which in a prior time would have been held in the great hall that was itself disappearing from country houses. Landowners continued to entertain, but the entertainment and hospitality were not fundamentally meant for retainers, the household, or the inhabitants of the surrounding area.[20] They were directed at those very much like the family whose seat it was – political fellows, those of similar sporting interests, kin, other landowners from near or far. This was the 'select company' whom Roger North claimed in 1698 would be mutually improved by the conversation that a desired architectural innovation – 'a gallery of a midle sort' – would afford.[21]

Social life in country houses seems to have become somewhat less openly and generously organized over the course of the century after the Restoration,[22] because of prolonged absences on the part of hosts, because of an unwillingness to mingle with different social groups, because of changes in the value accorded to specific social actions. There were of course enduring occasions for large and prolonged gatherings at country seats. Sir Edward Dering spent most of two months in the late 1670s entertaining family and gentry in Kent after the marriage of his eldest son, and some nobles like Viscount Yarmouth still held occasional open house in Charles II's reign. The Duke of Newcastle spent £2000 on a 'banquet to the countryside' to mark his adulthood in 1714. Others had large but elite gatherings. When the parish clerk of Ashover in Derbyshire travelled to Chatsworth in the 1670s and 1680s, he went to recite verses he made for the birthdays of the Earl of Rutland, where the company was clearly not otherwise socially mixed. The Earl of Cardigan celebrated his coming of age with a week-long house party in 1706 and was still holding his 'day' in 1710; these were also socially

20. Girouard, *Life in the English Country House*, pp. 149, 182, 189; Platt, *Great Rebuilding*, p. 41.
21. Quoted by Platt, *Great Rebuilding*, p. 79.
22. Girouard, *Life in the English Country House*, pp. 184, 189.

elevated occasions.[23] But such festivities were being complemented and even replaced by the mid-eighteenth century, either by substantial gatherings in urban surroundings or more exclusive ones collected for foxhunting or political strategy in country houses. The famous 'Norfolk Congress' that Sir Robert Walpole convened during his brief visits to the countryside featured Westminster allies and foreign visitors as much as local gentlemen. And although the latter drank, dined, and hunted with the rest, they left the table when high political business was conducted.[24]

Such notions of hospitality and entertainment also encouraged a rearrangement and different management of space within the country seat. The development of more varied entertainments, with several activities occurring in different parts of the house simultaneously, required easy movement from room to room and helped lead to the demise of the formal house where circulation was difficult. These gatherings and diversions – balls, assemblies, concerts, card-playing – contributed to the increasing cultural distance of landed from the rest of English society, and could as easily grace Roger North's Rougham as nearby Raynham Hall or far-off Stourhead in Wiltshire. The company present at these entertainments moved readily from one house to another, from house to county town to capital to resort, an instance of the mutuality of experience linking England's ruling order.[25]

Social life in the counties: other venues

The aristocratic country life that was nurtured by the country seat contained a curiously large number of activities that took landed families away from their principal residences. Although the landowner's identity to some degree continued to rest upon the social transactions of host and guest, the individualized round of visits

23. *Dering Diaries*, p. 114; Victor Stater, 'Continuity and change in English provincial politics: Robert Paston in Norfolk, 1675–1683', *Albion* 25 (1993), pp. 204–5; Romney Sedgwick, *The History of Parliament: The House of Commons 1715–1754*, 2 vols (New York, 1970), I, p. 332; 'The autobiography of Leonard Wheatcroft of Ashover 1627–1706', in D. Riden, ed., *A Seventeenth-Century Miscellany, Derbyshire Record Society* 20 (1993), pp. 78, 86, 92, 95, 98; *Eaton to Cardigan Letters*, pp. xv–xvii.

24. *Richmond–Newcastle Correspondence*, pp. 35, 38, 46, 51, 80; J.H. Plumb, *Sir Robert Walpole*, II, *The King's Minister* (London, 1960; reprinted 1972), pp. 81 n. 3, 87–9, 249.

25. Girouard, *Life in the English Country House*, pp. 189–95; see Jackson-Stops, *English Country House in Perspective*, pp. 80–91 for Stourhead.

and reception of visitors in the households of the great and not-so-great that were common in the sixteenth and early seventeenth centuries diminished. More impersonal patterns of visiting seem to have been emerging, the precursors to genteel tourism, exemplified by nineteen-year-old Walter Calverley's trip through the north in 1689 or by the journeying of the Ishams of Lamport, Northamptonshire, who sojourned as much in places as with people. Their excursions in 1672–73 (omitting the patriarch's trips to quarter sessions and to London) included a tour of Althorp House, a visit to the Spencer family tombs at Brington, attendance at two sets of races and Northampton's mayoral feasts, a trip to deliver a son to Oxford, and a two-week summertime circuit through the towns of Gloucester, Worcester, and Coventry.[26] These varied venues collectively exposed the Ishams to others with whom they shared the pursuit of edifying sights and pleasures, folk similarly engaged in fashioning and fastening on themselves their insignia as the kingdom's elite.

Their experience attests to the popularity of country-house visiting, which had roots dating from before 1600 but became commonplace after the mid-seventeenth and flourished in the eighteenth centuries.[27] When Viscount Cobham created his extensive landscape gardens at Stowe in the 1720s and 1730s, he hoped to attract royal visitors but 'was happy to entertain any aristocratic travellers' and even endorsed written guides to his house and grounds.[28] The first true guidebook to an English country seat was published in 1744, not long after the first catalogues of country-house pictures appeared.[29] While Norfolk's natural charm could not lure visitors before the late eighteenth century, starting in George I's day genteel tourists went around its grand houses, which led one newly transplanted landowner to enthuse in 1745 about the 'beautys' of what he acclaimed as the 'most improved part of England . . . both in the industry of the farmer, and magnificence of seats, of squire, knight & lord'.[30]

26. 'Calverley memorandum book', p. 46; *Isham Diary*, pp. 131, 155, 159, 161, 167, 217–21, 225–9.

27. Tinniswood, *Country House Visiting*, chs 3–4; Felicity Heal, *Hospitality in Early Modern England* (Oxford, 1990), pp. 208–9; Stone and Stone, *An Open Elite?*, pp. 327–8.

28. J.V. Beckett, *The Rise and Fall of the Grenvilles: Dukes of Buckingham and Chandos, 1710 to 1921* (Manchester, 1994), p. 24.

29. Gervase Jackson-Stops, ed., *The Treasure Houses of Britain* (New Haven, 1985), pp. 415, 417–18.

30. R.W. Ketton-Cremer, *Norfolk Assembly* (London, 1957), pp. 171–87; T. Wyndham to A. Windham, 1 September 1745, Norfolk Record Office, WKC 7/32/16, 404x2.

In its way, touring might reinforce a localist identity and even county pride, as one went the circuit of a shire's houses, although it seems that geography and the state of the roads would most often encourage regional itineraries that ignored county borders. It was in any case a different matter to visit a house than it was to visit the family in it, although the hospitality implied by the token glass of wine Celia Fiennes received at Bretby in Derbyshire in 1698 carries with it the ghostly remembrance of a time when one only did the latter.[31] The practice of visiting the house alone, however, characteristic and distinctive of eighteenth-century gentlefolk, did nothing to attach visitors to the absentee owners as individuals, only as symbols of a style of life made visible in the house.

As the eighteenth century progressed, before the cult of the picturesque induced the elite to travel for the sake of scenery, they went to view the contents, architecture, and grounds of great houses instead. More houses offered more – inside and out – that social expectations made it necessary to see.[32] As touring visitors, the landed read in the text a house presented them nothing different from what they observed at leisure when they were guests in other houses. What they read was in profound ways independent of their politics or faith. Whether one saw early eighteenth-century England as a latter-day Roman Republic because of its virtues or because of its decay, Palladian architecture, for example, spoke about the same ideals – of harmony and order in art as well as governance.[33] There may have been idealized tory and whig views of landscape, the former seeking to preserve and the latter to transform the traditional landscape, but in the first half of the eighteenth century neither one would have removed the country house from it. Nor did either view reject classical models as appropriate to their enterprises.[34]

In a development traceable to the second half of the seventeenth century, and occurring more or less concurrently across the kingdom, a good deal of elite socializing was starting to take place in venues other than the great country houses, a shift which may have weakened the landed's ties to a single country seat and its immediate neighbourhood, while strengthening bonds within the social group as a whole. Many of these were urban venues found in

31. Tinniswood, *Country House Visiting*, p. 65.   32. Ibid., p. 66.
33. James Lees-Milne, *The Earls of Creation: Five Great Patrons of Eighteenth-Century Art* (London, 1986; originally published 1962), pp. ix–xi; Tinniswood, *Country House Visiting*, pp. 75–7, 80–7.
34. Nigel Everett, *The Tory View of Landscape* (New Haven, 1994), chs 1–2.

virtually any provincial town, and not just a few centres of leisure.[35] A common place to gather, of course, was the great town house in London, but other arenas were more public ones, which grew crowded with structured activities. Race meetings grew in size, number, and complexity, organized foxhunting (not necessarily tied to a specific country seat) featured in the rural life of many elite men. In the towns after the Restoration, rural gentry and urban elites forged 'a powerful relationship . . . based on mutual economic, social and political benefits', which encouraged 'new types of élite urban ritual, especially in the areas of recreation and politics'.[36] By the mid-eighteenth century, many provincial towns – not just the best-known resorts – offered a well-defined round of activities, in which the landed eagerly and fully participated, removing them further from remaining hierarchical and paternalist rural associations, by placing them more exclusively in the company of their social equals.

The development of race meetings hints at an emergent cultural standardization within new country-based social activities. Although some political segregation took place at races, one party's meet was not differently structured or conducted from another's, and in the mid-eighteenth century whigs and tories were involved in the same recreations, although separately.[37] Moreover, the gatherings at Newmarket and Ascot, Epsom and Goodwood, no matter how partisan or how attached to social life in a particular locale, were of broader significance as affirmations of 'a sense of élite masculine identity' in surroundings where the landed men present were 'not constrained and defined by the roles of host and guest'.[38] This transcendence of roles, with an attendant freedom to define differently the relationship between participants, was a new phenomenon, or at least new in its availability, offered by the coffee house, the theatre and opera, the assembly rooms, and the pleasure gardens of the period.

35. Stone and Stone, *An Open Elite?*, pp. 308–15. For the urban venues see Borsay, *English Urban Renaissance*, parts III and IV; and cf. Angus McInnes, 'The emergence of a leisure town: Shrewsbury 1660–1760', *Past and Present* 120 (1988), pp. 53–85 and Peter Borsay and Angus McInnes, 'Debate: the emergence of a leisure town: or an urban renaissance?', *Past and Present* 126 (1990), pp. 189–202.

36. Peter Borsay, ' "All the town's a stage": urban ritual and ceremony 1660–1800', in Peter Clark, ed., *The Transformation of English Provincial Towns 1600–1800* (London, 1984), pp. 232–3.

37. Paul Kléber Monod, *Jacobitism and the English People 1688–1788* (Cambridge, 1989), p. 294.

38. Heal and Holmes, *Gentry*, p. 310.

Grand race meetings also differed only in scope from smaller ones in less noted places, competitions that were similarly structured and organized. Supporting local races and their attendant entertainments was in some degree construable as a gesture of loyalty to county society and an affirmation of the ties that cemented it,[39] yet these meets were held widely across the kingdom, unique to no region, and were clearly not 'provincial' events. They had the patronage of peers, drew spectators (many of high standing) from a wide geographical range, and featured horses from nationally known stables and breeding lines. Lists of mid-eighteenth-century subscribers to prizes for the Warwick races show that 30 per cent were of the rank of knight or above. Horses that raced in Glamorganshire during the 1760s came from as far off as Yorkshire.[40]

The recourse of the landed to county centres for races, assemblies, balls, or theatre sometimes coincided with the conduct of the political and administrative business that has often been seen as affirming local rather than class or national identity. Such business could even cause the suspension of social life. In a manner reminiscent of advertising blackouts prior to modern elections, one commentator in 1734 anticipated that there would 'be no visiting till after the [Canterbury] election' ten days away.[41] As this comment indicates, the Septennial Act, which extended the maximum life of a parliament from three to seven years, made parliamentary elections sufficiently rare yet weighty occasions that they garnered special attention – and even the suspension of pleasure. A similar sign of elections' uniqueness lay in their ability to increase gentry attendance at assizes when polls were in the offing, encouraging partisans to appear and assure candidates 'of their Votes and Interest'.[42]

In contrast to elections, routine provincial administration seems to have begun to take a back seat to pleasure in the eyes of much of the ruling elite. Even in extraordinary circumstances, with invasion threatening Scotland, the Duke of Newcastle quickly deferred going to the assizes for Sussex but continued for a week in August 1745 to hope he could attend the Lewes races. In less critical times, absent landowners returned to the country from the capital or

39. Borsay, *English Urban Renaissance*, p. 189.

40. Ibid., p. 190; Beckett, *Aristocracy*, p. 357; Nicholas Russell, *Like Engend'ring Like: Heredity and Animal Breeding in Early Modern England* (Cambridge, 1986), pp. 93–110; *Isham Diary*, pp. 99, 147–51, 155, 201, 231; Jenkins, *Making of a Ruling Class*, p. 267.

41. M. Milles to Mrs Lee Warner, 22 April 1734, Norfolk Record Office, Lee Warner box 8, 441x2.

42. *Ipswich Journal*, 29 July–5 August and 5–12 August 1727, reporting on assizes at Bury St Edmunds.

elsewhere primarily to look after their estates and find diversion and not to devote themselves to governing in their counties. They would sometimes grace summer and Easter quarter sessions and summer assizes, especially to enjoy the 'informal side of sessions', but they came to other magisterial meetings much less often, partly because they were often away from the countryside. The conduct of the more momentous business entailed entertainment in the form of magistrates' dinners or the ceremonial entry of judges into assize towns, and these events were those at which attendance mattered.[43]

Scores of mounted gentry would meet assize judges entering a county on circuit and happily dine with them, but many managed to avoid the next days' sessions of the court. Some months before he 'acted in any publick business' (sitting as a tax commissioner), Sir Walter Calverley joined his fellows in greeting first the Archbishop of York and then Yorkshire's high sheriff upon their entrances to the county in 1692.[44] When the Duke of Richmond in 1739 sought royal permission to remain in the countryside instead of leaving to review troops, it was not to take part at assizes but to enjoy the local horse races. A contemporary observed that at York the official business of assizes had been eclipsed by 'the grand meeting of the nobility and gentry of the North, and other parts of England . . . drawn thither by the hopes of being agreeably entertained . . . in horse-racing, balls, assemblies, etc.'[45]

The occasional high-profile appearances in the countryside, regardless of purpose, of a landed elite often non-resident had mixed effects. They made at best ambiguous statements about that elite's identification with any particular neighbourhood, county, or region, although if landowners took up magisterial or administrative duties the visits did make them locally visible. Sir James Lowther of Whitehaven, MP almost without interruption from 1694 until his death in 1755, only visited his northern estate during summers but then made a point of attending assizes and even serving as foreman of the grand jury. At times of crisis, country-dwelling aristocrats necessarily became involved in public affairs, as when, in autumn of 1745, the Duke of Richmond personally took 'affidavits against a man for talking Treason' – but he did so in the privacy of his house

43. *Richmond–Newcastle Correspondence*, pp. 170–3; Anthony J. Fletcher, *Reform in the Provinces: the Government of Stuart England* (New Haven, 1986) p. 99; Mingay, *Landed Society*, pp. 158–60.

44. Fletcher, *Reform in the Provinces*, p. 99; 'Calverley memorandum book', pp. 49–51.

45. Mingay, *Landed Society*, pp. 158–60; *Richmond–Newcastle Correspondence*, pp. 28–9; Borsay, *English Urban Renaissance*, p. 144.

at Goodwood.[46] The extent and the benefits of even a much more 'theatrical resumption of . . . local duties'[47] was none the less limited. It is difficult to imagine that more than minimal impact was made on a particular neighbourhood by the summertime visits of landlords, who even then spent most of their days out of public sight. In this isolation, eighteenth-century landowners comported and presented themselves in ways their ancestors had not: the attractions of provincial towns particularly removed the former from the immediate environs of their estates.

The paternalist relations of landowner and neighbourhood, characteristic of earlier generations, were difficult to sustain when one of the parties was absent or invisible. This attenuation of relations could obtain for gentry who were more consistently resident in the country than the 'summer visitor' sort of landowner. Once begun, Walter Calverley took an energetic part in Yorkshire's local government from the mid-1690s for about a dozen years. Then, just around the time he got married and, paradoxically, at the same time that he stopped visiting London so regularly as he had, he grew far less attentive to county affairs – or stopped recording this public service in his memorandum book. Perhaps local concerns seemed petty compared with what he had seen in London, perhaps marriage and family kept him busy, but in any case the withdrawal remains.[48]

Local reputation

In the process of carving images as landowners, the elite of the later seventeenth and early eighteenth centuries tended their provincial reputations, inactive though many were in the provinces' public matters. In this cultivation, they might seem occupied as their predecessors were, and one as wealthy and powerful as Sir James Lowther thought it worthwhile to have the locals made aware of 'his riches, power and abilities, and the want of such people in their country'. Rarely though he visited Cumberland in the 1730s, he valued the warm reception accorded him when he did so.[49] Yet

46. J.V. Beckett, 'A back-bench MP in the eighteenth century: Sir James Lowther of Whitehaven', *Parliamentary History* 1 (1982), pp. 81–3; *Richmond–Newcastle Correspondence*, p. 178.

47. Langford, *Public Life*, p. 381.

48. 'Calverley memorandum book'. In this context, it is notable that when Calverley was treasurer of his riding he hired another to transact the formal business involved: p. 120.

49. Beckett, *Aristocracy*, p. 356; Beckett, *Coal and Tobacco*, p. 18.

county identity was coming to weigh less in the overall definition of the gentleman than it once had, not because it was a matter of indifference but because it was diminished by other considerations. Although the trouble taken to make and preserve a county reputation seems in many ways unchanged on the surface, the motivation behind it was changing.

Displays of public magnificence, for example, and the provision of hospitality and bounty in the country, added to the givers' reputation and were still looked for from landowners, especially peers: the Earl of Shaftesbury (who distributed the odd sixpence to poor folk in London) gave £9 11s 8d each quarter toward the almshouses his grandfather had established at Wimborne in Dorset.[50] As men like him were less often in the country, however, they seem to have begun to shirk the duty of charity, channelled it impersonally, or else assumed it grudgingly, limiting their generosity by adopting 'new codes of civility' that de-emphasized this gesture.[51] The public bestowal of charity depicted in Gillis van Tilborch's painting *Tichborne Dole* (1670),[52] where Sir Henry Tichborne, Lieutenant of the New Forest, prepares personally to distribute bread to tenants and villagers, was a rare image by this time. For figures seeking to preserve past practices or for newly minted gentry and nobility, say, the occasional Christmas and birthday feasts in the countryside made claims to local respect, but these were noteworthy and effective events precisely because of the landlord's presence at them.

By contrast, William Heyricke in 1699 discontinued the family practice of providing a Whitsun preacher and a gift to the poor of the Old Hospital at Leicester, perhaps because someone in the town had offended him.[53] The behaviour of men like the third Lord Fitzwilliam or Sir John Verney at the century's turn was more characteristic in continuing the practice on a reduced scale. Absent in London, the former authorized Christmas doles to the local poor 'as usual'. He thereby demonstrated a semblance of personal paternalist concern that was none the less contradicted by its automatic, impersonal nature, and which revealed the progressive thinning of the elite's connection to neighbourhood community as the eighteenth century advanced. Not only could connection to neighbourhood and county thin, but it took on altered form where

---

50. Haley, *Shaftesbury*, pp. 209–10.
51. Heal, *Hospitality*, pp. 186, 190; Langford, *Public Life*, p. 380.
52. Jackson-Stops, ed., *Treasure Houses*, p. 147.
53. J. Cracroft to W. Heyricke [February 1699], Bodleian Library, MS Eng.hist.c.478, fol. 247.

it persisted. When Verney first inherited the family estate in the 1690s, he ordered his cook no longer to give food away at the gate, although a decade later he grew willing to provide Christmas open house to further his political career.[54] Other politically motivated charity flowed less personally, dispensed not at one's house but to new and often urban institutions. Thus, with an eye to his electoral interest, the Earl of Northampton contributed to the founding of the town of Northampton's hospital in 1743–44. A decade later, after the election of 1754, he gave the town corporation £200 for a new charity school – and £1000 for its 'sole use and benefit . . . as they shall judge most proper'.[55]

If provincial reputation was coming to rest less on one's hospitality and charity, it continued to depend on cutting a proper figure through one's house and grounds and in one's own person.[56] When William Hodgkinson, a former merchant with an estate, was made sheriff of Derbyshire for 1730, he expressed his intention to wear in office a thirty-year-old cloak and a wig of his own hair. This understandably alarmed his gentlemen colleagues. They hoped he 'wud carry it a little hansomely bothe for his own creditt and his friends' by abandoning his antiquated clothes and securing the services of a London tailor.[57]

Where Hodgkinson was oblivious to his attire and its impact on his and others' reputation, most even of the newly landed were much more self-conscious. Nowhere could self-consciousness be better translated into self-expression than in the country house. Here an owner could display his wealth, his taste, his own skill as a designer, and even use the grounds to make a visual statement about his character and beliefs.[58] In line with a long tradition, some gentry saw theirs as a distinctive life on account of its location in the countryside, rather than a specific county. To them, living a proper country life was of paramount importance. The Roman Catholic Sir James Simeon knew his son would be excluded from

54. *Fitzwilliam Correspondence*, pp. 26, 82, 97, 116, 135, 161, 189, 223, 254, 287. I am grateful to Dr Susan Whyman for the reference concerning John Verney.
55. Victor A. Hatley, 'Locks, lords and coal: a study in eighteenth century Northampton history', *Northamptonshire Past and Present* 6 (1980–81), p. 210.
56. Stone and Stone, *An Open Elite?*, pp. 299–310; Heal and Holmes, *Gentry*, pp. 137–40.
57. *Banks Papers*, p. 111.
58. Heal and Holmes, *Gentry*, pp. 298–9, 303–6; Stone and Stone, *An Open Elite?*, pp. 329–49; Lees-Milne, *Earls of Creation*; Douglas D.C. Chambers, *The Planters of the English Landscape Garden: Botany, Trees, and the Georgics* (New Haven, 1993); Gervase Jackson-Stops, 'A British Parnassus: mythology and the country house', in Jackson-Stops et al., eds, *Fashioning and Functioning*, pp. 217–38.

public life and so especially need an education appropriate for a gentleman in the country. While the boy Edward was abroad, Simeon worried that he was engaging in pursuits and learning things 'which will not soe sute . . . a country life. Tennis in particular', he noted, 'is very useful here.'[59]

Where provincial identity was expressed in positive ways through one's accoutrements, surroundings, and accomplishments, it was also defined in opposition to that of those who did not fit in. It could take expression in a reflexive distaste for outsiders who tried to take part in county affairs. This hostility drew on a vision (often ahistorical and fanciful) of county integrity now being breached. In Chester, men who had been opponents in the civil war joined in 1663 to endorse a local nominee as governor of the castle because 'the placing of a stranger (though otherwise deserving) . . . is not [as] pleasing to our county as if a gentleman of the same county were therein placed'. A similar objection arose in 1701 at the prospect of appointing as Norfolk's lord lieutenant 'a forrenor . . . whose power it can never be in to unite this coun[ty]'. The severe treatment that outsiders received at elections was so prevalent that a parliamentary candidate, spurned in 1681 by a borough that had previously chosen him, complained of treatment 'upon terms so severe as a stranger might have expected it'.[60]

The impulse to protect a county against the undue and uncontrollable influence of outsiders, shared by gentry and non-gentry alike, indicates the shire's continuing status for the former as a respected polity. In this context it is unsurprising that gentry continued to care about the making and marring of their county reputations. Yet it is noteworthy that concern about the presence of outsiders entails their service in the most prominent positions available, in the lieutenancy, a royal office like governorship of a castle, and in parliament. On the commission of the peace or the tax commissions, 'foreigners' could and would have to be borne.

Whether landowners lazily projected an image into the provinces from afar or cultivated it intensely and at first hand, they all

---

59. Simeon's draft on G. Webbe's letter to him, 5 December 1700 (NS), Bodleian, MS D.D.Weld.c.13/3/34.

60. P. J. Challinor, 'Restoration and exclusion in the county of Cheshire', *Bulletin of the John Rylands University Library of Manchester* 64 (1982), p. 362; Rosenheim, *Townshends of Raynham*, p. 194; Mark Kishlansky, *Parliamentary Selection: Social and Political Choice in Early Modern England* (Cambridge, 1986), p. 138. Outsiders in boroughs were different creatures and raised different issues than outsiders in county positions: see Perry Gauci, *Politics and Society in Great Yarmouth 1660–1720* (Oxford, 1996), pp. 48–54.

laboured to protect it from disparagement and unseemly exposure, which, though it occurred first in the country, had effect wherever one's reputation might be discussed by friends, relations, allies, or enemies. Undervaluation hurt in a society still much bound by honour, and its corrosive power did not stop at the county borders even if it originated within them. It also had material consequences, and for a group whose indifference to timely settlement of financial accounts is legendary, the landed assiduously avoided local disparagement on account of credit-related matters. Sir William Coventry in 1670 explained that a gentleman 'had rather borrow in London than in the country where his borrowing will be known to his discredit'. His point is made by the anxious complaints of Bassingbourne Gawdy when an unpaid creditor made 'a great noise in the eares of the country' about his debt. William Heyricke played to the same fears with his threat 'to acquaint the whole countrie' with his son's financial mistreatment of him, even 'to the scandall and disgrace of all my children'.[61] Lord Fitzwilliam admitted to shame for failing to pay a small bill due when he left the country. When the hundred where his estate lay was fined for failing to raise the hue and cry after a robbery, he lent it £50, at a time when he had little ready money, to save the hundred and himself from dishonour.[62]

The fictional squire George Selby grumbled unhappily in the mid-eighteenth century that he had 'lived fifty years in this county, [and] should think I might be known on my *own* account', rather than solely as his niece's uncle.[63] More than being opposed, it was being ignored in 'those parts where I am settled' (as Lord Brooke put it in 1749)[64] that generated disquiet among run-of-the-mill gentry and the highest nobility alike. A Gloucestershire man kept off the county bench had reason to complain when he learned that 'every Clothier . . . of Substance, is in Commission and Scarce any one Gentlemen [*sic*] of Fortune excepted but my self'.[65] Provincial reputation mattered because it affected reputation at Westminster and Whitehall. Eighty years before Brooke, the Earl of Derby worried that the king believed he was 'last in the affections' of the

61. Joan Thirsk and J.P. Cooper, eds, *Seventeenth-Century Economic Documents* (Oxford, 1972), p. 83; B. Gawdy to O. Le Neve, 28 April 1697, British Library, Additional MSS 27397, fol. 72; W. Herricke, 'My case truelie stated', 3 February 1693, Bodleian Library, MS Eng.hist.c.476, fol. 88.
62. *Fitzwilliam Correspondence*, pp. 103–4, 107, 142.
63. Samuel Richardson, *Sir Charles Grandison*, Jocelyn Harris, ed. (3 vols in one; Oxford, 1986; originally published 1753–54), I, p. 29.
64. Norma Landau, *The Justices of the Peace, 1679–1760* (Berkeley, 1984), p. 101.
65. Ibid., pp. 100–1, 139.

Lancashire gentry, who were rumoured to be at the beck of two of Derby's own deputy lieutenants instead.[66] And being overlooked could operate in reverse, so that the late-Stuart Duke of Newcastle was dismayed when a loyal address he promoted garnered no public notice from central government.[67]

The preservation or enhancement of county reputation was of course greatly at stake in parliamentary elections, however much these were dominated by questions of principle and party loyalty, and it was equally at risk when elections were occurring frequently (as between 1689 and 1715) or at long intervals (between 1715 and 1747). Viscount Cholmondeley worried that giving support for an unsuccessful candidate would make him appear to be 'a forward fool that shows his teeth and cannot bite'. That kind of consideration induced landowners with modest or uncertain influence to shroud their doings when they were active. Lord Fitzwilliam in 1700 directed his steward to enlist voters 'without any noise', hoping that there would be 'no notice taken that I concerne myselfe'. Even one as powerful as the Duke of Newcastle in the 1740s knew that electoral defeats in his home county of Sussex would constitute severe blows to his stature, and the whig losses for the county seats in Norfolk in the general election of 1734 deeply humiliated Sir Robert Walpole.[68]

Yet in his autobiographical sketch of 1680, Sir Edward Dering exposes a different side of the matter. Here he expressed pride that he and his son had together served Kent three times as knights of the shire, but he asserted that it was 'now time to set downe in quiet and leave other gentlemen to take their turnes'. As much as parliamentary service was a crucial measure of repute, Dering's willingness to yield his claim – perhaps the necessary action of a court supporter at a time of whig ascendancy – suggests that in his eyes his family's standing was not contingent on or defined by a continuous assertion of local political interest.[69] Walpole and Newcastle's chagrin at losses in their counties grew also from their

---

66. Barry Coward, 'The social and political position of the earls of Derby in later seventeenth-century Lancashire', in J.I. Kermode and C.B. Philips, eds, *Seventeenth-Century Lancashire: Essays Presented to J.J. Bagley, Transactions of the Historic Society of Lancashire and Cheshire* 132 (1982), p. 144.

67. PRO, SP 29/431/8 (I owe this reference to Victor Stater).

68. Hainsworth, *Stewards*, p. 141 and pp. 136–58 generally; *Fitzwilliam Correspondence*, p. 81; *Richmond–Newcastle Correspondence, passim*; Plumb, *Walpole*, II, pp. 320–2.

69. *Dering Diaries*, p. 116; Basil Duke Henning, *The History of Parliament: The House of Commons 1660–1690*, 3 vols (London, 1983), II, pp. 208–12.

anxiety at the broader unpopularity, and the potential loss of parliamentary influence, that the defeats portended.

The revivified militia of the Restoration era, an institution perhaps useful to the kingdom's security, contributed more regularly than did elections to a sense of county identity among its officers. It acted 'as a vehicle for the chauvinism of the gentry elite' in a way that electoral politics was not structured to do. Commission as a deputy lieutenant was reserved for county grandees and those well connected to the lord lieutenant, and party political loyalty was a necessary qualification for appointment in a way it was not for justices of the peace or land tax commissioners. In the ranks of the militia, the distinction between officers and common soldiers sustained the kingdom's broad social division between rulers and ruled, while the hierarchy of officers created and maintained gradations among gentry in a given county.[70] On the individual level, the participating gentry's avid adoption of military titles (less a legacy of civil war service than a measure of the militia's vitality) demonstrates their desire to find meaningful emblems of differentiation within their social group and against those outside it. The care bestowed on uniforms and units' colours further indicates that the lieutenancy constituted an important arena for display of provincial social standing.[71] Yet ironically the militia's new importance in provincial society between 1660 and 1690 derived from the centre, from powers bestowed on it by parliamentary legislation and from the use central government made of it. Although institutions of the county, the lieutenancy and militia both derived much of their meaning for the elite of provincial society through their associations with matters of national policy, status, and power.[72]

Recognizing the complicated loyalties and sense of duty evoked by office in the lieutenancy with its hybrid local and national character also illuminates the ways in which absentees among the landed – men who did not appear at lieutenancy meetings, for example – fostered and garnered county feeling and reputation. Deaths in landed families were obvious occasions for social displays that drew

70. Stephen K. Roberts, *Recovery and Restoration in an English County: Devon Local Administration 1646–1670* (Exeter, 1985), p. 151 for quotation; see also D.P. Carter, 'The Lancashire militia, 1660–1688', in Kermode and Philips, eds, *Seventeenth-Century Lancashire*, p. 177.

71. Fletcher, *Reform in the Provinces*, pp. 331–2. On uniforms in the Napoleonic era, see Linda Colley, *Britons: Forging the Nation 1707–1837* (New Haven, 1992), pp. 184–7.

72. Victor Stater, *Noble Government: The Stuart Lord Lieutenancy and the Transformation of English Politics* (Athens, Georgia, 1994), chs 4–5.

attention to the landed from local society, and even if the bereaved family was not itself in attendance. Although the children of elite families were often baptized in London, away from family estates, they were usually brought 'home' to be buried. The funeral rituals were clearly important moments for landed society and served as reminders of its essential community of interest in the face of mortality. When the body of Lord Yarmouth's daughter passed through Norwich on its way to the family seat in 1676, when the county was politically divided, 'all sorts of people, otherwise disagreing, here united, to doe [Lord Yarmouth] honour'.[73]

Where funerals were occasions for the temporary interment of political differences, they also were moments that exposed and maintained the separation between the layers of provincial life. On the death of his son in 1699, Lord Fitzwilliam prescribed the way the casket was to be received and the funeral conducted, gauging carefully the appropriate social gestures. He sent down gloves 'that if any gentlemen in the neighbour[hoo]d comes in to the funerall, or the tennants, they may have each a paire of gloves', but he would not provide them 'to all the mobb that are not my tennants'. With similar social sensitivity, Lady Fitzwilliam, although shattered by the death, remained sufficiently self-possessed to insist that the family's housekeepers stay secluded 'till they [had] their mourning' and could appear properly attired.[74]

Burials in family tombs at 'home' churches were actions that seem to bespeak identification with a traditional provincial world, and monuments often spoke to county-oriented accomplishments. The first Viscount Townshend wanted an inscription that recorded that he 'had the honour to serve the king as Lord Leiutenant [*sic*] for the County of Norfolk and County and City of Norwich'.[75] Yet funerals were also gestures made with an eye to metropolitan standards. After the later 1680s, when London-based undertakers broke the College of Heralds' hold over funeral ceremonial, metropolitan undertakers would assist with burials anywhere in the kingdom, which was not only convenient for gentry residing in town but also guaranteed the application of current taste to the ritual.[76] Sir Walter Calverley's careful record of the gifts given to those attending

73. M. Peckover to Lord Yarmouth, 4 December 1676, Norfolk Record Office, Bradfer-Lawrence, Ic/1.
74. *Fitzwilliam Correspondence*, pp. 61–4.
75. Draft will, 18 November 1678, Raynham Hall, box files, 'Norfolk wills (ii)'.
76. Paul S. Fritz, 'The undertaking trade in England: its origins and early development, 1660–1830', *Eighteenth-Century Studies* 28 (1994–95), pp. 244–6.

funerals shows his preoccupation with the visible and the tasteful at these affairs. When he went to the funeral of the wife of a cousin-by-marriage in 1711, he was gratified by receipt of 'an *a-la-mode* scarfe' and (as a pallbearer) of a pair of chamois leather gloves and 'an *a-la-mode* hatband, with a scutcheon'. In addition he several times recorded that individuals had or had not been 'invited' or 'bidden' to a funeral, and when his sister died, he recorded that his brother-in-law 'brought her out handsomely', observations together suggesting that the ritual had a keenly appreciated social meaning.[77]

Away from the country, local identity might be supported (in a similarly ambiguous way) by activities like the county feasts and feast sermons held in London in the late seventeenth and early eighteenth centuries. These were not intended solely for a gentry audience, but county landowners often subscribed to the charities being promoted and were expected to buy the published sermons, many of which urged the union of county fellows to 'further harmony among the whole commonwealth'.[78] Gentry were similarly expected to subscribe to county histories, which might be graced with engravings of 'their seats, monuments, or other particulars', and support for Sir William Dugdale's work on *The Antiquities of Warwickshire* (1656) has been attributed to a sense of solidarity and a disregard for political background on the part of the county's leading gentry.[79] Even absentee landowners with no active part in the militia or magistracy supported local projects as divers as the building of sessions houses and town halls, the development of harbour facilities, turnpikes, and canals, and the promotion of particular industries and trades.[80] When the third Viscount Townshend solicited the relocation of a divisional meeting of the Norfolk quarter sessions from Holt to Fakenham in 1738, he urged it as beneficial to the entire county, but his intention was to show his political muscle and help restore lost trade to a town near his country seat.[81]

77. 'Calverley memorandum book', pp. 74, 101, 126, 129.

78. Newton E. Key, 'The political culture and political rhetoric of county feasts and feast sermons, 1654–1714', *Journal of British Studies*, 33 (1994), pp. 223–56; idem, 'The localism of the county feast in late Stuart political culture', *Huntington Library Quarterly* 58 (1996), pp. 211–37; Langford, *Public Life*, p. 384.

79. *The Correspondence of the Reverend Francis Blomefield (1705–52)*, D.A. Stoker, ed., *Norfolk Record Society* 55 (1992 for 1990), p. 44, n. 32; Ann Hughes, *Politics, Society and Civil War in Warwickshire, 1620–1660* (Cambridge, 1987), pp. 300–1.

80. Langford, *Public Life*, pp. 207–32.

81. Norfolk Record Office, uncatalogued mss, Box M, P168C; Raynham Hall, box files, '3rd Viscount Townshend, correspondence', 1720s–1739 and 1723–63.

The county polity

Whether landowners were absent or present, the county was a principal unit around which both they and the English state organized politics and administration. The county may not have embraced or defined a fixed community for any social group, but it constituted a focus for public life. Central government by and large administered the kingdom on the basis of counties. Although some formal associations might extend beyond county borders, like commissions of sewers or turnpike and canal trusts, even these tended to be dominated by men who hailed from a single shire. Public statements, like petitions for a free parliament in 1659, addresses to Charles II on dissolving the Oxford Parliament, praise or reproach for Dr Sacheverell, and subscriptions supporting regiments raised during the '45, were made in the name of counties.[82] For many public figures among the landed, whether magnate, member of parliament, or mere gentry, the sentiments and conduct of a county community (however defined) constituted an important index of their own success or failure as public figures. And for central government, the service to the crown of lords lieutenant, who after all oversaw individual shires, was measured by the tractability of the population under their supervision.[83] Yet it did not require one's presence in the county for it to be an important arena of action.

Men of the greatest national standing were engaged with political issues and machinations that affected local reputation – their own, their party's, that of fellow landowners – as the correspondence of the second Duke of Richmond and the Duke of Newcastle in the 1730s and 1740s amply shows. With a general election in the offing in June 1747, Newcastle's letter to Richmond about electoral prospects discussed only Sussex constituencies. Their letters in general, although much consumed with discussions of ministerial policy, regularly assessed the balance of parties in Sussex and included accounts of assize meetings and borough mayoral elections, along with myriad requests for minor patronage. Neither spent most of his time in the county, but of the pair Newcastle spent less and yet

---

82. Ronald Hutton, *The Restoration: A Political and Religious History of England and Wales 1658–1667* (Oxford, 1985), p. 90; Tim Harris, *Politics under the Later Stuarts: Party Conflict in a Divided Society, 1660–1715* (London, 1993), pp. 106, 181–2; J.R. Western, *The English Militia in the Eighteenth Century: The Story of a Political Issue 1660–1802* (London, 1965), p. 113. Of course opinion was organized on the basis of towns and other interest groups as well.
83. Stater, *Noble Government, passim.*

had a powerful influence there, transmissible by correspondence and derived from his status in the government.[84] Indeed, the profile politicians like Newcastle or Sir Robert Walpole projected onto their counties – often from afar – was backlit by the strong light of office. It was principally as government ministers that they enjoyed the power that made it 'treason in this country' even to speak disrespectfully of them.[85]

Central office by the reign of George I and George II allowed so much access to such divers channels of power that county reputation could virtually be built upon it. This was not just true for the lord treasurer or a secretary of state but also for lesser members of parliament, minor central officeholders, people connected to the apparatus of the state. Holding local office now constituted a minor mark of status, a kind of lowest common denominator among those claiming the prerogative of rule, and consequential largely on this score alone. Some singular offices mattered more than others: the lord lieutenancy, the position as *custos rotulorum* (usually combined with the former), and the sheriff's office. This last position, financial burden though it was, still conferred honour, and Richard Steele plausibly made the appointment of his fictional creation Sir Roger De Coverley, named sheriff at age twenty-three in 1678, the 'publick Occasion of showing my Figure and Behaviour to Advantage'.[86]

The growth in the number of appointees to collective office – the commissions of the peace, the lieutenancy, the land tax commissions – shows that landowners still desired nominal membership in the basic institutions of county (but not parochial) administration. To rank in the commission of the peace was 'a point of pride for the great families, and of ambition for aspiring gentry'.[87] But it and others were increasingly inflated honours. There were about 3500 justices across the kingdom in 1702 and 8400 in 1761, while the number of deputy lieutenants per county was twice as high in the 1660s as the 1620s, and the 13,000 land tax commissioners in 1723 had swollen in number to some 25,000 in 1775.[88] Along with the growing conviction among the landed appointees to these positions that other bodies addressed the matters most important to

84. *Richmond–Newcastle Correspondence*, pp. 247–8 and *passim*.

85. R. Keeling to [Lady Diana Feilding], 15 July 1729, Norfolk Record Office, HOW 796/2, 349x3. The reference is to Walpole.

86. *The Spectator*, Donald F. Bond, ed., 5 vols (Oxford, 1965), I, p. 464.

87. Langford, *Public Life*, p. 396.

88. Landau, *Justices of the Peace*, p. 141; Stater, *Noble Government*, ch. 3; Fletcher, *Reform in the Provinces*, p. 329; Langford, *Public Life*, p. 423.

elite life, the large increase in the numbers of officeholders would have diluted the meaning of appointment.

Although diluted, however, the significance of office was not washed away. The *Bath Journal*, whose marriage notices usually described landed esquires without addition, reported in 1744, as if it were remarkable, that Paul Mereton, Esq., new husband of a rich bride, was 'in the commission of the Peace for Kent'.[89] More typically, since reputation is harder to acquire than dishonour is to suffer, it was omission or dismissal from county bodies like the magistracy, even if politically motivated, that drew attention and brought a feeling of disgrace. Sir Denny Ashburnham in Sussex could believe so little in his dismissal during James II's purges in the late 1680s that he went to the Crown Office in London to examine the new commission of the peace. At the same time in Durham, Sir Daniel Fleming was actually sitting on the bench during the reading of the commission when he mortifyingly 'observ[ed] that his name was left out'. William Blythe of Lincolnshire, left off the bench in 1660, admitted that he did not value 'the employment . . . in the least' but was still 'asshamed to appeare any where with such a disgrace on me'.[90]

As Blythe's remarks make clear, service in office was not necessarily prized highly, nor apparently even required. Being known to belong sufficed to demonstrate one's position, and being publicly named when the texts of commissions were read out helped to designate one a place among the elite. Incredibly fierce quarrels over precedence among justices frequently broke out at sessions under the Tudors and early Stuarts,[91] and their absence in our period shows that appearing and literally sitting on the bench had become a much less momentous enterprise. The huge reduction in the number of commissions of the peace annually issued by the lord chancellor, from 115 a year in 1676–80 to 32 in 1716–20, reduced the occasions for revising precedence,[92] helping to cause but also mirroring a decline in the magistracy's profile in provincial life.

Where their predecessors had worried and fought over who sat where at public meetings, late Stuart and early Hanoverian justices (especially those among the greatest landowners) cared less about such gauges of local standing and thus were frequently absent from these occasions. As the numbers of gentry justices, tax commissioners,

89. *Bath Journal*, 30 July 1744.
90. Fletcher, *Reform in the Provinces*, pp. 24, 26; Holmes, *Lincolnshire*, p. 81.
91. Heal and Holmes, *Gentry*, pp. 168–71.
92. L.K.J. Glassey, *Politics and the Appointment of Justices of the Peace 1675–1720* (Oxford, 1979), pp. 17–18.

and various trustees grew, the appointees were increasingly loath actually to take up the tasks of their office, and the landed elite as a whole grew more distant from the mechanics of provincial administration. By the mid-eighteenth century, the county cast a fainter shadow on the landed elite's public and private image than a hundred or a hundred and fifty years before, a sign of that elite's increased distance from provincial sources of illumination.

The distancing of the elite

The social and political experiences of landowners during the interregnum played some part in attenuating their ties with the county. The entire population felt central government's local weight during these years, above all through military presence, heavy taxation, and the activities of new administrative bodies.[93] For royalists, an expression of paramount loyalty to the crown necessarily subordinated alternative, local allegiances. For many gentry, royalist or otherwise, ties were stretched by flight into exile abroad or to other protected places. This was so with those Lincolnshire gentry who abandoned their county to 'sit safe' in London, and with Sir Edward Dering, who never held office, took an oath, or found arms under any interregnum regime, a feat he managed by living anywhere except his native Kent between 1648 and 1660.[94] Substantial time spent away from traditional bases, and in the company of others similarly placed, both loosened ties with native counties and bestowed shared experiences on men of disparate geographical origins.

For those gentry who remained in their counties in the 1640s and 1650s, the unsuccessful attempts of successive revolutionary regimes to centralize government forced some to look over their shoulders to Westminster as they went about business in the countryside. A large number of centrally authorized, centrally appointed, and externally staffed agencies appeared in the counties: county committees, triers and ejectors, subcommittees of accounts, sequestration committees, major-generals' commissioners, and the like. Despite the presence of men from pre war provincial establishments on these bodies, local administration experienced discontinuity of

93. G.E. Aylmer, *The State's Servants: The Civil Service of the English Republic 1649– 1660* (London, 1973), pp. 298–325.

94. Hughes, *Warwickshire*, pp. 158, 305; Holmes, *Lincolnshire*, p. 182; *Dering Diaries*, p. 111.

personnel, and men of lesser social status participated in provincial government in place of traditional rulers who had been disqualified or had withdrawn from it. The new governors understandably looked to the centre for validation of their authority, and some at least of the old governors looked to the centre with trepidation. The elite in the countryside as a whole became more keenly attuned (if not necessarily responsive) to the needs and desires of central authority, and less assertive of provincial independence.[95]

It was not possible to insulate localities from the salient events of civil war and interregnum. A flood of published materials brought news about national (especially parliamentary) affairs into the countryside. Unprecedented developments like the regicide, extraordinary levels of taxation, unrestrained political debate, the spirit of religious innovation – all these upset (and enthused) people of every station, but they were perhaps most disturbing to the social elite. Calls to abolish tithes, reform the common law, or allow women to preach had profoundly unsettling implications for the social order itself.[96] In word and deed both, the revolutionary era profoundly unsettled England's county polities – and the men who had traditionally dominated them.

The Restoration unsurprisingly saw an effort to re-secure that order, partly through the reanimation of local government, which took place in an 'atmosphere of investigation, of revenge and of taking stock' during the early 1660s and even with the use of 'self-consciously antiquarian' practices of government.[97] Leading figures resumed participation in provincial administration, and the numbers of gentry at least nominally associated with it grew appreciably after 1660. This re-engagement was not immediate or universal, however, and after the Restoration most of the deputy lieutenants of Dorset, Somerset, and Wiltshire were reportedly in London seeking reward for prior service to Charles II.[98] Within a decade or so, moreover, prominent landowners in other areas began backing away from the direct engagement in provincial governance, that is,

95. This and the next paragraph rely on David Underdown, *A Freeborn People: Politics and the Nation in Seventeenth-Century England* (Oxford, 1996), ch. 4; see also Andrew M. Coleby, *Central Government and the Localities: Hampshire 1649–1689* (Cambridge, 1987), part I; Hughes, *Warwickshire*, pp. 243–7, 274–90; Holmes, *Lincolnshire*, p. 193.

96. Hughes, *Warwickshire*, pp. 250–1; Holmes, *Lincolnshire*, pp. 198–9.

97. Roberts, *Recovery and Restoration*, p. 187; see also Underdown, *Freeborn People*, ch. 6.

98. P.J. Norrey, 'The restoration regime in action: the relationship between central and local government in Dorset, Somerset and Wiltshire, 1660–1678', *Historical Journal* 31 (1988), p. 790.

attendance at meetings, appearance at musters, and holding petty sessions. Whereas the landed elite's engagement with the centre rose during this era, its participation in local governance faltered. The steady if fluctuating growth of the commissions of the peace after the Restoration was not accompanied by activity in office by most justices.[99]

It was one thing to seek and receive the commission as justice, a far different matter actually to serve. Although historically most men appointed to be justices had not acted in their office, a decline in the proportion of those who did began in the 1680s and continued into the middle of the eighteenth century. For the kingdom as a whole during the century after 1730, men appointed were least likely to take the steps to qualify themselves for active service as magistrates between about 1735 and 1755. Regional studies have uncovered signs of elite withdrawal from magisterial business at diverse points dating from the late seventeenth century up to the 1740s and 1750s; there seems no evidence of increasing involvement anywhere.[100]

The origins of this retreat have been traced as far back as the interregnum when the commission's function as the principal agent of government in the county diminished in face of new administrative structures.[101] Displacement from county government before 1660 probably made some less willing to resume service (though accepting appointment) thereafter, at least once the new-old royal regime had been placed on sound footing. Thereafter many county grandees took no part in the regular administration of their counties because they were too often absent to do so, and because the ways to sustain a local reputation did not rely on magisterial activity as crucially as they had a hundred years before. The politicization and overt partisan competition within administrative institutions characteristic of the late 1670s and the 1680s repelled some former rulers of the counties, creating a psychological distance that precluded their wholehearted participation in local government. And perhaps the

99. Glassey, *Politics and Appointment*, pp. 15–17; Landau, *Justices of the Peace*, appendix A.

100. Landau, *Justices of the Peace*, pp. 320, 323, 395; Glassey, *Politics and Appointment*, pp. 267–9; Langford, *Public Life*, pp. 401–3; Stone and Stone, *An Open Elite?*, pp. 269–71; Jenkins, *Making of a Ruling Class*, pp. 88–9; James M. Rosenheim, 'County governance and elite withdrawal in Norfolk, 1660–1720', in A.L. Beier, David Cannadine, and James M. Rosenheim, eds, *The First Modern Society: Essays in English History in Honour of Lawrence Stone* (Cambridge, 1989), pp. 106–15; Holmes, *Lincolnshire*, p. 83.

101. J.S. Morrill, *Cheshire 1630–1660: County Government and Society during the English Revolution* (Oxford, 1974), pp. 223–6.

transplantation of this competition from the provincial to the parliamentary and national stage then and under the last two Stuarts
made conflict in the county seem less important.[102]

If inactivity and absence actually lessened gentry influence locally (and there is little to suggest that it did), such diminution did
not lead landowners to change their behaviour, which suggests that
a county reputation based on local public service had lost some
of its significance among persons quality. By the early and mid-
eighteenth century a gentleman's style and taste played such a large
role in defining his gentility and were displayed minimally enough
in local administration that engagement with the countryside as a
resident magistrate dropped to secondary importance in his life.
As absence from the county ceased to be a bar to reputation, many
greater gentry ignored sessions and shunned assizes too. But it is
important to remember that lesser figures on the bench also ignored
the call to service. Only one-third of Kent's justices appointed between 1743 and 1758 qualified themselves to act in that office within
five years of their appointment. When the commission numbered
over a hundred justices in many counties, and only a minority were
active, it was not just the grandees who refused to see this kind of
public service as necessary.[103]

A mental disengagement and diversion of elite energy into pleasure and leisure contributed to the gentry's withdrawal from direct
local governance in the eighteenth century, a retreat whose 'effect
in weakening deference patterns and paternalist values in the rural
areas must in the long run have been considerable' – even if as
yet unmeasured.[104] The elite's lessened participation reflected the
diminished sense of county identity amid proliferating alternative
identities, many based on national lines of demarcation: whig, tory,
investor in the Funds, member of a particular hunt, dissenter,
Roman Catholic, Anglican hot or cold or occasional, subscriber to
this opera or that publishing venture, visitor to Bath, or tourist to
Italy. Behind this proliferation of characteristics lay the growth of a
more national and metropolitan vision of the life proper to a gentleman, a product of the civil war years and a function of political,
economic, and social changes during the late seventeenth and early
eighteenth centuries. That Humphrey Prideaux, resident in the
kingdom's second largest city, Norwich, could speak of himself in

---

102. Glassey, *Politics and Appointment*, p. 24; Holmes, *Lincolnshire*, p. 83; G.C.F. Forster, *The East Riding Justices of the Peace in the Seventeenth Century* (York, 1973), p. 32.
103. Landau, *Justices of the Peace*, pp. 320, 328; Heal and Holmes, *Gentry*, pp. 187–9.
104. Stone and Stone, *An Open Elite?*, p. 275.

1686 as 'remote from the centre of affairs and in a great deal of quiet' indicates that a metropolitan perspective was taken for granted when assessing one's own cultural position.[105] Edward Laurence, trying to make good landlords of the gentry, knew it took incentives to lure 'the Lord of the Manor himself sometimes to come down and visit his Estate'. How little any such inducement might work appeared when the Devonshire commission of peace was renewed in the mid-eighteenth century and the lord lieutenant was so unfamiliar with the county gentry that from personal knowledge he could suggest no one as a new magistrate.[106]

'Remote control'

How could county administration continue effectively, and without seeing localities decay into disorder, in the absence of greater gentry whose sense of identity no longer required them to be energetic justices, tax commissioners, and the like? To begin with, some men of stature still willingly took part in local government, like the nominee of 'very pretty fortune' whose qualifications for the bench included residence in the county and willingness to serve actively,[107] or like the justices in Kent's commission in 1743, who were more likely to be active in office the larger the estates they possessed.[108] Second, when powerful members of the landed elite had concerns about the conduct of local business, much could be accomplished from afar, because absence from the countryside did not erase one's power there. In some measure, 'the county' had become a group of people rather than a place, and those who comprised this group operated as if their authority in the geographic shire was unaffected by distance from the region. 'London-based and London-minded' oligarchs determined much local business. Formal meetings were held in London by the lord lieutenant of Lincolnshire in the 1720s, in 1736 issues of 'navigation and drainage' were discussed there, and a decade later a scheme to found a hospital in Lincoln was prepared in and transmitted from the capital.[109]

105. *Prideaux to Ellis Letters*, p. 146.
106. Edward Laurence, *The Duty and Office of a Land Steward: Represented under Several Plain and Distinct Articles*, 2nd edn (London, 1731; reprinted New York, 1979), pp. 79–80; Landau, *Justices of the Peace*, p. 134.
107. *Richmond–Newcastle Correspondence*, p. 145.
108. Landau, *Justices of the Peace*, pp. 322–3.
109. Langford, *Public Life*, pp. 383–4; *Banks Papers*, p. 177. See also Key, 'Political culture and rhetoric of county feasts' and 'Localism of the county feast' on the ties of London and the county.

Third, to the extent that local administration was played out along lines dictated by absentee landed interests, effective communication between resident and absentee gentry played a critical role. Some of this communication was direct, some at a remove, and only through others acting on their behalf could landowners sustain contact with the locality. Family members on the scene – cousins, uncles, wives – performed some of this function, but they are distinguishable from other agents who gathered information, made contacts, and conducted business on the landowner's behalf. Ranging in status and skill from the most minor gentry to landed barristers to yeomen-tenants, these brokers guided landowners through marriage and financial markets, supported them in electoral conflicts, and acted as their surrogates in estate affairs and county administration. Some of them, like Robert Britiffe of London and Norwich, served a half-dozen families. William Busby, a barrister-broker for the Verney family, was a justice for Buckinghamshire who, tellingly, attended quarter sessions but generally avoided involvement in local politics.[110] Men like this have not been well studied, but they increased in number from the late seventeenth century in parallel with others who served the interests of the wealthy. By the end of the next century (and probably from its mid-point), true specialists – land agents, estate stewards, election agents – began to divide the brokers' more general functions, but until then, such individuals literally went where the grander gentry did not and met face-to-face with people they avoided, allowing landowners to exercise power by a kind of remote control.

More commonly, the absence of local grandees from the active bench and other provincial institutions was supplied by landed figures from below the county's topmost layer, some adopting apolitical stances like William Busby, but most showing no greater willingness to perform the magistracy's onerous duties than their more prominent fellows. Whatever their wealth and stature, moreover, the active were ambivalent about performing their duties. Sir Justinian Isham showed little reverence for his office when he sealed a warrant at his dinner table with a spoon, 'adding that that was a suitable seal for the occasion'. 'Ah hang it,' Sir Thomas Cave, MP for Leicestershire exhorted Ralph Verney in 1715; 'Leave thy Justice

---

110. Plumb, *Walpole*, I, pp. 310, 361; correspondence of Britiffe and Dacres Barret, Essex Record Office, D/DL C3; Susan E. Whyman, 'Sociability and Power: The World of the Verneys, 1660–1720' (unpublished Ph. D. dissertation, Princeton University, 1993), ch. 3.

Trade, and come and hunt in my open Air.' Thirty years later, Thomas Wyndham, an active magistrate, wrote to his cousin that he studied 'the Trade of a Justice and am reforming Forresters, more savage than Iroquois'.[111] Wyndham's remark, that of a younger son who had only recently acquired his estate, may betray insecurity about what his cousin would think of him for taking on this work, which at the same time gave Wyndham a mark of status distinction. But even so, his and Cave's description of magisterial office as a 'Trade' indicates the diminished prestige and significance it now had with some landed gentlemen. What gave them stature in the realm of public service was not readily found in county institutions.

The conceptions of service voiced by men like Isham help to explain why service on the bench was a minority occupation among appointed justices and a lower status one. This does not mean that there was recourse to the non-genteel to fill the bench, as there had been during the interregnum. The recruits who took up burdens abandoned by grandees were not in significant numbers either merchants or clergy,[112] whose heyday on the bench began around mid-century. Rather, they were gentlemen with landed estates, some of whom had simply never made it into the commission before, others possessing new accessions of property that made them seem likely defenders of local order.[113] Among these least socially prominent magistrates, the majority of working justices were to be found. On the commission of peace for Glamorganshire in 1722, the most active magistrates were from lesser families; in Buckinghamshire in 1735 only one of the fourteen active justices (out of a bench of 116) numbered among the top fifty landowners in the county.[114] In Norfolk in the mid- and late 1730s, two-thirds of justices who bothered to attend assizes came from the bottom of the commission.[115] In Kent, the obscurity of appointees appears in the fact that 11 per cent of those named to the bench from 1724 to 1761 cannot even be identified from county histories and published genealogies. Gentry justices of high status in Kent comprised just one-third of the total

111. *Isham Diary*, p. 85; Landau, *Justices of the Peace*, p. 288; T. Wyndham to A. Windham, 7 October 1743 and 23 June 1744, Norfolk Record Office, WKC 7/32/7, 9, 404x2.

112. W.M. Marshall, 'Episcopal activity in the Hereford and Oxford dioceses, 1660–1760', *Midland History* 8 (1983), p. 117.

113. Landau, *Justices of the Peace*, pp. 141–3, 185; J.M. Beattie, *Crime and the Courts in England 1660–1800* (Oxford, 1986), pp. 62–4; Jenkins, *Making of a Ruling Class*, pp. 89–90.

114. Jenkins, *Making of a Ruling Class*, p. 89; Langford, *Public Life*, pp. 401–2.

115. PRO, ASSI 35/174/15 and 35/178/16.

active magistrates at mid-century. Judicial office no longer symbolized the 'natural' authority of elite rural rulers.[116]

Such a shift to lesser-status magistrates was not only the result
of landowners turning their backs on service. It was also facilitated
by and contributed to central government's new outlook on the
magistracy. Where in the seventeenth century, even after 1660, central government saw magistrates as individuals, by the middle of the
next century they were viewed collectively; in appointments and
dismissals particular interests were subordinated to those of the
magistracy as a group. The survival of an alphabetical list of potential justices for Devon, prepared for the absent and uninformed
Duke of Bedford in 1754, aptly symbolizes the altered attitude
toward the commission of the peace as an institution, for in the
past candidates would surely have been arranged geographically, by
political interest, or in terms of social standing. Just as the interests
and demands of individual justices were subordinated to those of
the bench as a whole, so was the image projected by the bench (of
party identity, of patriotic zeal) less valued by ministers than performance of its administrative tasks – labour, it was recognized, that
'any gentleman could perform no matter what his ranking within
or alliances among England's upper orders'.[117]

This attitude helps to account for and was encouraged by an
increasingly non-political pattern of appointment and dismissal, a
strategy adumbrated early in the eighteenth century (if not before)
and consciously implemented by Lord Hardwicke as Lord Chancellor (1737–56). By the reign of George II, the requirements of county
administration, the need to secure magisterial efficiency in the face
of widespread reluctance to participate regularly, had 'established
the lesser justice as a permanent and numerically impressive fixture
on the bench'.[118] This establishment had also entailed much sacri-
fice of political tests for appointment to and retention on the commission of the peace. The dramatic slowing in the issuance of new
commissions that took place in the early eighteenth century, marginally attributable to the work involved in copying documents that
grew ever longer with the addition of names, also bespoke an
unwillingness to continue to make the bench a political plaything.
Once it had been this, during the rage of party when purges and
additions to the commission of the peace reshaped it in every county.
Yet even then local administration did not necessarily suffer, because

116. Landau, *Justices of the Peace*, pp. 313, 316, 318, 322, 385.   117. Ibid., p. 137.
118. Ibid., p. 316.

the minority of active justices 'bore the burden of county government regardless of the changes made in the list of their nominal but inactive colleagues'. In fact, the regulations of the commission from the mid-1670s to the accession of George I 'were to some extent notional operations, without much relevance to the real exercise of local power in the countryside'.[119]

Under the first two Hanoverians, moreover, even these 'notional' purges virtually came to seem unnecessary and ended, and although whigs dominated the commissions numerically, under Lord Chancellor Hardwicke many tories were put on. In 1743, he received lists of nominees to the county bench from a magnate who complimented the Pelhamites on their 'national ways of thinking'. These were particularly proper thoughts in wartime, when internal order had to be kept and the exclusion from administration of 'many Gentlemen of figure, purely for their being of one certain [party] complexion', was unjustifiable. Party loyalty obviously counted for little when in 1744 the Duke of Richmond readily confessed, as he nominated a Sussex justice, that he knew 'nothing of his polliticks, & very little of him'.[120] A century before, this would have been an outrageous admission and one unlikely to result in appointment.

Neither the numerical and modest social dilution of the commission, nor the hesitation of the swollen ranks to perform its tasks, weakened the magistracy as an instrument of social and legal order. In the first half of the eighteenth century, small groups, now much reliant on middling gentry, managed to conduct ably the bulk of magisterial work. Perhaps they were sufficiently more knowledgeable about their neighbourhoods to be able to perform critical magisterial functions of mediation and arbitration better than titled and grand justices.[121] All justices, regardless of status, benefited from reforms and innovations in county administration, which began in the 1690s to make it noticeably more routine. Mirroring the gradual changes in militia administration, these efficiencies included the use of printed forms, the appointment of salaried, semi-permanent treasurers, the establishment of standing committees of audit, as well as insistence on decorum at sessions and adherence to schedules for business. Recurrent service by jurors, including some members of the gentry on assize grand juries, helped to stabilize trial proceedings, and between quarterly meetings specific tasks were frequently

119. Glassey, *Politics and Appointment*, pp. 18–19, 268–9.
120. Landau, *Justices of the Peace*, pp. 107, 125–8; *Richmond–Newcastle Correspondence*, p. 145; Langford, *Public Life*, pp. 401–2.
121. Fletcher, *Reform in the Provinces*, p. 80; Landau, *Justices of the Peace*, pp. 325–8.

assigned to specific divisional and petty sessions. Legal prescription was even abandoned where desirable, in order to repair bridges, for example, without waiting for quarter sessions authority.[122]

Central government in the counties

By the end of the seventeenth century, both central authorities and political nation at large had come to acknowledge unreservedly the efficiency and superiority of 'a national system of provincial governance which relied for its implementation on local dignitaries'.[123] By the middle of the eighteenth century, the expansion of the propertied classes would complement these figures, even displace them, with others recruited from outside the landowning elite.[124] But this century, 1650 to 1750, still predominantly placed the implementation of governance in the hands of local dignitaries: 'dignitaries' because they were members of the landed order that had traditionally ruled, and 'local' because they were present with some regularity at routine meetings; these governors were provincial but not parochial. Their local connection but lack of parochialism is what made them attractive to their own kind as public figures.

Their appointments were based on both local and national imperatives, often coincident, but in action they did not subordinate national debates to local ones. On occasions of local governance, at the assizes, sessions, militia musters, and meetings of special commissions, active local governors (regardless of stature) were in fact transacting what was manifestly the kingdom's business and were doing so in settings that made apparent their accountability to 'a national system of government and law'.[125]

The local governors' involvement in national structures helped to create and affirm group cohesion among them, and several novel developments in the period worked to insinuate them (and the objects of their rule) further into the kingdom-wide system of governance than ever before. Part of the development lay in the fact that

122. G.C.F. Forster, 'Government in provincial England under the later Stuarts', *Transactions of the Royal Historical Society*, 5th series, 33 (1983), pp. 37–8; Rosenheim, 'County governance', pp. 119–22; Roberts, *Recovery and Restoration*, pp. 186–90; Fletcher, *Reform in the Provinces*, pp. 126–31, 140–2, 327–38; J.S. Cockburn, 'Twelve silly men? The trial jury at assizes, 1560–1670', in J.S. Cockburn and Thomas A. Green, eds, *Twelve Good Men and True: The Criminal Trial Jury in England, 1200–1800* (Princeton, 1988), pp. 158–81.

123. John Brewer, *The Sinews of Power: War, Money and the English State, 1688–1763* (Cambridge, Massachusetts, 1990; originally published London 1988), pp. 21–2.

124. Langford, *Public Life*, ch. 4.

125. Holmes, *Lincolnshire*, pp. 84–7; quotation at p. 85.

several local institutions were themselves becoming more 'national'. The lieutenancy under Charles II, when it was used effectively as an instrument of royal rule, was one. The ceremonial appearances of the militia gave public evidence of royal authority. On a structural level, by legislating royal authority over the militia and formalizing the monarch's final approval of deputies, the militia's enabling statutes of the 1660s made the lieutenancy more liable to national direction, as extensive purges of deputies in 1678–79 demonstrated. The practical tasks of the militia (notably when it was deployed in the 1660s against domestic subversion and Dutch threats), and the propaganda surrounding these activities, showed the lieutenancy to have been transformed from an agency of localism into a loyal tool of crown control.[126]

Yet that principal allegiance to the crown of lords lieutenant and their deputies did not prevent the decay of the militia by the mid-eighteenth century, so that in the face of the '45 the lord lieutenant of Cornwall had no idea even how to call his militia to muster.[127] Once a source of prestige and excitement, participation in lieutenancy and militia began to seem inessential and dull around the turn of the century. When statutorily authorized rates began to support the institutions, they became more settled and bureaucratic, a process symbolized in the use of printed forms for lieutenancy commissions by the early eighteenth century.[128] They also ceased to be important vehicles for the assertion of social standing. By the end of the seventeenth century, gentry assessed to supply men for the militia (as opposed to those acting as its officers) were never serving in person and sent substitutes instead, displaying a reluctance to mix with and expose their military ignorance to the lesser sort who were present at musters. In the reigns of George I and George II, the gentry's ties to the lieutenancy even as officers and deputies grew thin. Because the militia statutes only required a quorum of three deputies to conduct lieutenancy business, by the early eighteenth century a handful of figures performed the routine business of the lieutenancy in times of domestic calm or when a standing army was ready to hand to cope with internal disorder.[129]

126. Carter, 'Lancashire militia', pp. 169–71, 176–7; Fletcher, *Reform in the Provinces*, pp. 316–32; Stater, *Noble Government*, chs 4 and 5.

127. Colley, *Britons*, p. 81.

128. Commission for John Buxton, 12 January 1705, Cambridge University Library, Buxton MSS, box 37.

129. Carter, 'Lancashire militia', pp. 161–2; Western, *English Militia in the Eighteenth Century*, pp. 25, 96; Norfolk lieutenancy journals, 1676–1715 and 1715–50, Norfolk Record Office, NRS 27276, 372x7 and NRS 27308, 447x, respectively.

Where the traditional channels of the lieutenancy served to integrate gentry into a national polity in new ways, the land tax administration created in the 1690s and thereafter offered new avenues that had similar effect. Among the hordes of gentry named as commissioners, a small minority actually oversaw the machinery of assessment and collection or heard appeals and adjusted tax burdens, but that minority still comprised many hundreds of gentlemen. A place on the land tax commission was not terribly important to most gentry except as a means of keeping their own assessments down,[130] although the power of assessment could be a weapon against one's enemies. Yet the appointment of gentry as commissioners and the annual occurrence of the tax impressed national fiscal policy on the shape of landowners' provincial lives, especially so in the first years of the tax, when changes in enabling legislation called for annual reassessments. Landowners in some places clung to traditional methods of assessment and familiar local procedures, but despite sharp variations in the process of taxation, the 'general thrust of fiscal policy was in the direction of uniformity and universality'. Those who were engaged in tax administration implicated themselves and their inactive fellows in a structure of national governance, connecting them to the machinery of the state rather than alienating them from it.[131]

Because landlords almost universally gave their tenants allowances for paying the land tax, and thus themselves ultimately bore most of its burden, the mostly efficient and little-resisted collection of the tax intimates that the structure of governance associated with it was generally acceptable to the landed gentry. The unresisting payment also suggests that those who laid out their money generally approved the ends for which the tax was levied. Others were keenly aware that this and other taxes originated in legislative action at the centre, which far from tainting the imposition bestowed acceptability and legitimacy on it. The published acts themselves, dispatched from the capital for use in local administration, were significant, authoritative documents, so that William Chaplyn in 1690 sought from his employer Sir Richard Temple, then in London, the text of the new 'sweeping Taxes' to inform himself of

130. Colin Brooks, 'Public finance and political stability: the administration of the land tax 1688–1720', *Historical Journal* 17 (1974), p. 294.

131. Dennis Mills, 'Survival of early land tax assessments', in Michael Turner and Dennis Mills, eds, *Land and Property: The English Land Tax 1692–1832* (New York, 1986), p. 221; Brooks, 'Public finance and political stability', p. 283; Langford, *Public Life*, pp. 161–3, 232; quotation at pp. 162–3.

the particulars before the tax commissioners met.[132] Later in the decade, Lord Fitzwilliam studied the statute, took advice on it in London 'with councell as likewise with gentlemen', and then instructed his steward to use the law's loopholes to secure him lower assessments.[133]

While the predominant commissions authorized by parliament before the later eighteenth century were those for the provincial administration of the land tax, the occasional commissions for other purposes – to drain and reclaim land, to establish turnpikes – also drew the men they named into a national public life by the very act of naming them in statutes generated in parliament.[134] This national public life was itself being transformed. The concept of public service was changing with the growth of state institutions and the emergence of service to the bureaucratic state, rather than to the monarch, as a proper and sustaining profession. The respectability of paid state service grew between the 1680s and Queen Anne's death partly because civil servants were increasingly discouraged (and even prohibited) from political activism. As a result, and because they were no longer made political victims, these same figures began to be able to expect a measure of secure and continuous employment.[135] The creation of thousands of jobs in centrally administered agencies helped to emphasize a new concept of public service. The explanation offered for Charles Duncombe's removal as Cashier of the Excise in 1697 exemplifies the ideal. He was replaced by one of 'a greater forwardness to accomodate himself to what the public service requires'.[136]

The wars in the reigns of William III and Queen Anne, which raised questions about the meaning of public employment by calling forth an expanding civil service, gave rise to a new public servant in the form of the military officer. The numbers of officers grew to some four thousand around 1710, from about three hundred thirty years before, and although obscure men secured numerous commissions between 1688 and 1713, doing so cost enough money to guarantee that the numbers of socially elite officers would remain high. As more individuals from or directly connected to the

132. W. C[haplyn] to Sir Richard Temple, 2 February 1690, Huntington Library, STT 475.
133. *Fitzwilliam Correspondence*, pp. 5–15, 33–5; quotation at p. 15.
134. Langford, *Public Life*, pp. 208, 213–14.
135. Holmes, *Augustan England*, pp. 239–61.
136. G.E. Aylmer, 'From office-holding to civil service: the genesis of modern bureaucracy', *Transactions of the Royal Historical Society*, 5th series, 30 (1980), pp. 93–4.

landed order (gentry younger sons in particular) earned their livings in employment provided by the state, public service came to be conceived more in terms of central and less in light of local government activity. This shift helps to explain why the gentry elite often failed to participate in county government. No longer did they believe that seeking or promoting the public interest consisted primarily in unpaid, voluntary local service.[137]

Conclusion

When the Duke of Richmond sought to recommend one 'Nash of Walberton' for a magistrate knowing 'nothing of his polliticks, & very little of him', he did more than illustrate the depoliticization of the bench. Nash was 'an odd cub' who could be passed over on this account, but 'if other Gent[leme]n are putt in', Richmond asked, '& he left out, might not he complain?'[138] Asking this question makes inclusion in the commission of the peace almost appear to be a status entitlement in Richmond's mind. He seems to have been confident that if 'Nash of Walberton' chose to be an active justice after appointment, his political convictions would not adversely affect his service. The other values that Nash embraced as a member of the ruling order would presumably hold sway: belief in the rule of law, in the paramount value of property, in the need to maintain public order, in the excellence of existing social and political institutions. These would reliably induce him and others like him to courses of public action that did nothing to subvert the common interests of gentility everywhere and instead would sustain and strengthen them.

Although shared convictions did not free county governance from sources of conflict or create a realm of provincial harmony and good feeling, by the mid-eighteenth century local disputes and competitions competed with increasing numbers of other matters in the rank order of the landed's concerns. For some gentry they had pride of place, but they rated relatively low for many others, who had a panoply of activities to busy them, many places to go and pleasures to enjoy, whether these lay in beautifying their parks, saving their souls, making scientific experiments, improving their farmlands, navigating the ways of metropolitan life, or competing for national place and power.

137. Holmes, *Augustan England*, pp. 262–70.
138. *Richmond–Newcastle Correspondence*, p. 145.

The presence in the county of some men willing to govern allowed for the absence of those who were more inclined to rule. And for the many gentry and nobility who were in some degree both national rulers and local governors, their engagement with the local and regional public sphere was more distant and less defining, more peripheral and less profound an element in the composition of their lives. Their attachment to the provincial realm was often to its more private side, and when public service called it was more often now conceived as national service, even when conducted locally. Withdrawal from provincial life did not dilute the flavour of elite life, but only played its part in transforming it.

CHAPTER FIVE

Central Government and National Politics

Introduction

The emergence of party politics toward the end of the seventeenth century reflected division among landowners on issues of grave importance – but it also enhanced a sense of common identity among them. Further, and paradoxically, the inactivity of the elite and their partial eschewal of partisanship in local government also denoted the emergence of a ruling order conscious of and responsive to its immanence across the kingdom. The disengaged stance that many landed figures took when acting in provincial governance – even their withdrawal from local administration altogether – resulted from two simultaneous developments, the displacement of a political culture of consensus by overt partisanship, and the projection of elite political activity onto a national stage. Engagement in local government was of diminishing note in the calculations of some landed political actors, who simply no longer saw it as important to the maintenance of their image and power. For others it remained significant precisely because of its resonances with other affairs, specifically with the essentially nonpartisan maintenance and sustenance of the position, privileges, and power of landowners as a group, and with the advancement of party political interests at Westminster and Whitehall.

Civil war created two kingdom-wide coalitions, royalist and parliamentarian, that in transmuted form were perpetuated in later political contexts. The continued and frank use of all-encompassing rhetorical pairs to describe political actors (Old Cause or royalist, churchman or nonconformist, whig or tory, Hanoverian or Jacobite, to name the most notable) reveals how far the polarization of politics entailed their universalization. When party divisions began

130

to colour, even stain, elite political activity, the landed increasingly oriented that activity toward the political centre – toward a parliament and a governing ministry, toward the royal court (as had traditionally been the case), toward expanding or new state agencies like the Navy Office, Customs, Post Office, and Board of Trade, to name a few.[1] This greater attentiveness to the national was redefining the remaining localist orientation in elite political culture while it was redefining the landed's relationship to the political metropolis. There lay the arenas for political competition on policy – war and peace, religion, government finance, the uses and abuses of power. Politicians also competed for place, traditional ones in the church and royal establishment, and those flourishing in military and civil service. Competition encouraged political alignment toward the centre as the essential site for securing contracts, positions, and favour, and in the eighteenth century that alignment was increasingly toward ministry first and then monarch, or to ministry in preference to monarch.

The growing hold of national politics in landed life was caused partly by the anxious desire for order among those in the generations after the Restoration who had memories or fears of civil discord and who saw little in their vicious, crime-ridden society to make them confident of future security. Their desire for stability, permanence, and continuity with the past encouraged some to look to the centre – king, council, parliament, and central courts – for collaborators in their own efforts as the agents of order. Moreover, after 1689 the annual rhythms of parliamentary sessions tuned ears to the dramas of Westminster and Whitehall. The vast magnification of state finance and national taxation, the simultaneous growth of Great Britain as an island kingdom and an expanding empire, and the swelling ranks of state servants, military and civil, played their part in making elite political culture less an enterprise of counties and constituencies and more of the country as a whole.

England's more centralized political culture emerged from crises occurring in the middle and late seventeenth century, and it was shared by the landed classes no matter what their party affiliation or their specific positions toward the established church, the succession of the monarchy, or the nature of the constitution. Especially after the Glorious Revolution, English landowners 'united in their recognition of the necessity of supporting government'.[2] Critics of

1. Holmes, *Augustan England*, chs 8–9.
2. Colin Brooks, 'Public finance and political stability: the administration of the land tax, 1688–1720', *Historical Journal* 17 (1974), p. 282.

particular ministries and policies were not critics of basic political structures; quite the contrary, they endorsed the structures and accused those in power of subverting a fundamentally sound constitution. Plausible alternatives to existing modes of governance were in some sense unthinkable. Republican landowners were few even in the 1670s and 1680s and enjoyed little influence. Jacobites were a tiny minority among the landed and had no success in inducing most aristocrats to withhold cooperation from successive regimes. Understandably reluctant to oppose existing powers openly, the feeble support that Jacobite gentry gave various risings shows that real, as opposed to projected, rebellion was more likely to induce fear in them than resolve.[3]

Even among those at the radical margins, most gentry accepted 'a national ideology of a centralized state under a common law' – they differed as to who or what should sit at the centre, significant points of contention but not ones that erased common attitudes and interests among the landed. As significant, landowners, whether they liked it or not, were affected by the intensity of government centralization and their consequent inability 'to insulate the localities from Westminster', a failure increasingly manifest as central institutions grew in size and power.[4] New government positions in the capital, provinces, and colonies had to be filled, and filling them drew attention to the integration of all subjects' lives into a national fabric. Unable to insulate themselves from the fires of bureaucratic growth, many gentry sought to benefit by its warmth instead, gaining place for themselves and seeking it for others, and using the new instruments of state to secure their predominance in society.

So too did gentry and nobility increasingly see in parliament a singularly effective national institution for advancing their particular interests. The bulk of the 14,000 acts passed between 1688 and 1801 (as opposed to 2700 passed from 1485 to 1688) addressed limited problems and concerns, social and economic development in particular, and came prepared by local negotiation. But all bills, even if advanced by sophisticated provincial political elites, received critical scrutiny and ultimate approval from representatives of the whole kingdom in the parliamentary forum. In this way, local business was accomplished on a national plane, and insofar as landowners, whether in Kent or in Cumberland, pursued provincial concerns

---

3. Paul Kléber Monod, *Jacobitism and the English People 1688–1788* (Cambridge, 1989), pp. 270–1, 273, 281, 295.

4. Holmes, *Seventeenth-Century Lincolnshire*, p. 262.

via legislative means, they ultimately followed parallel procedures and in the same parliamentary locale.[5]

In two ways the parliamentary electoral process strengthened the translocal identification of the landed as a group that, despite internal divisions, shared activities and values that linked them horizontally as a social order. To begin with, elections were ideological, which reinforced landowners' broader-than-local sensibilities for three reasons. First, choices to parliament were increasingly resolved – both when contested and when not – on the basis of recourse to issues of national note or to matters resolved through national channels, more than over local affairs. Second, especially under the Hanoverians (when elections were somewhat less ideologically fraught), those issues were increasingly effectively spread through the kingdom by the national and provincial press. Finally, in fighting their political battles, gentry (and their parties) used a single language, 'the rhetoric of a political culture . . . shared [by] gentlemen throughout England'. It was not a language inaccessible to other elements in society, but talk of 'our known established lawes and fundamentall liberties'[6] resonated differently with urban freeman and rural forty-shilling freehold voters than with the landed gentry, even the slightest of whom was most likely to identify with those who sat in parliament rather than with those who elected them to sit.

Beyond the impact made by their ideological nature, elections clarified the relationship of local and national structures and circumstances and they highlighted the (mainly landed) candidates' national connections. In marked fashion toward the end of the period, parliamentary choices (never exclusively resolved on ideological bases) were determined by a candidate's ability to provide local services, influence local life, and help constituents to 'a reasonable share in the distribution of local offices'. In this context, however, it is essential to recognize that 'local services' were frequently supplied by or with assistance from the centre, and that 'local offices' meant offices that gave employment in or near the constituency but to which appointment came from the centre. The litany of the latter is impressive: 'government posts and contracts; legal offices and promotions; army commissions, discharges, and

5. Julian Hoppit, Joanna Innes, and John Styles, 'Towards a history of parliamentary legislation, 1660–1800', *Parliamentary History* 13 (1994), pp. 313–14; Stuart Handley, 'Local legislative initiatives for economic and social development in Lancashire', *Parliamentary History* 9 (1990), pp. 14–37.

6. Holmes, *Seventeenth-Century Lincolnshire*, p. 262 for both quotations.

transfers; local places, favours, and requests; appointments to post-masterships, tidewaiterships, and positions in the Excise among many others'.[7] When a landed constituency-patron was able to dispense or provide constituents access to such patronage, it emphasized his participation in national structures of rule and showed off his metropolitan contacts. The landed order could not help but recognize that political life was nationally divided and contentious *and* that central government and parliamentary authority and oversight could be neither avoided nor deflected. These acknowledgements together bred a sense of shared enterprise and an awareness of common relationships to sources of power among the rulers of England.

Party

The fact that open partisanship characterized political behaviour in the generations after the Restoration is a truism in English political history. Partisan identification could be fleeting and mutable, party loyalty was often diffuse, and attributions of factiousness rather than principled action still attached to party men, often by others equally partisan. None of these qualifications diminishes the fact that the politics of the landed in the late seventeenth and first half of the eighteenth century was significantly national in character because it was largely the politics of party.

This era differed from preceding ones in the scope of the discursive institutions of politics, which employed a language of political binarisms – an easy recourse to the division of all political players into friends and enemies, well affected and disaffected – that emerged in the civil war and characterized politics up to the middle of the next century. Powerful polarities generated on national axes in the 1640s and 1650s politicized local worlds along fault lines much defined by relations to the state. Shifts in the terminology that defined the poles – court/country, tory/whig – and the co-existence of several poles at one time, did nothing to diminish this tendency.[8] The political participants among the landed – which

7. Frank O'Gorman, *Voters, Patrons, and Parties: The Unreformed Electoral System of Hanoverian England 1734–1832* (Oxford, 1989), pp. 5–6, 46–51, 151–8; quotation on p. 51.

8. Mark Kishlansky, *Parliamentary Selection: Social and Political Choice in Early Modern England* (Cambridge, 1986); Ann Hughes, 'Parliamentary tyranny? Indemnity proceedings and the impact of the civil war: a case study from Warwickshire', *Midland History* 11 (1986), pp. 49–78, esp. pp. 67, 69; idem, *Politics, Society and Civil War in Warwickshire, 1620–1660* (Cambridge, 1987), pp. 289–90. But cf. David Underdown's

effectively means all of them – had long thought and acted in national terms and on national planes. Yet the sorting of people by the unending imposition of engagements, oaths, sacramental tests, and punitive taxation; the tarnishing of opponents with labels of reproach that derived from specific, traumatic historical episodes, usually the 1640s;[9] and the publicly advertised rifts that marked the world of party – all of these identify late Stuart and Hanoverian political activity as different from the elite politics of previous generations.[10]

The civil wars propagated religious and constitutional partisanship which gave rise to the adversarial politics that emerged in parliament in the 1640s, and to the transformation of parliamentary selections into elections that became most noticeable in the 1640s and 1650s.[11] Partisanship lasted long after the fighting stopped, and whatever the intentions of some conciliators, the Restoration settlement proved to be contentious and fomented an 'atmosphere of investigation, of revenge and of taking stock', which led in places to acts of local retribution and perpetuated divisions in local society and government.[12] A list like that drawn in 1662 naming forty-four members of the gentry in Derbyshire 'and how they stand affected' – some 'very Loyall', others 'Rigid Presbit[erian]' – illustrates how division was perpetuated.[13] Twenty years later, an analysis of politics in the borough of Aylesbury attributed the 'perpetuall feudes . . . demonstrated in . . . Electing Burgesses for Parliament' to the presence forty years earlier of a parliamentary garrison that 'impregnated [the community] with Schimsaticall Rebellious Principles'.[14]

The occasions for gentry and nobility to see the kingdom riven throughout along the same fault lines accelerated in the crisis of

reminder in *Revel, Riot and Rebellion: Popular Politics and Culture in England 1603–1660* (Oxford, 1985), pp. 242, 289 that not all fault lines were defined by relations to the state.

9. Tim Harris, *Politics under the Later Stuarts: Party Conflict in a Divided Society, 1660–1715* (London, 1993), p. 160.

10. Mark Knights's term 'factious party' is a reminder of the hybrid history of party politics: *Politics and Opinion in Crisis, 1678–81* (Cambridge, 1994), pp. 112–45.

11. Kishlansky, *Parliamentary Selection*, pp. 105–22.

12. Stephen K. Roberts, 'Public or private? Revenge and recovery at the restoration of Charles II', *Bulletin of the Institute of Historical Research* 59 (1986), pp. 187–8. See also Paul Seaward, *The Cavalier Parliament and the Reconstruction of the Old Regime, 1661–1667* (Cambridge, 1989); Joyce Lee Malcolm, 'Charles II and the reconstruction of royal power', *Historical Journal* 35 (1992), pp. 307–9, 317–24.

13. S.C. Newton, 'The gentry of Derbyshire in the seventeenth century', *Derbyshire Archaeological Journal* 86 (1966), pp. 6–8.

14. Charles Hamilton, 'The election in 1685 at Aylesbury', *Parliamentary History* 12 (1993), p. 71.

1679–81, which gave 'relevance to the language of party'. The contesting of three elections, voluminous activity in the press, and widespread petitioning and addressing all pulled localities into national politics and individuals into party camps.[15] Recent study has stressed the social inclusiveness of the politics of the Exclusion crisis but is in danger of losing sight of its distinctive meaning for landed society.[16] On the one hand, these events implicated participants in a broad political culture, making more clearly national the perspectives of the politically aware, gentry most notable among them because of the wide range of their contacts and connections. On the other hand, the omnipresent if low-level threat that popular participation in politics might get out of hand, while it did not deter elite whigs and tories from appealing to the activism of the lower orders, reminded party opponents of their shared positions of landed privilege and modified the impact of religious issues on their behaviour.

Partisan polarization in the constituencies had parallels in parliament, where it affected two houses overwhelmingly comprised of landowners. For this reason, the slow and discontinuous development of party in the parliaments of Charles II and James II is particularly significant in defining and assessing elite political culture. That evolution owed much to the interregnum's legacy of oppositional thought and behaviour, which informed the obstruction of government policy by members of the Cavalier House of Commons. The Earl of Danby's efforts in the 1670s to build a court interest responded to this and created further dissonances, which were most audible when crown legislation was being considered.[17] Some members denounced the sorting of political players into opposing camps and so resisted the labels whig and tory when they gained currency after 1681.[18] Yet in Herefordshire similarly inspired efforts to promote moderation unintentionally helped to spark party conflict there in the 1680s, and elsewhere even fervent advocates of 'accommodation', who crossed the lines of party to talk, dine, marry, and even

15. Knights, *Politics and Opinion*, p. 356.

16. Tim Harris, *London Crowds in the Reign of Charles II: Propaganda and Politics from the Restoration until the Exclusion Crisis* (Cambridge, 1987); idem, ' "Lives, liberties and estates": rhetorics of liberty in the reign of Charles II', in Tim Harris, Paul Seaward, and Mark Goldie, eds, *The Politics of Religion in Restoration England* (Oxford, 1990), pp. 217–41; idem, 'Party turns? or, whigs and tories get off Scott free', *Albion* 25 (1993), pp. 581–90; Gary S. De Krey, 'The first restoration crisis: conscience and coercion in London, 1667–73', *Albion* 25 (1993), pp. 565–80.

17. Knights, *Politics and Opinion, passim*; Derek Hirst, 'The conciliatoriness of the Cavalier Commons reconsidered', *Parliamentary History* 6 (1987), pp. 221–35.

18. Knights, *Politics and Opinion*, pp. 111–12.

ally tactic...   ...guage of

...story of min-
the mid-1690s
...illiam III's and
...not parties proved
...s of the 1740s were
...mbers in parliament
...ough opposition in the
still castigated as faction
...onstituted the legitimate terms
...contest, both locally and nationally. Par-
...y criticism of specific policies or of a ministry in general
was 'based on party: for as party provided a mechanism for governmental control of Parliament, it equally provided the means for
organized opposition'.[21]

Annual sessions affected the way landowners in parliament understood and exercised their roles as politicians by generating predictable means for members to concert their efforts. The Glorious
Revolution provides a benchmark here. Sittings under Charles II
were frequent but often capriciously cut short or postponed. After
1689 they recurred annually, began at regular seasons,[22] and lasted
several months, a predictability that eased the passage of legislation. The extensive committee work by members in the capital that
was entailed in passing local and private legislation constituted 'an
indispensable and continuous form of constituency organization' that
connected members to their points of origin and to one another.[23]

19. Newton E. Key, 'Comprehension and the breakdown of consensus in Restora-
tion Herefordshire', in Harris et al., eds, *Politics of Religion*, pp. 191–215; James M.
Rosenheim, '"Being taken notice of as engag'd in a party": partisan occasions and
political culture in Restoration Norfolk', in Carol Rawcliffe, Roger Virgoe, and Richard
Wilson, eds, *Counties and Communities: Essays on East Anglian History Presented to Hassell
Smith* (Norwich, 1996), pp. 259–74.

20. B.W. Hill, *The Growth of Parliamentary Parties 1689–1742* (London, 1976),
pp. 31–2, 81, 91–2, 215, 221–6; Harris, *Politics under the Later Stuarts*, p. 150; Henry Horwitz, *Parliament, Policy and Politics in the Reign of William III* (Newark, Delaware, 1977);
Geoffrey Holmes, *British Politics in the Age of Anne*, revised edition (London, 1987).

21. Clyve Jones, 'The House of Lords and the growth of parliamentary stability,
1701–1742', in Jones, ed., *Britain in the First Age of Party 1680–1750: Essays Presented to
Geoffrey Holmes* (London, 1987), p. 101; see generally Linda Colley, *In Defiance of
Oligarchy: The Tory Party 1714–60* (Cambridge, 1982).

22. From 1689 to 1722 sessions began in October–December with eight exceptions; in 1724–53 they began November–January in twenty-eight out of thirty-two
meetings: E.B. Fryde, D.E. Greenway, S. Porter, and I. Roy, eds, *Handbook of British
Chronology*, 3rd edn (Cambridge, 1986; reprinted with corrections 1996), pp. 577–9.

23. Colley, *In Defiance of Oligarchy*, p. 128 for quotation. See also Handley, 'Local
legislative initiatives', pp. 16–17; Holmes, *British Politics*, pt 2, 'The working of politics'.

Concerting activities in committee or on the floor was not a new practice in the eighteenth century and pre-dated the efforts of the Earl of Danby in the 1670s on behalf of his Anglican policy and the strategic planning of the Earl of Shaftesbury and opposition elements at the same time. Such ephemeral arrangements extended outside the chambers when members met at times of crisis to coordinate activity.[24] Under William III and Anne the whigs had the more formidable organization and more distinctive leadership, but the tories were always able to project a party identity. From at least the 1690s, each party regularly galvanized its followers with gatherings of high strategists between sessions, planning with key members as parliament assembled, and general conclaves that gave directions to the rank-and-file during sessions, along with the use of whips, proxy voting, and intra-cameral management. These methods emphasized that in the leaders' eyes parliamentary service was party service and made independence difficult.[25]

All these activities changed the parliamentary experience of gentry who sat in the Commons and of peers who took their seats in the Lords. Manipulation within the houses during daily sessions was open and expected in the eighteenth century, if not always effective.[26] For any party or sub-group, attendance was a leading concern. Party leaders could not accomplish goals without followers, whom they therefore marshalled more methodically than could be done in the late sixteenth or early seventeenth centuries, when sessions were short and adjournments unforeseen and abrupt. In the Augustan era calls for absentees to attend went down to gentry and lords in the country, and appealed to their sense of party loyalty, their hope of parliamentary success, and their fear of future electoral defeat.

Members' responses to demands for their attendance were in part conditioned by a sense of accountability and their awareness that responding to local concerns was for constituents a measure of

24. Harris, *Politics under the Later Stuarts*, chs 3, 4; Knights, *Politics and Opinion*, pp. 128–9, 134–5.

25. For this and the next paragraph see Geoffrey Holmes, *British Politics*, pt 2; idem, *The Making of a Great Power: Late Stuart and Early Georgian Britain 1660–1722* (London, 1993), pp. 342–6; Colley, *In Defiance of Oligarchy*, ch. 3; J. C. Sainty, 'The origin of the leadership of the House of Lords', *Bulletin of the Institute of Historical Research* 47 (1974), pp. 53–73; Clyve Jones, 'The parliamentary organization of the whig junto in the reign of Queen Anne: the evidence of Lord Ossulston's diary', *Parliamentary History* 10 (1991), pp. 164–8; idem, 'The House of Lords and parliamentary stability', pp. 85–110.

26. David Lemmings, 'Lord Chancellor Cowper and the whigs, 1714–16', *Parliamentary History* 9 (1990), pp. 166–7, 172.

effectiveness and of worthiness

... careful party-line organ-
...ation, demonstrated the significance attached
by eighteenth-century men of power to affairs at the nation's centre. Those landed men conducting parliamentary business in this
structured manner – so different from the course of parliamentary
business under the Tudors and early Stuarts – were redefining not
just what it meant to be parliament men but what it meant to be
the nation's governors.

Members of the landed order who sat in parliament could not
think of politics without taking party into account, even if they
wanted to set it aside. Party in parliament limited members' scope
for independent action and reminded them that they were embedded in a national political world. Sir James Lowther (1673–1755,
MP 1694–1702, 1708–55), always ambivalent about party, tried to
distance himself from partisan conflict, but as much as political
independence mattered to him, he still more wanted to use his seat
to promote his industrial and commercial ventures and raise his
local standing. He secured patronage for his constituents but curbed
his parliamentary independence to do so, and to have his cherished economic legislation pass too. Trapped by changes in the
nature of politics, his ambitions forced him to be a party player.[29]

Largely unconcerned about local reputation, Sir Richard Cocks
(*c.* 1659–1726, MP 1698–1702) was a country whig untempted by
office who claimed to be 'guided by reason, not party', but during
his public life party allegiance exercised an increasing 'gravitational

27. Handley, 'Local legislative initiatives'; Perry Gauci, *Politics and Society in Great
Yarmouth 1660–1722* (Oxford, 1000), pp. 51–2, 192–4; O'Gorman, *Voters, Patrons,
and Parties*, pp. 248–53.

28. Knights, *Politics and Opinion*, pp. 178–83; Jeremy Black, *The Politics of Britain
1688–1800* (Manchester, 1993), pp. 84–5.

29. J.V. Beckett, 'A back-bench MP in the eighteenth century: Sir James Lowther
of Whitehaven', *Parliamentary History* 1 (1983), pp. 79–97.

force' upon him. Although an idiosyncratic back-bencher in parliament, he was a party man, for national concerns lay at the heart of public life, in parliament and out. His published speeches to local grand juries dwelt on the need for political loyalty, his anti-papist pamphlets addressed national issues like the war with France, his economic arguments stressed the need for increased international trade, and he advocated moral reform because he believed that private immorality endangered the public sphere. His rather eccentric political writings, those of a man 'in water far too deep for him', none the less show him immersed in the national scene in politics rather than in provincial ponds.[30]

Even immersion in provincial ponds exposed a member of parliament to powerful currents. Someone like Viscount Perceval might complain about being 'pestered with petitions from persons in and about Weobley' in the late 1740s,[31] but an electoral patron had a reciprocal relationship with his constituency, an ideologically obligatory one that demanded response to requests. Patrons had to provide services to meet voters' expectations of what men of power did to justify its possession and exercise.[32] Services were harder to provide if one was not attached to the party in power but could satisfactorily consist of efforts to sustain a principle by attacking popery, placemen, or a prime minister. Yet the most common service considerations were material – promotion and expedition of constituents' practical interests – and sometimes what constituents wanted, the state – for reasons of limited resources, cost, or administrative efficiency – might not provide. Whether members aimed at grand political goals – to save the church, to preserve the succession – or hoped only to satisfy local interests and fulfil constituents' expectations, or both, no ambition could be attained by struggling against the party nature of parliament in a world of burgeoning government. Perhaps especially among gentry representing county constituencies, freedom of action was limited by a complex mix of private conviction, the demands of party, constituent interests, and personal advantage in what was none the less a party-oriented political process.[33]

30. David Hayton, 'Sir Richard Cocks: the political anatomy of a Country whig', *Albion* 20 (1988), pp. 221–46; quotations at pp. 225, 234, 244; Georges Lamoine, ed., *Charges to the Grand Jury 1689–1803, Camden Society*, 4th series, 43 (1992), pp. 81–8, 175–82.

31. Black, *Politics of Britain*, p. 69.

32. O'Gorman, *Voters, Patrons, and Parties*, pp. 141–62, 224–85, although mostly addressing a later era, is highly informative on these points.

33. Colin Brooks, 'Interest, patronage and professionalism: John, 1st Baron Ashburnham, Hastings and the revenue services', *Southern History* 9 (1987), pp. 51–70.

Elections

Starting in the last decades of

... through some
..., requiring the assistance of those with access
to patronage and favour.

Political choice at the constituency level was fraught throughout our period: in many boroughs the party character of annual
municipal elections in the early eighteenth century, as much as trien-
nial elections to parliament, guaranteed, as Gilbert Burnet put it,
that 'in every corner of the nation the two parties stand . . . listed
against one another'.[34] Even after the whigs' great triumph in 1715
unbalanced the scales in parliamentary elections, neither party
nor party contests disappeared in the constituencies, and local
alignments still guaranteed that candidates and voters in contested
elections had 'recourse to binary party terminology'.[35] Despite the
tendency in the 1740s to elevate the opposition of patriots and
ministerialists over that of tory and whig, the electoral activity of
the political elite continued along traditional, resonantly national
party lines until the fall of Walpole.[36]

This trajectory meant that although a general election included
choices made in nearly two hundred and seventy English and Welsh
(and starting in 1707 forty-five Scottish) constituencies, it was perceived as a national political exercise by the landed. At the end
of the seventeenth century, political actors recognized a national
political year governed by the sitting and rising of parliament. As a
permanent fixture of public life, parliament was more associated
(but not exclusively so) with the formulation of kingdom-wide public
policy.[37] The frequency of elections from 1689 to 1715 intensified

34. Hill, *Growth of Parliamentary Parties*, p. 17.
35. Colley, *In Defiance of Oligarchy*, p. 133.
36. Hill, *Growth of Parliamentary Parties*, ch. 12; Robert Harris, *A Patriot Press:
National Politics and the London Press in the 1740s* (Oxford, 1993), ch. 2.
37. Handley, 'Local legislative initiatives', pp. 14–37.

this agency, changing elite exercise of power by funnelling it to the centre and encouraging a conceptualization of governance as a national as well as an enduringly provincial matter. Each local election of representatives had a potentially national consequence, and for landowners, who were those most likely to stand at and bear the cost of elections, the regional and national view of electoral politics was stronger than that of any social group. The political consciousness of the landed, nourished by education, family connections, and often by residence in London, extended well beyond any single constituency they fought, a breadth of vision that the practice and structure of elections reinforced.

The frequency of general elections and contests diminished after 1715, but party gave continuing life to national electoral awareness, and although selection of candidates was a form of decentralized political decision-making, it contributed to a broad conceptualization of political action. At a time when partisanship touched every constituency during elections, those who attended meetings to select competing candidates (and for county constituencies these were likely to be gentry) had their politics illuminated by a national light. First, the timing of general elections and thus the occasion for meetings to hit upon candidates was not determined autonomously in a given constituency but rather at the centre. In the absence of a constitution that dictated intervals, here the engine for setting general elections was ostentatiously located in the hands of national figures – ministers and monarch. Second, the candidate-choosing meetings came more and more to be held not to seek consensus pairings but to choose party candidates, whigs or tories, for an anticipated contest. This was true even during the whig ascendancy after 1715: half of all constituencies were contested in the election of 1722 and almost three in ten as late as 1741.[38]

At one time candidate-selection meetings had included all shades of opinion and sought agreement on prospective members who could be selected unopposed. As with the meeting in Dorset in the mid-1670s to select a by-election candidate, many counties had had a 'usual meeting' for this purpose at a usual place – not two places.[39] Even before Charles II's reign, however, such gatherings were becoming volatile occasions politicized around ideological issues. During the crisis years of the late 1670s and 1680s, the anticipation

38. O'Gorman, *Voters, Patrons, and Parties*, pp. 108–9.

39. K.H.D. Haley, *The First Earl of Shaftesbury* (Oxford, 1968), pp. 386–7; Kishlansky, *Parliamentary Selection*, chs 2, 6, and esp. pp. 139–47.

of new parliaments led to prior planning.[40] Matters had changed in Dorset by 1681, when at a 'Muster' of tory gentry the majority 'did agree what persons should be put in nomination for the county and burroughs, who are most of them in men of differing sentiments from the three last parliaments'.[41] Still, in the late seventeenth century nomination of candidates could be haphazard and informal, with candidates canvassing privately beforehand but announc candidacy simply by turning up at the poll.[42] In the ages of and Walpole, however, meetings held for this purpose were single-party assemblies and not always even public. When soliciting freeholders' votes in September 1740 (eight months before the next election), the Whig gentry of Sussex chose 'rather to entertain att private houses than go to the towns ourselves; it is much easier and wholesomer, and what the freeholders amongst are used to, and like, as well'.[43]

By this late date, political decisions were even being removed from the provinces, where meetings that did occur were held to ratify choices made by London-based politicians. The referral to county meetings of selections decided elsewhere showed the continued need for local approval but also indicated where party power lay. Plans for the Norfolk county election of 1741, for example, were laid as early as February 1740 by whigs 'in town', who intended to inform the county of their design at assizes but still left one of the candidates in the county ignorant as to those 'with whom I may correspond' to receive instructions.[44]

It did not take contests between tory and whig to generate awareness of electoral politics as occurring on a national stage. In the eighteenth century, after all, parties often agreed to split representation. But the decision to compromise in this way itself represented a linking of opposites, a cancelling out of polarities, and it had first to be reached on each side by the agreement of partisans to submerge partisanship. Some proposed electoral accommodation to contribute 'to a national settlement', as one opined in 1681, or to 'preserv[e] the peace of the country', as Walpole himself claimed in 1740. But others found 'Elections very expensive' and welcomed

40. Kishlansky, *Parliamentary Selection*, ch. 5 and pp. 171–4.
41. R.G. Pickavance, 'The English Borough and the King's Government: A Study of the Tory Reaction 1681–85' (Oxford University D. Phil., 1976), p. 79.
42. Kishlansky, *Parliamentary Selection*, p. 183.
43. *Richmond–Newcastle Correspondence*, p. 46.
44. Sir R. Walpole to T. De Grey (and draft replies), 12 February and 6 March 1740, Norfolk Record Office, WLS XVI/1/2–3 and 5, 410x1; see also Rosenheim, *Townshends of Raynham*, pp. 207–8.

compromise to avoid the 'unnecessary expences, which contested elections doe occasion', a more plausible motive.[45] By and large, the local 'unanimity' created by agreements to eschew contests was tenuous, artificial, and specious: compromises to split representation were not neutralist rejections of party. Such pacts did not deny party but acknowledged it by ostentatiously setting party competition aside, just as 'safe seats' were not safe *from* party but safe *for* a party.

Concerted planning for elections began in the 1670s, but was ported in the next century, when predictability made it easier. First the frequent elections of the years 1695–1715 and then contests that were foreseen together led to increasingly systematic approaches to electioneering. Between 1702 and 1747, six of eleven general elections occurred after a sitting parliament had ended its statutory term, and three others took place after a monarch's death. In the former case parliament's end was foreseeable and in the latter new elections were predictably delayed by statute, so in both circumstances there was time to lay plans.[46] Parties established (and ignored) ground rules for pre-electoral manoeuvring and for use at the poll; in the absence of deep-pocketed patrons to finance elections, funds were amassed by subscription as early as the Exclusion years; the preparation and publication of pollbooks in the eighteenth century, some alphabetized for easier use, advertised support, served as evidence if results were challenged, and assisted in future contests.[47] The identification of 'an improper time' to be making plans for an election even confirms the existence of a protocol about electoral seasons.[48]

Relying on all this organization, candidates, patrons, and others of local influence could be absent from constituencies until polling

---

45. Kishlansky, *Parliamentary Selection*, p. 147; Sir R. Walpole to [T. De Grey], 21 April 1740 and H. L'Estrange to T. De Grey, 28 March 1740, Norfolk Record Office, WLS XVI/1/1 and XVI/1/25, 410x1; Basil Cozens-Hardy, ed., *The Norfolk Lieutenancy Journal 1676–1701*, *Norfolk Record Society* 30 (1961), pp. 64–6.

46. Holmes, *British Politics*, pp. 312–21; W.A. Speck, *Tory & Whig: The Struggle in the Constituencies, 1701–1715* (London, 1970), ch. 3; Kishlansky, *Parliamentary Selection*, pp. 180–91. By the second half of the eighteenth century, elections across England boasted the employment of election committees, professional election agents, and pre-poll canvassing: O'Gorman, *Voters, Patrons, and Parties*, pp. 67–105.

47. B. Wrench to T. De Grey, 26 March 1740, Norfolk Record Office, WLS XVI/1/24, 410x1; Kishlansky, *Parliamentary Selection*, pp. 186–7; S.W. Baskerville, P. Adman, and K.F. Beedham, 'Manuscript poll books and English county elections in the first age of party: a reconsideration of their provenance and purpose', *Archives* 19 (1991), pp. 384–403.

48. F. Wise to Lord Guilford, n.d. [1729], Bodleian Library, MS North.d.4, fol. 21a{verso}–21b; C. Townsend to Sir T. Drury, 24 November 1746, Norfolk Record Office, NRS 21138, 74x5.

day drew near. Many were energetic, but some never appeared. Lord Cholmondeley did not stir from London during the election of 1681 but still expected his tenants to back his candidates. James Lowther of Whitehaven attended none of the four elections he won for Carlisle between 1694 and 1701, and Robert Walpole safely begged off appearing at King's Lynn when his appointment to places of profit necessitated his re-election there in 1710 and 1721.[49] In these circumstances, landowners seeking influence depended greatly on the assistance of neighbours, friends, relatives, and employees. The estate steward often served as chief electoral agent, a logical choice to tend the constituency interest, considering his familiarity with tenants and neighbourhood. Published manuals did not describe political labour among a steward's duties, but one in eighteenth-century Cheshire simply assumed that his new employer would instruct him how to rally tenants and provide for voters 'that are poor & want horses'.[50] The planning for local elections, even in the capital, did not articulate national party strategy, and the long-distance selection of candidates rested with figures geographically linked to the constituencies affected. No London central office existed, and even ministers dispensing crown patronage to influence opponents and retain supporters at election time could only do it on a case-by-case basis.[51] Yet none of this prevented seeing elections as national phenomena, and because early modern elections took place over a period of weeks, the prolonged polling stimulated interest in results unfolding nationwide, which the mobile and well-connected aristocracy were best able to follow.[52] Voters may not have been expressing 'any kind of "national" sentiment' when they polled, as has been argued for the era after 1734,[53] but the landed were well situated to inform one another of progress county by

49. P.J. Challinor, 'Restoration and exclusion in the county of Cheshire', *Bulletin of the John Rylands University Library of Manchester* 64 (1982), pp. 376–7; Beckett, 'A back-bench MP', p. 81; R. Walpole to E. Rolfe, 17 January 1710 and 3 April 1721, Norfolk Record Office, GUN 1/2 and 1/6, 362x5.
50. Hainsworth, *Stewards*, ch. 7; S.W. Baskerville, P. Adman, and K.F. Beedham, 'The dynamics of landlord influence in English county elections, 1701–1734: the evidence of Cheshire', *Parliamentary History* 12 (1993), pp. 134–5; Geoffrey Holmes and W.A. Speck, *The Divided Society: Parties and Politics in England 1694–1716* (New York, 1968), pp. 158–60. For other agents in operation see also J.R. Burton, 'Two elections for Bishop's Castle in the eighteenth century', *Transactions of the Shropshire Archaeological Society*, 3rd series, 9 (1909), p. 261; *Richmond–Newcastle Correspondence*, p. 41; and O'Gorman, *Voters, Patrons, and Parties*, pp. 78–90 for a later era.
51. Colley, *In Defiance of Oligarchy*, pp. 122–4; *Richmond–Newcastle Correspondence*, *passim* provides numerous illustrations.
52. Holmes and Speck, *Divided Society*, p. 156.
53. O'Gorman, *Voters, Patrons, and Parties*, pp. 5–6.

county and assess success or failure on a global basis. They followed outcomes across the kingdom: in May 1705 Henry St John reported on 385 results of which he knew, in May 1708 the Earl of Manchester was given 'hopes of a very good Parliament', and in 1727 Lord Strafford saw tory resolve 'all over England' to secure a majority in the coming parliament.[54] All candidates were understood to be standing as part of a general endeavour to gain a party majority, and to this end gentry cooperated within and across constituencies through personal appearance, correspondence, and donations of money. Sir Charles Shuckburgh in July 1702, for example, hoped to make his personal contribution at contests in Gloucestershire, Warwickshire, and Northamptonshire.[55] This cooperation could take place on a substantial scale: in 1741 tories came to a Southampton election 'from all parts of England to support the cause of their political friends', about the same time that a party member proposed assembling a national network of constituency societies and a London-based committee to coordinate electoral strategy.[56]

Opinion and the political press

Such a proposal for a national party would have been unimaginable in a less-informed political environment or one populated by more introspective clusters of men: Augustan and Hanoverian political culture had broader horizons than that of early Stuart times. Nationally defined parties influenced electoral mechanics, and national politics were inextricably entwisted with provincial affairs as subjects of public discourse.[57] In the reigns of William III and Anne the press coupled local and national issues, 'transported the political

54. Holmes and Speck, *Divided Society*, p. 29; Colley, *In Defiance of Oligarchy*, p. 135. For other examples see Haley, *Shaftesbury*, pp. 499–500, 625–6 for 1679 and 1681; J.H. Plumb, *Sir Robert Walpole*, 2 vols (London, 1972; originally published 1956–60), I, *The Making of a Statesman*, p. 378 for 1722 and II, *The King's Minister*, pp. 318–23 for 1734.

55. Holmes and Speck, *Divided Society*, p. 156.

56. Romney Sedgwick, *The History of Parliament: The House of Commons 1715–1754*, 2 vols (New York, 1970), I, p. 254; Colley, *In Defiance of Oligarchy*, pp. 135–8.

57. For the press and politics see Jeremy Black, *The English Press in the Eighteenth Century* (London, 1987; reprinted Aldershot, 1991), ch. 1; Knights, *Politics and Opinion*, ch. 6; Gary S. De Krey, *A Fractured Society: The Politics of London in the First Age of Party, 1688–1714* (Oxford, 1985), ch. 6; G.A. Cranfield, *The Development of the Provincial Newspaper 1700–1760* (Oxford, 1962); Michael Harris, 'Print and politics in the age of Walpole', in Jeremy Black, ed., *Britain in the Age of Walpole* (New York, 1984), pp. 189–210; idem, *London Newspapers in the Age of Walpole: A Study of the Origins of the Modern Press* (London, 1987); Harris, *A Patriot Press*.

fury of the national macrocosm into the civic microcosm'; in the following reigns, it served as 'an agent of persuasion' to explain public affairs in partisan language that was meant to galvanize existing supporters and win over the uncommitted.[58] Both as a vehicle that brought metropolitan, national, and international news, taste and mores into the country-house drawing room, and as an instrument meant to shape opinion and political behaviour, the press had a role in forming the culture of England's ruling order, although it in some sense preached to the converted. Much more so than professionals, merchants, and shopkeepers, landowners already led cosmopolitan and politicized lives.

From the Restoration to the mid-1690s, with brief exceptions, government censorship limited the impact of published works, but manuscript newsletters effectively spread news, as they had done throughout the century. Temporarily freed by expiry of the Licensing Act in 1679, the press briefly but decisively voiced and shaped public opinion during a period of constitutional and political struggles.[59] Reinstated press laws were ineffective in the crisis of 1688–89, and the Licensing Act permanently lapsed in 1695, which allowed newspapers to flourish both in London and the provinces with the new century, intensifying ideological divisions as they prospered. The press made a useful tool in a political system where whigs and tories, despite disagreements over the need to impose limits on its exercise, valued the press's expression of different public voices.[60] These voices were well attended to by landowners.

Polemical literature enjoyed a wide readership, and the contents of eighteenth-century newspapers were accessible to more than a thin, well-educated section of society. Yet many political publications forthrightly addressed a cultivated, prosperous readership in which the landed elite were the major component. This was also the case with manuscript newsletters, which had a wide circulation in London through the coffee houses but when directed to the countryside were so costly that they were more restricted to the landed wealthy.[61]

58. De Krey, *Fractured Society*, p. 218; Black, *English Press*, pp. 115–16. See also Jonathan Barry, 'The press and the politics of culture in Bristol, 1660–1775', in Jeremy Black and Jeremy Gregory, eds, *Culture, Politics and Society in Britain, 1660–1800* (Manchester, 1991), pp. 49–81.

59. James Sutherland, *The Restoration Newspaper and Its Development* (Cambridge, 1986), pp. 12–24; Knights, *Politics and Opinion, passim*.

60. De Krey, *Fractured Society*, ch. 6; Black, *English Press*, ch. 1 and p. 115; Harris, 'Print and politics', pp. 196; Barry, 'Press and politics in Bristol', pp. 70–2.

61. Knights, *Politics and Opinion*, pp. 172–6; Sutherland, *Restoration Newspaper*, pp. 6–8.

Many publications in their content, cost, and style aimed at the elite. Roger North exaggeratedly implied that pamphlets, unlike ballads and broadsides, spoke only to 'Men of Fortune and Education', but in the provinces it was gentry who were exposed to the fullest range of publications.[62] Many London periodical publications purposefully sought a landed provincial and a metropolitan audience: the *British Mercury* boasted in George I's time that it was 'carefully distributed into all Parts not only of this City, but of the whole Nation'. Dissemination from London, expedited by an improved postal service, still would have been exceedingly expensive had not members of parliament, officeholders, and post office clerks used their franking privileges to spread publications. The landed origins and connections among these distributors ensured that country gentlemen were well supplied.[63]

By George II's reign papers and journals saturated the kingdom with news of public affairs that fed the broad curiosity of elites in the country for information and opinion from and about the metropolis. When country life grew tedious, as it could, such news broke up the long stretches of time. Provincial newspapers, which numbered twenty-four in 1723 and forty-two in 1746, intentionally carried little local matter but printed large amounts of foreign intelligence and tried to shape perceptions by focussing on national politics.[64] The provincial press provided ammunition for local ideological battlegrounds with its partisan conveyance of news under Queen Anne, and in Walpole's ascendancy played an integral and acknowledged role in political competition and persuasion: claims to impartiality convinced no one.[65] Whether newspapers advertised candidacies, tried to stir voters by publishing fragmentary election results, or called members to come up to parliament for new parliamentary sessions, they presented readers a vision of a political nation divided in party terms.[66]

62. Knights, *Politics and Opinion*, pp. 168–75, citing North on p. 169; Black, *English Press*, p. 47; Simon Targett, 'Government and ideology during the age of whig supremacy: the political argument of Sir Robert Walpole's newspaper propagandists', *Historical Journal* 37 (1994), pp. 289–317; Harris, *London Crowds*, pp. 98–100.

63. Harris, 'Print and politics', pp. 190–1.

64. Black, *English Press*, pp. 21, 300–5; Cranfield, *Provincial Newspaper*, pp. 13–21, 270–2; Harris, *A Patriot Press*, p. 15.

65. Barry, 'Press and politics in Bristol', pp. 51, 69–70, 72–3; Holmes, *Politics in the Age of Anne*, pp. 30–3; Holmes and Speck, *Divided Society*, pp. 66–76; Harris, 'Print and politics', p. 210.

66. De Krey, *Fractured Society*, p. 217; *Ipswich Journal*, 1–8 April 1721, p. 6 and 15–22 July and 29 July–5 August 1727.

To see the press as 'the critical mechanism in the national political culture',[67] however, relies on defining that culture more in terms of its popular element and in terms of discrete and unusual episodes of political crisis than this study does. Whatever its effect on others, the press was only pushing the landed further in a direction they had already taken,[68] and it is more helpful to see it as an important connection in 'a circuit of political communication' than as a critical mechanism. Although this circuit took in a broad array of groups, the gentry element in it had the most power to conduct political energy, connecting domains 'of traditional public concern . . . with parliamentary or related political activity'.[69] The press spoke to a population acted upon by public policy, but it spoke especially loudly to those who made and implemented that policy, the landed principal among them by virtue of their political and economic power and their embrace of an ideology of citizenship that demanded action in the public sphere.

Sites of association

The press manifested the intrusion of party into public life, which by the second third of the eighteenth century had created a political culture that was 'national in both scope and orientation'[70] and situated in constituencies and the metropolis. The ruling elite uniquely straddled both sites. Committed to the electoral system and parliament[71] for access to the sources of power that lay in the capital, they were also grounded in localities. In negotiating a relationship between these sites of political power, the landed had many occasions for partisan public association in country houses and coffee houses, town houses and taverns, west country quarter sessions and Westminster Hall, and by the mid-eighteenth century the gathering-places were as much urban as rural. Permanent parties and parliaments created a steady clientele for public establishments, and the coffee houses of the kingdom, often affiliated with a party, provided a natural base for political activity. Twenty-nine

---

67. Kathleen Wilson, 'Empire, trade and popular politics in mid Hanoverian Britain: the case of Admiral Vernon', *Past & Present* 121 (1988), p. 92.
68. Jeremy Black points out the pitfalls in taking '[c]risis, division and conflict' as the key features of politics: *The Politics of Britain*, pp. 2–3.
69. Harris, 'Print and politics', p. 203.
70. Wilson, 'Empire, trade and popular politics', p. 91.
71. O'Gorman, *Voters, Patrons, and Parties*, p. 17; see also chs 3, 5.

different whig clubs gathered in London during the era of exclusion; twenty years later, aided by the rise of the newspaper press, public venues habitually visited by politicians were even more dedicatedly political and more clearly an element of party organization. The landed men who figured among the tories and whigs congregating at the Sun Tavern or Cocoa Tree Chocolate House in London found and made them significant sites of cultural activity.[72]

Similarly, the aristocratic support extended to a body like the Honourable Artillery Company proclaimed affiliation on the broad basis of attachment to church and crown. In contrast, gentry support for the many county feasts held in London and other urban centres between the mid-1650s and Queen Anne's death gave visibility to some landowners' desire to show affiliation with provincial sentiment and local causes. Gentry contributed to the charities promoted in the feast sermons, which they bought when published. Ironically, the sermons, which were preached on occasions celebrating the country and county element in the identities of town dwellers, were in content anything but provincial. They addressed national political issues and openly acknowledged the division of the political nation into parties. As arenas for debate outside and in lieu of parliament, the county societies provided 'protopartisan' organization that heightened political energy generally and exemplified the new extra-provincial organizational practices of extra-parliamentary politics.[73]

Like the feasts, other practices were not gentry-driven but still contributed to the shaping of elite political experience. These included campaigns of petitioning and addressing parliament and crown. Gentry had limited involvement in producing but more in conveying these documents, generated any time from the 1670s to the 1740s. The petitions were not the spontaneous products of their signers, however, and landowners, while not principal promoters in the towns whence many came, helped in writing county addresses. After the Oxford Parliament was dissolved in 1681, over two hundred loyal addresses came to the crown, some from groups predominantly comprised of the landed elite – justices, deputy lieu-

72. Harris, *London Crowds*, pp. 100–2; Knights, *Politics and Opinion*, pp. 128–9; Harris, 'Print and politics', pp. 194–5; Linda Colley, 'The Loyal Brotherhood and the Cocoa Tree: the London organisation of the tory party 1727–1760', *Historical Journal* 20 (1977), pp. 77–95.

73. Newton E. Key, 'The political culture and political rhetoric of county feasts and feast sermons, 1654–1714', *Journal of British Studies* 33 (1994), pp. 223–56; idem, 'The localism of the county feast in late Stuart political culture', *Huntington Library Quarterly* 58 (1996), pp. 211–37.

tenants, militia officers. Tory squires later promoted many addresses to the queen after Dr Sacheverell's conviction in 1710.[74] One London publisher appointed to print addresses to George II at his accession promised to compile the names and addresses of local officeholders and to list 'any other Loyal Subjects' who subscribed or transmitted their names to him from the provinces. He presumed that he could sell this publication to those – readily found among the gentry – who wanted to advertise their connection to these public demonstrations of loyalty.[75]

For the nation at large, the monarchy and its court were still potent sources of political symbolism and power and played a major if reduced part in shaping the character of political society. The court remained a lure for ambitious and curious women and men of the aristocracy, people seeking material reward and the prestige or even psychological affirmation that could accompany association with the truly great.

Yet even though the court continued to give cues in the performance of national political ritual, and monarchy provided most of its symbolism, those disillusioned by, at odds with, or removed from the court created alternatives that challenged its mystique. They did so by turning to metropolitan as well as regional alternatives: for them, the substitute for a court-based, centralized culture of power did not lie only in provincial circles. When aristocrats boycotted or were pushed from George I's or George II's court, they went to that of the Prince of Wales or, under Queen Anne, to homes of social surrogates like the Duke of Marlborough. They adhered to their own national political calendar or observed existing celebrations in rivalry to the court, like the whigs who commemorated the birthday of William III in November 1703 with new clothes and noble attendance.[76] Celebrations of a different sort, like those honouring Admiral William Vernon as a national hero after 1739, were by and large out of aristocratic hands, but they too presented alternatives to 'official' rituals and constituted part of a vibrant national, extra-parliamentary political culture,[77] strikingly melded by national issues. Yet while it shook aristocrats out of any

---

74. Pickavance, 'English Boroughs and the King's Government', p. 150; Harris, *Politics under the Later Stuarts*, pp. 106–7; idem, *London Crowds*, ch. 7; idem, 'Party turns?', p. 586.

75. *Ipswich Journal*, 23–30 September 1727.

76. Robert O. Bucholz, *The Augustan Court: Queen Anne and the Decline of Court Culture* (Stanford, 1993), ch. 7, esp. pp. 226–7.

77. Wilson, 'Empire, trade and popular politics', p. 108.

complacency they had fallen into and at times audibly rattled the structures of their rule, before the later eighteenth century this extra-parliamentary politics did not consistently or materially threaten the oligarchic power of the landed order.

The sources of divisiveness in the ruling order

The resilience of the edifice of landed rule depended in part on the regime of law and order that nobility and gentry successfully directed throughout the kingdom.[78] It also derived from the limits placed on the raging national politics of party that after 1650 challenged, complemented, and also replaced the ideal of a localist politics of consensus. Landed politicians did not see everything in binary terms, and few questioned the basic fabric of political life. For the landed, political activity rested on tenets that sustained the group's privilege and power: the need for monarchical (and then Hanoverian) rule, the necessary part of parliament in government, the benefit of existing social and economic structures, the special place of Protestantism, and the virtue of the legal system.[79] Political contention within the landed elite arose more over content than fundamental structures; clashes of principle underlay party conflict, but so did agreement on principle. Public figures and writers used common language and appealed to the same principles, but they did so for different purposes and attached different meanings to their similar words. Wealthy men might be hostile to or admiring of the monied interest; supporters of monarchy might be Jacobites or Hanoverian; faithful Protestant gentry might believe in a comprehensive or an exclusive church.

There are two points to bear in mind when considering these three important sources of divergence among the landed elite. First, division occurred over matters of national policy, of national as well as regional or local import. Thus while generating rifts, preoccupation with these issues oriented aristocratic vision and thought onto cosmopolitan and metropolitan planes. Second, although the disagreements about church, monarchy, and economic interest were

78. Anthony J. Fletcher, *Reform in the Provinces: The Government of Stuart England* (New Haven, 1986), *passim* and esp. ch. 10. See also J.M. Beattie, *Crime and the Courts in England 1660–1800* (Cambridge, 1986), chs 1, 7–8, 11; Douglas Hay, 'Property, authority and the criminal law', in Douglas Hay, Peter Linebaugh, John G. Rule, E.P. Thompson, and Cat Winslow, eds, *Albion's Fatal Tree* (New York, 1975), pp. 17–64.

79. J.P. Kenyon, *Revolution Principles: The Politics of Party 1689–1720* (Cambridge, 1977), chs 4, 7, 8, 10, 11.

expressed forcefully, that force of expression was qualified in each instance – and in all instances weakened and even dissipated by the middle of the eighteenth century. As far as religion goes, the tensions between nonconformists and Anglicans, between high church and low, even between non-jurors and conformists, were mitigated by an underlying acceptance of Protestantism on all sides. On the dynastic issue, the support for the Stuarts on whatever basis (but especially on the principle of a hereditary, divine right, and indefeasible conception of monarchy) was noisier than it was deep or strong – and was finally put paid to among the landed by the rising in 1745.[80] And the conflict of land and money was more real in the polemics of the time than in the financial practices of the landed.

Of these three divisions, that pertaining to the landed–monied split had least bearing on the self-identity of landowners. In the public press and in parliamentary debates, there were clashes, especially noisy between 1688 and 1720,[81] about the ostensibly contradictory interests of the landed and the monied. The association of nonconformists with the latter interest, based on the legitimate perception that they were disproportionately represented among England's businessmen, especially in London, allowed easy elision of the whig party that dissenters favoured with the monied interest.[82] Self-proclaimed defenders of the landed interest argued that whig financiers and whig merchants in trades stimulated by wartime demand were fostering land-based continental war, and paying for it with a land tax, to further their own interests. Yet in the world of business after 1689, 'there was no clear division' of different trades or interests along party lines,[83] in the parliamentary world neither whig nor tory party was decisively pro- or anti-business,[84] and in the landed world tories showed themselves willing to invest in and profit from business and stocks. Few aristocratic families at any level prospered 'without some assistance from other sorts of income' besides land.[85] While a tory ministry in 1711 established property qualifications for members of parliament as a gesture against non-landed aspirants, it showed no greater anti-commercial bias than this. Government even by tories rested on a 'propertied consensus' that included those propertied in more than just land.[86]

80. Black, *Politics of Britain*, pp. 35–7.   81. Habakkuk, *Estates System*, pp. 564–5.
82. Grassby, *Business Community*, pp. 272–4.   83. Ibid., p. 207.
84. Harris, *Politics under the Later Stuarts*, pp. 197–9.
85. Stone and Stone, *An Open Elite?*, p. 210, and ch. 7 passim.
86. Langford, *Public Life*, p. 306.

Of the binary religious divisions that affected elite political life – juring and non-juring Anglican, conformist and nonconformist, Catholic and Protestant – the latter created the largest ostensible gap but was the least material in affecting the life of the landed order. It is true that outside Wales, the northeast, and Lancashire Catholicism until about 1700 'was a non-conformism of the gentry' and anti-popery was as strong a public sentiment as any in England: this combination would seem to make for anything but assertion of the common interest of the landed. But anti-Catholic fears grew more from imaginings about the monarch's leanings, papists in office, or the dangers of foreign invasion than from concrete fears based on the behaviour of English Catholics. The gentry-dominated domestic Catholic community was small, numerically stable (around 60,000), and undergoing a 'reconciliation with the general ethos of English society', that is, assimilating in some ways.[87] From the reign of Charles II to that of George II, the image of popery 'was often only dimly associated with the local recusant family', and as far as landed culture went, Catholic sensibilities seem little different from Protestant ones.[88]

As for Protestant landowners, at and after the Restoration a committed minority of them, working from a belief that the Church of England should be tolerant of a range of church practices, resisted the reimposition of a persecuting and narrow church establishment. Some were especially well motivated because liturgical narrowness squeezed their own consciences. This latter group, whether called Puritans or Presbyterians, were partial nonconformists by and large. As had historically been true, it remained 'comparatively rare for upper class Protestants to abstain completely from attendance at Church of England services',[89] which did not stop them from asserting others' right to do so – but also serves as a reminder that the religious divisions within the Protestant aristocracy were not cavernous compared to the doctrinal disagreements of Catholics and Protestants.

None the less, landowners who endorsed the concept of a more comprehensive church contended over this issue with the convinced Anglicans who supported a restrictive establishment that would demand uniform worship throughout the kingdom. In parliament in

---

87. John Bossy, *The English Catholic Community 1570–1850* (London, 1975), chs 5, 7–8, 12; quotations on pp. 100, 290.

88. John Spurr, 'Religion in Restoration England', in L.K.J. Glassey, ed., *The Reigns of Charles II and James VII and II* (London, 1997), p. 94.

89. J.T. Cliffe, *The Puritan Gentry Besieged, 1650–1700* (London, 1993), p. 82.

the early 1660s, Puritans and sympathizers tried to craft an inclusive solution to religious conflict. When efforts to arrive at a moderate church settlement failed, some aristocratic dissidents put nonconforming clergymen under their protection and tried to mitigate the effects of the punitive legislation that had been passed; others passed quietly into conformity. Through the reign of Charles II, the first group doggedly promoted comprehension, embraced royal indulgences when offered, and refused to bow before the image of a monolithic church. Because the settlement of 1689 provided only a limited measure of relief for dissenters, and because uncompromising Anglicans in parliament hoped to repeal even these concessions, struggle over the future direction of national religious policy continued.[90]

It continued with some vehemence because a group of influential figures refused to take oaths of allegiance to William and Mary. These non-jurors, adamant in their disassociation from an 'official' Church of England they saw now tainted by its acceptance of the new monarchs, were a loosely constituted group dominated numerically by over four hundred clergy who left or were thrown out of their livings. Only a quarter this many aristocratic families – those of ten peers and about a hundred gentry, including sixty who had recently supplied members of parliament – were non-jurors in the 1690s and many of them took the opportunity of James II's death in 1701 to subscribe the requisite oaths. Although a few notable figures found themselves unwilling to swear loyalty to George I in 1714, as a group within the landed elite the non-jurors' heyday was fleeting.[91]

As the ranks of gentry non-jurors were small, so too the numbers of completely nonconformist aristocrats were limited in size to begin with, and both their numbers and energies diminished over time. Among the Puritan gentry so visible in the first half of the century, religious conviction was not an inheritance that could be passed down like a house or lands: it was, wrote the Presbyterian Thomas Manton in 1658, 'a rare case to see strictness of Religion carried on for three or four descents'; 'where is such a succession to be found in the houses of our Gentry?' he asked.[92] It can in fact

---

90. Spurr, 'Religion in Restoration England'; idem, *The Restoration Church of England, 1646–1689* (New Haven, 1991), ch. 2; Ronald Hutton, *The Restoration: A Political and Religious History of England and Wales 1658–1667* (Oxford, 1985), pt. 3; Seaward, *The Cavalier Parliament*, ch. 7; Cliffe, *Puritan Gentry Besieged*, chs 3–4.

91. Monod, *Jacobitism and the English People*, pp. 138–45.

92. Cliffe, *Puritan Gentry Besieged*, p. 61.

be traced up to the end of the century in families like the Hampdens, Harleys, and Hobarts, but by about 1700, the Restoration era aristocratic patrons and protectors of dissent were dead 'and their places in the meeting-houses were seldom taken up by their sons and daughters'.[93]

Michael Watts argues that for this later generation an association with the meeting house 'was incompatible with their social and political aspirations',[94] which would make sense only if these aspirations differed from those of their forebears, who were not so impeded by these considerations from associating with others of like mind. The visible falling-off of landed association with dissent may have many explanations, including optical illusion. Where it became impossible to maintain a partly conformist minister in the church near one's country seat, it was easy to accommodate a domestic chaplain, as did at least seventy-three Puritan gentry families between 1650 and 1700, who gave support to at least ninety divines who had been deprived of fellowships or parish livings in the early 1660s. Few gentry took up the opportunity of licensing their houses or private chapels for dissenting meetings.[95] On the other hand, there are reasons why the numbers of nonconforming gentry (not the same as gentry sympathetic to nonconformity) might fall. From the beginning of Charles II's reign the association of dissent with political extremism encouraged conformity among the landed, who had much to lose by being labelled and then potentially prosecuted and punished as radicals. Then and through the eighteenth century, legislatively imposed disabilities that denied nonconformists full participation in public life also provided reasons to conform outwardly, whatever went on in one's private chapel. Disillusionment accompanying 'the experience of defeat' among Puritans in Charles II's reign, the 'more pronounced materialistic ethos which offered no encouragement to those who believed in the necessity of self-denial',[96] the latitude offered by low church interpretants within the Church of England in the first half of the next century – all of these made it more difficult to remain essentially presbyterian or congregational in outlook and easier to join the Church of England in full communion.

Ultimately, the efforts of landed protectors were less essential for the preservation of dissenting ways in religion. As important as

---

93. Michael R. Watts, *The Dissenters: From the Reformation to the French Revolution* (Oxford, 1978), pp. 346–66; quotation on p. 359.

94. Ibid., p. 360.   95. Cliffe, *Puritan Gentry Besieged*, pp. 193, 206–28.

96. Ibid., p. 61.

divisions derived from religious conviction were in the politics and society of Augustan England, those among Protestants did not create visible, impassable rifts among the landed or make occasional conformists unrecognizable compared to high churchmen. Divisions among Protestants were less virulent after the repeal in 1717 of tory legislation aimed at enforcing and better defining the second-class citizenship of nonconformists, and after the annual passage of indemnity acts to protect dissenters from prosecutions in the age of Walpole.[97]

The contest between conformity and dissent helped to define one of the axes along which partisans aligned in the English political world of the late Stuarts and early Hanoverians. The split between those who would swear allegiance to the new monarchs William and Mary and those non-jurors who felt their oaths to absent James II were binding defined another. Yet in both cases the depth of conflict and even the then- and now-recognized importance of the politics of religion can be exaggerated. The animus between proponents of the numerous circulating versions of orthodoxy and dissent, especially within a landed order where so many other bonds of commonality tempered such a division, was strictly limited. It was not, to be sure, the modern, literally murderous, often ethnically based antipathy of Jew and Muslim on the West Bank of the Jordan River, Muslim and Hindu in Bangladesh, or Ulster nationalist and Irish republican in Londonderry. After 1660, very few Protestants among the landed classes died in England for their religious convictions.

Where the landed did put their lives at risk was in associating with the Jacobite cause of the exiled James II, his son James the Old Pretender, and his grandson Charles Edward the Young Pretender.[98] Actually to appear on behalf of any of these was to court a charge of treason, although exile (and revokable exile at that) was as harsh a punishment as an energetic conspirator like Bishop Atterbury or a renegade minister like Viscount Bolingbroke received. The wisdom of hedging bets that led whig ministers in the 1720s to negotiate politically with known Jacobites, the common employment of double agents, and Robert Walpole's obsession with Jacobites (whether

97. G.M. Townend, 'Religious radicalism and conservatism in the whig party under George I: the repeal of the Occasional Conformity and Schism Acts', *Parliamentary History* 7 (1988), pp. 24–44; Black, *Politics of Britain*, p. 60.

98. This and the next two paragraphs draw on the argument of Harris, *Politics under the Later Stuarts*, ch. 8; for a contrasting view, see Monod, *Jacobitism and the English People*, esp. ch. 9.

cynically or delusionally bred in him) provide some of the breeding
ground for the fevered accusations and fabricated evidence that
constitute a good deal of the 'Jacobite activity' of the years from
1689 right up to 1745.[99]

There were of course supporters of the old Stuart cause to
be found among English landowners, but how that support was
manifested and how strong it was are matters on which historians
energetically disagree. The paucity of and difficulty in interpreting
surviving sources contribute to this controversy. So do the inconsistent behaviour of those who can be labelled Jacobites at some point
but not at others, as well as the very different identifiable strands of
Jacobitism.[100] Some called Jacobite sought an unconditional return
of the Stuarts, some expected some restrictions on the monarch,
still others seem to have been only marginally preoccupied with the
possibility of return at all. Indeed, the sociability of gentry Jacobites has been advanced both as a principal means whereby they
maintained the cause and as constituting them as a significant subculture within the landed classes. For these Jacobites 'organized politics and the Parliamentary opposition to Whig rule . . . were often
peripheral'.[101] For the more politically minded, Jacobites who were
Catholic took heart from a co-religionist, supporters of divine right
believed they had a religious duty to restore God's agent, opponents of the Glorious Revolution and later the Hanoverian succession saw in the cause a weapon to use variously against William III,
whigs and Walpole. Yet if these inconsistencies among Jacobites
complicate analysis for the historian, they also simplify it, since they
make evident Jacobitism's overall incoherence, its weakness as a
pro-Stuart political movement, and its greater significance as a means
of expressing opposition to prevailing powers.[102] None of this de-
nies the crucial part Jacobitism played in shaping the lives of individual genteel adherents to the cause, but for the ruling order as a
whole neither Jacobitism nor religious difference nor the unique
economic interests of the land created rifts so great as to cast totally
in the shadow those increasingly prominent common features of
the ruling order's profile.

99. Clyve Jones, 'Whigs, Jacobites and Charles Spencer, Third Earl of Sunderland', *English Historical Review* 109 (1994), p. 54; Plumb, *Walpole*, II, pp. 41, 298–9.
100. F.J. McLynn, 'The ideology of Jacobitism – Parts I and II', *History of European
Ideas* 6 (1985), pp. 1–18, 173–88; Monod, *Jacobitism and the English People*, chs 4–5.
101. Monod, *Jacobitism and the English People*, pp. 283–307; quotation on p. 283.
102. Harris, *Politics under the Later Stuarts*, pp. 228–9.

Nonpartisanship and consensus

Looking only at the ferocity of party warfare ignores the abstract positions shared by those in struggle. Opponents often employed the same language, as when condemning arbitrary government and popery, or acclaiming the rule of law and a properly constituted parliament.[103] They just disagreed about the way to apply their terms, as do advocates of 'family values' in the late 1990s. Although parties differed on matters of ideological substance in the early eighteenth century, party contests to an important degree constituted 'a stylised . . . conflict which took place within a social consensus; a manifestation of the confidence and fundamental political unison of England's landed elite'. Expressing party animosities served to release aggression, and by 'helping to make aristocratic oligarchy more difficult to discern, party rivalry afforded it some protection'. Paul Langford has discerned a separation of 'the sensibilities of the landowner from party politics'.[104]

Aside from the testimony of political thought, public behaviour shows that party animosity did not make division permanently irreconcilable within the fabric of elite life. Party fury undoubtedly split much social life in the eighteenth century, not only in the sports restricted to men but also at some assemblies, where the sexes mingled but sometimes parties did not. Local charities could also be infected with and their beneficial work curtailed by partisanship.[105] Yet civil intercourse still took place between political foes, and party sentiment grew more temperate under the second King George. A relative decline of party feeling among the landed even before then left the way open for more pleasant – and more cosmopolitan, metropolitan – distractions. 'Politics are no more,' declared Lady Mary Wortley Montagu in 1726, 'no body pretends to wince or Kick under their Burdens, but we go on cheerfully with our Bells at our Ears, ornamented with Ribands and highly contented with

103. Ibid., p. 101; idem, *London Crowds*, chs 5–7; idem, ' "Lives, liberties and estates" '.

104. Colley, *In Defiance of Oligarchy*, p. 12; John Cannon, 'The isthmus repaired: the resurgence of the English aristocracy, 1660–1760', *Proceedings of the British Academy* 68 (1982), p. 450; Langford, *Public Life*, p. 306. See also J.G.A. Pocock, *The Machiavellian Moment: Florentine Political Thought and the Atlantic Republican Tradition* (Princeton, 1975), pp. 402, 446–61 and J.C.D. Clark, *English Society 1688–1832: Ideology, Social Structure and Political Practice during the Ancien Regime* (Cambridge, 1985), pp. 121–41.

105. Langford, *Public Life*, pp. 120–1.

our present condition.' At mid-eighteenth century, 'politics occupied a strictly subordinate priority' in the Earl Waldegrave's social circle, where Horace Walpole observed that extravagant entertainments and beautiful women supplanted ministerial intrigue as topics of conversation.[106] For all the party-specific socializing, members of county society none the less occasionally congregated with their political opponents in social settings, and politicians at the centre did the same.[107] Although the royal courts most welcomed those of the ministerial party and saw less of those associated with opposition, rivals sometimes met at court, and Queen Anne early in her reign unsuccessfully tried to use ceremonial occasions to unite the aristocracy and set herself above party.[108]

In parliament itself, party lines were blurred over country issues like place bills and attacks on the standing army, and a unique problem like the investigation of the South Sea scandal saw 'the Names of Whig and Tory . . . in a manner lost, [and] all perswations and Party's [*sic*] unite and agree', just as the Scottish Duke of Dover was denied a seat in the House of Lords by a group of 'mixed whiggs and torys, courtiers and antecourtiers'. Regional solidarity in the reign of Queen Anne provided a means of bridging the social and political distance between tories and whigs, as attested by the occasional union in both spheres that northerners made at Westminster.[109] Most commonly, however, party was set aside over local projects. Occasionally adherents to one cause went separate ways, like Cheshire's whig members who split over a regional navigation bill in 1720, but more typical were Shropshire's representatives who cooperated legislatively, although maintaining segregated social worlds.[110] Parliamentary loyalties, in short, were often compartmentalized as men who opposed one another at the centre buried their differ-

106. *Montagu Letters*, II, p. 66; *The Memoirs and Speeches of James, 2nd Earl of Waldegrave, 1742–1763*, J.C.D. Clark, ed. (Cambridge, 1988), p. 44.

107. Clyve Jones, 'A Westminster Anglo-Scottish dining group, 1710–12: the evidence of Lord Ossulston's diary', *Scottish Historical Review* 71 (1992), p. 119; idem, 'The parliamentary organization of the whig junto', p. 165; Eveline Cruickshanks, 'Lord Cowper, Lord Orrery, the Duke of Wharton and Jacobitism', *Albion* 26 (1994), p. 31.

108. Bucholz, *Augustan Court*, pp. 204–7.

109. Clyve Jones, 'The new opposition in the House of Lords, 1720–3', *Historical Journal* 36 (1993), p. 311; idem, 'Parliament and the Peerage and Weaver Navigation Bills: the correspondence of Lord Newburgh with the Earl of Cholmondeley, 1719–20', *Transactions of the Historical Society of Lancashire and Cheshire* 139 (1989), p. 53; *Nicolson Diaries*, p. 6.

110. Jones, 'Parliament and the Peerage and Weaver Navigation Bills', pp. 31–61; Colley, *In Defiance of Oligarchy*, p. 125.

ences in the interests of the kind of comity evident in the will of
Joseph Banks I, MP (d. 1727), which with an apparent indifference
to party designated legacies to men in Lincolnshire whose names
'read like a catalogue of the nobility and gentry'.[111]

Elsewhere, contact across partisan divides occurred at diverse
times and places, unpredictably but without appearing remarkable.
This held true in Cheshire in the 1650s when royalist and parliamentarian gentry resumed a shared social life, when families exchanged country visits in the 1670s although in opposition politically,
or when Robert Harley and Thomas Tanner consorted with whigs
in pursuit of antiquarian and bibliophile interests in the early eighteenth century. It applied as the whig Earl of Derby kept up contacts
with tories in Cheshire after 1715, while the Earl of Carlisle tried to
make York's assemblies into non-partisan events in 1716, and when
the tory Earl of Cardigan hunted with whigs in the 1720s and
1730s.[112] This socializing neither compromised party integrity nor
anathematized those who took part. A shared occasion did not constitute treachery: because 'a Whig dines with a Jacobite, does not
make the Whig a Jacobite, and vice versa'.[113] Whig and tory gentry certainly organized distinct races and balls, joined different hunts and
patronized separate clubs, but they also attended the same operas,
plays, pleasure gardens, and assemblies, as well as sessions and
assizes. Although party set the terms of political life and sometimes
the tone of social life, party only invaded but did not wholly con-
quer the latter, the private and even the public associations of the
landed.

In fact, party had limited play in aspects of civic as opposed to
social life in ways that mark the underlying unity of England's landed
order. Party allegiance helped gentry into office, to be sure, especially lucrative office, but after appointment the political hetero-
doxy worthy of punishment was measured by as narrow a gauge as

111. *Banks Papers*, p. xxvi.
112. J.S. Morrill, *Cheshire 1630–1660: County Government and Society during the English Revolution* (Oxford, 1974), pp. 260–1; R.W. Ketton-Cremer, *Norfolk Portraits* (London, 1944), p. 41; Clyve Jones, 'Jacobitism and the historian: the case of William, 1st
Earl Cowper', *Albion* 23 (1991), p. 685; Sarah Markham, *John Loveday of Caversham
1711–1789: The Life and Tours of an Eighteenth-Century Onlooker* (Salisbury, 1984),
p. 128; Barry Coward, 'The social and political position of the Earls of Derby in later
seventeenth-century Lancashire', in J.I. Kermode and C.B. Philips, eds, *Seventeenth-
Century Lancashire: Essays Presented to J.J. Bagley, Transactions of the Historic Society of
Lancashire and Cheshire* 132 (1982), p. 150; Holmes, *Augustan England*, p. 273; *Eaton
to Cardigan Letters*, pp. xlviii–xlix.
113. Clyve Jones, '1720–23 and all that', *Albion* 26 (1994), p. 45, n. 8.

that of Jacobitism.[114] Moreover, 'party' was an ill-defined thing, lacking organizational fixity, and other imperatives sometimes overrode. The whigs who accepted local office late in James II's reign had not forgotten the persecution they suffered after 1681 from the king's friends, but they set aside resentment and took up positions to help govern the kingdom – and pursue their own ends of greater religious toleration.[115]

Fears about the societal dangers posed by partisan disputes fed an urge to set these disputes aside where feasible, an impulse felt in both central and local government. The landed's stake in the enforcement of law and in the collection of revenue to defend the nation was in the end upheld both through *and* despite party affiliation. Therefore the political elite accepted a significant measure of bipartisanship within institutions that sometimes pursued partisan policies. Religious questions had divided magistrates' benches and even interfered with civil administration under Charles II, but they rarely did so in the eighteenth century. Politically motivated dismissals from state service had sufficiently disrupted the work of bureaucracy in the 1690s and again from 1714 to 1717 that the practice was curbed thereafter.[116] By the 1720s and 1730s, and even in the face of the dismissal of large numbers of officers for political reasons just after George I's accession, even the military profession was less politicized and less disturbed by politics than in the previous thirty years, and presumably the stronger for it.[117] Both tory and whig saw common cause in protecting the existing social order, knowing that the too-blatantly partisan conduct of legal and fiscal proceedings invited resistance from the population. Group solidarity, the ties within a national ruling elite, at key moments superseded the bonds of party, just as they did those of locality at other times.

Cooperation in the counties

Cooperation between factions in the ruling elite occurred on the magistrates' bench, in machinery for the land tax, and in other commissions organized by county. It was found in the 1650s when administrative needs overrode republican ideology in the making

114. John Brewer, *The Sinews of Power: War, Money and the English State, 1688–1763* (Cambridge, Massachusetts, 1990; originally published London, 1988), pp. 74–5.

115. Mark Goldie, 'John Locke's circle and James II', *Historical Journal* 35 (1992), p. 570.

116. Brewer, *Sinews of Power*, pp. 74–5.   117. Holmes, *Augustan England*, p. 274.

of official appointments. In the 1660s, some formerly parliamentarian gentry remained in positions of local authority, and many commissions of the peace included figures whose presence defied their prior antipathy to the royalist cause.[118] Quarter sessions business in Wiltshire in 1661 was in the hands of those who had controlled it in the 1650s; in Hampshire over a third of the Protectorate's justices remained on the Restoration bench; men from parliamentary or republican backgrounds comprised 40 per cent of Lancashire's JPs in 1665 and a like proportion of its tax commissioners.[119]

The appointment in the early 1660s of officials who had served in the interregnum was meant to cultivate potential supporters of the restored regime. That consideration does not fully explain the persistence of mixed benches in following years, and here administrative aims prevailed. Although the period from the Exclusion years through the reign of Queen Anne saw party-based manipulation of the magistracy in virtually every county, purges most often spared active justices, that minority who 'bore the burden of county government regardless of the changes made in the list of their nominal but inactive colleagues'.[120] The administrative implications of political manipulation are seen in the hesitation of Suffolk's whig lord lieutenant to request the dismissal of a tory justice in 1706, for fear that if he did, none of the man's friends 'would ever act or appear . . . and . . . the sessions would fall'.[121] In a change of tack, purges ceased and ministers accomplished party ends after the 1720s simply by enlarging the commissions of the peace; supporters were added and exclusion (other than for death) grew rare. In 1743 the Earl of Ailesbury, who sought inclusiveness on the bench in Wiltshire, showed keen awareness of the broad danger posed by the opposite practice: 'the keeping out of many Gentlemen of figure, purely for their being of one certain [party] complexion . . . is surely a great national hurt'.[122]

118. Holmes, *Lincolnshire*, pp. 219, 223; Fletcher, *Reform in the Provinces*, pp. 12–13, 34.

119. P.J. Norrey, 'The restoration regime in action: the relationship between central and local government in Dorset, Somerset and Wiltshire, 1660–1678', *Historical Journal* 31 (1988), p. 804; Andrew M. Coleby, *Central Government and the Localities: Hampshire 1649–1689* (Cambridge, 1987), p. 90; B.G. Blackwood, *The Lancashire Gentry and the Great Rebellion 1640–60*, Chetham Society, 3rd series, 25 (1978), p. 76.

120. L.K.J. Glassey, *Politics and the Appointment of Justices of the Peace 1675–1720* (Oxford, 1979), *passim*, quotation at p. 268; James M. Rosenheim, 'Landownership, the aristocracy and the country gentry', in Glassey, ed., *Charles II and James VII and II*, pp. 158–60.

121. Fletcher, *Reform in the Provinces*, p. 30.

122. Norma Landau, *The Justices of the Peace, 1679–1760* (Berkeley, 1984), p. 107. See also Glassey, *Justices of the Peace*, pp. 267–9; Langford, *Public Life*, pp. 393–4.

Where applied, party tests influenced appointment to the commission much more than they guaranteed or predicted who would serve actively when named: long before the era of party, in 1662, Sir John Harper of Swarson in Derbyshire was acknowledged to be 'well affected to the Kinge and church but backwards in Actinge for eith[er]'.[123] After 1689, as the prosecution of religious nonconformists ceased to be a major concern of local justices, no new cause divided benches in a way that threatened the effective conduct of civil or criminal business. Here lay a key component in what Anthony Fletcher has called 'the triumph of the gentry'.[124] Significantly, the lieutenancy rather than the magistracy led the way in campaigns to discover and disarm the disaffected, whether whigs in the 1680s or, with increasing reluctance, non-jurors in the 1690s and suspected Jacobites under Anne, George I, and George II. Even where one party dominated the public sessions of the peace, there is little sign that the routine magisterial business of the countryside was conducted solely by adherents to a particular party: what mattered was that representatives of the kingdom's governing authority were in place and performing the tasks of local governance. And when a justice unwilling to confront a partisan majority of fellow magistrates absented himself from sessions and thus took no part in the criminal and administrative business settled there, he still had plentiful powers to try to keep the local peace and resolve disputes when he acted as a justice on his own or in tandem with just one other colleague.[125]

Partisan considerations of course sometimes affected the degree of a justice's enterprise, and quarter sessions and assizes continued to serve party ends, affording opportunities to announce parliamentary candidates, endorse addresses to the crown, listen to animated sermons, and deliver equally ideological jury charges. Often, however, the ideology expressed was that of class rather than party.[126] Similarly, where individual justices behaved in a partisan manner at

123. Newton, 'Gentry of Derbyshire in the seventeenth century', p. 6.
124. Fletcher, *Reform in the Provinces*, ch. 10.
125. Ibid., pp. 143–58, 316–48; J.R. Western, *The English Militia in the Eighteenth Century: The Story of a Political Issue 1660–1802* (London, 1965), pp. 52–71; Victor Stater, *Noble Government: The Stuart Lord Lieutenancy and the Transformation of English Politics* (Athens, Georgia, 1994), ch. 5.
126. See charges contained in Lamoine, ed., *Charges to the Grand Jury 1689–1803*; Sir Peter Leicester, *Charges to the Grand Jury at Quarter Sessions 1660–1677*, E.M. Halcrow, ed., *Chetham Society*, 3rd series, 5 (1953); *The Notebook of Robert Doughty 1662–1665*, James M. Rosenheim, ed., *Norfolk Record Society* 54 (1989), pp. 89–121.

an election, as many did, their influence as landed gentlemen rather than as working magistrates may have been greater. Sir Edward Ward's electoral clout, according to a contemporary, 'turned upon his being in the commission of the peace' – on his membership, not on his action in office. Sir Walter Calverley, a justice in Yorkshire who entertained freeholders from ten neighbouring parishes in 1710 in anticipation of the county election, led nearly two hundred of them to the poll in York, a sign of his landlordly rather than his magisterial power.[127]

Whatever the capacity of the meeting of quarter sessions to serve as a vehicle for political propaganda and even vengeance, the actual conduct of official county business by the mid-eighteenth century was freer from overtly and oppressively partisan wrangling and manipulation than at the end of the seventeenth century. Perhaps as a result, the proportion of appointees who bothered to qualify themselves to act, if Kent is a guide, fell from around half to about a third between the early and middle years of the eighteenth century. Among the greater landowners, comment on the politics of sessions under the Hanoverians had less urgency and virulence than fifty years before. Lord Lovell in 1732 considered only a controversy over relocating sessions worthy of a report to a county compatriot in London. In the 1730s William Stukeley the antiquarian believed that a 'country justice has but a very silly part to act'.[128]

Even the lieutenancy, which served partisan purposes more effectively than the commission of the peace, briefly received 'a non-party character' under Queen Anne, the result of the government's uneasiness about partisanship and its fear that when county institutions were excessively factious they were ineffective. To make it too partisan diminished the lieutenancy's prestige among the gentry (and lost their cooperation) by excluding those with an expectation of appointment that verged on a sense of entitlement. So both in the ranks of deputy lieutenants and among officers of the militia too, 'party men had to be combined with moderates whose only loyalty was to the crown as such'.[129]

127. B. Wrench to [T. De Grey], 22 March 1740, Norfolk Record Office, WLS XVI/1/22, 410x1 (emphasis added): 'Calverley memorandum book', p. 126.

128. Landau, *Justices of the Peace*, p. 320; Lovell to Sir R. Walpole, 22 July 1732, Cambridge University Library, Cholmondeley (Houghton) correspondence, no. 1897; Langford, *Public Life*, pp. 390–7; quotation on p. 392.

129. Western, *English Militia*, pp. 59–61; see also Rosenheim, *Townshends of Raynham*, p. 196.

The agencies of government

The reach of crown government grew in the late seventeenth and eighteenth centuries in ways that substantially affected gentry society, and many in the landed order took advantage of the public administration that expanded with that reach. Trying to expand power via borough politics was a controversial and doubtful undertaking for landowners, and the municipal history of Great Yarmouth from the Restoration to the 1720s demonstrates the difficulties that even the greatest landed families had in using the boroughs for political ends.[130] Looking to the centre offered a more productive alternative. Some landowners indeed had no truck with crown agencies like the Ordnance Office or shipyards, the Customs or Excise, and those disbarred by their politics were allowed none. But by the middle of the century the state claimed significance as a source of employment and means of advancement for the kin and connections of the landed exceeding that of local opportunity.

The rapid turnover of office in the early years of explosive growth in central administration, roughly coinciding with William's and Anne's reigns, at first discouraged officeholders from developing loyalty to department or government. But as the civil service began in the eighteenth century to apply relatively objective standards of employment, and offer substantial salaries and career ladders for advancement, departments became more formal and rule-bound, and employees grew attached to the institutions. The persistent ties of family and patronage with specific government branches fortified 'creeping departmentalism'.[131] These developments fostered loyalty to individual departments not far removed from and readily transformed into a patriotic attachment to the state. The landowners who sought access to the patronage of this budding civil service were committing themselves and their clients to institutions that were arguably conducting the business of kingdom and nation (rather than of a fortunate few) in a way that the royal court did not and never had.

The number of secure, full-time state employees – the 'new men of English government' – increased dramatically between 1680 and

130. Gauci, *Politics and Society in Great Yarmouth*.
131. Brewer, *Sinews*, pp. 69–70, and p. 85 for the quotation; G.E. Aylmer, 'From office-holding to civil service: the genesis of modern bureaucracy', *Transactions of the Royal Historical Society*, 5th series, 30 (1980), pp. 94–7.

1730, and they included large numbers of gentry. As the executive grew in the late seventeenth century, the figure of the professional administrator emerged, offering an opportunity for a gentry younger son to serve the nation, maybe less formidably than his father or older brother did, but while serving himself too. Government position, at least in the revenue services, provided the young man with status, reasonable income, and the chance to break a family's social fall or even to rise. In order to obtain one of the 12,000 offices estimated to exist in 1725, these members of landed society (including even the offspring of nobles in the topmost of these positions) required sponsorship, and even financial support in the form of money bonds. Greater gentry and nobles often provided these, and so where their immediate families may not have entered civil service, they themselves still pursued and exercised the patronage it spawned.[132]

Of all the elements of civil service, the central revenue establishments and the different systems of assessment and collection that landowners participated in and suffered under probably made the strongest impact in reorienting the landed's relations with metropolitan authority. The tax administration brought central government into the localities in an unprecedented way. As the Treasury under Charles II gained control over government spending and attained fiscal expertise, it gradually abandoned tax farming in favour of direct collection by central authorities. The introduction in the 1670s of new methods for collecting national taxes limited the power in the counties of tax commissioners (landed men named by parliament in the authorizing legislation), and bestowed it instead on royal appointees. Government collection demanded government supervision, and by the time William III called on his new kingdom's tax system, it relied on an infrastructure well embedded in the countryside yet fairly effectively controlled from the centre.[133]

The patterns of fiscal imposition gave prominence to a central orientation in the tax system. For all the attention the land tax garnered, it and other direct taxes were not the principal sources

132. Holmes, *Augustan England*, pp. 250–5 and part 3 generally; Brewer, *Sinews*, pp. xvii, 79–80.
133. Brewer, *Sinews*, pp. 91–5; C.D. Chandaman, *The English Public Revenue 1660–1688* (Oxford, 1975), pp. 28–31, 71–4, 183–6; Howard Tomlinson, 'Financial and administrative developments in England, 1660–1688', in J. R. Jones, ed., *The Restored Monarchy 1660–1688* (Totowa, New Jersey, 1979), pp. 100–3. For the local impact of changes in tax administration see Coleby, *Central Government and the Localities*, pp. 114–25, 169–71, 191–6.

of revenue for the later Stuart and first Hanoverian governments. Except during the reigns of William and Anne, indirect taxes were the predominant form of levy, which consigned revenue collection to the hands of centrally appointed officials.[134] This was not the case with the land tax, yet its administration also reinforced the tendency to acknowledge central authority, partly because it required an annual reauthorization that was one of the most charged political issues parliament regularly confronted. Its commissioners were also appointed by parliament in the authorizing statute. As a result, the tax figured both as an individual burden and as an instance of government intervention, rather like modern income tax. Its administration was essentially provincial, comprised of assessors and collectors from village elites and of tax commissioners (few of whom took an active part in administration) overwhelmingly drawn from the county gentry. Yet while the nomination of gentry commissioners year after year paid homage to local social hierarchies, the tax in operation placed participants in a direct relationship with central government and made the national administration familiar to them.[135]

Some gentry commissioners used metropolitan templates as guides to the procedures they should follow locally. Lord Fitzwilliam was surprised to learn that gentry in Northamptonshire's land tax commission who visited the metropolis did not 'consult with the commissioners in these parts to learne what methods they take'. Other commissioners, like those in Cumberland, deviated from legislative prescription and employed traditional assessments when levying the land tax, and there seems to have been room for local improvisation. But it is notable that Cumberland residents who objected to their rates appealed against them not to the quarter sessions, as was proper, but to those whom they believed to be empowered, the statutorily and centrally appointed tax commissioners.[136]

A measure of bipartisanship affected administration of the land tax.[137] From its inception the land tax in operation was only mar-

134. Following Chandaman, indirect taxation is here equated with the ordinary revenue and direct taxation with extraordinary supply: Chandaman, *English Public Revenue*, pp. 78, 138, 332–3, 348–63; Brewer, *Sinews*, pp. 95–101.
135. Brooks, 'Public finance and political stability', p. 300.
136. *Fitzwilliam Correspondence*, p. 33; J.V. Beckett, 'Local custom and the "new taxation"', *Northern History* 12 (1976), pp. 105–26, especially p. 122.
137. For this and the following paragraph see Brooks, 'Public finance and political stability', pp. 293–300; J.V. Beckett, 'Land tax administration at the local level 1693–1798', in Michael Turner and Dennis Mills, eds, *Land and Property: The English Land Tax 1692–1832* (New York, 1986), pp. 163–4; Langford, *Public Life*, pp. 423–4.

ginally affected by patronage or party and raised money with little conflict, possibly because parliament's appointment of commissioners aimed at thorough geographic coverage of the counties, not at political statement. The few active commissioners served with little regard for party affiliation; the occasional presence of grandees at general meetings seemed to develop consensus rather than division. Unlike the excise and other indirect taxes, the land tax's administration did not seem to contribute materially to the executive power manifest in the bureaucracy that grew around those levies. Land tax administration had its political component, and politicians at the centre derived some political credit by gratifying with appointments those gentlemen or aspirant gentlemen who valued the title of commissioner. But this was limited benefit indeed.

The overall ease of administration suggests that the land tax and its machinery were not believed to be fundamentally corrosive or harmful. None the less, they exemplify the proliferating linkages of central government and localities, which in other circumstances *could* seem malign. Unwelcome but tolerated, the tax enhanced the population's awareness of and involvement in 'a national administration which remained close and intelligible, and non- or bi-partisan'.[138] That the relations of provincials with the central government in this area were seen as generally benign is testimony to the state's success in tying together central government and the nation.

The case of John first Baron Ashburnham (1656–1710) demonstrates the effect of this linkage on the social identity and political career of a landowner who viewed bureaucratic growth dubiously and with hostility.[139] He had little concern for the politics of court and ministry and did not imagine his own interest could advance with that of the state. Placed between the conflicting demands of government and his constituents in the borough of Hastings, the tory Ashburnham translated the traditional, factional divisions of Hastings's civic politics onto a national plane, sometimes working with the borough's whig member to recommend clients for advancement.

In confronting the increasingly formalized career structure of state employment, Ashburnham was limited in his capacity to assist clients. He had no problem intervening effectively for those starting out: he could secure them training and then forward names of

138. Brooks, 'Public finance and political stability', p. 300.
139. Idem, 'Interest, patronage and professionalism', pp. 51–70.

candidates as vacancies occurred in the revenue services. After that point, however, the continued application of standards of competency and performance restricted his influence. Despite his best efforts, nothing Ashburnham did could prevent the dismissal of a tidewaiter whose appointment he had managed, and who came from the minor gentry essential to Ashburnham's local political interest. For reasons like this, Ashburnham rued the expanding power of state agencies and their intrusion into his life. But even so, and despite his dislike for the pressure put on him by his constituents, he solicited state positions for his supporters in Sussex.

Generally contemptuous of the state, he engaged with it in a way that marked him as a man of a transitional era, attempting with only limited success to shape the system he encountered. When he tried to bully the land tax commissioners in Westminster to lower his assessment, he found them so inspired by the imperatives of law and state that they ignored all private interests in executing their tasks, where he would have had them take into account his particular situation and status. Throughout his encounters with the patronage network, he never fully comprehended the larger framework enfolding his life – a kingdom becoming a great power steered by an increasingly impersonal state machine.[140]

Ashburnham's case illustrates the conflicting demands imposed by the evolving modern state on those participating in the ruling of the kingdom, demands recapitulated in the language of another landed man, Bernard Swainson, as he forwarded nominees for posts in the Excise Office in the 1740s. As he did he promised to propose only his 'own particular friends or those who shall be well deserveing or duely qualified'. Tersely but clearly he identified the attributes that mattered in assessing applicants – connection ('particular friends'), loyalty ('those . . . well deserving'), and training ('duely qualified'). And when, after Swainson died, another in turn recommended two men who had been 'instructed for the Excise', the label indicated how substantial a weight due qualification – that is, expertise – now carried.[141] This weight was a measure of the transformation of the landed experience. '[S]tate demands and state standards [had come] to dominate the established, customary processes of society', with the result that landowners, who like Ashburnham and Swainson played the patronage game with varying degrees of willingness, had

140. Idem, 'John, 1st Baron Ashburnham and the state, c.1688–1710', *Historical Research* 60, no. 141 (1987), pp. 64–79.

141. B. Swainson to A. Earle, 2 February 1744 and J. Spedding to same, 29 October 1746, Norfolk Record Office, BUL 4/66/1/5, 606x1 and BUL 4/77/6, 606x3.

no alternative but to participate if they hoped to have a place in the eighteenth century's changing political world.[142]

Conclusion

In what ways had that world changed since the Restoration? It had seen the elevation of parliament to an uncontested position of superiority in the political realm. It had seen the emergence of state institutions that had insinuated themselves inextricably into English daily life. It had seen both the rise and then the decline of party ideology and identity as determinative forces in the landed elite's political actions. It had seen all of these developments intensify existing tendencies among the landed to orient themselves toward the cosmopolitan in politics – toward the capital, toward central institutions, toward larger than local fields of thought.

More than any other element in society, England's landed elite benefited from the growth of state institutions and activity during the reigns of the last two Stuarts and of George I and George II, when the aristocracy's national identity solidified partly for the same reasons that Great Britain was forged as a nation after 1707: because the landed began 'to see this newly invented nation as a usable resource'.[143] Gentry between the reigns of Charles II and Anne came to accept the continuous, largely non-political service of state employees as a public good, and thus put their sense of commitment to the nation to use in the effort to gain state employment. Such service was above all necessary for effective prosecution of England's foreign wars under William III and Anne. Just as one outgrowth of war, the market in government stock, let gentry safely diversify their investments and thus perhaps mitigated country mistrust of both government and paper securities, so another consequence of war, the burgeoning of state offices that landowners and their relatives often filled, also had its role in changing attitudes to government. This growth made the existing social hierarchy nervously conscious of the visible arrival of a new class of public servants (and even spurred efforts to keep that group out of the House of Commons), but awareness of their appearance was in fact self-awareness, since so many public servants came from the landed order.[144] Gentry younger

142. Brooks, 'Interest, patronage and professionalism', p. 59.
143. Linda Colley, *Britons: Forging the Nation 1707–1837* (New Haven, 1992), p. 55 for quotation; see also Brewer, *Sinews*, p. 204.
144. Holmes, *Augustan England*, pp. 242, 254–5, 262, 266, 282–3.

sons who turned to employment in the military or the state bureau-cracy further honed landed identity by perpetuating 'a distinction between those who worked for the public good or as public servants and those who worked for private gain or profit'.[145]

In these circumstances, once-potent country ideology lost some of its power to shape landed identity, especially where its strands of thought encouraged a landed identity at odds with the metro-politan one otherwise being fostered. Country adherents expressed hostility to patronage and the ubiquitous placeman, to the 'meas-ures – standing armies, national debts, excise schemes – whereby the activities of administration [grew] beyond Parliament's con-trol'. Their humanist vision of the polity portrayed Britain as 'a democracy of the independent, an aristocracy of the leisured and well-born, a fixed hierarchy of the independent and dependent'.[146]

This vision was ceasing to accord with the character of English society and politics after the end of the seventeenth century. The politics of virtuous public independence articulated by a range of commentators both whig and tory lost ground in the reigns of the first two Georges, despite the appearance of powerful pleas for disinterested political service and the subordination of private to public interest. But these calls were being voiced at a time when social and economic developments made almost impossible a vir-tuous polity based on the leadership of the landed. The virtuous citizen pursuing the *vita activa* was out of place in a world of credit and commerce.[147]

An awareness of politics as an increasingly national exercise, a highly complicated set of negotiations between core and periphery that mostly favoured the former, accompanied an apparent decline in commitment *to* politics, insofar as politics was expressed through traditional public service. Gentry had once embraced magistracy as a duty; now they tended to shun it. Parliamentary seats that once had been assumed in shows of consensual selection as signs of attainment in the honour community were now far more avidly and instrumentally sought – and bought – as means of leverage and access. By the mid-eighteenth century, a politics emphasizing civic vir-tue was itself being transformed into a privately oriented politics, one

145. Brewer, *Sinews*, pp. 204–10, quotation on p. 206; Stone and Stone, *An Open Elite?*, pp. 225–8.

146. J.G.A. Pocock, *Politics, Language and Time: Essays on Political Thought and History* (New York, 1973), pp. 125, 138, and pp. 104–47 generally.

147. Shelley Burtt, *Virtue Transformed: Political Argument in England, 1688–1740* (Cambridge, 1992), *passim*; Pocock, *Machiavellian Moment*, ch. 13.

emphasizing personal virtues rather than those of the citizen. The concept of civic virtue in the public arena was losing its attraction and was being displaced both as a *desideratum* of public life and as an explanation of the nature of public life. In its place the virtues of sociability, the ideal of the gentleman of manners, the ideal of politeness, were being erected. Attendant upon those values was a growing disinclination among the landed to engage daily with the ranks of those their forebears had once served and rather to seek out the socially and culturally similar, a disinclination that the next chapter explores.

CHAPTER SIX

Cultural Separation and Cultural Identity

Introduction

The trauma of civil war made the English landed order wary of the power of popular political opinion and action. That wariness did not soon diminish, even though during the half-century 1675–1725 elite and non-elite segments of society met in the political arena, as the electorate grew and party politicians actively sought popular support.[1] In other areas, especially social and cultural ones, the barriers between upper and lower levels of society were raised. Contacts between elite and common folk, based on bonds of faith or local residence or communal politics, had once been frequent and sometimes close. The reigns of the last Stuart and first Hanoverian monarchs, however, saw literal and metaphoric distance grow between landowners and the rest of society, and the elite's separation from social inferiors helped its consolidation. The social and cultural distancing of landowners from the rest of the countryside was not new in 1650, nor was it universal and complete in 1750. Elite and common folk did not inexorably march away from one another, and because landed gentry had long been integral to rural society, more than isolated figures in a country house, their disengagement from that society was bound to be slow and incremental.[2] But it was taking place.

---

1. J.H. Plumb, *The Growth of Political Stability in England 1675–1725* (London, 1967), esp. ch. 2.

2. On the political interaction see Tim Harris, *London Crowds in the Reign of Charles II: Propaganda and Politics from the Restoration until the Exclusion Crisis* (Cambridge, 1987); John Patrick Montaño, 'The quest for consensus: the Lord Mayor's Day shows in the 1670s', in Gerald MacLean, ed., *Culture and Society in the Stuart Restoration* (Cambridge, 1995), pp. 31–51; Nicholas Rogers, *Whigs and Cities: Popular Politics in the Age of Walpole and Pitt* (Oxford, 1989); Frank O'Gorman, *Voters, Patrons, and*

Persistence of contact

In some spheres, separation was not pronounced and in others countervailing influences appear. In the early eighteenth century, an innovative project like the series of popularized histories produced by the bookseller Nathaniel Crouch appealed to high and middling cultures alike. In Georgian Bristol a large public gained access to a wide range of locally published works that addressed an amorphously defined social readership. In a 'scientific' discipline like medicine, lines were blurred between popular and elite practice, as the quality still swallowed popular medical beliefs and the less well-off were more exposed to the attentions and took more of the nostrums of professional medical practitioners.[3]

An old, community-oriented concept of social order was also at least partly resurrected by some of the gentry in the first generation after the Restoration. As cultural conservatives whose 'modes of thought and behaviour were deeply imbedded in the experiences of rural life', some gentry were well disposed to and involved in the customary practices and pastimes of the countryside.[4] Although contact between landlord families and the rest of country society grew rarer and more stilted, the Christian charitable impulse and the remnants of a tradition of hospitality guaranteed some continued interaction between the landed and their neighbours and dependants. Gentry-sponsored Christmas celebrations in the countryside under the later Stuarts notably retained features that medieval landowners would have recognized. In his later years Bulstrode Whitelocke, who died in 1675, stopped spending the holiday in London and returned instead to his Berkshire estate, where he entertained friends and neighbours with 'Great feasting', and less lavishly fed those 'who had given him a worke day in Harvest'. At the

Parties: The Unreformed Electoral System of Hanoverian England 1734–1832 (Oxford, 1989). The discussion of popular culture still begins with Peter Burke, *Popular Culture in Early Modern Europe* (New York, 1978), but see also Tim Harris, 'Problematising popular culture', in Harris, ed., *Popular Culture in England, c. 1500–1850* (New York, 1995), pp. 1–27.

3. Robert Mayer, 'Nathaniel Crouch, bookseller and historian: popular historiography and cultural power in late seventeenth-century England', *Eighteenth-Century Studies* 27 (1993–94), pp. 391–419; Jonathan Barry, 'The press and the politics of culture in Bristol, 1660–1775', in Jeremy Black and Jeremy Gregory, eds, *Culture, Politics and Society in Britain, 1660–1800* (Manchester and New York, 1991), pp. 62–5; Roy Porter, 'The people's health in Georgian England', in Harris, ed., *Popular Culture*, pp. 124–42.

4. Robert W. Malcolmson, *Popular Recreations in English Society 1700–1850* (Cambridge, 1973), p. 68; David Underdown, *Revel, Riot and Rebellion: Popular Politics and Culture in England 1603–1660* (Oxford, 1985), pp. 280–8.

same time, Sir Justinian Isham in Northamptonshire provided finely graded bounty – to local poor on Christmas, to labourers on Boxing Day, and to the 'more substantial inhabitants' on 27 December. Nearly thirty years later, the Yorkshireman Walter Calverley feasted all his tenants along with 'some of our relations' in the January after he inherited his estate (although he apparently stopped doing so shortly thereafter), and Lord Fitzwilliam at his seat at Milton, Northamptonshire, still had Christmas doles distributed to the poor in his neighbourhood.[5]

Late seventeenth-century landowners were less generous on other holidays, but some of them subsidized feasts, revels, and the red-letter days of the civic calendar with food, drink, music, and spectacle. Others commemorated family births and weddings with celebrations involving tenants and employees, although the occasions probably went unacknowledged when the family was absent. Still, as late as 1725 an observer claimed that at harvest feasts 'the Servant and his Master are alike, and every Thing is done with an equal Freedom. They sit at the same Table, converse freely together, and spend the remaining Part of the Night in dancing, singing, etc. without any Difference or Distinction.'[6]

This unusual and perhaps implausible description of egalitarian socializing was unlikely to be found where nobility were involved, a reminder that there were layers of distinction within the landed order. It also leaves a misleading impression that when elite and non-elite interacted on religious, commemorative, or recreational occasions, they did so on an equal footing, as members of a single customary world. But rural culture was never historically unified, and different groups participated in the same event from different positions on the cultural map. The landed elite, after all, rarely attended all local festivities in any year, and when present they inhabited the rural world on a superior, even remote, footing. Those who graced country activities never intended to abridge social distances by doing so, and such a crossing was especially unlikely to

5. *The Diary of Bulstrode Whitelocke 1605–1675*, Ruth Spalding, ed., *Records of Social and Economic History*, new series, 13 (1990), pp. 685, 699, 713, 763 (for quotation), 804, 820, 834; *Isham Diary*, p. 71; 'Calverley memorandum book', p. 73; *Fitzwilliam Correspondence*, pp. 26, 97, 135.

6. David Cressy, *Bonfires and Bells: National Memory and the Protestant Calendar in Elizabethan and Stuart England* (Berkeley, 1989), chs 5, 11. Cressy's use of urban evidence may maximize community and minimize individual roles in providing bonfires, although he acknowledges that one 'could mount, host or put on a bonfire, rather as one might give a party': p. 85; Malcolmson, *Popular Recreations*, pp. 49, 63–8, 81 (for quotation); Heal and Holmes, *Gentry*, pp. 287–9.

occur when the landed took part in ritual celebrations as spectators rather than as more active participants. In addition, many land-owners during the interregnum had seen social subordinates threat-en and displace the established order, and whether as a result or coincidence, the elite subsequently displayed less interest in many traditional festivals and rituals. Those aristocrats who frequented customary pastimes in the Restoration era did so in a manner that diminished their social interaction with other groups and deep-ened pre-existing cultural divisions between the 'respectable' and lower orders.[7]

Where the restored rulers of the countryside joined in popular rituals, they unsurprisingly manipulated them to promote obedi-ence to church and state. The joyous celebrations of coronation day in 1661 were carefully orchestrated around the nation, and in the 1670s the government used the Lord Mayor's Day pageantry in London to promote ideological consensus. Many traditional rituals persisted unaffected by gentry designs, and little effort – and none successful – was made to suppress rowdy observances like those of May Day and Shrovetide. But it is no coincidence that the Lord of Misrule was the element of Christmas celebrations that did not reappear after the suppressions of the interregnum, the taste of genuine misrule having soured appetites for even its simulacrum.[8]

It did not lie within the power of the landed to manipulate celebrations at will, especially in highly politicized times, but if they could not shape old ones, the kingdom's rulers did promote new commemorations, presumably (if not actually) less likely to occa-sion disorder or carry untoward messages. These notably included 30 January, the anniversary of Charles I's execution; 29 May, the date of Charles II's entry into London in 1660 and his birthday; 5 November, a traditional holiday of national deliverance; and, to a lesser degree, 23 April, the feast of England's patron St George and Charles II's coronation day. Those elite who participated in what might be called politically sanctioned celebrations did so in a dis-tanced way that anticipated the theatrical appearances to which their patronage of popular culture was brought – perhaps through fear of the populace's own demonstrations – by the mid-eighteenth century. Yet each of these days significantly marked a national and political anniversary, whose celebration, even when put to partisan

7. Ronald Hutton, *The Rise and Fall of Merry England: The Ritual Year 1400–1700* (Oxford, 1994), chs 4–6.

8. Underdown, *Revel, Riot and Rebellion*, pp. 281–3; Montaño, 'The quest for con-sensus'; Hutton, *Merry England*, pp. 242–3.

uses or appropriated by the 'mob', propounded images of a single if not united kingdom.[9]

Public separation

Ironically, the interests of a united kingdom in the Augustan era also contributed to the marked absence of landed gentry from the countryside, where their regular if not constant presence had been a feature of English social life for the past two centuries. The absenteeism of landlords, their families, and their establishments mightily contributed to and symbolized the gaps between high and popular culture. On the one hand, the absence of the landlord class became more pronounced – and more pronounced upon – from the late seventeenth century. As the landed spent less time in the countryside, their absence generated complaints that landlords were shirking their local duties for those at the centre or in favour of diversions. Their households often sucked country products away to London rather than consuming them in – and employing the labour of – the neighbourhood. When gentry spent it in the country, the eighteenth-century Christmas resembled Christmas past, but they increasingly held this traditional season of open house in London or elsewhere. Indeed, landed families were in rural residence so infrequently that they could not possibly fulfil the local functions expected of them.[10]

On the other hand, when the landed *were* in the country, they were becoming less visible to and more remote from tenants and local community, making only occasional contact with those they lorded over. On the occasions when they interacted with inferiors, the elite did so in ways that emphasized social distance and reflected and nurtured separate elite identity. Bulstrode Whitelocke and Sir Justinian Isham distinguished between provision for 'poor neighbours', for 'those who had given . . . a worke day in Harvest' and for 'the better sort' – who were all variously entertained on separate days. Sir Walter Calverley's graded celebrations of his wife's arrival in the country in 1707 illustrate the same point. He first

---

9. Hutton, *Merry England*, ch. 7; Cressy, *Bonfires and Bells*, ch. 11; Linda Colley, *Britons: Forging the Nation 1707–1837* (New Haven, 1992), pp. 19–22; E.P. Thompson, *Customs in Common: Studies in Traditional Popular Culture* (New York, 1991), ch. 2, esp. pp. 44–9, 71–5; Tim Harris, *Politics under the Later Stuarts: Party Conflict in a Divided Society 1660–1715* (London, 1993), pp. 185–6.

10. Langford, *Public Life*, pp. 378–82; Hainsworth, *Stewards*, pp. 13–18.

cared for 'all the neighbouring gentlemen and their ladyes', then two days later 'had my tenants and neighbours and wives at another entertainment on purpose'.[11] The phrase 'on purpose' underlines the segregation of the groups of diners and renders the presence of the peer group of 'neighbouring gentlemen and their ladyes' natural by comparison with that of tenants and lesser neighbours.

The party Nicholas Blundell held in 1712 after completing a major agricultural venture on his estate also demonstrates the subtle contextualization of landed identity. As a Catholic in a relatively remote part of the country, Lancashire, Blundell may have had less reason to stand on status distinctions than others of the squirearchy. He sometimes socialized with his tenants, and in preparing to celebrate the end of marling his fields he taught locals a sword dance and helped to make decorations and costumes. Yet he ultimately – and, in the context of this argument, unsurprisingly – provided entertainment for 'my Neighbours and Tenants' separately from that for the employees, the 'Marlers, Spreaders, Water-Baylis and Carters'. He differentiated between those he himself had 'eat and drunk with' and those who merely 'din'd here'. Similarly, when he commented that the marl-pit was decorated 'very much to the Satisfaction of the Spectators', he discriminated between participants and observers, where the latter included the 'Neighbours and Tenants' whose relatively equal status to Blundell was testified by the presents they brought his wife and by their corporeal presence at his table.[12]

Although the actions of Blundell and Calverley – from Lancashire and Yorkshire, respectively – made statements about the gap between the genteel and the common folk, these actions entailed social meetings, confrontation, physical presence. The message of many more gentry was commonly delivered by absence. As Paul Langford has argued, the greatest consequence of landowners' presence in the country was often the impact their servants had on the local labouring population, rather than any impression made by landlord or lady. Both the continuous intercession of stewards and bailiffs, and the emergence of an agrarian system that placed tenant farmers between landowners and those who actually worked the land, contributed to this distance. Many of the landed men did not go to quarter sessions when in the country, and often neither

11. *Whitelocke Diary*, p. 763; *Isham Diary*, p. 71; 'Calverley memorandum book', pp. 117–18.

12. *The Great Diurnal of Nicholas Blundell of Little Crosby, Lancashire, 2, 1712–1719,* J.J. Bagley, ed., *Record Society of Lancashire and Cheshire* 112 (1970), pp. 25–7.

men nor women attended personally to charity. By and large, the landed socialized within their group, with other landowners on their estates and in private houses. When travelling they went with quite small retinues. Only a few pursuits, like cockfights and cricket matches, saw social strata mix, and contemporaries sometimes questioned the propriety, and a modern observer might doubt the depth, of the social integration that occurred even there.[13]

The aristocracy showed their influence over such proceedings in the organization and structure they provided horse-racing and cricket before and during the eighteenth century. In other arenas, however, gentry more straightforwardly eschewed socializing with inferiors, perhaps a sign of status anxiety. Certainly there were reasons for insecurity, indications that traditional status markers had lost some of their meaning. A century of history had established the fact of social mobility, and civil war had shown that the power of tradition was frangible. Some forms of distinction between social ranks, like those based on ancient lineage, had lost some of their force and centrality in claims to status. Heralds' visitations after 1660 received little attention and came to a halt, and funeral monuments ceased to bear the family effigies that had once spoken of the importance of lines of descent. New financial and legal safeguards for land diminished the importance of heraldic symbolism in maintaining status, and although in the eighteenth century coats of arms adorned the plate, coaches, and liveries of aristocrats, they were used less as 'a vital claim to status based on lineage' and more as 'a matter of taste'.[14]

Growing concern with taste, with refinement and politeness, helped to construct an elite masculine identity that depended on separation from the boorish, even to some extent from the boors among the landed class itself.[15] Where heraldry no longer served as a separator, the 'language of politeness' emerging at the end of the seventeenth century did. It rewrote the definition of a gentleman (and to some extent that of a lady) in terms of manners more than in traditional terms of civic behaviour. A gentleman showed his taste in his social and cultural activities and interests, and Lawrence Klein argues that other elements of a gentleman's identity, 'political activity, estate management, local justice and so forth', were

13. Malcolmson, *Popular Recreations*, pp. 40–1, 49–50.
14. Heal and Holmes, *Gentry*, pp. 38–42; quotation on p. 40.
15. Thompson, *Customs in Common*, p. 43; Langford, *Public Life*, p. 383; Beckett, *Aristocracy*, pp. 346–7; Heal and Holmes, *Gentry*, pp. 308–10; Bruce Redford, *Venice & the Grand Tour* (New Haven, 1996), ch. 1.

'not so much excluded as left invisible'. While preceding chapters have suggested here that both political activity and estate management had a good deal of visibility within landed society, the singular image of the gentleman partaking in activities inextricably tied to the countryside was joined by the image of the gentleman in and of the town. The new insistence on the gentlemanly character of cultural expression was establishing a connection between it and elite social status that did a great deal 'to fortify the distinctions between patrician and plebeian in culture'.[16]

The proud and careful use of militia titles starting in the reign of Charles II provided a nominal means to distinguish within the ranks of the landed. Cultural and social distances were also geographically enforced on the hunting field (especially in the foxhunt), a major instance of social segregation considering the time aristocratic men devoted to the chase. At races, as in Cowbridge in the 1740s, separate prizes were offered on the basis of social standing. Social discrimination also took place in political contexts, as when the Duke of Richmond was cautioned to show strength at Lewes' municipal elections in 1742 but not to 'bring any but Gentlemen or very topping Fa[r]mers' with him. Richard Nash levelled ranks within Bath's assembly rooms but he exalted difference by dictating who was admitted in the first place. Coffee houses contrastingly admitted all sorts of customers, yet individual establishments had their particular identities too – political, occupational, and social.[17]

Separation whether within or as against the landed was motivated by notions of suitable behaviour as well as those of suitable companionship. When Thomas Wyndham came into a landed estate by indirect inheritance he declined to pursue a claim to some local property rights because he 'scorn[ed] to enter the lists unless with superiors'. He observed tellingly that he was

ill-qualify'd for petty country contests, few of which are worth the serious thought of an hour, yet custome obliges us to vindicate our claim to rights of no real value, while we despise both the person and injury, who seem to have nothing so much at heart as victory about NOTHING, and never appear so empty as when full of themselves.

16. Lawrence E. Klein, 'Liberty, manners, and politeness in early eighteenth-century England', *Historical Journal* 32 (1989), p. 588.
    17. Jenkins, *Making of a Ruling Class*, p. 267; *Richmond–Newcastle Correspondence*, p. 80; Kathleen Wilson, 'Citizenship, empire and modernity in the English provinces, c. 1720–1790', *Eighteenth-Century Studies* 29 (1995), p. 76; Bryant Lillywhite, *London Coffee Houses: A Reference Book of Coffee Houses of the Seventeenth, Eighteenth and Nineteenth Centuries* (London, 1963).

The plunder of my estate and encroachment of neihbours ought not
to disturb my rest, who am obliged for what they are pleas'd to per-
mit me to enjoy.[18]

Perhaps 'ill-qualify'd' and certainly disinclined to such 'petty country contests', Wyndham took the view that reputation with one's
tenants and lesser neighbours, whether gained from paternalist rule
or in battle over rights, mattered less than the figure he cut among
his equals and superiors in class-specific activities.

Not fully comforted by regaining their hereditary privileges in
parliament in 1660, the titled nobility were similarly keen to obtain
respect as well as rights, and with unprecedented alacrity they used
the medieval statutes of *scandalum magnatum*, by which any utter-
ances spoken to dishonour nobles were made defamatory. In the
generation after the Restoration, nobles brought numerous legal
actions in defence of their reputations, on the basis of words sometimes as vague as the charge that one was 'an unworthy man and
acts against law and reason'. Vague or not, such challenges to honour troubled nobles insecure in their social pre-eminence, although
juries and judges eased noble plaintiffs' distress by usually finding
for them and sometimes awarding them thousands of pounds in
damages. The chief justice of King's Bench went so far in 1670 as to
enjoin that words directed at a peer should be construed 'in the
worst sense' so that 'the honour of such great persons may be preserved'. In the late 1670s and 1680s, *scandalum magnatum* took on an
overt political cast, most famously as the Duke of York employed
it against his enemies. The political abuse of the procedure and
the end to large awards lessened its popularity by the end of the
century. Yet the decline of cases is best explained by a triumphant
peerage's diminished need to assert its stature in this fashion after
the reign of James II.[19]

Legally protected by the statutes, a narrow element of the landed
order could thus try to keep inferiors at bay. Less directly, distance
was maintained through several developments that weakened social
patterns which had traditionally brought gentry into contact with
other groups. The honour culture that once spurred much elite
charity was losing force. When Lord Fitzwilliam's son died in 1699
the father was willing to provide mourning gloves to his tenants

---

18. T. Wyndham to [Mr Jones], 10 December 1748, Norfolk Record Office, WKC
7/32/23, 404x2.

19. John C. Lassiter, 'Defamation of peers: the rise and decline of the action for
scandalum magnatum, 1497–1773', *American Journal of Legal History* 22 (1978), pp. 216–
36; quotations on pp. 224–5.

and any neighbouring gentlemen who attended the funeral, but he shut his purse to the poor, refusing 'to give to all the mobb that are not my tennants' and insisting that his steward was 'to be at no mannor of expences, not so much as a pot of ale'. Benevolent impulses found new outlets, even if not entirely diverted from the old. In the mid-1670s the Earl of Shaftesbury still had the remnants of meals presented to the poor at the gates of his house in Wimborne St Giles, and Sir John Norton, who died in 1687, was similarly a throwback to the past whose generous table first fed his guests, 'afterwards feasted the Hall, and [then] plentifully reliev'd the Poor at his Gate'.[20]

But generally speaking, the allowances and gifts that once paternalistically connected landlord with tenants and employees were withheld by estate stewards, who rightly saw that a 'Predecessor's favours' were quickly 'insisted on as Rights' and that the minor expenses they involved none the less 'amount to a Sume at the end'. When the squire of Shalston (Buckinghamshire) in 1731 provided bread, cheese, malt, and hops for rogation processors, he cautiously insisted that his largess was 'no custom but my free gift only'.[21] Similarly, before Sir William Robinson died in 1737 he was in the practice of making a Christmas gift of £5 to the poor of Topcliffe (Yorkshire) 'in order that they might not be troublesome in begging at the door, as they usually have been'. His son, who gave nothing in 1738 because he had not been in residence there that summer, continued the bounty thereafter but by 1746 had progressively reduced it to £2.10.0 and was determined 'to order this matter so, that this gift may not be claimed as due of right to the poor'.[22] In such fashion, gifts in kind and personal gestures that brought landed benefactors close to the lower orders were being replaced by cash, which was often directed to institutions rather than to known individuals. The Earl of Cardigan subscribed to the fund for clergymen's widows in the 1720s; Sir James Lowther underwrote almshouses and then a workhouse for the poor of Whitehaven in the 1730s and 1740s.[23]

20. *Fitzwilliam Correspondence*, p. 62; J.H. Bettey, 'Lord Shaftesbury's estate and gardening notebook, 1675', *Notes & Queries for Somerset and Dorset* 33 (1994), pp. 295–6; Heal and Holmes, *Gentry*, p. 284.

21. Thompson, *Customs in Common*, p. 39; Malcolmson, *Popular Recreations*, p. 58.

22. G. Hinchcliffe, 'The Robinsons of Newby Park and Newby Hall, Part 2', *Yorkshire Archaeological Journal* 64 (1992), p. 201.

23. *Eaton to Cardigan Letters*, pp. 99–100; Beckett, *Coal and Tobacco*, pp. 194–5. See also David Hayton, 'Moral reform and country politics in the late seventeenth-century House of Commons', *Past & Present* 128 (1990), pp. 66–8. Langford, *Public Life*, pp. 490–500 places the shift to institutional subscription later in the century and associates it with the middle class.

Where more formal and distanced giving testified to the elite's removal from the locality, it remained a distinguishing assertion of *noblesse*, and distinction continued to be what the gentle classes sought. Even new, fundamentally public, and socially mixed gatherings asserted distinctions. At theatre and opera, in assemblies and on promenades in provincial towns, in all sorts of public settings, mingling was truncated and unequal. Horse racing, which with landed patronage developed on a national scale in the late seventeenth century, remained essentially 'an aristocratic preserve' in the next century, especially at the most prestigious sites like Newmarket, even though meets were not limited to the elite. Gentry presence dominated, and the other diversions that grew up around race meetings were particularly directed at the elite. Grandstands that accommodated the quality at racecourses physically and socially divided the spectators into status groups, and they removed the upper orders from view.[24]

This shielding was part of a continuing shift whereby, as the eighteenth century progressed, the landed were conceived of and appeared more as observers than as persons whose activities others observed. The occlusion of aristocracy reversed historical patterns and perceptions. The lower orders saw the aristocracy's houses in town and country, saw their landscapes, saw their servants, their professional employees, their gamekeepers and game. But landowners were less visible than they had once been. They were mostly shuttered in their houses, curtained in their coaches, hidden in private pews at church, and more audible than seen when chasing foxes. Screened from view in the countryside and unobserved by the rural element that used to be more familiar with gentry actions and behaviour, the elite's profile in town was higher but still limited, since they lived in socially segregated neighbourhoods, were difficult to see in theatre boxes, and were protected by ticket and occasionally even costumed or masked at social events like assemblies and balls.[25]

The occasions when male members of the elite were truly prominent were more compelling for being stylized and dramatic. But

24. Beckett, *Aristocracy*, p. 357; Jenkins, *Making of a Ruling Class*, pp. 267–8; Mark Girouard, 'The country house and the country town', in Gervase Jackson-Stops, Gordon J. Schochet and Lena Cowen Orlin, and Elisabeth Blair MacDougall, eds, *The Fashioning and Functioning of the British Country House, Studies in the History of Art* 25, Center for the Advanced Study in the Visual Arts, Symposium Papers, vol. 10 (Hanover, New Hampshire, 1989), p. 318.

25. Langford, *Public Life*, pp. 382–3.

these legal, military, or political appearances were also infrequent. Sessions occurred quarterly, assizes twice a year, other civic events annually, and militia musters were growing rare by the early eighteenth century, while parliamentary general elections took place at long intervals after 1715 and gentry did not inevitably dominate them anyway.

The landed's sheer desire for privacy played its part in this separation of great from lesser. The desire also coincided with the diminished ability of even great magnates to orchestrate imposing displays of social power, and with their lessened need to do so to maintain status and position. Although many funerals, and not just of Puritans, were private, nighttime affairs, funeral cortèges could be occasions for show – if the person of note had died away from the location of burial. And the appearance of great figures in the provinces could still elicit public acclaim in the late seventeenth and early eighteenth centuries, although most frequently this occurred in towns, where the thanks owed to patrons or high stewards or members of parliament was readily acknowledged and demonstrations of gratitude were probably easier to organize.[26]

Whether in boroughs or on the level of the county, public salutations were rare, prearranged contrivances, sparked by events important enough to warrant the unusual effort involved. Such events, moreover, were often those royally recognized or connoting national achievements. The return of a magnate to his home county was worthy of attention in times of intense political strife but less so otherwise. The trips taken by Lady Anne Clifford from castle to castle after the mid-seventeenth century warranted the accolades of the local population, from gentry down and sometimes in groups of several hundred strong, because she was Westmorland's resident aristocrat. In counties distant from London, too, away from its regular pomp and ceremony, gentry may have been most inclined to turn out for visiting dignitaries like assize justices or the Archbishop of York, who was accompanied into Yorkshire by a group of gentlemen in 1692. Fifteen years later the Bishop of Carlisle gave gratuities to the 'Boyes, servants Ringers, prisoners, Waites, &c.' who saw him out of the county of Westmorland on his way to parliament. In less remote Norfolk, Sir Robert Walpole received public acclamation in 1725 after having been made Knight of the Bath, but in the modest market town of Aylsham. And his grander county reception

26. Beckett, *Aristocracy*, pp. 344–5.

in 1733 was specially concocted by friends to ease the pain of defeat in the excise crisis.[27]

Whatever the circumstances that account for them, such events of welcome and congratulation directed specifically at figures from landed society apparently went into decline in the eighteenth century, except perhaps at elections. Movements of politically engaged figures grew unpredictable, and thus difficult to stage-manage precisely, when they revolved around the uncertain timing of parliamentary gatherings and adjournments. More importantly, improved transportation made journeys speedier and easier, trips out of one's county grew more frequent, so arrival and departure diminished in significance and often took place largely unaccompanied and mostly unheralded. The desire to celebrate or to make public statements of loyalty or antipathy did not diminish but was displaced from individual grandees onto national heroes like Admiral Vernon or John Wilkes, or onto individual or group scapegoats, like the Catholic objects of the Gordon Riots. Absent, indifferent to any but social equals when present, disengaged from neighbourhood and neighbours, many of the most powerful of the landed classes, content in their sense of collective self, were no longer fitting objects for the adulation of their provincial communities.

House and landscape

Relative disengagement from the broader culture of the country threw landowning families onto their own devices and increasingly into their houses. There, architecture and the surrounding landscape's design, reflecting changes in landed identity and presentation and serving distinctively to express eminence and rank, further distanced the elite from the rest of society. Within the elite's own circles, an expanded definition of 'polite' society brought greater informality to the country house itself, which gardens and more distant grounds began to mirror. From the second third of the eighteenth century, newly designed rooms facilitated circulation and interaction of visitors and hosts, rather than their studied presentation

27. R.T. Spence, 'Lady Anne Clifford, Countess of Dorset, Pembroke and Montgomery (1590–1676): a reappraisal', *Northern History* 15 (1979), pp. 47–8; *Nicolson Diaries*, p. 714; 'Calverley memorandum book', p. 49; *Ipswich Journal*, 26 June–3 July 1725; J.H. Plumb, *Sir Robert Walpole*, II, *The King's Minister* (London, 1960; reprinted 1972), pp. 282–3.

in set-piece encounters. Yet the country-house owners' yearning for detachment from social inferiors saw them erect back stairways and shift their kitchens and offices to other locations, displacing domestic activity (and servants) from areas they inhabited themselves.

In the environment around the country house a preference for social segregation inspired the creation of landscapes on which the stamp of possession was ostentatiously placed, originally by garden avenues and radial axes and later with the purportedly naturalistic landscape park, all of which made sensible the estate's extent. Signs of agriculture and domestic production (cultivated fields, kitchen gardens) were also being banished from view along with the rural populace.[28]

The formal, geometric gardens common in the early seventeenth century lasted into the 1750s but in modified form, larger yet simpler and often removed from the front façades of houses. By the first third of the eighteenth century they featured grassy areas and irregularly planted 'wildernesses' near the house, from which straight paths led away. The walls of earlier gardens were removed and a ha-ha in front of the house often replaced the visual barriers that fences or hedges had created between gardens and parkland. Commonly boasting a temple or ruins, gardens invited exploration by the growing number of visitors from landed society who came touring country houses and grounds. A walk through the landscape both showed the house owner's individuality, since grounds were to be viewed in a prescribed order, and cultivated that of visitors, who could interpret on their own terms what they saw. Yet one went around in company, signalling that the 'visit was as much about being a member of a particular kind of social group as it was about being an individual'. John Cleland, who thought them exceptionally boring, characterized such excursions as a 'kind of land tax', suggesting that one paid for a sense of belonging by enduring the tedium. And as legislation imposed taxes, so too did taste and convention dictate the proprieties of building and landscape in ways that led the twenty-four-year-old Philip Yorke (son of Lord Chancellor Hardwicke) to praise in 1744 the appearance 'at proper intervals'

28. On these developments see Mark Girouard, *Life in the English Country House: A Social and Architectural History* (New Haven, 1978), chs 5, 7, esp. pp. 138–9, 142–3, 151; Stone and Stone, *An Open Elite?*, chs 9, 10; Douglas D.C. Chambers, *The Planters of the English Landscape Garden: Botany, Trees, and the Georgics* (New Haven and London, 1993); Tom Williamson, *Polite Landscapes: Gardens and Society in Eighteenth-Century England* (Baltimore, 1995); J.R. Wordie, *Estate Management in Eighteenth-Century England: The Building of the Leveson-Gower Fortune* (London, 1982), p. 40; Habakkuk, *Estates System*, pp. 60–1.

of features in the landscape or to criticize the windows in an Ionic temple that were 'a little against rule'.[29]

In a manner that contributed to and revealed shared tastes, land-owners with modest acres surrounding their houses could affordably adopt several elements of this new environmental design – grass plats, removal of walls, the avenue – creating surroundings as fash-ionable and culturally symbolic of status as those of their greatest neighbours.[30] The most desirable changes in the country-house environment, however, entailed the widest possible landscape, and for those who had them all, gardens and pleasure grounds near the house received less attention in the early eighteenth century than parks away from it. As early as 1700, Timothy Nourse had situated the ideal country house in a park 'at the least a Mile and a half over every way' (which is more than 1400 acres), but only in the 1720s and 1730s did this and other innovative ideas about landscape gain hold, although then the hold was strong. Joseph Spence (writing at mid-century) maintained that by the 1720s a new national taste had changed the meaning of the 'very name of Gardens' to denote 'the disposition of the Land, Water, Plantations and Views about our Villas in the Country'. By mid-century many country mansions had been isolated in the middle of inviting landscape parks, although it took until the end of the eighteenth century for that park virtually to define membership in the landed order.[31] Landowners began to value expanse more than intricacy, perhaps desirous of demonstrat-ing their control over the increasingly enclosed countryside around their seats. Bragging about his improvements at Gosfield Hall in Essex, Robert Nugent stressed their extent: 'the lawns are greater, the water is greater, the plantations are much greater'.[32]

Paintings of the landed estate, which had earlier featured views toward the country house, reflected this preference for expansive-ness as the century wore on, more commonly directing their gaze across the landscape.[33] The landscape park became the object

29. Williamson, *Polite Landscapes*, p. 67; Langford, *Public Life*, p. 382, citing *Memoirs of a Coxcomb* (1751); Joyce Godber, 'The Marchioness Grey of Wrest Park', *Bedfordshire Historical Record Society* 47 (1968), pp. 126, 129; Adrian Tinniswood, *A History of Country House Visiting: Five Centuries of Tourism and Taste* (Oxford, 1989), ch. 4, especially pp. 75–7.

30. Williamson, *Polite Landscapes*, ch. 2.

31. Chambers, *Landscape Garden*, pp. 67, 164; Williamson, *Polite Landscapes*, p. 118, and ch. 5.

32. J.V. Beckett, 'Gosfield Hall: a country estate and its owners 1715–1825', *Essex Archaeology and History* 25 (1994), p. 187.

33. David Mannings, 'The visual arts', in *The Cambridge Cultural History of Britain*, 5, *Eighteenth-Century Britain*, Boris Ford, ed. (Cambridge, 1992), pp. 143–4.

of close scrutiny and considered judgement, and country-house owners were assessed by some on the basis of landscape more than their houses. The antiquarian John Loveday of Caversham, although a careful describer of interiors, assessed the houses he assiduously visited in the 1730s by the settings in which he found them. Sites that were low-lying or somehow failed to provide an adequate prospect invariably disappointed him, but a place like Heythrop Hall (Oxfordshire) delighted him with its panoramic elevation and with the combined effect of house and landscape, 'the most elegant Work of Art' joined with 'Nature in great Variety, each adorning the other'. Mr Allworthy's house in Fielding's *Tom Jones* sat low enough on its hill to be sheltered from winds but 'high enough to enjoy a most charming prospect of the valley beneath'.[34]

New fashions in landscape reflected in part the conditions that favoured growth and consolidation of estates. They also showed the continued influence on elite taste of classical models unavailable to those with different education. Virgil's *Georgics* and other classical works encouraged landowners to create a landscape arcadia covered with grass, winding walks, and groves, where seats, temples, or grottoes afforded places for contemplation. Although adaptable in miniature by gentry even in suburban London, fully to implement new designs required acres as well as the appropriate intellectual training. The landscape style Stephen Switzer advanced in *Iconographia Rustica* (1718) could be adapted by any country landowner of moderate substance, but the pattern he envisioned – inner garden linked to an extensively planted landscape – was obviously inappropriate for the bourgeois aspirant to gentility.[35]

Creating the 'natural' landscape required considerable labour to eradicate underwood, cut mature trees, plant new ones, and remove walls and obstructions. Still, the land rarely had to be prepared from scratch, and using a deer park as raw material made landscape parks affordable for many families. Deer parks abounded. With its 'candid, wasteful display' of land it was an increasingly important index of landed status for several decades after 1660, and allowed anxious Restoration aristocrats to make aggressive assertions about their right to hunt. By the eighteenth century, such claims were

34. Sarah Markham, *John Loveday of Caversham 1711–1789: The Life and Tours of an Eighteenth-Century Onlooker* (Salisbury, Wiltshire, 1984), pp. 174–5; Henry Fielding, *Tom Jones* (New York, 1950; originally published 1749), p. 9; Stone and Stone, *An Open Elite?*, pp. 330–1.

35. Chambers, *Landscape Garden*, pp. 12–23, 129–30, 133–4, 139–40; Williamson, *Polite Landscapes*, pp. 50–2.

being made in other ways and with less bluster behind them, so the deer park, consisting essentially of a bounded expanse of trees and grass, could be made more open and 'natural' by pulling down its fences. Woodland belts and clumps of trees extended it, new or refigured bodies of water beautified it. In later years, livestock, symbols of the landed family's pedigree in an age preoccupied with breeding and heredity, often replaced deer, but never with the significant economic value (which deer parks had) as a source of provision.[36]

The rise of the landscape garden and park may be interpreted in part as a return to an agrarian vision of cooperation with nature on the part of the landed, a reaction against growing capitalist appropriation of the countryside. The nostalgia for the land supposedly embodied in the new landscape style has also been associated with opposition to Walpole and with traditional 'country' values, as against the vices of court and capital. It might be seen also as a balance to the improvement taking place in the open fields around it. While it would be unreasonable to deny that landscape was used for polemical ends, it is improper to emphasize the partisan subtleties of design. The anti-urban aspects visible in the landscape garden's prospects did not prevent landowners from sitting in urban residences while they considered their new designs and wrote instructions to their estate employees about the implementation of their plans. Whatever its possible oppositional associations, moreover, the new style was not the monopoly of any political group within the classically trained landed elite. Because the new taste for landscape gardening was bolstered by ancient authority, that made it a shared rather than a monopolized, partisan taste. As Jonathan Swift said, 'I suppose Virgil and Horace are equally read by Whigs and Tories', and Stephen Switzer explicitly promoted his landscape design as one that landowners could embrace regardless of party. Both the relative homogeneity of polite society and the increasing self-awareness of the landed elite worked in favour of wide adoption of new landscape fashions.[37] They were not so much significant for speaking in favour of one party and against another as for speaking to the kingdom at large about the ability of a wealthy order literally to remake the face of the land.

36. Chambers, *Landscape Garden*, p. 90; Williamson, *Polite Landscapes*, pp. 22–4, 93–4; quotation on p. 24; *AHEW*, V, pt 2, pp. 366–8; Nicholas Russell, *Like Engend'ring Like: Heredity and Animal Breeding in Early Modern England* (Cambridge, 1986); Habakkuk, *Estates System*, pp. 60–1.
37. Chambers, *Landscape Garden*, p. 3; Williamson, *Polite Landscapes*, p. 52.

The rural existence these fashions exalted was not pastoral escapism but constructive engagement with nature. Resting on the premise that the beautiful ought to be useful, landscape improvement went hand in hand with agricultural improvement. In both endeavours, too, the landlord's direct role was critical, regardless of who else might be involved in making decisions. As improving landlords communicated with one another throughout the nation, so did landscaping landlords take advantage of their social world and ingrained habits of travel and visiting to build up informal connections.[38] They employed various kinds of knowledge in the effort, combining science, art, and business in a way largely inaccessible to other social groups. Successful landscape practices depended on precise botanical knowledge, acquired in the realm of the new scientific discourse. And as increasingly capitalist, patriotic, and imperialist ventures brought hundreds of new plants to England, botany also implicated practitioners in an expansive vision of the world. Landowners shared their mutual interest in the components of landscape design, whether trees or shrubs, classical temples or waterworks, by correspondence, visits, and publications that connected them across the kingdom. Before market developments of the mid-eighteenth century allowed gentry to rely on metropolitan nurserymen to supply exotic plants, the gardening brotherhood of landscaping landowners exchanged rarities and even bequeathed plant collections to one another.[39]

Where different sorts of knowledge were required in remaking the physical environment, so were different figures involved in applying that knowledge. Design of the landscape took an architect like William Kent or a theorist like Batty Langley, and in the way that the professional estate steward emerged to assist the farming landlord in his productive endeavours, so did the professional gardener help landowners to shape their environment. By 1750, the label 'gardener' had come to denote a profession. The assignment of the label denominated an individual of specific qualifications, accountable to a standard of accomplishment defined in terms common to landowners anywhere. The progress of the profession is illustrated by James Shiells' advertisement for employment in 1760. Playing on an aristocratic connection, he promoted himself as former gardener to Lady Katherine Pelham, informing 'the Nobility and Gentry, that he surveys, and plans Estates neatly and accurately; lays

---

38. *AHEW*, V, pt 2, p. 558.
39. Chambers, *Landscape Garden*, pp. 2–3, 26, 97–9, 113–14, and ch. 8.

out Parks, Pleasure and Kitchen Gardens, in the most useful, elegant, and modern Taste; [and] Makes artificial Rivers, or Pieces of
Water, in the most natural and agreeable Manner'.[40] The gardener
like this is another example of the elite's use of specialists from
anywhere they could be located in the kingdom, individuals whose
very employment is testimony to the idiosyncratic yet collectively
more standard needs and activities of the ruling landed order.

Where (landscape) gardening brought like-minded country-house
owners together in a common set of pursuits, it also distanced them
from the surrounding population physically, visibly, and culturally.
The new elements of the country house's immediate environment
– ruins, summer houses, views, walks – were most fruitfully enjoyed
in isolation from adjacent society, and many had literary, historical,
and philosophical associations comprehensible only to a few. Fully
controlled acres encouraged owners to congratulate themselves on
the extent of their possessions and on their superior judgement in
selecting a location and making improvements that gave delight.
Even those without tens of thousands of acres could fully control
those they owned. The traditional aristocratic enterprise of tree-
planting, which flourished after the Restoration as an indispensable feature of 'improvement', demonstrated one's ownership of
the land but also screened out the world.[41] New vistas signalled the
exclusivity of the landowner's realm by denying any sight of farm-
houses, village, or agricultural workers.

The manipulation of landscape to remove most signs of the
populace allowed for purely aesthetic appreciation of distances un-
populated by workaday folk and devoid of squalor. The desire for
predictable horizons or a larger deer park led some to relocate roads,
like Lord Townshend, who obtained a private Act of Parliament to
do so in the 1660s. Others like the Earl of Orford at Chippenham,
Sir Robert Walpole at Houghton, and Sir Richard Temple at Stowe
even moved villages, not historically unprecedented dislocations
but uncommon before the 1720s. The Earl of Southampton maintained privacy at Stratton House in Hampshire, which lay close to
the main London–Winchester road, by obtaining licence to enclose
part of it in 1664, and his son-in-law later added to his seclusion by
razing the hamlet of Stratton to enlarge his deer park. Such reloca-
tions powerfully expressed the magnates' separation from local community; more subtly but equally clearly, the shift of kitchen garden

40. Ibid., pp. 135–7; quotation on p. 140.
41. Keith Thomas, *Man and the Natural World: Changing Attitudes in England 1500–
1800* (Harmondsworth, 1984), pp. 205–12.

to a location distant from the house represented the landowner's 'divorce from the humdrum details of agricultural and domestic production'.[42]

Within the house that divorce was effected too, by layouts that provided separation of servants from landed residents and guests. The cultural separation of elite and common taste that the former's appreciation of an artificially natural landscape betokened was reproduced in the decor as well. Here landowners displayed their taste and cultivation in the furniture and silver, china and chimney-pieces, carvings, mouldings, and wallpaper that filled and covered their rooms. The unusual possessions they collected and tended did the same, only more forcefully. Merchants with taste might acquire expensive plate but were less likely to pick up the antique sculptures (real or fake) a European traveller could buy. Young men especially tended to return from European tours with works of visual art and books that then went on display. William Windham returned home in the early 1740s from his tour with over two dozen gouaches by a single artist, along with many other paintings, a collection of engravings, and works on architecture and classical antiquities. This was by no means atypical.[43]

Strategies of separation

However it was manifest, distance was growing, even if only via use of a private withdrawing room or study or retreat into a parcel of garden adjacent to one's country house: what it meant to be a member of England's ruling elite more and more entailed disengagement from rather than involvement with those whom one ruled. And while landowners gained separation from the rest of society by creating protected residential zones, they continued to try to control commoners' behaviour as it affected the country-house environment. One strategy for doing so heightened the exclusivity attached to any kind of hunting. In the face of mounting pressure on uncultivated land suitable for the chase, and in reaction to calls for the gentry to relinquish their privileges, lawyers and legislators

42. Rosenheim, *Townshends of Raynham*, pp. 171–2; Williamson, *Polite Landscapes*, pp. 57–8; Schwoerer, *Lady Rachel Russell*, p. 49; Habakkuk, *Estates System*, p. 61.

43. Barbara M. Benedict, 'The "curious attitude" in eighteenth-century Britain: observing and owning', *Eighteenth-Century Life*, new series, 14, no. 3 (1990), pp. 59–98; R.W. Ketton-Cremer, *Felbrigg: The Story of a House* (London, 1982; originally published 1962), pp. 126–7; Jeremy Black, *The British Abroad: The Grand Tour in the Eighteenth Century* (New York, 1992), ch. 12.

exalted the landed's exclusive game rights after the Restoration, apparently with better success than under the Tudors and early Stuarts. From the 1660s, a full two generations before the Black Act (1723) created many new capital offences in its attack on poaching, a set of new laws extended the gentry's control over game and at least in some places was vindictively applied against offenders. Legislation in 1671 disqualified from hunting many non-gentle landholders, and all those of non-landed wealth, by requiring £100 p.a. in freehold or £150 p.a. in leasehold property to qualify for possession of arms. Sons and heirs of esquires and above could hunt regardless of property, lords of manors of high status could appoint gamekeepers with broad powers of seizure, and a single justice was empowered to convict offenders on a single witness's testimony. The act's class bias was overt and heralded a sharp decline in the previously common practice of gentry-led deer-stealing, a reduction that reflected landowners' awareness of their 'need to respect private property, consolidate their class interests, and adhere to more appropriate standards of behaviour'. These laws prevented wealthy urbanites from hunting but more significantly affected (and surely offended) tenant farmers and small rural freeholders by erecting a boundary between greater and lesser men of property.[44]

The impact of the civil wars lay behind the symbolism of this legislation in more ways than one. It was not only in reaction against the disorders of the 1640s and 1650s that gentry passed this legislation. Influenced by their time on the Continent, where game rights were carefully guarded, some exiled gentry had returned to their estates in 1660 possessing new attitudes to leisure and determined to enjoy life. Outdoor recreation rose in the scale of elite male values, to the extent that these pursuits even detracted from gentlemen's fulfilment of domestic and civic duties. Male aristocrats poured their energy into hunting, perfecting their skills with horses, dogs, and guns, and applying scientific expertise to gamekeeping and horse-breeding. These occupations not only absorbed agricultural resources, they damaged landowners' relations with other elements

44. Roger B. Manning, *Hunters and Poachers: A Social and Cultural History of Unlawful Hunting in England, 1485–1640* (Oxford, 1993), pp. 232–6; quotation on p. 234; *AHEW*, V, pt 2, pp. 367–71; Stephen K. Roberts, 'Juries and the middling sort: recruitment and performance at Devon quarter sessions, 1649–1670', in J.S. Cockburn and Thomas A. Green, eds, *Twelve Good Men and True: The Criminal Trial Jury in England, 1200–1800* (Princeton, 1988), p. 191; Langford, *Public Life*, pp. 331–5; Beckett, *Aristocracy*, pp. 342–3; Joyce Lee Malcolm, 'The creation of a "true antient and indubitable" right: the English Bill of Rights and the right to be armed', *Journal of British Studies* 32 (1993), pp. 237–41.

of rural society, especially in the effort to guard land over which to hunt. A squirearchy preoccupied with preserving game not only united in enforcing the laws that governed its taking but united in preserving the appearance of privilege.[45] In the eighteenth century the shared passion for hunting grew so intense that it sometimes overrode party allegiance and heightened social sensibilities. When tories and whigs would hunt together, they did so in carefully defined, restricted circles. The desire of nobility in Northamptonshire to enjoy sporting fellowship apart from the local squirearchy led them to form hunting 'confederacies' around 1730, to which they contributed as much as £150 p.a. The Charlton Hunt controlled by the Duke of Richmond in the 1730s and 1740s, perhaps both England's premier sporting event and its most important social event outside London, was highly exclusive and dominated by peers.[46]

Foreign travel

England's ruling order was distinguished from those it ruled by its relationship to land – as epitomized by the game laws and the practices of the hunt as much as by the country house and its environs. But belonging to landed society also meant absorption in an increasingly national high culture as well. On the part of men, education at university or an inn of court had once served to break down gentlemen's localist intellectual predilections. Now the Grand Tour in some measure took its place.[47] Restricted until the later eighteenth century almost exclusively to men, its duration alone demanded substantial financial resources. Of a selection of Norfolk tourists, Henry Lee Warner travelled for two and a half years (1713–16), both Ashe Windham (1693–96) and the second Viscount Townshend (1694–97) for three, William Windham for four (1738–42), and Thomas Coke, future Earl of Leicester, for five years and nine months (1712–18).[48]

Typically, the tour included several constant features beyond expense of time and money, creating for aristocratic tourists a shared

45. Langford, *Public Life*, pp. 331–5; *AHEW*, V, pt 2, pp. 366, 369–70.

46. *Letters of Eaton to Cardigan*, pp. xlviii–xlix, 153–4; *Richmond–Newcastle Correspondence*, pp. xxxiv–xxxv.

47. This section relies on Redford, *Venice & the Grand Tour*; Black, *The British Abroad*, and idem, *The British and the Grand Tour* (London, 1985).

48. Andrew Moore, *Norfolk and the Grand Tour: Eighteenth-Century Travellers Abroad and Their Souvenirs* (Fakenham, Norfolk, 1985).

foreign experience that conferred yet another blaze of elite status and shaped identity in a way that increased the distance between landed and bourgeois culture. In some ways too the tour, like modern mandatory military service, provided both a break with the tourist's prior upbringing and a later source for reminiscence. Since most who toured did so in their youth and only once, the tour was formative and noteworthy because of its singularity as well as its class specificity. In pressing his father for permission to travel for several months after completing his studies abroad, young Edward Simeon pleaded that it was 'fort probable que ce sera l'unique occasion que je'auray de contenter ma curiosité'.[49]

The pull of classical Rome, the projection of the French (and to a lesser degree the Dutch) as models of taste, and a taste for Europe developed by some aristocratic royalist exiles together account for a rise in elite travel to Europe after 1660. Yet because the late seventeenth-century tour exposed travellers to the influences of Catholicism and autocracy at a time when each potentially threatened English life, its popularity remained muted until about 1700. The gradual recession of the threat of Catholics, Jacobites, and tyrannical political models, and Britain's avoidance of continental war for twenty-five years after 1713, helped to bring an increase in foreign travelling that renewed fighting did little to diminish after 1739.[50]

The tour's attractiveness also grew because of the decline of earlier patterns of upbringing. Formerly a combination of home rearing and formal education at universities and inns had given the landed elite distinctive training 'in manners, morals, piety and learning, a synthesis of medieval charity and humanist and Protestant scholarship'.[51] As the seventeenth century waned and the gentry's grip on society grew stronger, reliance on academic learning (which some blamed for provoking civil war) seemed less necessary. The civic knowledge that helped to maintain control of society, and the civility, politeness, and refinement that distinguished elite from social inferiors, partly displaced institutional education as attributes of gentility. Europe was clearly one place to acquire these. Direct contact with the Roman classical world delivered a civic education, and a stay in Paris provided social and cultural adornments, which

49. E. Simeon to Sir J. Simeon, 29 April 1701 [NS], Bodleian Library, MS D.D. Weld.c.13/47.

50. Redford dates the heyday of the Italian tour as 1700–60: *Venice & the Grand Tour*, pp. 14–15.

51. Heal and Holmes, *Gentry*, p. 275.

made Italy and France the two most popular stops on a gentleman's tour. Yet experience of any different society was thought to bestow a fuller understanding of England's ways and the light of comparison by which to judge them. William Graves in the late 1740s thought that the study of foreign polities and the acquaintance through travel with 'things of virtuoso-kind' constituted 'the marks of gentility and a polite education'.[52]

Most tourists would have seen Paris and made an Italian journey that included Rome, Venice, Florence, and Naples, but many also visited northern, central and eastern Europe, and some never set foot in France or Italy. Edward Simeon's father – a Roman Catholic at that – was not alone in thinking Italy so far south as to be unhealthy. He bargained with his son to substitute a trip to Lyons and five weeks in Paris for a venture there.[53] Regardless of their destination, however, all tourists encountered new and different manners, customs, foods, and institutions. According to contemporary opinion some of these encounters improved travellers by broadening or polishing them, while other experiences corrupted, perhaps especially the unfettered accommodation of desire in which so many indulged. Gaining sexual experience in a temperate fashion (the loss of virginity seems to have been expected) and even engaging in behaviour considered dubious or taboo at home (sexual debauchery, bouts of gambling or drinking) also gave tourists a measure of shared identity, both during and after their continental sojourns, if only as members of a (temporarily) risqué species.[54]

All aspects of foreign travel encouraged reflection on the aristocratic British life from which most tourists came. Touring additionally involved a measure of estrangement for all travellers no matter where they went, and it is easy to imagine that this alienation was conducive to the formation of shared sentiments and attitudes – of having been tested, of having gained sophistication and breadth, of having enjoyed rare and superior experiences. The introduction to autocratic institutions, the observation of foreign economies, and the exposure to Catholicism sustained the conviction most already had of England's superiority. Not all observers were unthinking critics of everything foreign. Some were seduced, not just sexually

52. Black, *The British Abroad*, p. 293; see also Jenkins, *Making of a Ruling Class*, p. 246.
53. Sir J. Simeon's draft reply to E. Simeon's to him, 29 April 1701 [NS], Bodleian Library, MS D.D. Weld.c.13/47.
54. Redford, *Venice & the Grand Tour*, pp. 17, 21–2; Black, *British Abroad*, p. 253; idem, *The British and the Grand Tour*, p. 205.

but spiritually conquered by Rome, or even atheism. A few saw England compare unfavourably to foreign states and cultures. Yet for the majority of travellers continental touring surely heightened awareness of being English – and landed English at that. In this the experience demonstrably served as a rite of passage.

The world of high culture

However powerfully the Grand Tour could serve as cultural cement within landed society, it bonded only a minority of this group and generally the wealthiest section. Other cultural experiences, however, more transitory, affordable, and mundane, ones entered into with little necessary planning or self-consciousness of social or cultural position, also emerged in the eighteenth century to bind together elite men and women into a coherent social order. And although unselfconscious when they entered upon them, members of the elite came away from these experiences with greater exposure to a world they shared with others like them.

The literary realm constituted one arena for such experiences, especially from the late seventeenth century on. That period in particular saw the agents of high culture working to deny 'the designations "literature" or "learning" to texts they regarded as debased' and thus effectively to exclude many non-elite readers and authors from their intellectual world.[55] These cultural agents did accept the utility of publishing enterprises that aimed at providing watered down, popular versions of classical history and literature, but they would not respect these as works of literary art, unlike the literary journals that first appeared at the end of the seventeenth century and represented a commercial appropriation of high-toned coterie literary practices. An inclination to restrict select intellectual products to certain hands was perhaps in effect when Sir John Lowther, aware that many in the country could use the books he sent from London, nevertheless instructed his agent in 1697 to lend only to specified individuals 'being publick persons', whereas 'to any others . . . I would not have you lend any for a practice of that kind would make everyone expect it' – an expectation he was unwilling to meet.[56]

---

55. Mayer, 'Nathaniel Crouch', p. 416.
56. Margaret J.M. Ezell, 'The *Gentleman's Journal* and the commercialization of Restoration coterie literary practices', *Modern Philology* 89 (1992), pp. 323–40; *Lowther Correspondence*, p. 423.

In agricultural writing, authors who addressed themselves to land-owners seeking agricultural improvement spoke little of personal interaction between gentry and their neighbours. And Walter Blythe's books of husbandry, *The English Improver* (1649) and *The English Improver Improved* (1652), which addressed a wide social audience, were dismissed by Restoration gentry because they were 'deliberately written in simple language'. Ralph Austen's *Treatise of Fruit Trees* of 1653 highlighted parliamentary schemes to ease agricultural poverty, but the mostly unaltered edition of 1665 was dedicated to Robert Boyle and gave short shrift to the victims of that poverty and to small-holders in general. It condescended to husbandmen, whose needs were to be addressed through impersonal statutes, anonymous offi-cials, and simplified texts. Books such as Austen's gave legitimacy to a prevalent eighteenth-century perspective on English society that construed it along the bifurcated lines of cultural learning and cultural illiteracy.[57]

A new literary product of the late seventeenth century, the novel, offered 'simple language' to a decidedly non-elite readership, and consequently drew opprobrium as debased writing. When Richard Steele objected to the practice of 'reading but for pleasure . . . [and] the transient satisfaction of what one does', he may have had in mind both the newspaper and the novel as formats that most con-tributed to this sad state of affairs.[58] With similar condescension to that of literary critics, the antiquaries and historians of the late seventeenth and eighteenth centuries increasingly shunned oral tradition as an historical source, partly suspecting its evidential value but particularly mistrusting its vulgar social origins.[59]

Cultural distancing also occurred in the realm of music. As with the new landscape style, no political party monopolized the emer-gent corpus of musical classics in the eighteenth century, although some public music resonated with tory overtones, especially the sacred music whose revival figured prominently in the growing music canon. Tory MPs acted as stewards for the Three Choirs Festival in the 1740s, and tory gentry appeared prominently at the provincial music festivals. Yet the development of a cult around Henry Purcell in the 1720s and 1730s actually saw the politically distinct identities

57. *AHEW*, V, pt 2, pp. 560–1.

58. Ian Watt, *The Rise of the Novel: Studies in Defoe, Richardson and Fielding* (Ber-keley, 1957), pp. 48–9; see also J. Paul Hunter, *Before Novels: The Cultural Contexts of Eighteenth-Century English Fiction* (New York, 1990).

59. D.R. Woolf, 'The "common voice": history, folklore and oral tradition in early modern England', *Past & Present* 120 (1988), pp. 47–52.

of groups of musical commentators dissolve. Both whigs and tories adulated the English virtues found in Purcell's music, and some patriotically contrasted it with 'decadent' Italian opera (which none the less had enthusiastic supporters among the landed). 'Members of the two parties found a kind of common ground in xenophobia but on a broader plane, in the sense that the music pointed toward a higher moral and civic order.'[60] Thomas Tudway, who collected music for Edward Harley, son of the first Earl of Oxford, did so in affirmation of a politically transcendent church music tradition. Arthur Bedford's call for regeneration in *The Great Abuse of Musick*, (1711), dedicated to the Society for the Propagation of Christian Knowledge, drew on the nation's heritage and promoted the music of Tallis and Byrd as an antidote to the commercialized and debased contemporary music commonly found on the stage and in the street.[61]

Bedford (who voted whig but worked with tories) and others like him were sufficiently bipartisan to create and nurture a distinctly elite and national musical canon. Many gatherings drew from landed society without political distinction, like the music performed in Norfolk's towns or the Salisbury festival which attracted 'most of the best families within many Miles of this Place, to the Amount of more than 300 persons the first Night, and near as many the second'. Such festivals set apart the landed elite. Although the Three Choirs Festival was held by rotation in three urban centres, it was mainly a landed affair, and municipal officials and urban rulers had little stake in the performances, described in 1726 as 'Consorts for the Gentry'.[62]

The audience for much publicly performed music (itself a new phenomenon), or at least the audience essential for much of its success or failure, was clearly a landed one. Provincial benefit concerts, critical to the financial survival of professional musicians, were underwritten by gentry patrons and coincided with quarter sessions, race meetings, or other local events that brought gentry into the towns where concerts were held. John Vanbrugh's attempt to produce all-sung Italian opera in 1705 foundered after five days because the singers were 'lik'd but indifferently by the Gentry', proof of the group's importance in making a musical success.[63] As

60. William Weber, *The Rise of Musical Classics in Eighteenth-Century England: A Study in Canon, Ritual, and Ideology* (Oxford, 1992), pp. 90–102; quotation on p. 96.

61. Ibid., ch. 2.

62. Ibid., pp. 118–20; Trevor Fawcett, *Music in Eighteenth Century Norwich and Norfolk* (Norwich, 1979).

63. Fawcett, *Music in Norwich*, pp. 9–11; Robert D. Hume, 'The sponsorship of opera in London, 1704–1720', *Modern Philology* 85 (1988), p. 424.

Italian opera began to flourish a handful of years later, it did so with the patronage of London-based gentry and nobility, an instance of the 'cultured Englishman's [*sic*] liking for all things Italian'.[64] To name as the 'Opera of the Nobility' a company set up in the 1730s to rival Handel's troupe indicates a strong imaginative association between this musical form and an elite divided in its company loyalty but united in its passion for the music. The association was pronounced enough that the aristocratic liking for Italian opera, which gentlemen often brought back from their tours abroad, continued to draw condemnation in the 1720s and 1730s from social critics who found the preference for this Catholic art unrefined and unpatriotic. The assistance patrons gave such an expensive, foreign, and unnatural music (it did after all employ castrati) seemed especially pernicious because it deprived indigenous music of support it deserved. Criticism like this, however, did little to diminish the growing hold of Italian music in general and opera in particular.[65]

Other styles of eighteenth-century music that relied on landed support were immune to such criticism. Handel's oratorios presented a highly acceptable nationalist message expressed in a unique style. Performed in London during Handel's lifetime as Lenten substitutes for opera, they had sponsorship of neither church nor civic establishment and so depended crucially on audience support, which their stories and messages helped to garner. Unlike the opera, oratorios provided familiar, identifiable tales. The libretti were based on biblical texts and celebrated national safety or national victories, portraying in amorphous religious terms the history of the Jews as an English epic. Taken together the oratorios established a basis for their audiences to 'relate to the biblical tradition and communicate about their faith but not necessarily be divided along sectarian lines' – a non-sectarianism that permeated the public world of music even more after the failure of the '45.[66]

In the realm of music, then, diverse forces and styles operated to nourish a sense of national identity in listeners, among them the landed classes for whom the music resonated longer and more

64. Paul Langford, *A Polite and Commercial People: England 1727–1783* (London, 1989), p. 315.
65. Nicholas Anderson, 'Music', in *The Cambridge Cultural History of Britain*, 5, pp. 277–8; John Lord Hervey, *Some Materials towards Memoirs of the Reign of King George II*, Romney Sedgwick, ed., 3 vols (London, 1931; reprinted New York, 1970), I, pp. 273–4; Black, *British and the Grand Tour*, p. 205.
66. Colley, *Britons*, pp. 31–2; Weber, *Musical Classics*, pp. 120–3, 128–9; quotation on p. 123.

deeply. The growing consciousness of a national musical heritage, the celebration of great national events by musical compositions (from those of Purcell through to the commemoration of the Treaty of Aix-la-Chapelle by Handel's *Music for the Royal Fireworks*), and the play of nationalistic themes in oratorios and anthems reminded the landed of their positions as the kingdom's ruling order. And the contrasting appreciation some of them had for esoteric, foreign styles of music (even where it opened them to criticism) strengthened their own sense of possessing tastes distinctive from those of other social classes.

In other areas, the foreign influences – culinary, artistic, architectural, even literary – that historically coloured landed life put aristocrats increasingly at odds with xenophobic elements in the nation, while enhancing a landed sense of group identity. Openness to things foreign was not unqualified or universal among the highest ranks of society, only more pronounced than among their inferiors. Although undeniably selective and neither uncontroversial nor a total erasure of native influence, the process of 'Frenchification' and 'Italianizing' none the less further drew together and set apart the elite. It did so, too, without necessary regard for party: pious Jacobites made their way to St Germain; oligarchic whigs made their way to Venice. Part of the explanation for this receptivity lay in the elite's encounter with the world beyond England, directly through foreign touring but vicariously as well. Painting and sculpture, music and architecture, fashions in clothing and the decorative arts were all dominated by continental tastes. Half of the more expensive paintings sold in London auction rooms between 1714 and 1760 were by Italian masters.[67] Things foreign – and costly – such as tea and coffee, porcelain, silk, and calicoes, were to some extent defined as things tasteful.

The taste for things foreign signalled the cosmopolitanism and superiority of its devotees. It made apparent that they were rich enough, sufficiently educated, and possessed of ample leisure to develop and apply discernment in consumption. If manuals on *politesse* were actually aimed at non-elite individuals, who could learn in them how to behave politely,[68] it was all the more important for the gentry and nobility to demonstrate their gentility in other ways. They did this individually by purchasing products of both material

---

67. Colley, *Britons*, pp. 165–7.
68. Lawrence E. Klein, 'Politeness for plebes: consumption and social identity in early eighteenth-century England', in Ann Bermingham and John Brewer, eds, *The Consumption of Culture 1600–1800: Image, Object, Text* (London, 1995), pp. 362–82.

and intellectual culture on a vaster scale than other social groups, intimation of their precocious acceptance of the commodification of culture so characteristic of the modern world. Interested in but not so obsessed with novelty as the middle class came to be, aristocrats predominantly consumed to maintain their status and reputation by revealing their refined tastes.[69] While the taste for things foreign and for things luxurious, and the often-excessive consumption of both, opened the landed to social criticism, this reprimand did little to alter behaviour. Indeed, criticism may have fostered a defensive solidarity among elite consumers, forced either to justify their behaviour in the face of others' strictures or to deny that the criticisms applied to them at all.[70] By the mid-eighteenth century, a strong faith in their own tastes supported the elite in indulging them.

Religion

Unlike a shared belief in the culture of consumption, shared religious belief undeniably allowed communion across social lines. Among Catholics these ties were strongest, although in the mid-eighteenth century they might also be found among early adherents to Methodism, and they obviously characterized the relations of Lord Willoughby of Parham, a nonconformist notable for his social relations with those beneath him.[71]

In the northern lowlands of England and in the countryside south of the Trent, Catholicism was mostly a faith 'of the gentry and of individual choice' and had relatively little consequence for a generally conforming Protestant population. In Lancashire and the northern uplands in general, however, Roman Catholic gentry sustained closer connections with local communities than did aristocrats elsewhere. Here, Roman Catholic gentry were the moving force in the formation of Catholic congregations prior to 1700, making their influence felt among both their servants and their tenants.

---

69. J.E. Wills, Jr, 'European consumption and Asian production in the seventeenth and eighteenth centuries', in John Brewer and Roy Porter, eds, *Consumption and the World of Goods* (London, 1993), pp. 133–47; Colin Campbell, 'Understanding traditional and modern patterns of consumption in eighteenth-century England: a character-action approach', in ibid., pp. 49–52; John Brewer, ' "The most polite age and the most vicious": attitudes towards culture as a commodity, 1660–1800', in Bermingham and Brewer, eds, *Consumption of Culture*, pp. 341–61.

70. Jeremy Black, *The English Press in the Eighteenth Century* (London, 1987; reprinted Aldershot, 1991), pp. 266–7.

71. P.J.W. Higson, 'A dissenting northern family: the Lancashire branch of the Willoughbys of Parham, 1640–1765', *Northern History* 7 (1972), pp. 32–5.

A number of Catholic landlords probably offered the latter favourable leases along with secure tenure through the generations. William and Nicholas Blundell at Little Crosby in Lancashire from the mid-seventeenth to early eighteenth centuries clearly adopted such a concessionary policy with their Catholic tenants, but in the case of the former notably demanded the appropriate deference from them. Tenants 'undeserving' of generous treatment were those who failed in this respect.[72]

Their liability to prosecution for recusancy may have encouraged some Roman Catholic gentry and nobility in these practices, yet they were targeted relatively rarely on this basis through the period. In Charles II's reign few fines were ever levied against them and sequestration of estates was easily avoided. The practice of doubling the land tax assessments on Roman Catholics (introduced in 1693) had more consequence than the retention of the anti-Catholic laws to which they remained technically liable. A more general decline of religious animosities toward the middle of the eighteenth century lessened the vulnerability of Catholic landlords to disgruntled neighbours or tenants. And even when more apparent, their vulnerability did not make Catholic landowners into soft or anti-entrepreneurial landlords, whatever generosity some of them showed. Others were as willing as their Protestant counterparts to enclose land and fight with their tenants.[73]

Shared belief could alleviate some of the strains but did not erase the distinctions between landlord and tenant. By helping to direct, pay for, and organize the arrangements necessary for worship, the Catholic landed elite took a crucial part in the survival of Catholicism that no other group could play. This paternalist underwriting of a marginally placed faith may have done nothing to forge links between Catholic and Protestant components of the landed order, but it also served as a powerful reminder that, relative to their co-religionists, Catholic aristocrats walked upon an elevated stage.

In the case of nonconformists, the place of the 'besieged' Puritan gentry was ambiguous. At least in the 1660s, the boundary between nonconformist and Anglican could be blurred and the practice of qualified nonconformity no source of controversy.[74] Most

---

72. John Bossy, *The English Catholic Community 1570–1850* (London, 1975), pp. 84–5, 149, 168–81.

73. Heal and Holmes, *Gentry*, pp. 149–50; Bossy, *English Catholic Community*, pp. 103–4; Jenkins, *Making of a Ruling Class*, p. 178.

74. John Spurr, *The Restoration Church of England 1646–1689* (New Haven, 1991), pp. 186–7.

gentry and nobility of a Puritan persuasion 'remained in communion with the Church of England' after the Restoration but also retained connections with nonconformists.[75] In many instances, this continued connection took place through chaplaincies bestowed on dissenting ministers. The relatively private context for worship found in a chapel may have limited the numbers of the lower orders who attended conventicles like that held in the London house of the Dowager Countess of Exeter. Yet Lady Frances Hobart had a chapel in her house in Norwich that reportedly accommodated two hundred and even conventicles held in country houses attracted large enough numbers (sixty Presbyterians and Independents at Great Houghton in Yorkshire in the 1660s) to indicate an attendance consisting of more than persons of quality alone.[76]

It seems that differences in religion could play little part in creating bonds of commonality among the landed elite; quite the contrary. Yet the potentially divisive power of religion was moderated in three ways. First, the generation of committed Puritans, of whatever stripe, that survived civil war, revolution, and restoration was not perpetuated into the eighteenth century. Where the elite fought over religious politics (occasional conformity, the Bangorian controversy) up to and beyond the mid-eighteenth century, they increasingly did so from opposite pews rather than separate houses of worship. And where gentry retained affiliation with the chapel, it sometimes represented nothing more than a family inheritance. A squire in Glamorgan excused his nonconformity (which he used to seek exemption from the office of sheriff in 1746) by explaining that he was a dissenter because his father had been one. Protestant denominational affiliation can have mattered little if those who had vetted this man for the shrievalty either did not know or did not care that he was a dissenter.[77] Although J.T. Cliffe believes that 'moderate conformists could take comfort from the fact that upper-class patronage still survived' at the end of the seventeenth century, he finds that even among the seventy county families he identifies as dispensers of this patronage 'few . . . were prepared to throw in their lot completely with the nonconformists'.[78]

Second, the curiosity and scepticism about religion (not to mention the irreverence) expressed by many lay people cut some of the

75. J.T. Cliffe, *The Puritan Gentry Besieged, 1650–1700* (London, 1993), p. 109.

76. Ibid., ch. 9, esp. pp. 111, 113; Michael R. Watts, *The Dissenters: From the Reformation to the French Revolution* (Oxford, 1978), pp. 346–66.

77. Watts, *Dissenters*, p. 360; Jenkins, *Making of a Ruling Class*, pp. 178–80.

78. Cliffe, *Puritan Gentry Besieged*, p. 204.

virulence from religious disagreement and debate. The injection of 'civility' into religion around the turn of the century was not immediately apparent, in the political realm especially, but private devotion, like much of elite intellectual life, was undergoing 'a cultural sea-change' all the same.[79] It was not that atheism bloomed but that denominationalism lost a good deal of its bite. Even those who were strong proponents of Christianity might have little time for institutionally defined shibboleths and texts, might be 'lukewarm towards the church, or even hostile'. Some of this scepticism took aim at the clergy and charged them with 'priestcraft' in a way that defined them as an order apart.[80]

Third, far more than a craft, the ministry was becoming increasingly clearly a profession; if the clergy were 'losing the battle to define the values of English society', one of the groups to whom they were losing were the landed – from which social order many of them came.[81] The clergy's professionalism laid the basis for connections between parson and squire, through patrons' willing perpetuation of clerical 'dynasties' that passed livings from father to son and through the recruitment of kin of gentry and nobility into clerical positions. In the early eighteenth century, improvement in the value of some parish livings helped make the ministry a more socially acceptable and agreeable career for landowners' sons, whose assumed reliability and tractability also made them appropriate objects of patronage. They desired positions in the upper clergy most of all, where they served as the church's administrators – canons and prebends, deans and even bishops. Yet gentry offspring willingly accepted parish livings too.[82]

Popular beliefs

To argue that English aristocrats became culturally removed from others in the social hierarchy is not to suggest that they lived in isolation or that English society was riven by an impassable gulf between the culture of the elite and that of other ranks. Cultures abutted on, interacted, and were even integrated with one another – reflection on the ties created by common religious belief underscores this interpenetration. None the less, the landed elite were

---

79. Heal and Holmes, *Gentry*, p. 377; see also Spurr, *The Restoration Church*, ch. 5.
80. John Spurr, 'Religion in Restoration England', in L.K.J. Glassey, ed., *The Reigns of Charles II and James II and VII* (London, 1997), pp. 115–18; quotation on p. 115.
81. Ibid., p. 118; idem, *The Restoration Church*, pp. 195–209.
82. Holmes, *Augustan England*, ch. 4.

holding themselves more aloof from the cultural activities of their social inferiors in 1750 than they had a hundred years before, an aloofness partly revealed in denunciations some of them directed at a once more-congenial popular culture.

By contrast with the late sixteenth century, when religious objections were raised against the most raucous popular events like parish wakes, those of the elite who did censure aspects of popular culture in their turning from them did not primarily raise religious objections. Gentry who were hostile to 'the old popular rituals, and the notions of community they represented' rejected them as 'barbarous survivals, unsuited to a disciplined commercial society'. When the upper orders assailed popular culture in the eighteenth century they attacked its disorder and irrationality, not its ungodliness. Those who most closely scrutinized it at the turn of the seventeenth century were probably not hostile observers at all but antiquaries and natural scientists interested in recording the phenomena of popular life rather than eliminating them. When magistrates in Gloucestershire did begin in the early eighteenth century what later turned into a wider campaign to suppress village wakes, they characteristically condemned these large, overwhelmingly plebeian public events for the licence and disorder they produced. Growing anxiety about such revels ultimately led to efforts to tame or erase them that lasted into the mid-nineteenth century. Limited though such actions against popular diversions were, they still attest to an elite ethos that derived from a conviction that such behaviour was morally wrong and from political and social anxiety that gatherings of common people were potentially seditious and clearly inappropriate in a progressing nation.[83]

In the 1690s a more straightforwardly religious concern with the moral well-being and immoral behaviour of society's lower levels took institutional form in Societies for Reformation of Manners. Through the first two decades of the next century these institutions thrived, perhaps because society seemed especially corrupt to their adherents, perhaps because William and Mary's initial support encouraged reformers not to fear any possible repercussions from correcting the lower orders' behaviour. Little of the societies' attention fell on the rituals and pastimes of popular culture, however: eradicating vice, profanity, and, more mundanely, Sunday trading fully occupied the moral reformers. They focussed on saving souls

83. Underdown, *Revel, Riot and Rebellion*, p. 283 for quotation; see also Hutton, *Merry England*, pp. 235–8; Langford, *Public Life*, p. 382; Malcolmson, *Popular Recreations*, pp. 146–8.

by prosecuting the morally debauched, and they targeted popular sabbath day recreations only minimally, and general revelry not at all. The crusade for reformation of manners was strongest around London, but even its limited spread from metropolis to the provinces shows the influence that cultural concerns and patterns of life in the capital had on the entire kingdom. The societies moreover sought participation from the landed because they believed in the power of good examples to stimulate personal reform and hoped that those set off at the top of society would serve as models for all. This short-lived movement, lasting scarcely a decade, sought landed participation but attracted only modest, unenthusiastic support from gentry, who were repeatedly criticized by its propagandists for this apathy and animosity. Yet a substantial portion of the 117 members of parliament from 1689 to 1702 categorized as moral reformers were gentry and belonged to a Society for Reformation of Manners or similar group like the Society for the Propagation of Christian Knowledge and the Society for the Propagation of the Gospel.[84]

The movement for reform cut across party lines in parliament and out, and where it attracted gentry adherents they ranged from extreme whig to high tory on the political spectrum, even though the societies were politically controversial. It has been suggested that the moral reformers in the Commons constituted an important link between country ideologues of the 1670s and their counterparts of the 1730s, all of them critics more of a political than a social status quo. More broadly, some contemporaries decried the reformers as enemies to national institutions, enemies whose mere existence falsely implied the presence of serious shortcomings in the established order of church and state. Yet the societies presented themselves as agencies propounding ideals of order and submission among 'lewd and vicious persons possessed [of] a leveling spirit'. Proponents believed that their campaign to provoke higher morality in the persons they targeted could provide 'a social cement, an instrument of civil peace'. They also deemed moral reformation a balm to heal party divisions.[85] Even in the case of a

---

84. D.W.R. Bahlman, *The Moral Revolution of 1688* (New Haven, 1957), ch. 1; Robert B. Shoemaker, 'Reforming the city: the reformation of manners campaign in London, 1690–1738', in L. Davison, T. Hitchcock, T. Keirn, and R.B. Shoemaker, eds, *Stilling the Grumbling Hive: The Response to Social and Economic Problems in England, 1689–1750* (New York, 1992), pp. 99–120; T.C. Curtis and W.A. Speck, 'The Societies for the Reformation of Manners: a case study in the theory and practice of moral reform', *Literature and History* 3 (1976), pp. 45–64; Hayton, 'Moral reform'.

85. Bahlman, *Moral Revolution*, pp. 42 (for quotation), 83; Hayton, 'Moral reform', pp. 88–9.

movement construed by many in partisan terms, ambiguous feelings about party and a hopeful nonpartisan vision informed its goals and led the societies to cast their appeals in terms that sought to set aside partisanship – and that helped to shape national elite identity in doing so.

This identity also took on the form of distinctive intellectual attitudes that landowners adopted, none monopolized or held by all of them, but some of which affected their assessment of the society around, and did so in ways that further separated them culturally from those below them. A growing acceptance of the superiority of modern over ancient knowledge and practices, an intellectual fashion more pronounced after 1750, had social and cultural ramifications for the separation of 'superior' from 'inferior' even before then. Sceptical about society's inevitable degeneration from its classical past, the educated elite of the eighteenth century grew increasingly persuaded of the necessity of improvement in all aspects of life, which the simple 'visibility of progress' showed to be feasible.[86] Possessed of ample resources of time, money, and power, the landed were better placed than any other group to try to translate such convictions into reality.

Scepticism about and even rejection of once-popular beliefs set the elite more and more apart from common folk. This is not to identify 'progress' with modern 'science' or posit an innate hostility between the period's scientific and popular knowledge, but the scepticism and rejection tended to rest on rational bases and have improving goals. Such was the case with the largely futile efforts made under the later Stuarts to reform the kingdom's systems of measures and weights (although these attempts mostly sought to regularize crown income).[87] In the mid-1730s the witchcraft laws passed under James I were finally repealed, a sign of official denial of the phenomenon itself. Calendar reform in the mid-eighteenth century both acknowledged and contributed to the fragmenting of what shared traditional culture still remained. The enabling act decreed, almost without exception, that events fixed to a specific date should remain with their New Style counterpart. Commemoration of Charles I's death, for example, stayed on 30 January New Style and was not removed to 10 February. Many common people, however, continued to follow Old Style dates for consequential

86. David Spadafora, *The Idea of Progress in Eighteenth Century Britain* (New Haven, 1990), esp. chs 2, 4–5; the phrase is found on p. 49.
87. Julian Hoppit, 'Reforming Britain's weights and measures 1660–1824', *English Historical Review* 108 (1993), pp. 82–3, 92–4.

occasions like parish feasts and even Christmas. Reform thus unintentionally created a gap between popular and official observances that paralleled the emerging difference between a popular seasonal calendar and a polite one that revolved around political, social, and legal demarcations. In the eyes of the instigators of reform, resisters to change were credulous, irrational, and ignorant, while those accepting it were educated, rational, and well informed. The reasons offered for the change underlined this separation of elite and popular culture. Reform was urged both on the practical grounds of conformity with the Continent and because science in the form of astronomical observation justified and even demanded it. Pamphlets that explained the reform's scientific rationale actually widened the gap between uninformed and educated understanding of the calendar.[88] Assertion of the scientific nature of the calendar change also placed its adherents clearly on the 'rational' side of the relatively novel but rapidly growing divide between science and unreasoning 'superstition'.

The trajectory of astrological beliefs also illustrates the gulf between the culture of the quality and commoners that the application of the label 'superstitious' expressed.[89] Into the middle of the seventeenth century, most of society accepted to some degree the tenets of judicial astrology, that practice of predicting and advising about particular events on the basis of the stars' and planets' positions. But astrology's association with radicalism during the interregnum opened it to attack at the Restoration, when press licensors censored and suppressed almanacs and other works. The contemporary charge of 'instilling . . . superstitious belief'[90] was levelled at publishers and practitioners alike. The state and the church establishments, with aid from the Royal Society, together rapidly managed to marginalize and discredit astrologers among England's elite.

The connection between astrology and 'enthusiasm' tarred the former with the latter's inherent vulgarity, an association that was anathema to all elements of a politically divided Restoration ruling order. Antipathy to astrology provided a reason to suspend differences in recognition of the interests the elite shared. For all the strenuous efforts of astrology's adherents, the practice could not be

---

88. Langford, *Polite and Commercial People*, pp. 281–7; Robert Poole, ' "Give us our eleven days!": calendar reform in eighteenth-century England', *Past & Present* 149 (1995), pp. 95–139.

89. Patrick Curry, *Prophecy and Power: Astrology in Early Modern England* (Princeton, 1989).

90. Ibid., p. 47.

made to seem scientific, and it continued to lose credibility with the educated elite readership, at whom much published argument in its favour was none the less directed. By the time Jonathan Swift devastatingly satirized the astrologer John Partridge between 1707 and 1709, English astrology was no longer a 'respectable metropolitan pursuit' and soon enough its ideas became anathema in elevated circles. Where astrology was seen at the Restoration as a frightening phenomenon with subversive potential and ties to radicalism, by Swift's day it obviously posed no threat to state or society and had become risible.[91]

What are conventionally seen as advances in natural science intensified the aristocracy's turning from 'common knowledge' and from common folk. It was not an absolute turning away, but a decisive one in terms of cultural message. 'Your credulity is not ours, our rationally derived beliefs are not yours', was the message sent by these intellectual developments. While the discipline of natural history, for example, greatly depended on popular lore for its initial progress in the early modern era, much of this folk knowledge was rejected in the seventeenth and eighteenth centuries. Initially it was the ungodly and superstitious character of common beliefs about the natural world that rendered them questionable. By the late seventeenth century and into the next their irrationality offered the greater grounds for rejection. The disjuncture of popular and learned views of the natural world was signalled and intensified by changes in the nomenclature applied to it. Among the quality and the educated, Latin names for plants displaced English ones. Labels that polite society thought suggestive (for plants such as 'naked ladies', 'priests ballocks', and 'prick madam') began to be discarded, and names 'which preserved the tradition of a plant's supposedly religious or protective significance' were often dropped. In short, the learned tried to fix and standardize a new terminology to replace the unstable vernacular one, which common folk found useful but which undercut the elite's project to control scientific (and public) discourse.[92]

Conclusion

Enlightenment in England (perhaps best symbolized by belief in progress and rejection of 'superstition' and 'vulgar errors') generally

91. Ibid., pp. 91, 157, 160.
92. Thomas, *Man and the Natural World*, ch. 2, esp. pp. 73–87; quotation on p. 84.

implied a move from rusticity toward cosmopolitan urbanity. It was a move made by many of the landed order of England, and although partly an abstract move, it was also partly literal, because towns alone offered the opportunities to acquire the many components of enlightened gentility: 'taste, elegance, society, knowledge, science'.[93] The traditional architecture of the urban landscape was replaced by fashionable, classically inspired Renaissance designs, a rejection of the 'pull of locality' in favour of a more cosmopolitan, international style and theory of architecture. From the mid-seventeenth century, the more evidently shared economic, social, and political interests of town elites and landed gentry induced the latter to spend more time in the provincial town, exposed to its far from provincial culture. The consequent interaction of urban and country elites provided energy to many towns, 'reshaping their cultural life and guaranteeing them renewed prosperity'.[94]

This reshaping notably provided landowners with powerfully attractive and increasingly available entertainments like dancing and dining, card playing and conversation in the late seventeenth and eighteenth centuries. Such urban leisure was not to everyone's taste: Lady Mary Wortley Montagu, when looking for places to live in the north, complained of 'the Inconvenience and disagreablenesse of a Country Town', and the Countess of Deloraine, 'quit[e] tierd of staing . . . so long in Lincoln', welcomed the prospect of a short summer visit to Warwickshire in 1734. Bath, that quintessential site of leisured resort, had its detractors too, and where the Earl of Chesterfield went on eloquently about its diversions at some times, at others he found none to mention. Two landed women, Elizabeth Lady Townshend in 1707 and Mary Windham seventeen years later, both unhappily separated from their husbands, found Bath a 'hatefull place', 'a most dismal place, sad, wet, [with] cold weather & but very indifferent company', where 'all which they call divertion' was wearying and in fact the source of 'a great deal of trouble and uneasiness'.[95]

93. Roy Porter, 'Science, provincial culture and public opinion in enlightenment England', in Peter Borsay, ed., *The Eighteenth Century Town 1688–1820: A Reader in English Urban History* (London, 1990), p. 254.

94. Peter Borsay, '"All the town's a stage": urban ritual and ceremony 1660–1800', in Peter Clark, ed., *The Transformation of English Provincial Towns 1600–1800* (London, 1984), pp. 228–58; quotation on p. 233; idem, 'Culture, status, and the English urban landscape', *History*, 2nd series, 67 (1982), pp. 1–12, esp. pp. 5–9.

95. *The Letters of Philip Dormer Stanhope 4th Earl of Chesterfield*, Bonamy Dobrée, ed., 6 vols (London, 1932; reprinted New York, 1968), II, *August, 1712 to April, 1745*, pp. 290–3, 309–11, 357; *Banks Papers*, p. 162; *Montagu Letters*, I, pp. 182–3; E. Townshend

Yet even if hateful and boring for some and rejected by others, town life offered to all the landed both ritual and routinized conduct that reinforced a sense of shared social identity. In towns with parliamentary representation, growing gentry interest played its part in the elaboration of political and celebratory ritual surrounding elections. In towns primarily devoted to leisure, daily routines prevailed so strongly that few could resist being 'drawn into company'. And in any urban venue that offered the most modest of organized entertainment, not only did performers follow expected patterns of conduct, but audiences also engaged in carefully coded, stylized, and repeatable behaviours that bound them performatively and psychologically together.[96] There were proper ways to dress for a function, arrive at it, and behave while it took place.

Towns were of course also places to make connections and identify prospects, to proclaim taste, and to gain polish, civility, and refinement. In provincial urban settings and not just in London, gentry were introduced to – and then imported into their country houses – many new ideas, activities, fashions, and foods that helped to define the landed way of life.[97]

Beyond novelty and diversion, towns also afforded convenient and protected venues to attain and assert intellectual superiority, and as judicial occasions like assizes had pulled sixteenth-century landowners into towns, in the eighteenth century scientific lectures and other educational offerings did the same. In order to flower in these ways, provincial urban culture necessarily had to suspend or overcome the violent political partisanship that characterized much of public life in the late seventeenth and early eighteenth centuries. The cultural occasions just noted, where divided elites (rural and urban) came together on non-controversial grounds, served this purpose and fostered a measure of urban political stability as well.[98] Although this function of provincial urban culture probably had its greatest consequences for the lives of townspeople, it had its impact on the landed elite as well, reminding its members of their common interests. To put it simply, landed engagement with the public cultural or political life of York or Newcastle, Bristol or

to Lord Townshend, April–May [1707], Raynham Hall, uncatalogued manuscripts box 1 and box file 'Second Viscount 1696–1735'; M. Windham to Mrs Windham, 19 April 1724, Norfolk Record Office, WKC 7/26/73.
    96. Borsay, 'All the town's a stage', pp. 233–4, 240–1.
    97. Langford, *Polite and Commercial People*, pp. 99–108; Girouard, 'The country house and the country town', pp. 323–7.
    98. Barry, 'Press and politics of culture in Bristol', pp. 50–1.

Shrewsbury encouraged withdrawal from the countryside, made more pronounced the distance between elite and non-elite sectors of English society, and contributed yet another element to the making of landed identity. But in this cultural process the impact of provincial towns was dwarfed by that of London, to which attention finally turns.

CHAPTER SEVEN

The Influence of the Metropolis

Introduction

The metropolis of London has figured in English life in many ways, but ever since the royal court settled there, and maybe as early as when the law courts became fixed, it has especially drawn the kingdom's prominent landowners. Of course, England's landed elite did not respond to it in identical ways, and time spent there did not afford the only exposure to urban life. During the Augustan and early Hanoverian era, many gentry and nobility visited the towns of provincial England, which underwent an energetic transformation, particularly in the eighteenth century. The 'triumph of the gentry' that marked local governance at the end of the Stuart dynasty was partly brought about in county towns, whose administrative functions drew visitors and residents, spurred the development of cultural amenities, and supported a wide variety of crafts and trades. The growth of provincial towns that were not county seats was even more explosive, sparked by economic development unrelated to local administration.[1]

Despite the importance of town life for the landed elite, this chapter argues that London, potentially yielding more wide-ranging and even intense experience than provincial society, played a greater role in shaping what has here been identified as the landed's uniquely metropolitan identity. It is not just that London's population even

1. Anthony J. Fletcher, *Reform in the Provinces: The Government of Stuart England* (New Haven, 1986), ch. 10; Peter Borsay, *The English Urban Renaissance: Culture and Society in the Provincial Town 1660–1770* (Oxford, 1989); Alan Everitt, 'Country, county and town: patterns of regional evolution in England', in Peter Borsay, ed., *The Eighteenth Century Town: A Reader in English Urban History, 1688–1820* (London, 1990), pp. 83–115.

in 1750 was twice that of the kingdom's other nineteen largest towns combined,[2] but that in this period several developments intensified the metropolitan experience for elite society. Exposure to London grew more usual and prolonged for landed men, women, and children. In temporal terms, life in the city[3] bulked larger than ever before. The landed when in town were becoming more geographically segregated (although not isolated) from the rest of the urban population, a result of the growth of fashionable and relatively exclusive residential enclaves. In addition, the landed savoured a London in many ways socially and culturally different from that which other groups enjoyed. Theirs was mostly a luxurious and leisured life, and their experience of the city's hardships was on a reduced scale compared with that of most urban residents. Moreover, when back in the country, the landed remained intimately connected to town through many channels. Among the quality, whatever their internal differences of wealth or faith or party precept, and regardless of whether they bemoaned or celebrated metropolitan life, what was in many ways an elite-specific experience of the metropolis helped to weld them into a distinctively visible and self-aware social group.

Going to town and settling there

Even if there had been nothing qualitatively new about life in the late Stuart and early Hanoverian metropolis, the physical and demographic expansion of London would have altered the impact it made on elite existence. But the qualitative experience did change, in part simply because more gentlemen and noblemen came to the urban area more often, for longer periods, and brought their wives and children with them. Regular visits to London had historically been fairly common among greater gentry and nobility, but, having been discouraged by royal proclamation in the 1630s and by political upheavals in the 1640s, they grew habitual among the lesser and middling gentry only slowly. They were none the less pronouncedly on the increase by the end of the 1650s. With the Restoration, visits became normal among all the landed, and recourse to the capital intensified so much that when landowners were absent from their

2. Calculation based on the figures in E. Anthony Wrigley, 'Urban growth and agricultural change: England and the Continent in the early modern period', in Borsay, ed., *The Eighteenth Century Town*, p. 42.

3. In this chapter 'city' refers to metropolitan London and 'City' to the corporate borough bounded by walls.

country estates, London was assumed to be the principal site of their relocation.[4]

In specific instances, the accession of wealth or the acquisition of public office or metropolitan connections allowed individuals to experience London differently at separate points in their lives. It is therefore important to compare the metropolitan experiences of the landed across generations bearing such particularities in mind. Yet there is no escaping the impression that extended residence in the capital became a common feature of eighteenth-century landed life. This impression is borne out by examples of relatively rustic fathers and more cosmopolitan sons, of an early generation that lived in rented accommodations and of later ones that bought London houses, of household heads who came to town wifeless but whose successors travelled and settled there *en famille*. Although it was still the wealthier landowners who went most frequently to town, more minor gentry – those outside the elite described by membership in parliament, for example – regularly did too. The lack of comment sparked by journeys to London, whether for brief or long sojourns, indicates their unremarkable nature. Distance was no bar: Yorkshire's leading gentry adopted what their chronicler calls a 'peripatetic lifestyle' with the capital a frequent stop. The middling squire Walter Calverley went from Yorkshire to London six times in a little more than three years in the 1690s, and two decades later was willing to stay there for as long as six months and also as little as a fortnight. In the years just before 1700, William Massingberd of Gunby, Lincolnshire, spent an average of nine weeks a year in the city. And people who lived in London expected landowning friends and relatives to visit town often and more than briefly.[5]

England's road system expedited these visits, because its expansion in the eighteenth century featured the establishment and improvement of provincial connections to the capital. This was so much the case that in 1750 all major towns in the provinces had regularly scheduled passenger stagecoach services to London. By the 1720s, the gentry of Glamorgan had abandoned their county to such a degree that those seeking news of them had to write to town, and leading families went so predictably in the 1730s that Sir Edmund Thomas

4. Lawrence Stone, 'The residential development of the West End of London in the seventeenth century', in Barbara C. Malament, ed., *After the Reformation: Essays in Honour of J.H. Hexter* (Philadelphia, 1980), pp. 175–6; Heal and Holmes, *Gentry*, pp. 224–5.

5. Roebuck, *Yorkshire Baronets*, p. 53; 'Calverley memorandum book', pp. 46–55, 119, 133–5; Holmes, *Seventeenth-Century Lincolnshire*, pp. 78–9.

was amazed to learn one year that his neighbour did *not* plan to come up. In light of these practices, the traditional complaint that absentee landowners' extravagance in London caused poverty in the countryside may have seemed more credible when voiced at this time.[6]

HOUSING

In line with London's growing popularity among the landed, the stock of housing available to visitors expanded from about the mid-seventeenth century as the result of two building booms. One occurred around the time of the Restoration and provided for landed figures rushing back to the capital with the end of the revolutionary era. The boom also compensated for the loss of suitable dwellings resulting from the decay of elite residences in and near the Strand. In 1657 the Earl of Southampton revived plans drawn in the 1640s to build a mansion on his Bloomsbury land, which when completed in 1660 was set in a neighbourhood improved by the replacement of wooden tenements with brick buildings that Southampton rented out.[7] In the following years building occurred in the area north of St James's Palace (Leicester Fields and St James's Square) and further away in Golden Square, Soho Square, and Bloomsbury Square. The London fire displaced some luxury shops from the City to such neighbourhoods, adding to their select character, but by the early eighteenth century these districts, fashionable thirty or forty years before, had lost cachet with the most elite.

In the mid-1710s, the Peace of Utrecht and the change of dynasty ushered in a new era of construction, when several noble landowners led the way in building up northwest Westminster. The next decades featured development of the streets off Piccadilly and of what became the most fashionable squares of early Hanoverian London: Cavendish Square, Grosvenor Square, and Hanover Square. The expansion was so marked that when Sir Robert Walpole left office in the early 1740s and began to make social visits (something he had been spared as prime minister), 'he could not guess where he was, finding himself in so many new streets and squares'.[8] Moreover,

6. J.A. Chartres, 'City and towns, farmers and economic change in the 18th century', *Historical Research* 64 (1991), p. 148; Jenkins, *Making of a Ruling Class*, pp. 243–4; J.V. Beckett, 'Absentee landownership in the later seventeenth and earlier eighteenth centuries: the case of Cumbria', *Northern History* 19 (1983), p. 87.

7. Lawrence Stone, *Family and Fortune: Studies in Aristocratic Finance in the Sixteenth and Seventeenth Centuries* (Oxford, 1973), pp. 94–5, 108, 111–12, 237–8; idem, 'Residential development', p. 194; Schwoerer, *Lady Rachel Russell*, pp. 28–9.

8. *Walpole Correspondence*, xxiv, p. 228.

while planned developments, including one around Berkeley Square after 1739, spread fashionable residential areas unevenly around Westminster, newly built single or small groups of terrace houses helped to connect the grand squares to one another and to provide affordable housing for landowners coming to London.[9]

The large projects were taken on by contractors who secured decades-long ground leases from the landowners, most of whom were noblemen. But prospective inhabitants also built for themselves. Upon being made commissioner of the privy seal in 1669, Sir Edward Dering moved to London and successively built two houses in Russell Street (renting one out before living in it) and a third in Gerard Street behind Leicester Gardens, where he settled with his family in 1679.[10] Building extended beyond Westminster. Daniel Defoe claimed in the 1720s that since the Great Fire two thousand houses for the wealthy (though not all of them landowners) had been built 'in the little Towns or Villages of the County of *Middlesex*, West of *London* only'.[11]

In places like Chiswick or Hammersmith, not to mention those that Defoe explicitly omitted in his count – Chelsea, Kensington, Knightsbridge, Marylebone, and Paddington – the vibrant activities of West End and City were not distant. A resident of Parson's Green in the mid-eighteenth century did complain that he was 'much out of the way of [town] & it's news here', but even four miles removed from the metropolis's heart he was geographically better placed than his country correspondent both to obtain information of town and to enjoy its offerings.[12] As available housing increased, expectations rose, and many of the landed abandoned sets of rooms for the burgeoning numbers of row houses being erected. Taking lodgings in another's house may have been wise for those first coming to town or uncertain of success there, but for those with more substantial means and for neophytes once they gained experience, mere lodgings would not suffice. It was difficult to put up an entire

9. *Survey of London*, 29–30, *The Parish of St James Westminster, Part One, South of Piccadilly* (London, 1960); 31–2, *The Parish of St James Westminster, Part Two, North of Piccadilly* (London, 1963); 33–4, *The Parish of St Anne Soho* (London, 1966).

10. Stone, 'Residential development', pp. 199–203; John Summerson, *Georgian London*, revised edition (Baltimore, 1962), pp. 98–112; George Rudé, *Hanoverian London* (Berkeley, 1971), pp. 9, 12–14, 40–4; Alison Adburgham, *Shopping in Style: London from the Restoration to Edwardian Elegance* (London, 1979), pp. 29, 38; *Dering Diaries*, pp. 111–16.

11. Daniel Defoe, *A Tour Thro' the Whole Island of Great Britain*, G.D.H. Cole, ed., 2 vols (London, 1927; originally published 1724–27), I, p. 392.

12. H. Marriott to Sir T. Drury, 2 October 1746, Norfolk Record Office, NRS 21138, 74x5.

family in a set of rooms rather than in a house, and in the more chic parts of the eighteenth-century metropolis houses were anyway more commonly found to rent than were smaller accommodations.

London not only offered better accommodation but grew more attractive as a place for the landed to live after the mid-seventeenth century. The spread of town news, fashion, and gossip by well-developed postal services, which distributed them privately, and by the newspaper and serial press, which made them public, aroused interest in the doings of the metropolis and inspired gentry visits. Improved transportation gave quicker and more comfortable access to London and made it easier to get around town once there. Advances in lighting and provision of water also made urban life safer, healthier, and more pleasant, while coincidentally extending social life into the evening hours.[13] More and greater amenities like these encouraged entire families, or at least husbands and wives, to come to town: the expansion of housing and other improvements probably both stimulated and responded to demand. Where once a parliament man up for the session or a landowner pursuing legal business stayed alone in rooms hired by the week, even gentry of relatively modest means were increasingly expected to bring their wives with them and to live in houses rented by the month or year.

The elder Robert Walpole was content to live alone in the capital in a room above a linen-draper's, costing a pound a week, where his son the prime minister began his public life living in Westminster (and then moved to Chelsea) with his wife, who often remained in town when he had to leave. Joseph Banks I (1665–1727), the successful Sheffield attorney and whig MP, who established his family on a landed estate in Lincolnshire, happily lived in Boswell Court off Fleet Street in the City when he came to the metropolis. His son Joseph II (1695–1741) on election to parliament in 1728 purchased a house in St James's Square, Westminster. Sir William Leveson-Gower, a political lightweight while member for Newcastle-under-Lyme from 1675 to 1691, resided primarily in Staffordshire, annually came to London, and lived in rooms. His son passed virtually all his time in town after entering parliament in 1692, and while he was apparently less interested in London's consumer goods than his father, he none the less bought a house in Dover Street, Westminster.[14]

13. Stone, 'Residential development', pp. 177–81.
14. J.H. Plumb, 'The Walpoles: father and son', in J.H. Plumb, ed., *Studies in Social History* (London, 1955), pp. 192–3; *Banks Papers*, pp. xvii, xxviii; J.R. Wordie, *Estate Management in Eighteenth-Century England: The Building of the Leveson-Gower Fortune* (London, 1982), pp. 77–8.

PROFILES OF VISITORS, PATTERNS OF VISITING

Landed women apparently went more frequently to London after the Restoration than before. Separation of married couples, with wives left in the country, seems responsible for generating the mass of surviving correspondence between elite spouses from the late sixteenth and first half of the seventeenth centuries. No comparable amount appears after 1660, when wives more automatically accompanied their husbands, even on diplomatic missions abroad and especially on the journeys to town that new coach technology made more bearable.[15] Women, married or single, were stereotypically depicted as being particularly possessed by 'the prejudices in favour of this good Town of London'. A neighbour of *The Spectator*'s Sir Roger de Coverley had a wife 'always hankering after the Diversions of the Town', and if George Etherege's *The Man of Mode* (1676) is any guide, a young woman would even pretend to accept in marriage a man she disliked, if the ruse would get her 'up to London'. For Jane Lowther, when it became clear in 1699 that her father would never go back to town, a claim of illness that needed metropolitan care justified her own return to the city.[16]

With greater accommodation and more comfortable travel available, children also routinely joined their parents in an urban locale that offered them great edification, both through schooling and the mere experience of urban living. It was presumably to the intended benefit of the heir to the Hotham baronetcy that, after his father's death, the family relocated from Yorkshire to London during his minority. In similar vein, one squire wrote of his teenaged son and a friend that they 'both want a little of London'; another took the opportunity of half a year in town to have his merely five-year-old son learn to dance and to speak French.[17] Although by no means confined to London, the 'new world of children' was a highly urbanized one to which the metropolis contributed significantly. Under the influence of new ideas about how best to rear children, parents in the late seventeenth century willingly exposed them to

15. Heal and Holmes, *Gentry*, p. 70; Joyce Godber, 'The Marchioness Grey of Wrest Park', *Bedfordshire Historical Record Society* 47 (1968), pp. 7–9.

16. *Banks Papers*, p. 183; *The Spectator*, Donald F. Bond, ed. (Oxford, 1965), II, p. 11; George Etherege, *The Man of Mode; or, Sir Fopling Flutter* (1676), in John Harold Wilson, ed., *Six Restoration Plays* (Boston, 1959), p. 115; *Lowther Correspondence*, p. 657. See also Beckett, *Aristocracy*, p. 366 and G.E. Mingay, *English Landed Society in the Eighteenth Century* (London, 1963), p. 156.

17. Roebuck, *Yorkshire Baronets*, p. 100; *Banks Papers*, p. 17; 'Calverley memorandum book', pp. 133–4. See also Plumb, 'Walpoles: father and son', p. 188; Godber, 'Marchioness Grey', pp. 12–13.

the new sights and experiences of which towns, and especially London, had so many. By the eighteenth century, children served as their parents' companions in unprecedented ways, visiting with them an array of attractions that had simply not existed before, including lectures, pleasure gardens, and collections of rarities. Family attachments, perhaps more easily indulged and more freely expressed than ever before, played a part in bringing children to London and giving substance to an increasingly meaningful social unit, the nuclear family. Sir Robert Walpole's uncle, Horatio, a man of rising importance in the tory party, came alone to town in 1711 on parliamentary business but quickly asked his political masters for temporary release to fetch his family before the session began. For the eighteenth-century gentry of southwest Wales, travel to town was very much a family affair.[18]

The rhythm of London life profoundly shaped elite behaviour and consciousness. Uncertain, hesitant, difficult to follow for forty years after mid-century, from the 1690s this rhythm became clearer and more pronounced and grew increasingly so under the Hanoverian kings, whose own foreign travels, for example, helped to set the metropolitan beat. Part of what it came to mean to belong to landed society in the mid-eighteenth century was to be in town at generally certain times of year, rarely before mid-autumn or after late spring, sometimes coming as late as November and departing as early as March. When Joseph Banks II negotiated to rent his house in St James's Square to the Prussian ambassador in 1731, the parties agreed on six months' rent of £180 from November to May, continuing thereafter at £20 per month for 'the summer season, when people goe in to the contry again'. Thomas Potter, barrister of the Inner Temple, took a summer trip to the Continent in 1737 'merely to look about . . . any where else but in London during the long Vacation'. Late autumn, winter, and early spring were, contrastingly, more desirably spent in the city than the country; this may have been the case with winter most of all for some time. It was for a winter stay that one of William III's chaplains, John Herne, believed he could lure his landowning brother to the city. Resumption of

---

18. J.H. Plumb, 'The new world of children', in Neil McKendrick, John Brewer, and J.H. Plumb, *The Birth of a Consumer Society: The Commercialization of Eighteenth-Century England* (Bloomington, Indiana, 1982), pp. 286–315; Heal and Holmes, *Gentry*, p. 46; Walpole to the Earl of Oxford, 1 December [1711?], British Library, Loan 29/160, unfoliated at time of consultation (papers have now been recatalogued as two volumes, Additional MSS 70262 and 70263); David W. Howell, *Patriarchs and Parasites: The Gentry of South-West Wales in the Eighteenth Century* (Cardiff, 1986), pp. 175–6.

her former pattern of spending this season in London signalled Lady Rachel Russell's psychological recovery from the execution of her husband in 1683, and was a routine she maintained into her old age.[19]

Various matters determined whether a landed household – and what elements of it – made a stay in London, and for how long and where. For many of the men, business imperatives, the legal term, or political developments most affected the timing of visits, while they might be less relevant for women. One common reason for both sexes to visit the metropolis, to participate in its social season, was clearly connected to the meeting of parliament. In late 1741 the Duke of Richmond planned to go to London 'Parliament or no Parliament' because he had 'business of my own in town', but his wife's coming depended entirely on the start of the session, which heralded the social season.[20] Contrarily, when male heads of household returned to their country business, wives sometimes stayed behind in the capital, which necessitated distinctive arrangements to supply them with money. The author of a guide for estate stewards published in 1683 in fact provided in a model set of accounts an exemplary entry for £15 paid to 'my Lady at her going out of Town'.[21]

Complaints about the dullness or quiet of the town often coincided with periods when parliament was out of session, rural recreations beckoned, and summer heat made the city unhealthy. Before late autumn the town could be deserted, as Lord Chesterfield complained it was one late September and declared it would remain until parliament met.[22] But many landed figures of either sex and any age were loath to leave London once there. After all, if everyone among the social elite had left town, there would have been no one left to observe just how dull it had become.

Some landowners so enjoyed the metropolis that they allowed their country estates to become secondary residences, although this was rare. After 1706, Sir James Lowther resided permanently in

19. *Banks Papers*, p. 134; Sarah Markham, *John Loveday of Caversham 1711–1789: The Life and Tours of an Eighteenth-Century Onlooker* (Salisbury, Wiltshire, 1984), p. 286; J. Herne to R. Herne, 31 March 1694, Cambridge University Library, Buxton MS, box 37; Schwoerer, *Lady Rachel Russell*, p. 155.

20. *Richmond–Newcastle Correspondence*, p. 80.

21. [Stephen Monteage,] *Instructions for Rent-Gatherers Accompts &c. made easie* (London, 1683), p. 19; see also *Fitzwilliam Correspondence*, p. 18.

22. *The Letters of Philip Dormer Stanhope 4th Earl of Chesterfield*, Bonamy Dobrée, ed., 6 vols (London, 1932; reprinted New York, 1968), III, *April, 1745 to August 1748*, pp. 1014–15.

London as long as he lived, making only summer visits to his northern estates. Once Robert Walpole entered parliament in 1700 he only returned to the country for brief stays, not so difficult to do when Norfolk was his destination, but some were as short as two weeks. Lord Fitzwilliam, who considered himself a private country gentleman and heard the siren call of the land, none the less remained in London between 1697 and 1709, ignoring his country estate despite annual vows and preparations to visit it. When his eldest son died in London, no member of the family went with the body to Northamptonshire, and significantly it was neither business nor politics but seemingly only an habituation to metropolitan life as a whole that kept Fitzwilliam in town.[23]

London as focal point: politics, law, and business

Against the specificity that determined individual decisions about the timing, duration, and frequency of visits to London ran a defining undercurrent shared by aristocrats at large, an undercurrent driven by much more than the tides of the political and social seasons. As Peter Roebuck has pointed out, by the time that George I came to the throne it had become 'increasingly difficult to arrange purely private concerns without visiting the capital'.[24] Part of what it meant to belong to landed society was to have one's life moulded in many ways by London-based institutions that were doubly central to it, first as instruments of a singular and integrating state and second as institutions that intruded into one's everyday activities and assessment of priorities, demanding attention and claiming prominence in elite life. While some compelling events and institutions of rule could be found in the towns of the provinces (like parliamentary elections or sessions of the peace), we have already seen that these had to vie for the attention of the landed, and often unsuccessfully, with the rewards proffered by one's country seat: recreation, renovation, the satisfactions of ownership. When in winter the provincial towns might offer diverting respite from a country seat that might be cold, dark, and quiet, that was when London often presented stiff competition of its own.

23. Beckett, *Coal and Tobacco*, pp. 26–7; idem, 'A back-bench MP in the eighteenth century: Sir James Lowther of Whitehaven', *Parliamentary History* 1 (1982), p. 81; Plumb, 'Walpoles: father and son', p. 192; *Fitzwilliam Correspondence*, pp. 61–4.
24. Roebuck, *Yorkshire Baronets*, p. 53.

London's centrality to many aspects of English life prior to the mid-seventeenth century intensified in the ensuing years. The metropolis's magnetism in the arenas of government and politics grew synergistically, especially with the continued expansion of government agencies that had commenced in the 1640s and 1650s. A supplicant in the country who sought access to the Navy Office, or Excise, or to more traditional channels of power and influence, benefited by the presence in London of 'any friend there, proper, whose assistance you coud ask for me in this affair'.[25]

The expansion of state bureaucracy made the metropolis more visible as the site where the work of government was done, where one sought to enrol in that work, and where appeals against that work or its consequences were to be made.[26] Parliament's meetings further enhanced this visibility. In one hundred and two years, from 1653 to 1754, the body was called into formal session one hundred times. This rate was unprecedented over a long period and had only been parallelled in the mid-fifteenth century, when the nature of a parliamentary session was very different, not least because it frequently assembled away from the metropolis.[27] More to the point, no group aside from parliament's employees (doorkeepers, custodians, and so on) and the victuallers and hostellers around the Palace of Westminster was more affected by this early modern frequency of meeting than the landed figures who predominantly comprised the members of the two houses of parliament. Meetings of the body played important parts in making the London sojourn routine for many of the landed, and whatever different private reasons they had for coming to the city, attendance at the legislature gave them a common, public, and national one.

THE COURT

Not merely the centre of national decision-making and legislation as effected in parliament, London was also the centre of political planning and scheming. Much of these revolved around the court

25. *Banks Papers*, p. 143. For the transformative power of the city, see E. Anthony Wrigley's classic exposition, 'A simple model of London's importance in changing English society and economy, 1650–1750', in Wrigley, *People, Cities and Wealth: The Transformation of Traditional Society* (Oxford, 1988), pp. 133–56.

26. G.E. Aylmer, *The State's Servants: The Civil Service of the English Republic 1649–1660* (London, 1973); Henry Roseveare, *The Treasury, 1660–1870* (London, 1973); C.D. Chandaman, *The English Public Revenue 1660–88* (Oxford, 1975).

27. E.B. Fryde et al., eds, *Handbook of British Chronology*, 3rd edn (Cambridge, 1986; reprinted with corrections 1996), pp. 569–71, 575–9.

under the later Stuarts. But they spilled over both then and under the next dynasty into private residences, taverns, coffee houses and elsewhere, especially because the evolution of two political parties tended to create an 'out' group unwelcome at court.

Lord Hervey's experience attests to contemporary awareness that the eighteenth-century political world even of those who were 'in' extended well beyond the court. Although Hervey was actually pursuing pleasure, he told the king that he stayed twice a week in town (rather than at Hampton Court) 'to pick up news, to hear what people said, to see how they looked, and to inform Their Majesties what was thought by all parties of the present posture of affairs'.[28] That he perceived a need to bring political news to Hampton Court serves as a reminder that public business was conducted in many places and that those clustered around the monarch had no exclusive claim to the political attentions of the great of the land. Even before George I came to England, the court was being overwhelmed by the state as an employer, and it was being diminished as a fount of political reward by ministries to which the ambitious had to attach themselves. The world of commerce also overshadowed it as a place of material reward. Those seeking advancement continued to make their way to London in order to gain it, but the days were gone when the monarch's position as patron of all patrons made court itself the ultimate destination of the ambitious.

Stuart kings may have been too much involved in day-to-day politics to be effective national figures who garnered loyalty and affection from their kingdoms, but perhaps their successors were too little involved to become the universal and magnetic objects of landed politicians' attention. Moreover, the social attachments that had once made court lively were disappearing in a post-revolutionary political world where traditional ritual symbolism and strictly personal allegiances counted for less with the ruling elite. The court was fading as the centre of social life in the Augustan era because many found more rewarding sociability in the West End. Limited access to court also diminished its attraction: after Queen Mary's death, William III was absent from the realm for nearly 40 per cent of the rest of his reign.

Queen Anne tried to restore lustre to the court by reviving royal ceremonial but had little success with the landed elite. She maintained the Stuart outdoor traditions of hunting and racing but

---

28. John Lord Hervey, *Some Materials towards Memoirs of the Reign of King George II*, Romney Sedgwick, ed., 3 vols (London, 1931; reprinted New York, 1970), I, p. 221.

offered limited indoor entertainment, and that of slight appeal. Aristocrats reluctantly attended her twice- or thrice-weekly gatherings in the royal apartments, which the queen's ill-health made unpredictable and her formality made dull. The party character of court occasions drove whigs away toward the end of Anne's reign, and tories were similarly put off under her successors, when opposition whigs also turned from the monarchs' courts to their rivals in those of the Princes of Wales. Finally, the distance of Windsor, Hampton Court, and (to a lesser degree) Kensington Palace from the West End, and the problems in communicating with the formal and shy Queen Anne, the private George I, and the stiff, unlikable George II made attendance at court an uninviting prospect for many.[29]

Diminished as a focal point of public employment and social life, the court also declined as a centre of culture. Its uneven patronage of cultural talent encouraged artists to look outside for aristocratic patronage in individual homes and the age's private clubs. The failure to attract artists to court in turn drove off the artists' traditional customers and audience, the landed. By 1700, the court offered much less than it historically had to those subjects who set the kingdom's tone socially, culturally, and politically. Between 1717 and 1720 George I's court briefly came to life, although not with high culture. Unprecedentedly, the king dined in public and held assemblies, evening receptions, and even morning *levées*. He also established a public table at court where members of parliament and others of quality came and fed at royal expense. All this the king undertook, however, only in a successful effort to compete for popularity with the Prince of Wales, from whom he was estranged. But when the two reconciled in 1720, George I returned to his reclusive ways and the life of court grew dull once more.[30]

Despite some revival under George II and his queen Caroline, the court was becoming a marginal, alien, mostly symbolic institution in the eyes of many of the landed, a self-referential and closed world. Speaking in 1733 of George II's household, Lord Hervey asserted that 'in no Court was there ever less to be got', while Sir

29. Robert O. Bucholz, *The Augustan Court: Queen Anne and the Decline of Court Culture* (Stanford, 1993), pp. 244–6, 249–50; Rudé, *Hanoverian London*, pp. 77–8; Fryde et al., eds, *Handbook of British Chronology*, p. 45; J.M. Beattie, *The English Court in the Reign of George I* (Cambridge, 1967), pp. 257–62; *The Memoirs and Speeches of James, 2nd Earl of Waldegrave, 1742–1763*, J.C.D. Clark, ed. (Cambridge, 1988), p. 4.

30. Bucholz, *Augustan Court*, ch. 7; William Weber, *The Rise of Musical Classics in Eighteenth-Century England: A Study in Canon, Ritual, and Ideology* (Oxford, 1992), pp. 110–12; Beattie, *Court of George I*, pp. 264–76.

Robert Walpole observed that it was 'as little the fashion to speak well of [George II] in his palace as in the country; and that by his awkward, simple, proud conduct, even among all those whose interest it is to be friends to his power, there is not one to be found who is a friend to his person'.[31] These conditions were not likely to make landowners eager to enter the courtly world.

The court's diminished allure for landowners in the eighteenth century was more than offset by other metropolitan opportunities and excitements, however. The decline of the court's magnetism certainly did not prompt an exodus from London. Instead, the landed spent more of their time in town away from the court, gaining and exercising political power through an attachment to party and state, and promoting their fortunes in the financial markets and professions. A variety of public venues more than compensated for the loss, because they offered even more than court did and provided it day in and day out. Thus it was increasingly outside court 'that art was commissioned, business transacted, political plots laid, and the beau monde displayed'.[32] Withdrawal from the court discouraged the landed elite gathered in London from seeing themselves as members of a group defined by its vertical relationship to the monarchy. And as they then gathered in alternative venues, this detachment provided the perspective for seeing themselves as similarly inclined individuals who together comprised a most singular social grouping.

THE LAW

The metropolis was thus a hub (though not the sole location) of elite political, social, and artistic cultures that were in the process of redefinition. The same could be said about its place within a national legal culture that permeated to all corners of the island but none the less radiated from the centre. An eager and highly susceptible landed elite received encouragement from country lawyers to pursue litigation at Westminster, which they took little convincing to do, since for generations men of honour and standing had involved themselves directly and energetically in their own legal affairs.[33]

---

31. Hervey, *Memoirs*, I, p. 208 for quotations; see also Bucholz, *Augustan Court*, pp. 241–8; *Waldegrave Memoirs*, pp. 2–5, 16, 18–19.
32. Robert O. Bucholz, ' "Nothing but ceremony": Queen Anne and the limitations of royal ritual', *Journal of British Studies* 30 (1991), p. 313.
33. Holmes, *Lincolnshire*, p. 51; Stone, *Crisis of the Aristocracy*, pp. 240–2.

Provincial law was not necessarily inadequate, but the metropolis offered unique legal services or those that were simply seen as superior. London-based barristers, though expensive, had distinctive credentials as well as special knowledge unavailable in the countryside. Landowners went to confer with lawyers in the capital and even called their country attorneys to the metropolis for consultation on complicated local matters. Walter Calverley's negotiations for the purchase of tithe rights on his Yorkshire estate involved a month in town meeting with his lawyers, negotiating with other parties, and taking advantage of immediate recourse to the law courts.[34]

The metropolis was the increasingly obvious centre for all sorts of legal transactions (conveyancing, settlements, probate) as well as litigation, and when in town landowners were frequently occupied with their lawyers and in the courts. While legal papers could always be sent up to and signed in the countryside, the danger of miscarriage, the ease of correcting faulty documents, and the clarifying benefit of direct consultation together warranted the time and expense of a trip to the capital, even if these alone were reasons to come. In the late seventeenth century William Massingberd travelled annually from Lincolnshire to pass a couple of months in London pursuing litigation. The action of Wycherley's *Country Wife* (1675) was largely set in motion by Mr Pinchwife's trip to London to pay his sister's £5000 marriage portion and pursue a suit at law, even though his fears for the virtue of the new wife accompanying him would have made staying in the country an otherwise reasonable decision.[35]

The unique credentials that made London barristers indispensable for conduct of the business of the landed were of course acquired by study at and qualifications provided through the inns of court. These remained attractive destinations for some landed sons, even though few crossed the hurdles to the bar and even though fewer students *in toto*, and fewer from the landed classes in particular, came to the inns after 1650 than had in the previous century. These declining numbers reached their nadir in 1745–49. Yet between 1688 and 1714 more sons from the social elite enrolled each year at the inns than did at Oxford. During this era some seventy-five sons of substantial landowners (peers, baronets, knights, and esquires) were annually entering and dominating the inns, where heirs to

---

34. 'Calverley memorandum book', pp. 53–5, 64; *Fitzwilliam Correspondence*, p. 56.
35. *Banks Papers*, p. 91; Holmes, *Lincolnshire*, p. 78; William Wycherley, *The Country Wife* (1675), in John Harold Wilson, ed., *Six Restoration Plays* (Boston, 1959), p. 14.

landed estates comprised nearly half the student body. Moreover, better than half of the landed group of law students were university alumni, suggesting that residence at the inns gave sons of the landed specific elements of education (perhaps social attributes rather than intellectual ones) that the university failed adequately to supply.[36]

That these elements of education were uniquely metropolitan is suggested by the regional pattern of decline in admissions to the inns. The greatest drop off between the late sixteenth and early eighteenth century occurred in counties closest to London, where landowners were especially beset by taxation and other economic burdens for fifty years after the Restoration. These financial strains may have made the cost of sending sons to the inns appear to be a questionable outlay, especially when geographic proximity allowed these young men relatively easy experience of London society in other ways. For gentry sons living in the north, by contrast, residence at an inn carried the double advantage of legal education and exposure to the metropolis together. Strikingly, the counties of Durham, Cumberland, and Northumberland were the only ones experiencing an increase in admissions over the period.[37]

BUSINESS

Legal and political affairs were far from providing the only material reasons – or even excuses – for coming to town year in and year out. Part of what drew gentry and nobility to London was its position as the kingdom's premier place of business, not merely the outlet for landowners' agricultural products, but home to the money markets and the increasingly sophisticated and wealthy banks of the age.[38] Sometimes London was simply the most convenient place to meet, and personal contact the best way, to conduct affairs. Disturbed lest its length 'shall be troublesome', the agent of Essex squire Dacres Barrett cut short a letter to his employer with the promise that 'what remayns when in London I will acquaynt you'.[39]

What kind of business the landed were transacting is not always evident, partly because distinctions that seem clear today were non-existent or blurred then, like the difference between personal and

36. David Lemmings, *Gentlemen and Barristers: The Inns of Court and the English Bar 1680–1730* (Oxford, 1990), ch. 1.

37. Ibid., pp. 28–30.

38. Frank T. Melton, *Sir Robert Clayton and the Origins of English Deposit Banking, 1658–1685* (Cambridge, 1986), pp. 223–5; D.M. Joslin, 'London private bankers, 1720–1785', *Economic History Review*, 2nd series, 7 (1954–55), pp. 167–86.

39. R. Britiffe to D. Barrett, 29 October 1697, Essex Record Office, D/DL C3/9.

other expenses or between different sources of income. Many land-owners had estate business that involved transfers of land and the disposal of estate-generated products, different affairs from those financial matters that involved their investments and paper securities. Whatever its type, the London business that helped to spur gentry trips to town was generally that which could not be performed indirectly or from elsewhere. Such was the 'money affair of moment' that prevented Edward Wortley Montagu, eager to live outside London, from doing so for several years, a preoccupation similar to the 'business' (predominantly legal matters) that Lord Fitzwilliam recurrently invoked to explain why he could not visit his lands in Northamptonshire. On yielding his parliamentary seat at Carlisle in 1702, James Lowther used the pressure of London affairs to explain the decision, an excuse he presumably offered to electors in the belief that they too assigned transcendent importance to metropolitan business over local concerns.[40]

London as focal point: marriage, medicine, and material goods

Obviously, business reasons were less likely to explain the presence in London of landed women than of landed men, but both sexes shared various interests demanding or benefiting from metropolitan attention, marriage constituting a major one. Landed families who socialized with one another in town inevitably discussed marriage prospects and made matrimonial arrangements. Although other urban locales, and even country houses, gave opportunities for single people to meet, London offered more. It was, for example, the only place where a couple like Mary Pierrepont and Edward Wortley Montagu, pursuing a clandestine courtship, could hope to encounter one another in as many as nine different houses.[41] London was not just a place to make matches but also somewhere to get married. Many partners from country families apparently found it convenient – perhaps prestigious – to undergo the ceremony in the capital, often a location where neither bride's nor groom's family permanently resided.[42]

40. *Montagu Letters*, I, p. 92; *Fitzwilliam Correspondence*, pp. 51, 55; Beckett, 'A back-bench MP', p. 81.
41. *Montagu Letters*, I, pp. 74–5.
42. D. Michell to Sir E. Harley, 1 December 1673, British Library, Additional MSS 70012, fol. 98; 'Calverley memorandum book', p. 71; *Eaton to Cardigan Letters*, p. xv.

By contrast, it was also a place to hide a marriage unwelcome to one family, as that between the second Earl Waldegrave's brother and the daughter of Lord Gower in 1751, and also where clandestine marriages occurred with extraordinary frequency until the Marriage Act was passed in 1753.[43] London was central to matrimony in other than social ways. The increasingly complicated task of preparing the settlements that accompanied so many marriages among the elite were in the hands of conveyancers, many in town. Marriage portions, although they might sometimes be accumulated by sales of land or by saving, were most frequently raised on mortgage, and the large sums involved were almost invariably raised in the capital, or at least through London agents. They were often paid in town as well, since that was where the kingdom's banking facilities lay.[44]

London frequently served as the site where the most valued products of marriages, the offspring, were born, a reflection of the city's status as a medical centre where the best doctors and latest knowledge were available. Elite women regularly planned to have their babies delivered in town.[45] Home to the Royal College of Physicians, nominal monopolists of the practice of 'physic', London also abounded with apothecaries and surgeons who vied with and complemented the work of physicians. The capital (and the kingdom at large) benefited from the slow fusion between 1660 and 1740 of these three groups of practitioners into a single medical profession, a process Geoffrey Holmes has called 'the coming of "the doctor"'. The development was accompanied by progress in the area of medical training, some of it obtained through observation at the hospitals of London, which increased in number from two under Queen Anne to seven by mid-century.[46]

The towering medical figures of the age, Dr Radcliffe, Dr Sloane, and Dr Mead, practised in the capital, where the Royal College's influence also meant that doctors from the highest social origins and of greatest reputation were most likely to practice as well.[47] Ample medical advice and more-than-competent ministration could be had

---

43. Lawrence Stone, *Road to Divorce: England 1530–1987* (Oxford, 1990), ch. 4; *Waldegrave Memoirs*, p. 41.

44. Susan Staves, *Married Women's Separate Property in England 1660–1833* (Cambridge, Massachusetts, 1990), ch. 3, especially pp. 58–9; Habakkuk, *Estates System*, pp. 65–70, 120–1.

45. D. Michell to Sir E. Harley, 22 February 1675, British Library, Additional MSS 70120; *Banks Papers*, p. 164.

46. Holmes, *Augustan England*, ch. 6. The old hospitals were St Thomas's and Bart's; the new were Guy's, St George's, the London, the Middlesex, and the Westminster Infirmary; Bart's was also completely rebuilt beginning in 1729: ibid., p. 200.

47. Ibid., ch. 7, esp. pp. 218–22.

in the provinces, especially in towns, and much it came from professionals, but the care obtainable in London was of a different order. When Lord Guilford was seriously ill in 1734, an anxious Prince of Wales quite naturally planned a 'scheme of sending for [him] to town', and Lady Rachel Russell moved from Bedfordshire to Hertfordshire in 1684 to be closer to a London doctor, later wintering in London to benefit her son's health.[48] When Jane Lowther sought her excuse to leave Cumberland and return to town on her own, she complained of ear trouble, refused both local advice and that which was sent from London doctors by mail, and so went off to the capital for treatment in person. Lady Betty Aislaibie's family took her to town and used the services of two London doctors in a vain effort to save her from smallpox, and the capital was the principal place where the bold few who underwent them (notably among the elite) had inoculations against the disease.[49]

London doctors were both consulted by letter and sent for in person when the sick could not come to town, a further confirmation of the landed's faith in metropolitan expertise. Lady Rachel Russell appealed to the highest authority she knew, Dr Hans Sloane, to send the best London obstetric doctor to Leicestershire to help her pregnant daughter, who rallied under this man's care and promptly went to London for further attention.[50] When Lord Fitzwilliam learned that his country lawyer was ill, he went to the man's London physician and relayed to Northamptonshire the doctor's advice, unavoidably limited in scope because 'at this distance 'twas impossible to direct' – a clear instance of the need to be in London to benefit maximally from it.[51]

In the person of professionals like doctors and lawyers, expertise resided in town and served as a powerful stimulus to bring to the city those who could afford the best services. More generally, it appears that metropolitan ways were conceived as intrinsically expert ones by many elite minds. This was apparent even in mundane arenas, as in a Lancashire gentlewoman's insistence on sending her personal linen to be laundered in town, or in the preference for sending purchases down to the country by London-based carriers, who knew 'how to packe up goods safe and deliver them [more] carefully then

48. C. Montagu to [Lord Guilford], 13 August 1734, Bodleian Library, MS North.d.4, fols 96–96v; Schwoerer, *Lady Rachel Russell*, p. 155.

49. *Lowther Correspondence*, p. 657; *Banks Papers*, p. 162; Godber, 'The Marchioness Grey', p. 10; *Montagu Letters*, II, p. 49, n. 3.

50. Schwoerer, *Lady Rachel Russell*, pp. 61, 227–8.

51. *Fitzwilliam Correspondence*, p. 184.

any countrey man can'.[52] Only London talent could properly alter the Countess of Deloraine's gown or make Joseph Banks's shirts. Provincial shortcomings are exemplified by one early eighteenth-century observation that Yorkshire could not even supply a coachman capable of the journey from country to city, much less one who knew how to drive in the streets of London.[53]

In some matters the superior skills and knowledge of the metropolis were transferable into the provinces, through oral report, writing, or personal contact. The correspondence of Lord Fitzwilliam and his steward Francis Guybon supplies many examples of the solicitation and then application of London expertise. Work on the floors of Fitzwilliam's hen house was deferred until he could bring down the recommendations of experienced fowl-keepers in town, and repairs to his leaky roof at Milton were put off until a London-based surveyor could give an opinion. When Fitzwilliam's country housekeeper fell ill, he asked for information on her condition so that 'what advise can be had here in towne shall immediately be gott, and what things shall be prescribed shall forthwith be sent downe if they are to be had for money'. In this case, the value of a service that included both a written transfer of metropolitan knowledge and the physical dispatch of town commodities warranted the cost in this landowner's eyes, but sometimes what the city held was too dear. When the London lawyers to whom Fitzwilliam spoke about a provincial legal problem wanted to consult his country attorney in town, he decided it was not worth the expense.[54]

The metropolitan corner on expertise and the association of the city with the best also rested on a metropolitan near-monopoly of desirable, status-bestowing, luxurious commodities. Although these could be purchased by people with sufficient money, they could not be put to proper use in appropriate context by just anyone. It was not a single item that bestowed and sustained status but rather the deployment of many items in the approved manner. And the provinces sometimes lacked the accessories of life that allowed the elite to act with the decorum and nuanced good taste that set them apart from the rest of society; London did not. Writing from the provinces as late as 1734, one might have to apologize in a condolence letter for failing to use 'black paper & wax', unavailable in the country; London could supply it. Town was where even modest Puritan gentlewomen bought their clothes and the only place for the fashionable to purchase gloves for a wedding. Although she recognized it was a

52. Stone, 'Residential development', p. 183; *Fitzwilliam Correspondence*, p. 122.
53. *Banks Papers*, pp. 162–5; *Montagu Letters*, I, p. 238.
54. *Fitzwilliam Correspondence*, pp. 16, 18, 34–5, 56.

strange request, one gentlewoman sought 'a hunderd of pens reddy made' from a friend going to London, since she was 'tired to death' with those inferior ones found in the country.[55] Local craftsmen seeking landed patronage knew that they had to compete against metropolitan producers and products, leading one country carpenter to promise in 1717 that he would make sash windows for the house of Joseph Banks I at Revesby in Lincolnshire 'as cheap and as good as you can have from London'. Banks took up the offer, but fearing that the carpenter had 'not seen the newest fashioned' sash windows, planned to send a model from London first, the capital thus literally providing the pattern for elements of country life.[56]

The city was the expected source for high-quality goods, from a fancy new carriage down to four 'best' close stools. Only some local artisans could provide products 'as good as you can have from London' by imitating the fashions set there, and even they could be undercut on cost. Others lacked the skill, materials, or facilities to do so. While a local carpenter made satisfactory windows for the front of the Banks home, the hangings and most other furnishings came from town – along with various spices then unavailable in the country. Colours for the paint to be used on the Earl of Cardigan's country-house renovations were mechanically ground in town and were thus cheaper (and so preferable) to the hand-ground ones found in the country. Despite the increasing availability of luxury goods in the eighteenth-century provincial town, a failure in the supply of London coffee could create domestic crisis.[57] Country gentry who would not have thought to procure a pocket watch locally at the turn of the century might have to be patient while a relative secured one in London, but once found it was dispatched with confidence in its high quality and with a seven-year guarantee.[58] Although these circumstances may have been altering at mid-eighteenth century, as the 'urban renaissance' saw a wide expansion in the crafts practised and thus the products sold in country towns,[59]

55. J. Ancaster to Lord Guilford, 29 May [1734], Bodleian Library, MS North.d.4, fol. 88; J.T. Cliffe, *The Puritan Gentry Besieged, 1650–1700* (London, 1993), p. 172; 'Calverley memorandum book', p. 115; *Banks Papers*, p. 153.

56. *Banks Papers*, pp. 32, 34, 38.

57. Rosenheim, *Townshends of Raynham*, pp. 78–9; *Banks Papers*, pp. 21–2, 49; 'Calverley memorandum book', p. 95; *Letters of Eaton to Cardigan*, p. 121.

58. J. Herne to R. Herne, 1 November 1691, Cambridge University Library, Buxton MS, box 37.

59. Peter Borsay, 'The English urban renaissance: the development of provincial urban culture *c.*1680–*c.*1760', in Borsay, ed., *The Eighteenth Century Town*, pp. 159–87 and idem, *English Urban Renaissance*.

the belief that London still afforded the highest quality and greatest variety of goods, especially for the grandest of the land, inculcated and reinforced buying habits that magnified the importance of the capital.

London events

Beyond commodities out of the ordinary, extraordinary occasions drew attention to affairs in town and brought landed folk there. Visits in person were the best means to show refinement and share fully in the new and growing wonders of the world – both important in maintaining elite identity. Rare commodities could be dispatched, but rare events had to be experienced directly, and not just for participants to display character. Frequently they were held to be instructive occasions, and when not, there was no pretence that anything other than curiosity and the desire for entertainment sparked a visit. When *The Spectator*'s Sir Roger de Coverley hastily and unexpectedly came to town, he was eager merely 'to get a Sight of Prince *Eugene*'.[60]

Such an incident was unique to the capital. When events took place throughout the kingdom, sometimes in response to 'ceremonial cues' given by the court,[61] they none the less were carried out most grandly in the metropolis. The entire kingdom gave thanks for the victory at Ramillies at the end of 1706, but only in London did commons, lords, and monarch make a three-hour procession from Westminster to St Paul's.[62] Singular observances included public royal occasions like coronations, weddings, and funerals, along with more private court events like the occasion of touching for scrofula that Samuel Pepys attended in April 1661 or the celebration of George II's birthday, which the Welsh gentlewoman Mrs Campbell proudly attended eighty years later.[63] Bulstrode Whitelocke, who had prudently left the city when suspected of ties to Venner's Rising, probably returned there with his family in April 1661 specifically to view the coronation, which included the last royal entry associated with such festivities, a cavalcade of king, peers, and others 'going in great gallantrie from the Tower to Whitehall' the day before the

---

60. *The Spectator*, II, p. 549.   61. Bucholz, *Augustan Court*, p. 209.
62. *Nicolson Diaries*, pp. 405–6.
63. *The Diary of Samuel Pepys*, Robert Latham and William Mathews, eds, 11 vols (Berkeley, 1970–83), II, p. 74; Howell, *Patriarchs and Parasites*, p. 176.

ceremony.[64] From the early 1660s to early 1680s the royal weddings of Charles II and Catherine of Braganza, of Princess Mary and the Prince of Orange, and of Princess Anne and Prince George of Denmark each in its way enlivened London. The subsequent intermission between royal weddings for two generations helps explain the gala atmosphere around the marriage of Princess Anne and William of Orange in 1734. Then, a long parade of nobility and royal officials and householders passed before galleries stuffed with several thousand 'people of quality', dressed and bejewelled for the occasion, an event eagerly anticipated in and reported to the provinces.[65]

London was a place of edification and intellectual exchange as well as one of social exchange and public enjoyment. The city's schools and freelance teachers were numerous but here the provinces were also quite well provided.[66] Unlike them, however, the metropolis offered unmatched opportunities for enlightenment and mental stimulus in less formal ways. Sir James Simeon enumerated the exotic animals on view in the metropolis (dromedaries, tigers, leopards), emphasizing that seeing them 'would enlarge [his son's] knowledge in what the Lord & nature doth produce'.[67] In like manner, the fourth Earl of Chesterfield thought his teenaged son would benefit from attending a trial in the Court of King's Bench.[68]

While providing myriad opportunities for education, London none the less was not self-evidently the centre of England's intellectual world, which in this era had no single geographic focus, except insofar as the kingdom's scholars were concentrated at the universities. It was, however, the centre of publishing, the source of useful or diverting works routinely circulated to the country, whether newspapers, journals, or books, all of them products of 'a national culture based on London common to all propertied groups, no matter how bitter their mutual hatred'.[69] For those among the landed who shared an interest in scholarly learning – the 'virtuosi' who cherished the 'idea of a community of the learned'[70] and among whom the landed element was numerous – London supplied more

64. *The Diary of Bulstrode Whitelocke 1605–1675*, Ruth Spalding, ed., *Records of Social and Economic History*, new series, 13 (1990), p. 627.
65. Hervey, *Memoirs*, I, pp. 263–71; quotation at p. 270; *Banks Papers*, pp. 150, 152, 161.
66. Holmes, *Augustan England*, ch. 3.
67. Draft, c. 12 June 1700, Bodleian Library, MS D.D. Weld.c.13/4/1.
68. *Chesterfield Letters*, III, p. 740.
69. Jenkins, *Making of a Ruling Class*, p. 233. For an example of the dissemination of works from London, see *Lowther Correspondence*, p. 423.
70. *Nicolson Diaries*, p. 11.

than literature. It furnished ways and places for face-to-face contact between interested parties and for first-hand observation of the novelties the modern world afforded. John Aubrey admitted that his *Brief Lives* could not have been written without 'the moderne advantage of Coffee-houses . . . before which, men knew not how to be acquainted, but with their owne Relations, or Societies'.[71]

Provincial visitors routinely sought intellectual stimulus in these coffee houses and elsewhere. Their trips to town at the turn of the century encouraged the Fullers of Brightling Park in Sussex to develop what became a continuing involvement with the Royal Society. Sir Charles Kemys around 1690 spent time in London discussing a new translation of Pascal, and John Loveday of Caversham on a London visit in 1738 made a point of dining with Dr Richard Mead, physician and collector, in order to see his collections of art and antiquities, containing 'nothing but what is truly curious, nothing trifling'. Bishop Nicolson of Carlisle eagerly visited institutions like the Royal Society, the library at Cotton House, the Royal Library, and the College of Arms, as well as individuals ranging from famous collectors and scholar-bishops to physician-naturalists, botanists and the uncategorizable keepers of extraordinary cabinets and museums. For Nicolson, every stay in London in the early part of the century 'was filled with a double exhilaration, high politics on the one hand, intense intellectual discovery on the other'.[72]

The cultivation of virtuosity and erudition fostered a sense of identity within the landed order by discouraging thinking in terms of a fragmented group. It placed value on learning – or at least the patina that the landed were expected to acquire – which added to the sense that gentlemen (and gentlewomen) in different parts of the kingdom, from Cornwall to Cumberland, were connected to one another by shared values and endeavours.

Negative perceptions

What, then, was the landed elite's perception of the advantages and disadvantages of metropolitan life, the shaping or misshaping done

71. Cited by K. Bennett, *Times Literary Supplement*, 27 May 1994, p. 15.

72. R.V. Saville, 'Gentry wealth on the Weald in the eighteenth century: the Fullers of Brightling Park', *Sussex Archaeological Collections* 121 (1983), p. 123; Jenkins, *Making of a Ruling Class*, pp. 232–3; Markham, *Loveday of Caversham*, pp. 326–7; *Nicolson Diaries*, pp. 17, 698–703.

by it, the lessons taught or to be avoided there? That landowners thought that metropolitan life had a negative side is evident, yet even this conviction and the stronger belief some held that the capital was truly nefarious demonstrate how large the city bulked in their lives. Those who disliked the undue influence of the corrupting metropolis testify to its part in shaping perceptions just as do those who valued it. Good or bad, it could not be ignored.

For some gentry, following a long tradition, the town was held to be inferior to the country, which many early modern moralists considered to be 'the natural sphere of gentry activity'. In the late sixteenth century, a gentleman going to London risked criticism for leading a solitary life there and abandoning the duty he had to live on his estate and 'conduct his life in and through his family and household'.[73] Perhaps the lingering impact of such an attitude led to the general condemnations of the place that could still issue from gentry lips: Sir William Doyly, arranging a marriage in the city in the 1660s, vowed to spend no more time than he had to 'in this damd place'.[74]

Well into the eighteenth century various commentators insisted – although with a shrillness that suggests they were losing the battle – on the superior attractions of country life. John Gay, born into the gentry of Devonshire, sharply criticized the artificiality and corruption of the city in works like *Trivia or the Art of Walking the Streets of London* (1716), and *The Beggar's Opera* (1728) depicted the deleterious effect of city life on all and sundry, including the landed classes.[75] More moderately, those whose occupations kept them from the country regretted the denial. A courtier writing in 1737, after being occupied with a 'succession of royall diverssions', reflected that where residence at court brought honours, 'a quiet country life [was] certainly more agreable', and a younger son consigned to a merchant's existence in town longed for the 'Paradise' of country-house life.[76]

Unlike courtiers or younger sons for whom London life might seem more a fate than a joy, landowners and heirs to land had both

---

73. Raymond Williams, *The Country and the City* (Oxford, 1973), esp. chs 1–8; Heal and Holmes, *Gentry*, pp. 282–3, 311–18; quotations on pp. 283, 311.
74. Sir W. Doyly to Lady Doyly, 5 April 1664, Norfolk Record Office, FEL 608, 554x1.
75. Isaac Kramnick, *Bolingbroke and His Circle: The Politics of Nostalgia in the Age of Walpole* (Ithaca, New York, 1968), pp. 223–30.
76. W. Irby to [Lord North and Guilford], 19 July 1737, Bodleian Library, MS North.d.4, fols 133–4; J. Windham to K. Windham, 4 August 1724, Norfolk Record Office, WKC 7/26/57, 404x2.

the luxury of metropolitan visits and the freedom to return to a permanent country seat. Yet even for them, metropolitan life could be a distraction from the care of estate and rural population that some still believed were the proper objects of elite attention. And metropolitan life presented challenges and difficulties even for members of the elite who most valued life there and perhaps derived satisfaction from overcoming the obstacles it presented.

Among the challenges of urban residence, financial ones ranked high. Most landowners found it expensive, and even the most frugal, those who shunned luxury, evaded temptations, and laid out only on necessities, still confronted high prices for the goods they could not avoid purchasing. Landed families could keep down housekeeping charges by consuming their own country produce and by retaining a reduced household, but many items had to be acquired locally, and unless one bought a house in London, rent had to be paid. That cost even forced some to move, like Sir Edward Dering, whose young family set up house in the City, 'but finding London chargeable for housekeeping' moved to Croydon in the mid-1650s. Fifteen years later, appointment as a commissioner of the privy seal, a desire to serve the king, and hopes of advancing his children drew him back to town, where he discovered to his dismay that 'the difference of expence between living in the country upon one's owne and leaving the country to live in the towne' consumed his annual salary of £650.[77]

Despite all the building that went on through the period, rents were apparently rising, chiefly inflated by shifting assessments of what were desirable neighbourhoods. Urban landlords frequently adjusted prices, because fashion in this matter changed rapidly and renters willingly took short leases and moved often. From 1696 on, James Brydges, first Duke of Chandos, moved house periodically both for the sake of convenience and to ensure that he lived in a manner appropriate to his growing stature. He settled successively in Red Lion Square, Golden Square, and Albemarle Street, while also first renting a suburban house at Sion Hill and then buying his own mansion of Canons Park, Edgeware.[78]

Housing alone did not make London expensive. Sir William Leveson-Gower, who went to London to acquire consumer goods unavailable at home and for the social life and entertainment, in six months in the late 1670s spent nearly £1000 just with suppliers

77. *Dering Diaries*, pp. 110–11.
78. Joan Johnson, *Princely Chandos: James Brydges 1674–1744* (Wolfeboro, New Hampshire, 1989), pp. 61–2.

of basic provisions (wine merchant, butcher, grocer, and so on).[79] Sir Thomas Hanmer spent £100 a week during a month and a half in town in the winter of 1700–1, and the more modest outlays of Sir Thomas Chester, who came from Gloucestershire for four months in early 1735 with his wife and servants, ran close to a thousand pounds.[80]

The nobility spent even more lavishly. When the state of the ninth Earl of Derby's finances were calculated in 1677 he owed £4200 (nearly 40 per cent of his outstanding debt) to 'several tradesmen in London', and on an even larger scale, the payments made for the Duke of Newcastle by his financial trustees in 1741 included more than £11,000 to discharge London debts. These the duke was none the less continuing to amass: more than half of the £45,000 in new indebtedness he accumulated in the next decade may have come from London expenses, and by 1751 London-derived 'Book Debts' of £17,500 comprised over a quarter of the £65,000 he owed altogether. John first Baron Ashburnham spent on approximately the same scale over a half dozen years after 1710, when he laid out an annual average of £4300 during his residence in London.[81] It is difficult to imagine anyone incurring so much debt in Warwick, Chichester, Abingdon, Rotherham, Bury St Edmunds, Saxmundham, or Topsham, to name just a few of the many provincial towns that developed squares or built town halls, boasted urban theatres, musical gatherings, or assemblies in the period of urban renaissance.[82]

By far the greatest burden on the finances of William Nicolson, Bishop of Carlisle, involved his annual residence in London when attending parliament each winter. Because he lived in the north, travel expenses (some £50 round trip in 1706) exceeded rent in his case and made up a large portion of costs that annually ran between 20 and 40 per cent of his net income.[83] When the young Philip Stanhope, future Earl of Chesterfield, tried to lure a friend to join him in Holland for two or three summer months in 1714, the cheapness of life in The Hague as compared to London was a point in favour of the proposal.[84] It was 'very inconvenient but . . . less expensive than living in London' for Edward Townshend (who

79. Wordie, *Estate Management*, pp. 77–8.
80. Mingay, *English Landed Society*, p. 157.
81. Barry Coward, *The Stanleys, Lords Stanley and Earls of Derby 1385–1672: The Origins, Wealth and Power of a Landowning Family*, Chetham Society, 3rd series, 30 (1983), p. 211; Ray A. Kelch, *Newcastle, a Duke Without Money: Thomas Pelham-Holles 1693–1768* (Berkeley, 1974), pp. 101–2, 136; Mingay, *English Landed Society*, p. 158.
82. Borsay, *English Urban Renaissance*, pp. 323–49.
83. *Nicolson Diaries*, pp. 56–8.   84. *Chesterfield Letters*, II, p. 10.

had £350 a year from ecclesiastical preferments) to commute while attending the Closet in the 1740s, and he did not bring his wife to town for medical attention because, as he put it bluntly, 'we cannot afford it'.[85]

Other aspects of urban life occasionally diminished appreciation of the pleasures that landed residents had purchased by these sometimes extravagant, sometimes unaffordable outlays. Those unhabituated to London might find it noisy, like the fictional Sir Roger de Coverley, who could not get the urban cries 'out of his Head, or go to sleep for them the first Week that he [was] in town'.[86] The complaint of noise could imply bustle and crowdedness as well, and aristocratic socializing made for a busy schedule, especially in the eighteenth century.[87] The demands on one's company and one's time might sometimes diminish enjoyment of metropolitan social life, whose turmoil nearly overwhelmed some of those first encountering it. The young Mary Pierrepont had 'very little time at [her] own Disposal' because she was expected 'to run into Visits, Noise, and Hurry, which serve rather to trouble than compose the thoughts of any reasonable Creature'. Her correspondence suffered as a result: 'I'll swear', she wrote in 1711,

> this town is such a place, and one is so hurryd about, tis with vast difficulty to get pen, ink, and paper, and perhaps when they are all in readynesse, whip, there comes some impertinent visiter or another and puts all into Confusion again.

Nearly twenty years later, as Lady Mary Wortley Montagu, she explained that the activities that yielded subjects for her letters left 'very little time . . . to make observations, much less to write them down'.[88]

Compared to such psychological irritants, the city's disease and crime posed actual dangers. As it had done historically, London's propensity to breed disease helped to set the rhythms of urban life for the landed elite, who had other places to go and the wherewithal to leave it when London grew dangerous. Plague ceased to empty the city after the 1660s, but summer-time remained a season that cleared the town of its leading figures partly because it was one associated with ill-health. Although home to the kingdom's best medical advice

85. E. Townshend to Lord Townshend, c. 12 November 1747, Raynham Hall, box files, '3rd Viscount Townshend, family correspondence'.

86. *The Spectator*, II, p. 474.

87. Mark R. Wenger, ed., *The English Travels of Sir John Percival and William Byrd II: The Percival Diary of 1701* (Columbia, Missouri, 1989), p. 33.

88. *Montagu Letters*, I, pp. 20, 75, 90, II, p. 58.

and care, London could be a sickly place, where there was 'allmost an impossibility of keeping entirely clear of the Infection',[89] and only love itself induced an otherwise healthy Edward Wortley Montagu to live in a city where he rarely had good health.[90] When Lady Cardigan fell ill in town, the air of Northamptonshire was quickly prescribed as 'the best phisick' for her, and the Duke and Duchess of Ancaster invited a country couple in London on the death of their child to visit them if 'the towne's smoaky air' proved damaging to their health.[91]

As for crime, many contemporaries believed that it was omnipresent and growing in the late seventeenth and early eighteenth centuries. While the countryside was not immune to it, that which occurred in London drew most attention, and around 1700 the town seemed to be beset by theft, immorality, and even criminal violence.[92] During the decades either side of 1700 the town experienced levels of offences that the rest of the country shared only in the 1770s, with some of the blame being assigned to the release of sailors and soldiers into the population with the cessation of war in 1697. Yet peace and war alike, London stood out from the rest of England, not just because it offered rich pickings but because the mechanisms of informal control that reduced the amount and mitigated the impact of property crime in smaller communities were largely absent or unavailing there.[93]

In the 1720s the city was beset by gangs (or fear of them), and the apparent increase in violent crime following the peace of 1748 prompted Henry Fielding's *Enquiry into the Causes of the Late Increase of Robbers* (1751), which took London as its point of focus. The crime wave also sparked appointment of a parliamentary committee of investigation and passage of the Murder Act of 1752, which cited in its preamble the rising incidence of murder 'particularly in and near the Metropolis'.[94] Greater London provided flourishing conditions for robbery and highway crime, and the better-off were visible and recurrent targets. The capital's radiating roads carried valuables and goods to all parts of the kingdom, and both the mails and coach travellers made tempting targets. London's extensive area of settlement, including the rich suburbs, offered victims as

89. Ibid., II, pp. 114–15.   90. Ibid., I, p. 92.
91. *Letters of Eaton to Cardigan*, p. 118; *Banks Papers*, p. 140.
92. J.M. Beattie, *Crime and the Courts in England 1660–1800* (Oxford, 1986), p. 14; Ian A. Bell, *Literature and Crime in Augustan England* (London, 1991), p. 14.
93. Beattie, *Crime and the Courts*, pp. 14–15.
94. Ibid., pp. 149, 156–8; quotation on p. 78.

well as safety for criminals. For the gentry and nobility who jour-
neyed regularly to and from town, often conveying jewels and other
valuables when they did, life in town involved a significant measure
of risk. Perhaps these adversities and vulnerabilities, shared by those
wealthy enough to constitute tempting targets, made up another
strand of mutual identity among the landed classes. That landowners
continued to flood the West End in any event indicates how strong
was the capital's lure and how important a role things metropolitan
played in elite life.[95]

Positive receptions

While the litany of the disadvantages of living in London is extensive, it is not so long as one recounting its attractions. For all that
any member of the landed classes understood that living in town
was not without its trials, and for all that some contemporaries even
despised and tried to avoid the city, its allure was irresistibly potent.
In all sorts of ways London was superior both to country life and to
other cities, the great capitals of Europe included.

Unlike the sixteenth- and early seventeenth-century pastoral vision
of the country house, which emphasized its actual occupation, a late
seventeenth- and eighteenth-century arcadian view, created partly
by urban-based writers, presented the country house as an idealized
location. A restricted focus on the house's inner family undermined
the claim of the house to be the model of social completeness, since
it excluded rather than assimilated 'discordant elements' in the surrounding world. The rural world of employee and tenant, formerly
depicted in stereotyped and implausibly bucolic terms, was now
conveniently left out. Preserving and advancing the family associated
with the house became the central task of its owners, but this could
be achieved outside the country house itself, even in the city, where
a virtuous gentleman could live as long as he maintained the country house.[96]

Although life in London for many landed men often pressed
public business on top of social demands, it could be freer than life

---

95. On this last point see Jenkins, *Making of a Ruling Class*, ch. 9.

96. William Alexander McClung, 'The country-house arcadia', in Gervase Jackson-
Stops, Gordon J. Schochet and Lena Cowen Orlin, and Elisabeth Blair MacDougall,
eds, *The Fashioning and Functioning of the British Country House, Studies in the History of
Art* 25, Center for the Advanced Study in the Visual Arts, Symposium Papers, vol. 10
(Hanover, New Hampshire, 1989), pp. 277–8, 281.

in the country. The Earl of Cardigan's steward thought it possible his master 'may perhaps find more time to look [his accounts] over in London than in the country'.[97] Where the rural way had once been credited as the superior mode of living, the provinces even before the mid-eighteenth century were less self-evidently natural or advantageous as the site for elite action. If *The Spectator* mocked the urgency of gentle ladies' desire to go up to town, it equally satirized the country gentleman, 'a morose Rustick, that frowns and frets at the Name of [London and] . . . wonders how any one can be pleased with the Fooleries of Plays and Operas'.[98]

It was partly as a 'centre of professional cultural production and marketing' – material as well as intellectual – and as a centre of fashion that the landed classes happily turned to London.[99] As the latter, London's hold over imaginations, young and old, female and male, was intensified by the increasing sway of fashion in the period, which not only intruded locally but induced many a visit to the capital. A *Spectator* 'correspondent' observed that one lady's 'whole Time and Thoughts are spent in keeping up to the Mode both in Apparel and Furniture'. Fashion dictated utility, which meant replacing even durable items on a regular basis, a bondage to taste that the magazine satirized as breeding the absurd opinions that 'an old-fashion Grate consumes Coals, but gives no Heat' and that wine drunk from last year's glass was indistinguishable from beer.[100]

Despite the emphasis on fashion, some asserted that life in town need not empty one's pocket, and Edward Waterhouse in the *Gentleman's Monitor* went so far as to declare that a family could 'live as handsomely and cheap in London as in any part of England'.[101] One like John first Baron Gower (1675–1709), although resident almost entirely in London as an adult, lived frugally even when he held ministerial office from 1702 to 1706. Prior to that, in the 1690s, he was spending less, despite owning a house near Westminster Hall, than his father, a political 'dabbler', had done in the late 1670s.[102] The many examples of piles of London debt (much of Andrew Archer's £12,000 amassed over a dozen years, for example) seem to contradict claims about the town's affordability, but desire

97. *Letters of Eaton to Cardigan*, p. 75.   98. *The Spectator*, II, p. 11.

99. Jonathan Barry, 'The press and the politics of culture in Bristol, 1660–1775', in Jeremy Black and Jeremy Gregory, eds, *Culture, Politics and Society in Britain, 1660–1800* (Manchester, 1991), p. 50.

100. *The Spectator*, III, p. 111; Christopher Breward, *The Culture of Fashion: A New History of Fashionable Dress* (Manchester, 1995), pp. 83, 112, and chs 3–4 *passim*.

101. Stone, 'Residential development', p. 181.

102. Wordie, *Estate Management*, pp. 77–8.

to live in the city could skew perceptions. It might have been true, as Lord Fitzwilliam thought when considering the future of his late lawyer's widow, that the town offered 'cheape enough liveing for retired private people', but the typical landed visitor to London was neither retired nor private. In the end, however, Edward Wortley Montagu's judgement surely isolated the most important consideration, that no matter how small one's fortune, 'if you like the town it is better living on a little there than not at all'.[103]

For those with much, of course, the metropolis had extensive offerings, more than anyone could take in and enough surely to prove daunting to some. Members of the landed elite did not all participate in London's social life equally, but only rare figures failed to do so to some degree, and participation was part of what generated elite identity. The sheer ease of amusement, the frequency of entertainment, were important elements of London's draw for the landed. Joseph Banks II relished his return from a therapeutic stay in Bath to a London where he and his wife could 'trail out every other day whilst we stay in town to see some fine thing or another'. Yet the communal character of these diversions was equally if not more important than their diversity. Banks encouraged his wife to plan the days when they would 'trail out' by making 'some parties of that kind before I come ... for 2 or 3 coaches to go togather makes the thing more lively'.[104]

Preoccupied though he was with pursuing suits at law when he annually visited town from Lincolnshire, William Massingberd found plenty of time for sightseeing, shopping, and visiting taverns and coffee houses.[105] London's distractions helped to rescue Sir Marmaduke Constable from intolerable boredom when a crippling accident deprived him of the hunting that previously supplied his principal pleasure in life.[106] Lady Rachel Russell retrospectively thought that in the 1660s she had enjoyed 'all too well ... the esteemed diversions of the town' (including visits, walks in the park, and attending plays), in which family connections enmeshed her and which an allowance from her father let her enjoy.[107] Without Lady Rachel's self-criticism, Lady Mary Wortley Montagu in the 1720s reported being surrounded by entertainments, some new since

103. Heal and Holmes, *Gentry*, pp. 140–1; *Fitzwilliam Correspondence*, p. 151; *Montagu Letters*, I, p. 83.

104. *Banks Papers*, p. 163.   105. Holmes, *Lincolnshire*, pp. 78–9.

106. Peter Roebuck, 'Absentee landownership in the late seventeenth and early eighteenth centuries: a neglected factor in English agrarian history', *Agricultural History Review* 21 (1973), p. 2.

107. Schwoerer, *Lady Rachel Russell*, p. 29.

Lady Rachel's time: 'Public places flourish more than ever', she observed, with 'Assemblys for every day in the week, besides Court, Operas, and Masquerades'. Two years later 'not a street in Town' lacked assemblies, and 'some spirited Ladys [went] to seven in a Night'. Such amusements provided gauges of the quality of metropolitan life. To say that 'The Town improves daily' was to speak of the quantity of fashionable people around, as well as to invoke the gaiety and brilliance of their company.[108]

Perhaps part of the lustre of these social occasions derived from their exclusive and readily observable settings, as open to view (at least metaphorically) as country houses in their landscape gardens. The gatherings of aristocracy were not randomly scattered around the conurbation, nor were they concentrated around the great town houses of lay and clerical magnates as in the sixteenth and early seventeenth centuries. Lady Mary obviously referred to the stylish areas of the city when she said that no street was without its assembly. The building booms in London and its suburbs starting in the late seventeenth century effected a geographic concentration of landed families in newly developed, thickly settled neighbourhoods.[109]

Residential segregation intensified elite identification with one another. In these circumstances a certain reinforcement of regional identity might occur,[110] but by and large it was minimal, since urban neighbours usually hailed from different removes. More importantly, the landed's life in London did not revolve exclusively around places of residence, so if there had been a tendency for landed families to group with others from their native counties, this inclination would not have restricted their socializing. Even private gatherings where those from the same county did regularly associate constituted circles that abutted and overlapped one another, rather than remaining disconnected. The socially exclusive public arenas, many of them new in the period, like the opera house and assembly rooms, threw together members of the landed order without regard to their geographic origins but in a manner encouraging mutual identity. So did open-air venues like Kensington Gardens, which grew more exclusive when fenced in under George II, and St James's Park, which George Rudé calls 'the public place among all public places

---

108. *Montagu Letters*, II, pp. 29, 46, 72 for quotations; see also I, p. 71, II, pp. 52, 66, 73–4.

109. M.J. Power, 'The social topography of Restoration London', in A.L. Beier and Roger Finlay, eds, *London 1500–1700: The Making of a Metropolis* (London, 1986), pp. 202–4.

110. Jenkins, *Making of a Ruling Class*, p. 242.

where men and women of fashion paraded in order to see and be seen'.[111] Social segregation also spilled over into the greater metropolitan area, so that aristocrats and gentry tended to patronize the spas of Epsom and Tunbridge Wells (best known for their company and amusements), while serious drinkers of water and lesser members of polite society went to Dulwich and Sydenham, which were also near enough to town to be inexpensively visited on foot in a single day.[112]

Increasingly close contact with varied London activities on the part of many late Stuart and Hanoverian gentry made time spent in the country appear contrastingly to some 'as a tedious and regrettable interlude'. Those consigned to the provinces received sympathy for not knowing 'how to spend your time in your old castle after so much politeness' and were given counsel on how to avoid 'the ennui of the country'.[113] In 1733 even the bustling town of Bath yielded to Joseph Banks II 'no gallantrys of any kind that I hear of, nor no hangeing or drowning' – in short, nothing to compare with the gratifying 'chitt chatt' his wife sent him from town. Sixty years earlier the spa at Bristol had been equally dull for the first Viscount Townshend and his wife.[114] After making 'country excursions' in the summer of 1733 and discovering no news worth reporting, the Earl of Chesterfield eagerly anticipated his return to London, if only to sit 'quietly in my easy chair, by a good fire, in St James's Square'.[115] When he resigned from office fifteen years later, Chesterfield expressed a desire to end his days in the capital, enjoying 'the comforts of social life, instead of groaning under the load of business'.[116]

'Inquisitive after the news of London'

Many of London's attractions were the material commodities and social occasions already itemized, but the landed also possessed a growing psychological conviction that London was central to the scheme of life's values. For those stuck in a countryside 'barren of any sort of news', national affairs and the world of the metropolis seemed naturally to provide subjects for conversation. These included

111. Rudé, *Hanoverian London*, pp. 72–3.   112. Ibid., p. 73.
113. Jenkins, *Making of a Ruling Class*, p. 244.
114. *Banks Papers*, p. 146; Townshend to Sir E. Harley, 12 June 1671, British Library, Additional MSS 70011, fol. 262.
115. *Chesterfield Letters*, II, p. 272.   116. Ibid., III, pp. 1101–2, 1118.

'elections or the intented [*sic*] wedding' of the Princess Royal, about which friends located in town, like 'you ladys that corryspond with the court ladys', could provide precise intelligence.[117]

While local and national or public and private spheres had no strict separation, it is clear that London's political, economic, and social life were distinguishable from those of the provinces. They figured very prominently among the matters that counted with gentry and nobility, partly because knowledge of them served as a kind of social and cultural demarcation. In town, by contrast with the country, the landed more or less invariably encountered events of substance. Where individuals could not be sure about the interest that their private affairs (or even the public affairs of their localities) held for others of their social standing, they had greater confidence that London concerns, being national ones, were or had a claim to be of moment to all. So when the Marquess of Beaufort was in France in the early 1740s, the ageing Lady Mary Wortley Montagu characterized him as 'too much an Englishman [by which of course she meant English gentleman] not to be inquisitive after the news of London'.[118] What seemed 'chitt chatt' had weight because of its source, which accounts for the suggestion that reports on London's social activity approximated to an account of 'the general state of the Nation'.[119]

It was important to remain current with metropolitan developments by any means at hand. Even those well placed in the provinces recognized the difficulty in obtaining comprehensive information there, especially before the eighteenth century. In 1685, writing from Oxford, which was scarcely an isolated backwater, Humphrey Prideaux knew that a friend in Ireland would 'have a more exact account' of the suppression of Monmouth's rebellion 'from London then [*sic*] I am able to give you from this place'.[120] Those of the landed who were not in town, or who, even when there, did not have direct access to special news, obtained it in different measure from legal and commercial agents and employees, from friends and families, and of course from the press. There were always many to thank for the 'kind continuance of intelligence as to publick affairs'.[121] By 1700, London's newspapers would be readily available in the countryside, and whether or not they supplied unimpeachable

117. *Banks Papers*, p. 150.   118. *Montagu Letters*, II, p. 284.
119. *Banks Papers*, p. 146; *Montagu Letters*, II, p. 66.
120. *Prideaux to Ellis Letters*, p. 143.
121. W. Bumpstead to [Lord North and Guilford], 10 March 1744, Bodleian Library, MS North.d.5, fols 80–80v.

information, and regardless of the origin of their stories and the preponderance of foreign news in their pages, they provided by definition a metropolitan perspective on the events of the day.[122]

As provincial papers emerged in turn, they were skewed toward town with the City-based economic data, news from the seat of government, and even the figures from London's bills of mortality that they contained. The appearance of these items, along with accounts of the 'Promotions, Deaths and Marriages of the Nobility, Gentry and Clergy, and of the Days when some of the Royal Family go to the Play House, or take the Air', indicates clearly what publishers believed would interest their provincial readers. That the advances and checks to the aristocratic course of life should be fodder for the press underscores the aristocracy's pre-eminence in English society, and shows that they were perceived by others as a discrete social group.[123]

Even in its eighteenth-century maturity, the press had its limitations as a source of information. Private correspondence, that intimate 'converse of the pen' whose power as communication rested on the cultural consensus of correspondents, was also on a practical level a key source of information about the metropolis.[124] Sometimes it was more timely or provided a clearer perspective on events, helping recipients in the country to make decisions and take action about politics, investments, and other business. Before tax commissioners met in Buckinghamshire in 1690, for example, or in Lincolnshire in 1717 they wanted copies of the respective acts sent to them, in the latter case because the text had been 'quite alterd to what it was before' and so required careful study prior to local implementation.[125] London-based landowners (especially parliament men) helpfully supplied eagerly awaited publications like the 'votes' that Joseph Banks II promised to supply a Peterborough coffee house in the 1720s.[126] Yet in the later seventeenth and early eighteenth centuries, these accounts of parliamentary actions, along with the *Gazette*, furnished only limited news, and manuscript newsletters

122. *AHEW*, V, pt 2, p. 465.
123. G.A. Cranfield, *The Development of the Provincial Newspaper 1700–1760* (Oxford, 1962), pp. 71 (citing *The Bee*, vol. 1 [1737], p. 242), 94–7; Jeremy Black, *The English Press in the Eighteenth Century* (London, 1987; reprinted Aldershot, 1991), pp. 298–9.
124. Bruce Redford, *The Converse of the Pen: Acts of Intimacy in the Eighteenth-Century Familiar Letter* (Chicago, 1986), p. 6.
125. W. Chaplyn to Sir R. Temple, 2 February 1690, Huntington Library, Stowe Collection, Temple Correspondence 1689/90–1690, Box 33, STT 475; *Banks Papers*, pp. 43–6; quotation on p. 45.
126. *Banks Papers*, p. 100.

were still circulated to and valued in the countryside for the supple-
mentary intelligence they supplied.[127]
Indeed, private accounts from London could be more valuable
than either newspapers or newsletters. Samuel Pepys, for example,
wrote to his father in advance of and to augment the 'news-booke'
account of the robbery and murder committed by the Earl of Dorset's two sons in early 1662.[128] At times of political crisis, personal
correspondence may have run ahead of the press and was nearly
essential for a full understanding of public affairs. Despite the newspapers' useful provision of timely reports on national events, gentry
in the countryside sought inside information and additional details
from friends and relatives who were on the scene and perhaps
better in the know. Typically, then, John Herne in London in 1699
casually assumed that the 'votes' would have delivered to his brother,
a Norfolk squire, the outline of recent public events, like the parliamentary debate about the commission given to 'one Captain Kid'.
It fell to John, however, to supply particulars otherwise unavailable
and set them in the publicly shrouded context of political intrigue.
And because he was privy to what ''tis said' (as only one on the scene
could be), he could also predict the impact of the parliamentary
debate.[129] In a parallel way, Lord Albemarle Bertie in 1738 assumed
that a country correspondent would see how public affairs went 'by
the prints' but could learn only from him 'that yt is thought it will
be a very short session, and that whoever wants private bills shud
get them in as soon as they can, for some think the House will be
up the middle of April'.[130]
Lord Chesterfield, no slouch as a letter-writer, valued news as
one of a letter's requisite components and clearly believed it was to
be had in town not country.[131] In similar vein, a Lincolnshire gentlewoman writing to London would 'not pretend to exchange northern for southern news', convinced that 'it would be as improper as
to fill my paper with an account of what was done in the last century,
as to trouble [her addressee] with the trivial occurrences that happen here'.[132] '[A]ll the towne newse' could be an account like one
a Leicestershire squire's brother promised of the fireworks held to
celebrate the Peace of Ryswick, and it was only when a metropolitan

127. J. Beveridge to W. Hayrick, 11 December 1683, Bodleian Library, MS.Eng.
hist.c.478, fol. 225.
128. *Diary of Samuel Pepys*, III, pp. 34–5.
129. J. Herne to R. Herne, 5 December 1699, Cambridge University Library,
Buxton MSS, box 37.
130. *Banks Papers*, p. 179.   131. *Chesterfield Letters*, II, p. 269.
132. *Banks Papers*, pp. 150, 167.

letter-writer had 'nothing to amuse you with' that she or he failed as a correspondent.[133] Information from the capital was no less valued when gossip, since the flow of 'chitt chatt' understandably centred on the carryings-on of the landed themselves. Moreover, where in one letter of early 1668 a baronet in town could report on a scandalous duel between two peers, four days later he might send with praise a new poem 'not only above all moderne attempts in verse but equall to any of the antient poets' – the just-published *Paradise Lost*.[134]

Conclusion

London's imprint on the lives of the elite was perhaps deeper in the mid-eighteenth century than in later years, when the city grew so gigantic and unmanageable as to be frightening. The invention of the telegraph and railway so improved postal and electronic communications in the nineteenth century as to obviate some of the need to come to the capital. The emergence of other true metropolises had some of the same effect. But beginning in the latter part of the seventeenth century, the location of so many weighty public events in the capital helped to direct a significant share of the attention of the publicly minded there during the crises and party fights that continued into the early eighteenth century. The availability in London of so many necessary and desired services and commodities as the eighteenth century progressed had the same impact on the more privately oriented and materially minded. Among both of these the landed elite was a well-represented group. At a time when landowners were less connected to rural communities and less engaged by county governance than in previous generations (although perhaps more attached to their country seats and the provincial towns), they were also freer to spend swathes of time in the capital. If news of the metropolis was news of the nation, this was largely the case because for the nation's leaders the metropolis provided a focal point of their activities and their mental attention. London had become a location in which and from which they could rule.

---

133. H. Marriott to T. Drury, 2 October 1746, Norfolk Record Office, NRS 21138, 74x5; B. Herricke to W. Herricke, 27 November 1697, Bodleian Library, MS Eng. hist.c.476, fol. 99.

134. Sir. J. Hobart to J. Hobart, 18 January 1668, Bodleian Library, MS Tanner 45*, fol. 254; J.M. Rosenheim, 'An early appreciation of *Paradise Lost*', *Modern Philology* 75 (1978), pp. 280–2.

CHAPTER EIGHT

Conclusion

Until the end of the nineteenth century, as John Beckett has observed, 'the ownership of land . . . determined a person's standing within the community'.[1] Yet despite owning among them some 60 to 70 per cent of the land of England in about 1690, the gentry and nobility of England in the middle and later seventeenth century were decidedly anxious about their status as the kingdom's elite social order. This book has traced some of the means whereby they regained confidence by the middle of the eighteenth century.

The civil wars and revolutionary events of the 1640s and 1650s did much to shake the certainty that the landed elite had once felt about its position as a body of 'natural rulers'. This trauma grew only partly from the aggressive and in some ways effective challenge made to the historic ruling order from below during that period. For the ruling order divided seriously against itself during those decades as well. While it regained a measure of cohesion in the face of the worst excesses of 1649–53, that did little to heal the rifts generated by the insistent need so many encountered to choose sides both in war and peace. Religious divisions exacerbated those more clearly political and constitutional ones and left the landed elite as a whole vulnerable both in fact and in spirit.

Even at the Restoration, when the upside-down world was supposedly restored to its natural and God-given position, the landed aristocracy did not immediately retake the reins of rule with full conviction. Many of the steps taken in the 1660s and 1670s to resecure its rule, like the passage of the Game Acts and a settlement of the militia that placed control in royal hands, can be seen as anxious

---

1. J.V. Beckett, 'Landownership and estate management', in G.E. Mingay, ed., *Agrarian History of England and Wales*, VI, *1750–1850* (Cambridge, 1989), p. 545.

gestures not confident ones. It was an unsettled world that elicited publication of *A Vindication of the Degree of Gentry* (1663), which was both an attack on hereditary honours and a defence 'in Reason and Religion [of] the several distinctions among men'.[2]

Landed uncertainty during the Restoration about their status as the most distinguished sector of the population was the product of recent history and was enhanced by two secular developments of those years. One was 'the fall of rents', which seemed to put landed income and therefore elite subsistence itself at risk. Serious reconsideration of the management of estates and the relations of landlord and tenant were necessary to overcome the hardships. While an observer of the economic crisis in Kent around 1670 identified macroeconomic forces behind it (the 'loss of the cloth trade', the 'extreme and disproportionate weight of taxes . . . ever since 1646', the 'almost incredible increase of sheep in Ireland'), he also spied social causes: 'insolence and carelessness of servants', brandy-drinking, the failure of justices of the peace to bind apprentices to farm labour.[3] The other, although later and less contemporarily apparent development of concern was a demographic crisis within the ranks of the landed that put the elite at risk of failing to perpetuate itself.

Uncertain in their station (though not uncertain about entitlement to it) and even at times doubtful of their capacity to rule, the late seventeenth-century landed elite took other steps to regroup besides the practical ones of disarming enemies and keeping a vigilant eye out for dangers from below.[4] As this book has suggested, they redefined what it meant to be a landowner and did so in three essential ways. On the one hand, they jettisoned for good and all some of the older meanings and practices that had characterized both their immediate and much more distant past. They also retained some of these in modified forms or with better understanding of them. And they defined and adopted new meanings and practices of what it meant to be a governor of English society.

On the first score, landowners generally moved away from past behaviour in four areas. First, and most prompted by the lessons

2. *A Vindication of the Degree of Gentry: In opposition to Titular honours, and the humour of Riches, being the measure of honours. Done by a Person of Quality* (London, 1663), sig. A5v.

3. Joan Thirsk and J.P. Cooper, eds, *Seventeenth-Century Economic Documents* (Oxford, 1972), pp. 85–6.

4. The events so simplified here were complicated by the fact that the gravest threat to the rule of the late Stuart landed order came from an unexpected source above – the crown.

of revolution, they shunned paternalism as a policy of landlordship. This shift, by no means entirely novel in 1650,[5] can be identified in the increasing preference for a policy of leasing land to large tenants at rack rents. It likewise appears in the emparking of new lands, the wholesale removal of villages in the process of developing the landscape, and in the abandonment of occasions of personal contact with tenants and employees, like the payment of direct doles or hosting of feasts in the great hall. The landed proprietor separated from employee and tenants. Instead of observing the moral economy of the agrarian community, he became an improver who 'knew his own' and put it to his own and his family's profitable ends.

Second, the landed elite by 1750 had backed away from behaviour characteristic of past generations by a more general retreat from engagement, and even preoccupation, with the purely local and provincial. This is not to suggest that even before the societal crisis of the 1640s landowners were insular and introspective, but in 1750 they were inclined to be even less so. They travelled more, were fed by a press that self-consciously ignored the parochial, and were citizens of an expanded nation and empire.[6]

In two other ways, landowners as a group had by 1750 turned their backs on the past: by receding from what now appeared to be the excesses of egregious partisanship and of egregious sectarianism. The power in society of religious and political institutions made them significant instruments of landed rule, and both party politics and religious faith and practice continued to contribute important components of landed identity. But within landed society itself they did not serve as yardsticks by which to measure the cloth of one's own suit or with which to beat one's landed neighbour. A tightly defined religious discipline was appropriate for the lower orders. But a broad Protestantism[7] rather than a carefully prescribed denomination of it (or perhaps even just a Christianity that stretched to Deism on one side and took in an Anglicized Catholicism on the other) served as a sufficient common ground of belief for those of the quality. In the political realm, the attempts to create 'broad-bottomed' governments, the failure of any significant number of gentry or nobility to rally to the Jacobite cause in the '45, and the

5. Andrew McRae, *God Speed the Plough: The Representation of Agrarian England, 1500–1660* (Cambridge, 1996).

6. Linda Colley, *Britons: Forging the Nation 1707–1837* (New Haven, 1992); Kathleen Wilson, *The Sense of the People: Politics, Culture and Imperialism in England, 1715–1785* (Cambridge, 1995).

7. Colley, *Britons*, ch. 1.

re-entry of tories to ministerial office in George III's reign do not signal the end to political contention among those aristocrats who ruled England. But taken together they indicate much fire had gone out of the 'rage of party' so evident one and two generations earlier.

Three other elements that had historically helped to define landed identity remained present but not unchanged by the mid-eighteenth century. The education of the landowner continued to be distinctively based on Latin language and literature, and instruction remained by and large impractical, if that is taken to mean relatively devoid of instruction in those areas to which aristocrats would be like to apply themselves. Although notionally available to them, accounting, agricultural science, engineering, even recent history were all subjects that young men of the ruling order pursued outside the walls of educational institutions, if at all. They did, however, learn to conduct themselves in the manner of gentlemen and their sisters learned the conduct of a lady. Partly in reaction to a turning toward private tuition and away from school, inn of court, and university in the late seventeenth and early eighteenth centuries, educational institutions (especially the grammar schools) adopted elements of a non-classical curriculum. But for the landed elite this was of marginal consequence.

The landed order also remained a country-house elite. As in earlier and later ages, landowners delighted in building and rebuilding, displaying their wealth and taste in this way. The architectural styles, the interior design and decor, and the surrounding landscape of rural seats were all washed by the waves of fashion. On the one hand, the audience to whom all this was displayed grew more self-enclosed because owners frequently cut themselves off from and made invisible the surrounding rural population. On the other hand, the practice of country-house visiting blossomed. As a result, in the mid-eighteenth century there were gentle folk unknown to houses' owners making pilgrimages to and tours through many country seats, a practice unimaginable a century before.

The limited accessibility of country houses to a select segment of the population serves metonymically to illuminate a final constant feature of the ruling order: its limited openness. Beset by demographic pressures, the landed elite none the less survived by recruiting from within.[8] Having partly brought on demographic crisis through mechanisms that maintained social exclusivity but made

---

8. Lawrence Stone and Jeanne C. Fawtier Stone, *An Open Elite? England 1540–1880* (Oxford, 1984).

reproduction through marriage difficult (insistence on social manners, close scrutiny of partners, the complexities of entail and use of marriage contracts), the landed suffered but survived with the consequences. Fortunately, the expansion of non-agricultural economic opportunities at a time of depressed farm prices, and then a recovery of the latter, allowed many of the landed to prosper and avoid the financial hardships which, if combined with the demographic ones, might well have forced an opening of their ranks.

Finally, in three new ways the landed adaptably embraced as part of their constitutive identity what one might identify as the central, the metropolitan, and the cosmopolitan in the world around them. In the first instance, although some among the landed became embroiled with and resisted the growth of state power at the end of the seventeenth century, by the mid-eighteenth century landowners not only took part in its expanded activities but took advantage of the opportunities it offered for positions, patronage, and profits. If central government in the eighteenth century was heavily dependent on local cooperation and lacking in bureaucratic organization, it none the less was much more present and intrusive in English lives in 1750 than in 1650. And the dependence of central government on 'the local aristocracy'[9], far from being a reliance on narrow provincials, placed it in the hands of those who were among the most accepting of state agency in the entire population.

As for the landowners' metropolitan character in the second instance, London's imprint on the lives of the elite by the mid-eighteenth century stained far more intensely than a hundred years before. And, as hinted at the end of the last chapter, the metropolitan dye now coloured aristocratic life perhaps more deeply than it would when changed in the next century by the emergence of other huge cities and of extraordinarily rapid communications. In the period studied here, the capital both loomed ominously and lured irresistibly. In both ways it played a major role in forging into a coherent ruling order those who were themselves helping, partly through London's facilities, to forge the nation.

Thirdly, the elite displayed a quickening openness to the expanding horizons of the world around them. Openness to its commercial opportunities helped them to survive financially, but, more than this, the growing cosmopolitanism of landowners – and the sense it bred in them of their superior place in the world at large – helped to generate new confidence. Here two developments simultaneously

9. Jeremy Black, *The Politics of Britain 1688–1800* (Manchester, 1993), p. 24.

built their conviction. On the one hand, foreign travel, especially as a Grand Tour, took partly-formed, impressionable young men and, by prolonged exposure and even instruction, ultimately made the case for the excellence of England. It was an excellence much improved by an admixture of things foreign – foreign foods, fashions, art, and much more – but one none the less grounded quintessentially in an English (or now British) constitution, and in native commerce and common sense. On the other hand, conviction of superiority also rested on the successful appropriation of the goods of the world. This was an acquisition in which elite women significantly participated with men and one that fed on an emerging culture of consumption. The growth of that culture of consumerism, however, and the increasing accumulation of goods were all too frequently accompanied by the appropriation of other peoples. Their consumption of the world of goods very materially helped the elite to redefine its identity, and in doing so it demonstrated to others, and reminded the landed order itself of, the power of the 'natural rulers' of England. This effective demonstration not only enabled the landed elite to continue their rule of English society, but it also encouraged them, for good and ill, to see themselves as the natural rulers of the world.

Bibliography

Printed primary sources

AUGHTERSON, KATE, ED., *Renaissance Women: Constructions of Femininity in England* (London, 1995).

The Bachelor's Directory: Being a Treatise of the Excellence of Marriage. . . . (London, 1694; 2nd edn, 1696).

The Letters and Papers of the Banks Family of Revesby Abbey 1704–1760, J.W.F. Hill, ed., *Lincoln Record Society* 45 (1952 for 1948–49).

The Correspondence of the Reverend Francis Blomefield (1705–52), D.A. Stoker, ed., *Norfolk Record Society* 55 (1992 for 1990).

The Great Diurnal of Nicholas Blundell of Little Crosby, Lancashire, 2, *1712–1719*, J.J. Bagley, ed., *Record Society of Lancashire and Cheshire* 112 (1970).

'Memorandum book of Sir Walter Calverley, Bart.', S. Margerison, ed., in *Yorkshire Diaries & Autobiographies of the Seventeenth and Eighteenth Centuries, Surtees Society* 77 (1886 for 1883), pp. 43–148.

The Letters of Philip Dormer Stanhope 4th Earl of Chesterfield, Bonamy Dobrée, ed., 6 vols (London, 1932; reprinted New York, 1968).

The Poems and Prose of Mary, Lady Chudleigh, Margaret J.M. Ezell, ed. (Oxford, 1993).

The Diaries of Lady Anne Clifford, D.J.H. Clifford, ed. (Stroud, 1990).

COZENS-HARDY, BASIL, ED., *The Norfolk Lieutenancy Journal 1676–1701, Norfolk Record Society* 30 (1961).

DEFOE, DANIEL, *A Tour Thro' the Whole Island of Great Britain*, G.D.H. Cole, ed., 2 vols (London, 1927; originally published 1724–27).

The Diaries and Papers of Sir Edward Dering Second Baronet 1644 to 1684, Maurice F. Bond, ed., House of Lords Records Office Occasional Publications, no. 1 (London, 1976).

The Notebook of Robert Doughty 1662–1665, James M. Rosenheim, ed., *Norfolk Record Society* 54 (1989).

The Letters of Daniel Eaton to the Third Earl of Cardigan 1725–1732, Joan Wake and Deborah Campion Webster, eds, *Northamptonshire Record Society* 24 (1971).

ETHEREGE, GEORGE, *The Man of Mode; or Sir Fopling Flutter* (1676), in John Harold Wilson, ed., *Six Restoration Plays* (Boston, 1959).

FIELDING, HENRY, *Tom Jones* (New York, 1950; originally published 1749).

The Correspondence of Lord Fitzwilliam of Milton and Francis Guybon, his Steward 1697–1709, D.R. Hainsworth and Cherry Walker, eds, *Northamptonshire Record Society* 36 (1990 for 1988).

HERVEY, JOHN, LORD, *Some Materials towards Memoirs of the Reign of King George II*, Romney Sedgwick, ed., 3 vols (London, 1931; reprinted New York, 1970).

The Diary of Thomas Isham of Lamport (1658–81) kept by him in Latin from 1671 to 1673 at his Father's command, N. Marlow, trans. and Sir Gyles Isham, ed. (Farnborough, 1971).

LAMOINE, GEORGES, ed., *Charges to the Grand Jury 1689–1803*, Camden Society, 4th series, 43 (1992).

LAURENCE, EDWARD, *The Duty and Office of a Land Steward: Represented under Several Plain and Distinct Articles*, 2nd edition (London, 1731; reprinted New York, 1979).

LEICESTER, SIR PETER, *Charges to the Grand Jury at Quarter Sessions 1660–1677*, E.M. Halcrow, ed., *Chetham Society*, 3rd series, 5 (1953).

LOCKE, JOHN, *Some Thoughts Concerning Education*, J.L. Axtell, ed. (Cambridge, 1968; originally published 1693).

The Correspondence of John Lowther of Whitehaven 1693–1698: A Provincial Community in Wartime, D.R. Hainsworth, ed., *Records of Social and Economic History*, new series, 7 (1983).

The Complete Letters of Lady Mary Wortley Montagu, Robert Halsband, ed., 3 vols (Oxford, 1965–76).

[MONTEAGE, STEPHEN,] *Instructions for Rent-Gatherers Accompts &c. made easie* (London, 1683).

The London Diaries of William Nicolson Bishop of Carlisle 1702–1718, Clyve Jones and Geoffrey Holmes, eds (Oxford, 1985).

The Diary of Samuel Pepys, Robert Latham and William Mathews, eds, 11 vols (Berkeley, 1970–83).

Letters of Humphrey Prideaux sometime Dean of Norwich to John Ellis sometime Under-secretary of State 1674–1722, Edward Maunde Thompson, ed., *Camden Society*, new series, 15 (1875).

RICHARDSON, SAMUEL, *Sir Charles Grandison*, Jocelyn Harris, ed., 3 vols in one (Oxford, 1986; originally published 1753–54).

The Correspondence of the Dukes of Richmond and Newcastle 1724–1750, T.J. McCann, ed., *Sussex Record Society* 73 (1984 for 1982–83).

The Spectator, Donald F. Bond, ed., 5 vols (Oxford, 1965).

THIRSK, JOAN AND J.P. COOPER, EDS, *Seventeenth-Century Economic Documents* (Oxford, 1972).

A Vindication of the Degree of Gentry: In opposition to Titular honours, and the humour of Riches, being the measure of honours. Done by a Person of Quality (London, 1663).

The Memoirs and Speeches of James, 2nd Earl of Waldegrave, 1742–1763, J.C.D. Clark, ed. (Cambridge, 1988).

The Yale Edition of Horace Walpole's Correspondence, W.S. Lewis et al., eds, 42 vols (New Haven, 1937–83).

WENGER, MARK R., ED., *The English Travels of Sir John Percival and William Byrd II: The Percival Diary of 1701* (Columbia, Missouri, 1989).

'The autobiography of Leonard Wheatcroft of Ashover 1627–1706', in D. Riden, ed., *A Seventeenth-Century Miscellany, Derbyshire Record Society* 20 (1993), pp. 71–117.

The Diary of Bulstrode Whitelocke 1605–1675, Ruth Spalding, ed., *Records of Social and Economic History*, new series, 13 (1990).

WYCHERLEY, WILLIAM, *The Country Wife* (1675), in John Harold Wilson, ed., *Six Restoration Plays* (Boston, 1959).

Secondary sources: books

ADBURGHAM, ALISON, *Shopping in Style: London from the Restoration to Edwardian Elegance* (London, 1979).

AMUSSEN, SUSAN, *An Ordered Society: Gender and Class in Early Modern England* (Oxford, 1988).

AYLMER, G.E., *The State's Servants: The Civil Service of the English Republic 1649–1660* (London, 1973).

BAHLMAN, D.W.R., *The Moral Revolution of 1688* (New Haven, 1957).

BEATTIE, J.M., *Crime and the Courts in England 1660–1800* (Oxford, 1986).

——, *The English Court in the Reign of George I* (Cambridge, 1967).

BECKETT, J.V., *The Aristocracy in England 1660–1914* (Oxford, 1986).

——, *Coal and Tobacco: The Lowthers and the Economic Development of West Cumberland, 1660–1760* (Cambridge, 1981).

——, *The Rise and Fall of the Grenvilles: Dukes of Buckingham and Chandos, 1710 to 1921* (Manchester, 1994).

BELL, IAN A., *Literature and Crime in Augustan England* (London, 1991).

BLACK, JEREMY, *The British Abroad: The Grand Tour in the Eighteenth Century* (New York, 1992).

——, *The British and the Grand Tour* (London, 1985).

——, *The English Press in the Eighteenth Century* (London, 1987; reprinted Aldershot, 1991).

——, *The Politics of Britain 1688–1800* (Manchester, 1993).

BLACKWOOD, B.G., *The Lancashire Gentry and the Great Rebellion 1640–60*, Chetham Society, 3rd series, 25 (1978).

BORSAY, PETER, *The English Urban Renaissance: Culture and Society in the Provincial Town 1660–1770* (Oxford, 1989).

BOSSY, JOHN, *The English Catholic Community 1570–1850* (London, 1975).

BRAUER, GEORGE C., JR, *The Education of a Gentleman: Theories of Gentlemanly Education in England, 1660–1775* (New York, 1959).

BREWARD, CHRISTOPHER, *The Culture of Fashion: A New History of Fashionable Dress* (Manchester, 1995).

BREWER, JOHN, *The Sinews of Power: War, Money and the English State, 1688–1763* (Cambridge, Massachusetts, 1990; originally published London, 1988).

BUCHOLZ, ROBERT O., *The Augustan Court: Queen Anne and the Decline of Court Culture* (Stanford, 1993).

BURKE, PETER, *Popular Culture in Early Modern Europe* (New York, 1978).

BURTT, SHELLEY, *Virtue Transformed: Political Argument in England, 1688–1740* (Cambridge, 1992).

BUSH, M.L., *The English Aristocracy: A Comparative Synthesis* (Manchester, 1984).

CANNADINE, DAVID, *The Decline and Fall of the British Aristocracy* (New Haven, 1990).

——, *Lords and Landlords: The Aristocracy and the Towns 1774–1967* (Leicester, 1980).

CANNON, JOHN, *Aristocratic Century: The Peerage of Eighteenth-Century England* (Cambridge, 1984).

CHAMBERS, DOUGLAS D.C., *The Planters of the English Landscape Garden: Botany, Trees, and the Georgics* (New Haven, 1993).

CHANDAMAN, C.D., *The English Public Revenue 1660–1688* (Oxford, 1975).

CLARK, J.C.D., *English Society 1688–1832: Ideology, Social Structure and Political Practice during the Ancien Regime* (Cambridge, 1985).

CLAY, C.G.A., *Economic Expansion and Social Change: England 1500–1700*, 2 vols: I, *People, Land and Towns*; II, *Industry, Trade and Government* (Cambridge, 1984).

——, *Public Finance and Private Wealth: The Career of Sir Stephen Fox 1627–1716* (Oxford, 1978).

CLIFFE, J.T., *The Puritan Gentry Besieged, 1650–1700* (London, 1993).

COLEBY, ANDREW M., *Central Government and the Localities: Hampshire 1649–1689* (Cambridge, 1987).

COLLEY, LINDA, *Britons: Forging the Nation 1707–1837* (New Haven, 1992).

——, *In Defiance of Oligarchy: The Tory Party 1714–60* (Cambridge, 1982).

CORRIGAN, PHILIP AND DEREK SAYER, *The Great Arch: English State Formation as Cultural Revolution* (Oxford, 1985).

COWARD, BARRY, *The Stanleys, Lords Stanley and Earls of Derby, 1385–1672: The Origins, Wealth and Power of a Landowning Family, Chetham Society*, 3rd series, 30 (Manchester, 1983).

CRANFIELD, G.A., *The Development of the Provincial Newspaper 1700–1760* (Oxford, 1962).

CRESSY, DAVID, *Bonfires and Bells: National Memory and the Protestant Calendar in Elizabethan and Stuart England* (Berkeley, 1989).

CURRY, PATRICK, *Prophecy and Power: Astrology in Early Modern England* (Princeton, 1989).

DE KREY, GARY S., *A Fractured Society: The Politics of London in the First Age of Party, 1688–1714* (Oxford, 1985).

DICKSON, P.G.M., *The Financial Revolution in England: A Study in the Development of Public Credit 1688–1756* (London, 1967).

EVERETT, NIGEL, *The Tory View of Landscape* (New Haven, 1994).

EZELL, MARGARET J.M., *The Patriarch's Wife: Literary Evidence and the History of the Family* (Chapel Hill, North Carolina and London, 1987).

FAWCETT, TREVOR, *Music in Eighteenth Century Norwich and Norfolk* (Norwich, 1979).

FLETCHER, ANTHONY, J., *A County Community in Peace and War: Sussex 1600–1660* (London, 1975).

——, *Gender, Sex and Subordination in England 1500–1800* (New Haven, 1995).

——, *Reform in the Provinces: The Government of Stuart England* (New Haven, 1986).

FORSTER, J.C.F., *The East Riding Justices of the Peace in the Seventeenth Century* (York, 1973).

FRYDE, E.B., D.E. GREENWAY, S. PORTER, AND I. ROY, EDS, *Handbook of British Chronology*, 3rd edn (Cambridge, 1986; reprinted with corrections 1996).

GAUCI, PERRY, *Politics and Society in Great Yarmouth 1660–1720* (Oxford, 1996).

GIROUARD, MARK, *Life in the English Country House: A Social and Architectural History* (New Haven, 1978).

GLASSEY, L.K.J., *Politics and the Appointment of Justices of the Peace 1675–1720* (Oxford, 1979).

GRASSBY, RICHARD, *The Business Community of Seventeenth-Century England* (Cambridge, 1995).

GREAVES, RICHARD L., *Deliver Us from Evil: The Radical Underground in Britain, 1660–1663* (New York, 1986).

——, *Enemies Under His Feet: Radicals and Nonconformists in Britain, 1664–1677* (Stanford, 1990).

HABAKKUK, JOHN, *Marriage, Debt, and the Estates System: English Landownership 1650–1950* (Oxford, 1994).

HAINSWORTH, D.R., *Stewards, Lords and People: The Estate Steward and His World in Later Stuart England* (Cambridge, 1992).

HALEY, K.H.D., *The First Earl of Shaftesbury* (Oxford, 1968).

HANS, NICHOLAS, *New Trends in Education in the Eighteenth Century* (London, 1951).

HARRIS, FRANCES, *A Passion for Government: The Life of Sarah, Duchess of Marlborough* (Oxford, 1991).

HARRIS, MICHAEL, *London Newspapers in the Age of Walpole: A Study of the Origins of the Modern Press* (London, 1987).

HARRIS, ROBERT, *A Patriot Press: National Politics and the London Press in the 1740s* (Oxford, 1993).

HARRIS, TIM, *London Crowds in the Reign of Charles II: Propaganda and Politics from the Restoration until the Exclusion Crisis* (Cambridge, 1987).

——, *Politics under the Later Stuarts: Party Conflict in a Divided Society, 1660–1715* (London, 1993).

HAY, DOUGLAS, PETER LINEBAUGH, JOHN G. RULE, E.P. THOMPSON, AND CAL WINSLOW, *Albion's Fatal Tree: Crime and Society in Eighteenth-Century England* (New York, 1975).

HEAL, FELICITY, *Hospitality in Early Modern England* (Oxford, 1990).

HEAL, FELICITY AND CLIVE HOLMES, *The Gentry in England and Wales 1500–1700* (Stanford, 1994).

HENNING, BASIL DUKE, *The History of Parliament: The House of Commons 1660–1690*, 3 vols (London, 1983).

HILL, B.W., *The Growth of Parliamentary Parties 1689–1742* (London, 1976).

HILL, CHRISTOPHER, *The English Bible and the Seventeenth-Century Revolution* (London, 1993).

HOLLINGSWORTH, T.H., *The Demography of the British Peerage*, supplement to *Population Studies* 18 (1964).

HOLMES, CLIVE, *History of Lincolnshire*, VII, *Seventeenth-Century Lincolnshire* (Lincoln, 1980).

HOLMES, GEOFFREY, *Augustan England: Professions, State and Society, 1680–1730* (London, 1982).

——, *British Politics in the Age of Anne,* revised edition (London, 1987).

——, *The Making of a Great Power: Late Stuart and Early Georgian Britain 1660–1722* (London, 1993).

HOLMES, GEOFFREY AND W.A. SPECK, *The Divided Society: Parties and Politics in England 1694–1716* (New York, 1968).

HORWITZ, HENRY, *Parliament, Policy and Politics in the Reign of William III* (Newark, Delaware, 1977).

HOULBROOKE, RALPH A., *The English Family 1450–1700* (London, 1984).

HOWELL, DAVID W., *Patriarchs and Parasites: The Gentry of South-West Wales in the Eighteenth Century* (Cardiff, 1986).

HUGHES, ANN, *Politics, Society and Civil War in Warwickshire, 1620–1660* (Cambridge, 1987).

HUNTER, J. PAUL, *Before Novels: The Cultural Contexts of Eighteenth-Century English Fiction* (New York, 1990).

HUTTON, RONALD, *The Restoration: A Political and Religious History of England and Wales 1658–1667* (Oxford, 1985).

——, *The Rise and Fall of Merry England: The Ritual Year 1400–1700* (Oxford, 1994).

JACKSON-STOPS, GERVASE, *The English Country House in Perspective* (New York, 1990).

——, ED., *The Treasure Houses of Britain* (New Haven, 1985).

JENKINS, PHILIP, *The Making of a Ruling Class: The Glamorgan Gentry 1640–1790* (Cambridge, 1983).

JOHNSON, JOAN, *Princely Chandos: James Brydges 1674–1744* (Wolfeboro, New Hampshire, 1989).

KELCH, RAY A., *Newcastle A Duke without Money: Thomas Pelham-Holles 1693–1768* (Berkeley, 1974).

KENYON, J.P., *Revolution Principles: The Politics of Party 1689–1720* (Cambridge, 1977).

KETTON-CREMER, R.W., *Felbrigg: The Story of a House* (London, 1982; originally published 1962).

——, *Norfolk Assembly* (London, 1957).

——, *Norfolk Portraits* (London, 1944).

KISHLANSKY, MARK, *Parliamentary Selection: Social and Political Choice in Early Modern England* (Cambridge, 1986).

KNIGHTS, MARK, *Politics and Opinion in Crisis, 1678–81* (Cambridge, 1994).

KRAMNICK, ISAAC, *Bolingbroke and His Circle: The Politics of Nostalgia in the Age of Walpole* (Ithaca, New York, 1992).

LANDAU, NORMA, *The Justices of the Peace, 1679–1760* (Berkeley, 1984).

LANDERS, JOHN, *Death and the Metropolis: Studies in the Demographic History of London 1670–1830* (Cambridge, 1993).

LANGFORD, PAUL, *A Polite and Commercial People: England 1727–1783* (London, 1989).

——, *Public Life and the Propertied Englishman 1689–1798* (Oxford, 1991).

LARMINIE, VIVIENNE, *Wealth, Kinship and Culture: The Seventeenth-Century Newdigates of Arbury and Their World* (Woodbridge, Suffolk, 1995).

LEES-MILNE, JAMES, *The Earls of Creation: Five Great Patrons of Eighteenth-Century Art* (London, 1986; originally published 1962).

LEMMINGS, DAVID, *Gentlemen and Barristers: The Inns of Court and the English Bar 1680–1730* (Oxford, 1990).

LILLYWHITE, BRYANT, *London Coffee Houses: A Reference Book of Coffee Houses of the Seventeenth, Eighteenth and Nineteenth Centuries* (London, 1963).

MCKENDRICK, NEIL, JOHN BREWER, AND J.H. PLUMB, *The Birth of a Consumer Society: The Commercialization of Eighteenth-Century England* (Bloomington, Indiana, 1982).

MCRAE, ANDREW, *God Speed the Plough: The Representation of Agrarian England, 1500–1660* (Cambridge, 1996).

MALCOLMSON, ROBERT, *Popular Recreations in English Society 1700–1850* (Cambridge, 1973).

MANNING, ROGER B., *Hunters and Poachers: A Social and Cultural History of Unlawful Hunting in England, 1485–1640* (Oxford, 1993).

MARKHAM, SARAH, *John Loveday of Caversham 1711–1789: The Life and Tours of an Eighteenth-Century Onlooker* (Salisbury, 1984).

MELTON, FRANK T., *Sir Robert Clayton and the Origins of English Deposit Banking, 1658–1685* (Cambridge, 1986).

MINGAY, G.E., *English Landed Society in the Eighteenth Century* (London, 1963).

——, *The Gentry: The Rise and Fall of a Ruling Class* (London, 1976).

MONOD, PAUL KLÉBER, *Jacobitism and the English People, 1688–1788* (Cambridge, 1989).

MOORE, ANDREW, *Norfolk and the Grand Tour: Eighteenth-Century Travellers Abroad and Their Souvenirs* (Fakenham, Norfolk, 1985).

MORRILL, J.S., *Cheshire 1630–1660: County Government and Society during the English Revolution* (Oxford, 1974).

NORTON, RICTOR, *Mother Clap's Molly House: The Gay Subculture in England 1700–1830* (London, 1992).

O'DAY, ROSEMARY, *Education and Society 1500–1800: The Social Foundations of Education in Early Modern Britain* (London, 1982).

O'GORMAN, FRANK, *Voters, Patrons, and Parties: The Unreformed Electoral System of Hanoverian England 1734–1832* (Oxford, 1989).

PARKER, R.A.C., *Coke of Norfolk: A Financial and Agricultural Study 1707–1842* (Oxford, 1975).

PLATT, COLIN, *The Great Rebuilding of Tudor and Stuart England: Revolutions in Architectural Taste* (London, 1994).

PLUMB, J.H., *The Growth of Political Stability in England 1675–1725* (London, 1967).

——, *Sir Robert Walpole*, 2 vols: I, *The Making of a Statesman* (London, 1956; reprinted 1972); II, *The King's Minister* (London, 1960; reprinted 1972).

POCOCK, J.G.A., *The Machiavellian Moment: Florentine Political Thought and the Atlantic Republican Tradition* (Princeton, 1975).

——, *Politics, Language and Time: Essays on Political Thought and History* (New York, 1973).

POINTON, MARCIA, *Hanging the Head: Portraiture and Social Formation in Eighteenth-Century England* (New Haven, 1993).

REDFORD, BRUCE, *The Converse of the Pen: Acts of Intimacy in the Eighteenth-Century Familiar Letter* (Chicago, 1986).

——, *Venice & the Grand Tour* (New Haven, 1996).

ROBERTS, STEPHEN K., *Recovery and Restoration in an English County: Devon Local Administration 1646–1670* (Exeter, 1985).

ROEBUCK, PETER, *Yorkshire Baronets 1640–1760: Families, Estates and Fortunes* (Oxford, 1980).

ROGERS, NICHOLAS, *Whigs and Cities: Popular Politics in the Age of Walpole and Pitt* (Oxford, 1989).

ROSENHEIM, JAMES M., *The Townshends of Raynham: Nobility in Transition in Restoration and Early Hanoverian England* (Middletown, Connecticut, 1989).

ROSEVEARE, HENRY, *The Treasury, 1660–1870* (London, 1973).

RUDÉ, GEORGE, *Hanoverian London* (Berkeley, 1971).

RULE, JOHN, *The Vital Century: England's Developing Economy 1714–1815* (London, 1992).

RUSSELL, NICHOLAS, *Like Engend'ring Like: Heredity and Animal Breeding in Early Modern England* (Cambridge, 1986).

SCHWOERER, LOIS G., *Lady Rachel Russell: 'One of the Best of Women'* (Baltimore, 1988).

SCOTT, W.R., *The Constitution and Finance of English, Scottish and Irish Joint-Stock Companies to 1720*, 3 vols (Gloucester, Massachusetts, 1968; originally published 1912).

SEAWARD, PAUL, *The Cavalier Parliament and the Reconstruction of the Old Regime, 1661–1667* (Cambridge, 1989).

SEDGWICK, ROMNEY, *The History of Parliament: The House of Commons 1715–1754*, 2 vols (London, 1970).

SLATER, MIRIAM, *Family Life in the Seventeenth Century: The Verneys of Claydon House* (London, 1984).

SMAIL, JOHN, *The Origins of Middle Class Culture: Halifax, Yorkshire, 1660–1780* (Ithaca, New York, 1994).

SPADAFORA, DAVID, *The Idea of Progress in Eighteenth Century Britain* (New Haven, 1990).

SPECK, W.A., *Tory & Whig: The Struggle in the Constituencies, 1701–1715* (London, 1970).

SPURR, JOHN, *The Restoration Church of England, 1646–1689* (New Haven, 1991).

STATER, VICTOR, *Noble Government: The Stuart Lord Lieutenancy and the Transformation of English Politics* (Athens, Georgia, 1994).

STAVES, SUSAN, *Married Women's Separate Property in England, 1660–1833* (Cambridge, Massachusetts, 1990).

STONE, LAWRENCE, *The Crisis of the Aristocracy 1558–1641* (Oxford, 1965).

——, *Family and Fortune: Studies in Aristocratic Finance in the Sixteenth and Seventeenth Centuries* (Oxford, 1973).

——, *The Family, Sex and Marriage in England 1500–1800* (London, 1977).

——, *Road to Divorce: England 1530–1987* (Oxford, 1990).

STONE, LAWRENCE and JEANNE C. FAWTIER STONE, *An Open Elite? England 1540–1880* (Oxford, 1984).

STOYE, JOHN, *English Travellers Abroad 1604–1667: Their Influence in English Society and Politics*, revised edition (New Haven, 1989).

SUMMERSON, JOHN, *Georgian London*, revised edition (Baltimore, 1962).

Survey of London, 44 vols to date, 1900– : 29–30, *The Parish of St James Westminster, Part One, South of Piccadilly* (London, 1960); 31–2, *The Parish of St James Westminster, Part Two, North of Piccadilly* (London, 1963); 33–4, *The Parish of St Anne Soho* (London, 1966).

SUTHERLAND, JAMES, *The Restoration Newspaper and Its Development* (Cambridge, 1986).

THIRSK, JOAN, ED., *The Agrarian History of England and Wales*, V, *1640–1750*, 2 pts (Cambridge, 1985).

THOMAS, KEITH, *Man and the Natural World: Changing Attitudes in England 1500–1800* (Harmondsworth, 1984).

THOMPSON, E.P., *Customs in Common: Studies in Traditional Popular Culture* (New York, 1991).

——, *Whigs and Hunters: The Making of the Black Act* (London, 1975).

TINNISWOOD, ADRIAN, *A History of Country House Visiting: Five Centuries of Tourism and Taste* (Oxford, 1989).

UNDERDOWN, DAVID, *A Freeborn People: Politics and the Nation in Seventeenth-Century England* (Oxford, 1996).

——, *Revel, Riot and Rebellion: Popular Politics and Culture in England 1603–1660* (Oxford, 1985).

VINCENT, W.A.L., *The Grammar Schools: Their Continuing Tradition 1660–1714* (London, 1969).

WARD, W.R., *The English Land Tax in the Eighteenth Century* (London, 1953).

WATT, IAN, *The Rise of the Novel: Studies in Defoe, Richardson and Fielding* (Berkeley, 1957).

WATTS, MICHAEL R., *The Dissenters: From the Reformation to the French Revolution* (Oxford, 1978).

WEBER, WILLIAM, *The Rise of Musical Classics in Eighteenth-Century England: A Study in Canon, Ritual, and Ideology* (Oxford, 1992).

WESTERN, J.R., *The English Militia in the Eighteenth Century: The Story of a Political Issue 1660–1802* (London, 1965).

WILLIAMS, RAYMOND, *The Country and the City* (Oxford, 1973).

WILLIAMSON, MARILYN, *Raising Their Voices: British Women Writers, 1650–1750* (Detroit, 1990).

WILLIAMSON, TOM, *Polite Landscapes: Gardens and Society in Eighteenth-Century England* (Baltimore, 1995).

WILSON, CHARLES, *England's Apprenticeship 1603–1763*, 2nd edn (London, 1984).

WILSON, KATHLEEN, *The Sense of the People: Politics, Culture and Imperialism in England, 1715–1785* (Cambridge, 1995).

WORDIE, J.R., *Estate Management in Eighteenth-Century England: The Building of the Leveson-Gower Fortune* (London, 1982).

WRIGLEY, E.A. AND R.S. SCHOFIELD, *The Population History of England 1541–1871: A Reconstruction* (Cambridge, Massachusetts, 1981).

Secondary sources: articles

AGNEW, JEAN-CHRISTOPHE, 'Consumer culture in historical perspective', in John Brewer and Roy Porter, eds, *Consumption and the World of Goods* (London, 1993), pp. 19–39.

ANDERSON, NICHOLAS, 'Music', in *The Cambridge Cultural History of Britain*, 5, *Eighteenth-Century Britain*, Boris Ford, ed. (Cambridge, 1992), pp. 274–303.

AYLMER, G.E., 'From office-holding to civil service: the genesis of modern bureaucracy', *Transactions of the Royal Historical Society*, 5th series, 30 (1980), pp. 91–108.

BARRY, JONATHAN, 'The press and the politics of culture in Bristol, 1660–1775', in Jeremy Black and Jeremy Gregory, eds, *Culture, Politics and Society in Britain, 1660–1800* (Manchester, 1991), pp. 49–81.

BASKERVILLE, S.W., P. ADMAN AND K.F. BEEDHAM, 'The dynamics of landlord influence in English county elections, 1701–1734: the evidence of Cheshire', *Parliamentary History* 12 (1993), pp. 126–42.

——, 'Manuscript poll books and English county elections in the first age of party: a reconsideration of their provenance and purpose', *Archives* 19 (1991), pp. 384–403.

BECKETT, J.V., 'Absentee landownership in the later seventeenth and early eighteenth centuries: the case of Cumbria', *Northern History* 19 (1983), pp. 87–107.

——, 'A back-bench MP in the eighteenth century: Sir James Lowther of Whitehaven', *Parliamentary History* 1 (1982), pp. 79–97.

——, 'Cumbrians and the South Sea Bubble, 1720', *Transactions of the Cumberland and Westmorland Archaeological Society* 82 (1982), pp. 141–50.

——, 'Estate management in eighteenth-century England: the Lowther–Spedding relationship in Cumberland', in John Chartres and David Hey, eds, *English Rural Society, 1500–1800: Essays in Honour of Joan Thirsk* (Cambridge, 1990), pp. 55–72.

——, 'Gosfield Hall: a country estate and its owners 1715–1825', *Essex Archaeology and History* 25 (1994), pp. 185–92.

——, 'Landownership and estate management', in G.E. Mingay, ed., *Agrarian History of England and Wales*, VI, *1750–1850* (Cambridge, 1989), pp. 545–640.

——, 'Land tax administration at the local level 1693–1798', in Michael Turner and Dennis Mills, eds, *Land and Property: The English Land Tax 1692–1832* (New York, 1986), pp. 161–79.

——, 'Local custom and the "new taxation"', *Northern History* 12 (1976), pp. 105–26.

——, 'Regional variation and the agricultural depression 1730–1750', *Economic History Review*, 2nd series, 35 (1982), pp. 35–51.

BECKETT, J.V. AND CLYVE JONES, 'Financial improvidence and political independence in the early eighteenth century: George Booth, 2nd Earl of Warrington (1675–1758)', *Bulletin of the John Rylands Library* 68 (1982–83), pp. 8–35.

BENEDICT, BARBARA M., 'The "curious attitude" in eighteenth-century Britain: observing and owning', *Eighteenth-Century Life* 14, new series, (1990–91, pp. 59–98).

BETTEY, J.H., 'Lord Shaftesbury's estate and gardening notebook, 1675', *Notes & Queries for Somerset and Dorset* 33 (1994), pp. 295–8.

BONFIELD, LLOYD, 'Marriage settlements and the "rise of great estates": the demographic aspect', *Economic History Review*, 2nd series, 32 (1979), pp. 483–93.

BORSAY, PETER, ' "All the town's a stage": urban ritual and ceremony 1660–1800', in Peter Clark, ed., *The Transformation of English Provincial Towns 1600–1800* (London, 1984), pp. 228–58.

——, 'Culture, status, and the English urban landscape', *History*, 2nd series, 67 (1982), pp. 1–12.

——, 'The English urban renaissance: the development of provincial urban culture *c*.1680–*c*.1760', in Peter Borsay, ed., *The Eighteenth Century Town: A Reader in English Urban History, 1688–1820* (London, 1990), pp. 159–87.

BORSAY, PETER AND ANGUS MCINNES, 'Debate: The emergence of a leisure town: or an urban renaissance?', *Past and Present* 126 (1990), pp. 189–202.

BREWER, JOHN, ' "The most polite age and the most vicious": attitudes towards culture as a commodity, 1660–1800', in Ann Bermingham and John Brewer, eds, *The Consumption of Culture 1600–1800: Image, Object, Text* (London, 1995), pp. 341–61.

BROOKS, COLIN, 'Interest, patronage and professionalism: John, 1st Baron Ashburnham, Hastings and the revenue services', *Southern History* 9 (1987), pp. 51–70.

——, 'John, 1st Baron Ashburnham and the state, c.1688–1710', *Historical Research* 60, no. 141 (1987), pp. 64–79.

——, 'Public finance and political stability: the administration of the land tax 1688–1720', *Historical Journal* 17 (1974), pp. 281–300.

BUCHOLZ, ROBERT O., ' "Nothing but ceremony": Queen Anne and the limitations of royal ritual', *Journal of British Studies* 30 (1991), pp. 288–323.

BURTON, J.R., 'Two elections for Bishop's Castle in the eighteenth century', *Transactions of the Shropshire Archaeological Society*, 3rd series, 9 (1909), pp. 259–66.

CAMPBELL, COLIN, 'Understanding traditional and modern patterns of consumption in eighteenth-century England: a character-action approach', in John Brewer and Roy Porter, eds, *Consumption and the World of Goods* (London, 1993), pp. 40–57.

CANNON, JOHN, 'The isthmus repaired: the resurgence of the English aristocracy, 1660–1760', *Proceedings of the British Academy* 68 (1982), pp. 431–53.

CARTER, D.P., 'The Lancashire militia, 1660–1688', in J.I. Kermode and C.B. Phillips, eds, *Seventeenth-Century Lancashire: Essays Presented to J.J. Bagley, Transactions of the Historic Society of Lancashire and Cheshire* 132 (1982), pp. 155–81.

CHALLINOR, P.J., 'Restoration and exclusion in the county of Cheshire', *Bulletin of the John Rylands University Library of Manchester* 64 (1982), pp. 360–85.

CHARTRES, J.A., 'City and towns, farmers and economic change in the 18th century', *Historical Research* 64 (1991), pp. 138–55.

COCKBURN, J.S., 'Twelve silly men? The trial jury at assizes, 1560–1670', in J.S. Cockburn and Thomas A. Green, eds, *Twelve Good Men and True: The Criminal Trial Jury in England, 1200–1800* (Princeton, 1988), pp. 158–81.

COLLEY, LINDA, 'The Loyal Brotherhood and the Cocoa Tree: the London organisation of the tory party 1727–1760', *Historical Journal* 20 (1977), pp. 77–95.

COOPER, J.P., 'Ideas of gentility in early-modern England', in J.P. Cooper, *Land, Men and Beliefs: Studies in Early-Modern History*, G.E. Aylmer and J.S. Morrill, eds (London, 1983), pp. 43–77.

——, 'Social distribution of land and men in England, 1463–1700', in J.P. Cooper, *Land, Men and Beliefs: Studies in Early-Modern History*, G.E. Aylmer and J.S. Morrill, eds (London, 1983), pp. 17–42.

COPE, S.R., 'The stock exchange revisited: a new look at the market in securities in London in the eighteenth century', *Economica* 45 (1978), pp. 1–21.

COWARD, BARRY, 'The social and political position of the earls of Derby in later seventeenth-century Lancashire', in J.I. Kermode and C.B. Phillips, eds, *Seventeenth-Century Lancashire: Essays Presented to J.J. Bagley, Transactions of the Historic Society of Lancashire and Cheshire* 132 (1982), pp. 127–54.

CRUICKSHANKS, EVELINE, 'Lord Cowper, Lord Orrery, the Duke of Wharton and Jacobitism', *Albion* 26 (1994), pp. 27–40.

CURTIS, T.C. AND W.A. SPECK, 'The Societies for the Reformation of Manners: a case study in the theory and practice of moral reform', *Literature and History* 3 (1976), pp. 45–64.

DAVIES, MARGARET GAY, 'Country gentry and falling rents in the 1660s and 1670s', *Midland History* 4 (1977), pp. 86–96.

DE KREY, GARY S., 'The first restoration crisis: conscience and coercion in London, 1667–73', *Albion* 25 (1993), pp. 565–80.

EVERITT, ALAN, 'Country, county and town: patterns of regional evolution in England', in Peter Borsay, ed., *The Eighteenth Century Town: A Reader in English Urban History, 1688–1820* (London, 1990), pp. 83–115.

EZELL, MARGARET J.M., 'The *Gentleman's Journal* and the commercialization of Restoration coterie literary practices', *Modern Philology* 89 (1992), pp. 323–40.

FINLAY, ROGER AND BEATRICE SHEARER, 'Population growth and suburban expansion', in A.L. Beier and Roger Finlay, eds, *London 1500–1700: The Making of a Metropolis* (London, 1986), pp. 37–59.

FORSTER, J.C.F., 'Government in provincial England under the later Stuarts', *Transactions of the Royal Historical Society*, 5th series, 33 (1983), pp. 29–48.

FRITZ, PAUL S., 'The undertaking trade in England: its origins and early development, 1660–1830', *Eighteenth-Century Studies* 28 (1994–95), pp. 241–53.

GIROUARD, MARK, 'The country house and the country town', in Gervase Jackson-Stops, Gordon J. Schochet and Lena Cowen Orlin, and Elisabeth Blair MacDougall, eds, *The Fashioning and Functioning of the British Country House, Studies in the History of Art* 25, Center for the Advanced Study in the Visual Arts, Symposium Papers, vol. 10 (Hanover, New Hampshire, 1989), pp. 305–28.

GODBER, JOYCE, 'The Marchioness Grey of Wrest Park', *Bedfordshire Historical Record Society* 47 (1968), pp. 7–163.

GOLDIE, MARK, 'John Locke's circle and James II', *Historical Journal* 35 (1992), pp. 557–86.

HABAKKUK, H.J., 'The rise and fall of English landed families, 1600–1800, I–III', *Transactions of the Royal Historical Society*, 5th series, 29 (1979), pp. 187–207; 30 (1980), pp. 199–221; 31 (1981), pp. 195–217.

HAINSWORTH, D.R., 'Fathers and daughters: patterns of marriage and inheritance among the later Stuart gentry', in L.O. Frappell, ed., *Principalities, Powers and Estates* (Adelaide, 1979 [recte 1980]), pp. 15–21.

HAMILTON, CHARLES, 'The election in 1685 at Aylesbury', *Parliamentary History* 12 (1993), pp. 68–72.

HANDLEY, STUART, 'Local legislative initiatives for economic and social development in Lancashire', *Parliamentary History* 9 (1990), pp. 14–37.

HARRIS, MICHAEL, 'Print and politics in the age of Walpole', in Jeremy Black, ed., *Britain in the Age of Walpole* (New York, 1984), pp. 189–210.

HARRIS, TIM, ' "Lives, liberties and estates": rhetorics of liberty in the reign of Charles II', in Tim Harris, Paul Seaward and Mark Goldie, eds, *The Politics of Religion in Restoration England* (Oxford, 1990), pp. 217–41.

——, 'Party turns? or, whigs and tories get off Scott free', *Albion* 25 (1993), pp. 581–90.

——, 'Problematising popular culture', in Tim Harris, ed., *Popular Culture in England, c.1500–1850* (New York, 1995), pp. 1–27.

HATLEY, VICTOR A., 'Locks, lords and coal: a study in eighteenth century Northampton history', *Northamptonshire Past and Present* 6 (1980–81), pp. 207–18.

HAY, DOUGLAS, 'Property, authority and the criminal law', in Douglas Hay, Peter Linebaugh, John G. Rule, E.P. Thompson, and Cal Winslow, eds, *Albion's Fatal Tree* (New York, 1975), pp. 17–64.

HAYTON, DAVID, 'Moral reform and country politics in the late seventeenth-century House of Commons', *Past & Present* 128 (1990), pp. 48–91.

——, 'Sir Richard Cocks: the political anatomy of a Country whig', *Albion* 20 (1988), pp. 221–46.

HENSTOCK, ADRIAN, 'Town houses and society in Georgian country towns, Part 1: architecture', *Local Historian* 14 (1980), pp. 68–75 and 'Part 2: houses and society', *Local Historian* 14 (1980), pp. 149–55.

HIGSON, P.J.W., 'A dissenting northern family: the Lancashire branch of the Willoughbys of Parham, 1640–1765', *Northern History* 7 (1972), pp. 31–53.

HINCHCLIFFE, G., 'The Robinsons of Newby Park and Newby Hall, Part 2', *Yorkshire Archaeological Journal* 64 (1992), pp. 185–202.

HIRST, DEREK, 'The conciliatoriness of the Cavalier Commons reconsidered', *Parliamentary History* 6 (1987), pp. 221–35.

HOLDERNESS, B.A., 'Credit in English rural society before the nineteenth century, with special reference to the period 1650–1720', *Agricultural History Review* 24 (1976), pp. 97–109.

HOLMES, CLIVE, 'The county community in Stuart historiography', *Journal of British Studies* 19 (1979–80), pp. 54–73.

HOLMES, G.S., 'Gregory King and the social structure of pre-industrial England', *Transactions of the Royal Historical Society*, 5th series, 27 (1977), pp. 41–68.

HOPPIT, JULIAN, 'Reforming Britain's weights and measures 1660–1824', *English Historical Review* 108 (1993), pp. 82–104.

HOPPIT, JULIAN, JOANNA INNES, AND JOHN STYLES, 'Towards a history of parliamentary legislation, 1660–1800', *Parliamentary History* 13 (1994), pp. 312–21.

HORN, PAMELA, 'The contribution of the propagandist to eighteenth-century agricultural improvement', *Historical Journal* 25 (1982), pp. 313–29.

HUGHES, ANN, 'Local history and the origins of the English civil war', in Richard Cust and Ann Hughes, eds, *Conflict in Early Stuart England* (London, 1989), pp. 224–53.

——, 'Parliamentary tyranny? Indemnity proceedings and the impact of the civil war: a case study from Warwickshire', *Midland History* 11 (1986), pp. 49–78.

HUME, ROBERT D., 'The sponsorship of opera in London, 1704–1720', *Modern Philology* 85 (1988), pp. 420–32.

IMPEY, OLIVER, 'Eastern trade and the furnishing of the British country house', in Gervase Jackson-Stops, Gordon J. Schochet and Lena Cowen Orlin, and Elisabeth Blair MacDougall, eds, *The Fashioning and Functioning of the British Country House, Studies in the History of Art* 25, Center for the Advanced Study in the Visual Arts, Symposium Papers, vol. 10 (Hanover, New Hampshire, 1989), pp. 177–92.

JACKSON, R.V., 'Growth and deceleration in English agriculture, 1660–1790', *Economic History Review*, 2nd series, 38 (1985), pp. 333–51.

JACKSON-STOPS, GERVASE, 'A British Parnassus: mythology and the country house', in Gervase Jackson-Stops, Gordon J. Schochet and Lena Cowen Orlin, and Elisabeth Blair MacDougall, eds, *The Fashioning and Functioning of the British Country House, Studies in the History of Art* 25, Center for the Advanced Study in the Visual Arts, Symposium Papers, vol. 10 (Hanover, New Hampshire, 1989), pp. 217–38.

JENKINS, J.P., 'The demographic decline of the landed gentry in the eighteenth century: a south Wales study', *Welsh Historical Review* 11 (1982), pp. 31–49.

JONES, CLYVE, '1720–23 and all that', *Albion* 26 (1994), pp. 41–53.

——, 'The House of Lords and the growth of parliamentary stability, 1701–1742', in Clyve Jones, ed., *Britain in the First Age of Party 1680–1750: Essays Presented to Geoffrey Holmes* (London, 1987), pp. 85–110.

——, 'Jacobitism and the historian: the case of William, 1st Earl Cowper', *Albion* 23 (1991), pp. 681–96.

——, 'The new opposition in the House of Lords, 1720–3', *Historical Journal* 36 (1993), pp. 309–29.

——, 'Parliament and the Peerage and Weaver Navigation Bills: the correspondence of Lord Newburgh with the Earl of Cholmondeley,

1719–20', *Transactions of the Historical Society of Lancashire and Cheshire* 139 (1989), pp. 31–61.

——, 'The parliamentary organization of the whig junto in the reign of Queen Anne: the evidence of Lord Ossulston's diary', *Parliamentary History* 10 (1991), pp. 164–82.

——, 'A Westminster Anglo-Scottish dining group, 1710–12: the evidence of Lord Ossulston's diary', *Scottish Historical Review* 71 (1992), pp. 110–28.

——, 'Whigs, Jacobites and Charles Spencer, Third Earl of Sunderland', *English Historical Review* 109 (1994), pp. 52–73.

JOSLIN, D.M., 'London private bankers, 1720–1785', *Economic History Review*, 2nd series, 7 (1954–55), pp. 167–86.

KEY, NEWTON E., 'Comprehension and the breakdown of consensus in Restoration Herefordshire', in Tim Harris, Paul Seaward, and Mark Goldie, eds, *The Politics of Religion in Restoration England* (Oxford, 1990), pp. 191–215.

——, 'The localism of the county feast in late Stuart political culture', *Huntington Library Quarterly* 58 (1996), pp. 211–37.

——, 'The political culture and political rhetoric of county feasts and feast sermons, 1654–1714', *Journal of British Studies* 33 (1994), pp. 223–56.

KLEIN, LAWRENCE E., 'Liberty, manners, and politeness in early eighteenth-century England', *Historical Journal* 32 (1989), pp. 583–605.

——, 'Politeness for plebes: consumption and social identity in early eighteenth-century England', in Ann Bermingham and John Brewer, eds, *The Consumption of Culture 1600–1800: Image, Object, Text* (London, 1995), pp. 362–82.

LASSITER, JOHN C., 'Defamation of peers: the rise and decline of the action for *scandalum magnatum*, 1497–1773', *American Journal of Legal History* 22 (1978), pp. 216–36.

LEMMINGS, DAVID, 'Lord Chancellor Cowper and the whigs, 1714–16', *Parliamentary History* 9 (1990), pp. 163–74.

——, 'The student body of the inns of court under the later Stuarts', *Bulletin of the Institute of Historical Research* 58 (1985), pp. 149–66.

LERNER, JOSHUA, 'Science and agricultural progress: quantitative evidence from England, 1660–1780', *Agricultural History* 66 (Fall 1992), pp. 11–27.

LIPPINCOTT, LOUISE, 'Expanding on portraiture: the market, the public, and the hierarchy of genres in eighteenth-century Britain', in Ann Bermingham and John Brewer, eds, *The Consumption of Culture 1600–1800: Image, Object, Text* (London, 1995), pp. 75–88.

McCLUNG, WILLIAM ALEXANDER, 'The country-house arcadia', in Gervase Jackson-Stops, Gordon J. Schochet and Lena Cowen Orlin, and Elisabeth Blair MacDougall, eds, *The Fashioning and Functioning of the British Country House, Studies in the History of Art* 25 (Hanover, New Hampshire, 1989), pp. 277–87.

McINNES, ANGUS, 'The emergence of a leisure town: Shrewsbury 1660–1760', *Past and Present* 120 (1988), pp. 53–85.

McLYNN, F.J., 'The ideology of Jacobitism – Parts I and II', *History of European Ideas* 6 (1985), pp. 1–18, 173–88.

MALCOLM, JOYCE LEE, 'Charles II and the reconstruction of royal power', *Historical Journal* 35 (1992), pp. 307–30.

——, 'The creation of a "true antient and indubitable" right: the English Bill of Rights and the right to be armed', *Journal of British Studies* 32 (1993), pp. 226–49.

MANNINGS, DAVID, 'The visual arts', in *The Cambridge Cultural History of Britain, 5, Eighteenth-Century Britain*, Boris Ford, ed. (Cambridge, 1992), pp. 107–47.

MARSHALL, W.M., 'Episcopal activity in the Hereford and Oxford dioceses, 1660–1760', *Midland History* 8 (1983), pp. 106–20.

MAYER, ROBERT, 'Nathaniel Crouch, bookseller and historian: popular historiography and cultural power in late-seventeenth century England', *Eighteenth-Century Studies* 27 (1993–94), pp. 391–419.

MELTON, FRANK T., 'Absentee land management in seventeenth-century England', *Agricultural History* 52 (1978), pp. 147–59.

MILLS, DENNIS, 'Survival of early land tax assessments', in Michael Turner and Dennis Mills, eds, *Land and Property: The English Land Tax 1692–1832* (New York, 1986), pp. 219–31.

MINGAY, G.E., 'The size of farms in the eighteenth century', *Economic History Review*, 2nd series, 14 (1962), pp. 469–88.

MONOD, PAUL, 'The politics of matrimony: Jacobitism and marriage in eighteenth-century England', in Eveline Cruickshanks and Jeremy Black, eds, *The Jacobite Challenge* (Edinburgh, 1988), pp. 24–41.

MONTAÑO, JOHN PATRICK, 'The quest for consensus: the Lord Mayor's Day shows in the 1670s', in Gerald MacLean, ed., *Culture and Society in the Stuart Restoration* (Cambridge, 1995), pp. 31–51.

MORGAN, VICTOR, 'Cambridge University and "The Country" 1560–1640', in Lawrence Stone, ed., *The University in Society*, 1, *Oxford and Cambridge from the 14th to the Early 19th Century* (Princeton, 1974), pp. 183–245.

MOTLEY, MARK, 'Educating the English gentleman abroad: the Verney family in seventeenth-century France and Holland', *History of Education* 23 (1994), pp. 243–56.

NEWTON, S.C., 'The gentry of Derbyshire in the seventeenth century', *Derbyshire Archaeological Journal* 86 (1966), pp. 1–30.

NORREY, P.J., 'The restoration regime in action: the relationship between central and local government in Dorset, Somerset and Wiltshire, 1660–1678', *Historical Journal* 31 (1988), pp. 789–812.

PARKER, R.A.C., 'Direct taxation on the Coke estates in the eighteenth century', *English Historical Review* 71 (1956), pp. 247–8.

PHILLIPS, A.D.M., 'A note on farm size and efficiency on the north Staffordshire estate of the Leveson-Gowers, 1714–1809', *North Staffordshire Journal of Field Studies* 19 (1979), pp. 30–8.

PHYTHIAN-ADAMS, CHARLES, 'Introduction: an agenda for English local history', in Charles Phythian-Adams, ed., *Societies, Cultures and Kinship, 1580–1850: Cultural Provinces and English Local History* (Leicester, 1993), pp. 1–23.

PLUMB, J.H., 'The new world of children', in Neil McKendrick, John Brewer, and J.H. Plumb, *The Birth of a Consumer Society: The Commercialization of Eighteenth-Century England* (Bloomington, Indiana, 1982), pp. 286–315.

——, 'The Walpoles: father and son', in J.H. Plumb, ed., *Studies in Social History* (London, 1955), pp. 179–207.

POOLE, ROBERT, '"Give us our eleven days!": Calendar reform in eighteenth-century England', *Past & Present* 149 (1995), pp. 95–139.

PORTER, ROY, 'The people's health in Georgian England', in Tim Harris, ed., *Popular Culture in England, c.1500–1850* (New York, 1995), pp. 124–42.

——, 'Science, provincial culture and public opinion in enlightenment England', in Peter Borsay, ed., *The Eighteenth Century Town 1688–1820: A Reader in English Urban History* (London, 1990), pp. 243–67.

POWER, M.J., 'The social topography of Restoration London', in A.L. Beier and Roger Finlay, eds, *London 1500–1700: The Making of a Metropolis* (London, 1986), pp. 199–223.

ROBERTS, STEPHEN K., 'Juries and the middling sort: recruitment and performance at Devon quarter sessions, 1649–1670', in J.S. Cockburn and Thomas A. Green, eds, *Twelve Good Men and True: The Criminal Trial Jury in England, 1200–1800* (Princeton, 1988), pp. 182–213.

——, 'Public or private? Revenge and recovery at the restoration of Charles II', *Bulletin of the Institute of Historical Research* 59 (1986), pp. 172–88.

ROEBUCK, PETER, 'Absentee landownership in the late seventeenth and early eighteenth centuries: a neglected factor in English agrarian history', *Agricultural History Review* 21 (1973), pp. 1–17.

ROSENHEIM, JAMES M., ' "Being taken notice of as engag'd in a party": partisan occasions and political culture in Restoration Norfolk', in Carol Rawcliffe, Roger Virgoe, and Richard Wilson, eds, *Counties and Communities: Essays on East Anglian History Presented to Hassell Smith* (Norwich, 1996), pp. 259–74.

——, 'County governance and elite withdrawal in Norfolk, 1660–1720', in A.L. Beier, David Cannadine, and James M. Rosenheim, eds, *The First Modern Society: Essays in English History in Honour of Lawrence Stone* (Cambridge, 1989), pp. 95–125.

——, 'An early appreciation of *Paradise Lost*', *Modern Philology* 75 (1978), pp. 280–2.

——, 'Landownership, the aristocracy and the country gentry', in L.K.J. Glassey, ed., *The Reigns of Charles II and James VII and II* (London, 1997), pp. 152–70.

RUSSELL, FRANCIS, 'The hanging and display of pictures, 1700–1850', in Gervase Jackson-Stops, Gordon J. Schochet and Lena Cowen Orlin, and Elisabeth Blair MacDougall, eds, *The Fashioning and Functioning of the British Country House, Studies in the History of Art* 25, Center for the Advanced Study in the Visual Arts, Symposion Papers, vol. 10 (Hanover, New Hampshire, 1989), pp. 133–53.

SAINTY, J.C., 'The origin of the leadership of the House of Lords', *Bulletin of the Institute of Historical Research* 47 (1974), pp. 53–73.

SAVILLE, R.V., 'Gentry wealth on the Weald in the eighteenth century: the Fullers of Brightling Park', *Sussex Archaeological Collections* 121 (1983), pp. 129–47.

SHOEMAKER, ROBERT B., 'Reforming the city: the reformation of manners campaign in London, 1690–1738', in L. Davison, T. Hitchcock, T. Keirn, and R.B. Shoemaker, eds, *Stilling the Grumbling Hive: The Response to Social and Economic Problems in England, 1689–1750* (New York, 1992), pp. 99–120.

SPENCE, R.T., 'Lady Anne Clifford, Countess of Dorset, Pembroke and Montgomery (1590–1676): a reappraisal', *Northern History* 15 (1979), pp. 43–65.

SPURR, JOHN, 'Religion in Restoration England', in L.K.J. Glassey, ed., *The Reigns of Charles II and James VII and II* (London, 1997), pp. 90–124.

STATER, VICTOR, 'Continuity and change in English provincial politics: Robert Paston in Norfolk, 1675–1683', *Albion* 25 (1993), pp. 193–216.

STONE, LAWRENCE, 'Libertine sexuality in post-Restoration England: group sex and flagellation among the middling sort in Norwich in 1706–07', *Journal of the History of Sexuality* 2 (1991-2), pp. 511–26.

——, 'The residential development of the West End of London in the seventeenth century', in Barbara C. Malament, ed., *After the Reformation: Essays in Honour of J.H. Hexter* (Philadelphia, 1980), pp. 167–212.

——, 'The size and composition of the Oxford student body 1580–1909', in Lawrence Stone, ed., *The University in Society*, 1, *Oxford and Cambridge from the 14th to the Early 19th Century* (Princeton, 1974), pp. 3–110.

TARGETT, SIMON, 'Government and ideology during the age of whig supremacy: the political argument of Sir Robert Walpole's newspaper propagandists', *Historical Journal* 37 (1994), pp. 289–317.

THOMAS, DAVID, 'The social origins of marriage partners of the British peerage in the eighteenth and nineteenth centuries', *Population Studies* 26 (1972), pp. 99–111.

TOMLINSON, HOWARD, 'Financial and administrative developments in England, 1660–1688', in J.R. Jones, ed., *The Restored Monarchy 1660–1688* (Totowa, New Jersey, 1979), pp. 94–117.

TOWNEND, G.M., 'Religious radicalism and conservatism in the whig party under George I: the repeal of the Occasional Conformity and Schism Acts', *Parliamentary History* 7 (1988), pp. 24–44.

TRUMBACH, RANDOLPH, 'The birth of the queen: sodomy and the emergence of gender equality in modern culture, 1660–1750', in Martin B. Duberman, Martha Vicinus, and George Chauncey, Jr, eds, *Hidden from History: Reclaiming the Gay and Lesbian Past* (New York, 1989), pp. 129–40.

TURNER, MICHAEL, 'The land tax, land and property: old debates and new horizons', in Michael Turner and Dennis Mills, eds, *Land Tax and Property: The English Land Tax 1692–1832* (New York, 1986), pp. 1–35.

WALLBANK, M.V., 'Eighteenth-century public schools and the education of the governing elite', *History of Education* 8 (1979), pp. 1–19.

WASSON, ELLIS ARCHER, 'The House of Commons, 1660–1945: parliamentary families and the political elite', *English Historical Review* 106 (1991), pp. 635–51.

WILLS, J.E., JR, 'European consumption and Asian production in the seventeenth and eighteenth centuries', in John Brewer and Roy Porter, eds, *Consumption and the World of Goods* (London, 1993), pp. 133–47.

WILSON, KATHLEEN, 'Citizenship, empire and modernity in the English provinces, c. 1720–1790', *Eighteenth-Century Studies* 29 (1995), pp. 69–96.

——, 'Empire, trade and popular politics in mid-Hanoverian Britain: the case of Admiral Vernon', *Past & Present* 121 (1988), pp. 74–109.

WOOLF, D.R., 'The "common voice": history, folklore and oral tradition in early modern England', *Past & Present* 120 (1988), pp. 26–52.

WRIGLEY, E. ANTHONY, 'A simple model of London's importance in changing English society and economy, 1650–1750', in E. Anthony Wrigley, *People, Cities and Wealth: The Transformation of Traditional Society* (Oxford, 1988), pp. 133–56.

——, 'Urban growth and agricultural change: England and the Continent in the early modern period', in Peter Borsay, ed., *The Eighteenth Century Town: A Reader in English Urban History, 1688–1820* (London, 1990), pp. 39–82.

Index